HEALTHCARE

OPERATIONS

MANAGEMENT

SECOND EDITION

HEALTHCARE

OPERATIONS

MANAGEMENT

SECOND EDITION

DANIEL B. MCLAUGHLIN
AND
JOHN R. OLSON

AUPHA

Health Administration Press, Chicago, Illinois

Association of University Programs in Health Administration, Arlington, Virginia

Your board, staff, or clients may also benefit from this book's insight. For more information on quantity discounts, contact the Health Administration Press Marketing Manager at (312) 424–9470.

16   15   14   5   4   3

Library of Congress Cataloging-in-Publication Data

McLaughlin, Daniel B., 1945-
  Healthcare operations management / Daniel B. McLaughlin and John R. Olson. -- 2nd ed.
    p. cm.
  Includes index.
  ISBN 978-1-56793-444-1 (alk. paper)
  1. Medical care--Quality control. 2. Health services administration--Quality control. 3. Organizational effectiveness. 4. Total quality management. I. Olson, John R. II. Title.
  RA399.A1M374 2012
  362.1068--dc23

                    2012004601

Acquisitions editor: Janet Davis; Project manager: Amy Carlton; Typesetting: Virginia Byrne

Cover illustration by Scott Miller. Copyright 2012.

Found an error or a typo? We want to know! Please e-mail it to hap1@ache.org, and put "Book Error" in the subject line.

For photocopying and copyright information, please contact Copyright Clearance Center at www.copyright.com or at (978) 750–8400.

Health Administration Press	Association of University Programs
A division of the Foundation of the American	in Health Administration
College of Healthcare Executives	2000 North 14th Street
One North Franklin Street, Suite 1700	Suite 780
Chicago, IL 60606–3529	Arlington, VA 22201
(312) 424–2800	(703) 894–0940

To my wife, Sharon, and daughters, Kelly and Katie,
for their love and support throughout my career.
—Dan McLaughlin

To my wife, Julie, and my daughters, Katelyn and Samantha,
you are my constant source of inspiration!
—John Olson

The first edition of this book was coauthored by Julie Hays. During the final stages of the completion of this book, Julie Hays unexpectedly died. As Dr. Christopher Puto, dean of the Opus College of Business at the University of St. Thomas, said, "Julie cared deeply about students and their learning experience, and she was an accomplished scholar who was well respected by her peers." This book is a final tribute to Julie's accomplished career and is dedicated to her legacy.
—Dan McLaughlin and John Olson

BRIEF CONTENTS

DETAILED CONTENTS

PREFACE

This book is intended to help healthcare professionals meet the challenges and take advantage of the opportunities found in healthcare today. We believe that the answers to many of the dilemmas faced by the healthcare system, such as increasing costs, decreasing profitability, inadequate access, and poor quality, lie within organizational operations—the nuts and bolts of healthcare delivery. The healthcare arena is filled with opportunities for significant operational improvements. We hope that this book will encourage healthcare management students and working professionals to find ways to improve the management and delivery of healthcare to increase the effectiveness and efficiency of tomorrow's healthcare system.

Manufacturing organizations have successfully employed the programs, techniques, and tools of operations improvement for many years. Leading healthcare organizations have begun to employ the same tools. Although many operations management texts are available, few focus on *healthcare* operations, and none takes an *integrated* approach. Students interested in healthcare process improvement have difficulty seeing the applicability of the science of operations management when most texts focus on widgets and production lines rather than on patients and providers.

This book covers the basics of operations improvement and provides an overview of the significant environmental trends in the healthcare industry. We focus on the strategic implementation of process improvement programs, techniques, and tools in the healthcare environment with its complex web of reimbursement systems, physician relations, workforce challenges, and strong governmental regulations. This integrated approach will help healthcare professionals gain an understanding of strategic operations management and, more important, its applicability to the healthcare industry.

How This Book Is Organized

We have organized this book into five parts:

1. Introduction to Healthcare Operations
2. Setting Goals and Executing Strategy
3. Performance Improvement Tools, Techniques, and Programs

4. Applications to Contemporary Healthcare Operations Issues
5. Putting It All Together for Operational Excellence

Although this structure will be helpful for most readers, each chapter stands alone and can be covered or read in any order that makes sense for a particular course or student.

The first part of the book, Introduction to Healthcare Operations, provides an overview of the challenges and opportunities found in today's healthcare environment (Chapter 1). We follow with a history of the field of management science and operations improvement (Chapter 2). Next, we discuss two of the most influential environmental changes facing healthcare today, evidence-based medicine and pay-for-performance (Chapter 3).

In Part II, Setting Goals and Executing Strategy, Chapter 4 highlights the importance of tying the strategic direction of the organization to operational initiatives. This chapter outlines the use of the balanced scorecard technique to execute and monitor these initiatives to achieve organizational objectives. Typically, strategic initiatives are large in scope, and the tools of project management (Chapter 5) are needed to successfully manage them. Indeed, the use of project management tools can help to ensure the success of any size project. Strategic focus and project management provide the organizational foundation for the remainder of this book.

The next part of the book, Performance Improvement Tools, Techniques, and Programs, provides an introduction to basic decision-making and problem-solving processes and describes some of the associated tools (Chapter 6). Almost all performance improvement initiatives (e.g., Six Sigma, Lean) follow these same processes and make use of some or all of the tools in Chapter 6. Good decisions and effective solutions are based on facts, not intuition. Chapter 7 provides an overview of data collection and analysis to enable fact-based decision making.

Six Sigma, Lean, simulation, and supply chain management are more specific philosophies or techniques that can be used to improve processes and systems. The Six Sigma (Chapter 8) methodology is the latest manifestation of the use of quality improvement tools to reduce variation and errors in a process. The Lean (Chapter 9) methodology is focused on eliminating waste in a system or process. Many healthcare decisions and processes can be modeled and optimized or improved by using computer simulation (Chapter 10).

The fourth section of the book, Applications to Contemporary Healthcare Operations Issues, begins with an integrated approach to applying the various tools and techniques for process improvement in the healthcare environment (Chapter 11). We then focus on a special but important case of process improvement, patient scheduling in the ambulatory environment (Chapter 12). Supply chain management extends the boundaries of the system to include both upstream suppliers and downstream customers, and this is the focus of Chapter 13. The need to "bend" the healthcare cost inflation curve downward is one of the most pressing issues in healthcare today and the use of operations management tools to achieve this goal is addressed in Chapter 14.

Part V, Putting It All Together for Operational Excellence, concludes the book with a discussion of strategies for implementing and maintaining the focus on continuous improvement in healthcare organizations (Chapter 15).

We have included many features in this book that we believe will enhance student understanding and learning. Most chapters begin with a vignette, called Operations Management in Action, that offers real-world examples related to the content of the particular chapter. Throughout the book we use a fictitious but realistic organization, Vincent Valley Hospital and Health System, to illustrate the various tools, techniques, and programs discussed. Each chapter concludes with questions for discussion, and Parts II through IV include exercises to be solved.

We have included many examples throughout the text of the use of various contemporary software tools essential for effective operations management. Healthcare leaders and managers must be experts in the application of these tools and stay current with their latest versions. Just as we ask healthcare providers to stay up to date with the latest clinical advances, so too must healthcare managers stay current with these basic tools.

Healthcare Reform

As this book goes to press, the US Supreme Court is reviewing a number of aspects of the Patient Protection and Affordable Care Act (ACA). As a result, some or all of the law may be repealed. Throughout this book, we use examples from the ACA that are well-supported health policy initiatives (e.g., accountable care organizations, medical homes). We feel that even if the ACA is completely repealed, these concepts will be reinstituted as federal regulations or as part of new healthcare reform legislation because they have now become an important part of healthcare delivery in the United States. Therefore we believe they still will be useful as background and context for making improvements in healthcare operations and as a part of this book.

Student Resources

We have developed an extensive companion website with links to a vast amount of supplementary material. This website, ache.org/books/Ops Management2, provides links to material we have developed, as well as other supplemental material. In particular, we have developed, and make available, various Excel templates, tutorials, exercises, and PowerPoint presentations for each chapter. Additionally, links to many of the cited articles and books

www.ache.org/books/OpsManagement2
can be found on this website. Finally, the site provides links to a wide variety of information and material related to specific topics, including videos, webcasts, web demonstrations, exercises, and tutorials. Because new and valuable information is constantly being added to the web, we encourage readers to share any relevant sites they find so that we can include them on the companion website. A password is not necessary for access.

Instructor Resources

For instructors who choose to use this book in their courses, accompanying resources are available online. For access information, e-mail hap1@ache.org. Contained in these resources are answers or discussion points for the end-of-chapter questions and exercises; teaching tips; and recommended teaching cases, with links to sources as needed.

We hope that this text is helpful to you and your organization on your journey along the path of continuous improvement. We are interested in your progress whether you are a student of healthcare administration, new member of the health administration team, seasoned department head, or physician leader. Please use the e-mail addresses on the companion website to inform us of your successes, and let us know what we could do to make this a better text so that we, too, can continuously improve.

—Dan McLaughlin
—John Olson

Acknowledgments

A number of people contributed to this work. Dan McLaughlin would like to thank his many colleagues at the University of St. Thomas Opus College of Business. Specifically, Dr. Ernest Owens provided guidance on the project management chapter, and Dr. Michael Sheppeck assisted on the human resources implications of operations improvement. Dean Chris Puto and associate dean Michael Garrison encouraged and supported this work. Former US Senator Dave Durenberger, of the National Institute of Health Policy, provided an impetus for this book, as he strongly feels that system change in US healthcare must come from within—this is what much of this book is about.

The outstanding professionals at Hennepin County Medical Center in Minneapolis, Minnesota, also provided much of the practical and realistic examples in this book, and they continue to be an outstanding healthcare resource for all of the residents of Minnesota.

John Olson would like to thank his many colleagues at the University of St. Thomas Opus College of Business; specifically, Victor Sandler, for all of his insights related to the costs of delivering effective care; John McCall, for the tremendous conversations that helped him think through the many difficult issues surrounding healthcare; and the staff of the Center for Business Excellence, for managing programs of high quality that help transform the way our healthcare professionals think about their profession.

The dedicated employees of the Veterans Administration have helped him to embrace the challenges that face healthcare today, in particular Christine Wolohan, Lori Fox, Susan Chattin, Eric James, Denise Lingen, and Carl (Marty) Young of the continuous improvement group, who are helping to create an organization of excellence. Working with people who are dedicated to serving our veterans has been an honor; their service is truly amazing.

Finally, this book still contains many passages that were written by Julie Hayes and are a tribute to her skill and dedication to the field of operations management.

INTRODUCTION TO HEALTHCARE OPERATIONS

THE CHALLENGE AND THE OPPORTUNITY

Overview

The challenges and opportunities in today's complex healthcare delivery systems demand that leaders take charge of their operations. A strong operations focus can reduce costs, increase safety, improve clinical outcomes, and allow an organization to compete effectively in an aggressive marketplace.

In the recent past, the success of many organizations in the US healthcare system has been achieved through executing a few key strategies: First, attract and retain talented clinicians; next, add new technology and specialty care; and finally, find new methods to maximize the organization's reimbursement for these services. In most organizations, new services—not ongoing operations—represented the key to success.

However, that era is ending. Payer resistance to cost increases and a surge in public reporting on the quality of healthcare are strong forces driving a major change in strategy. The passage of the **Patient Protection and Affordable Care Act (ACA)** in 2010 provided a culmination of these forces. Although portions of this law may be repealed or changed, the general direction of health policy in the United States has been set. To succeed in this new environment, a healthcare enterprise must focus on making significant improvements in its core operations.

This book is about improvement and how to get things done. It provides an integrated system and set of contemporary operations improvement tools that can be used to make significant gains in any organization. These tools have been successfully deployed in much of the global business community for more than 30 years and now are being used by leading healthcare delivery organizations.

Patient Protection and Affordable Care Act (ACA)
The Patient Protection and Affordable Care Act was passed by Congress in 2010 and signed into law by President Obama. It contains policies to increase access to health insurance and to improve the operations and outcomes of the American healthcare system. Its common name has been shortened to the Affordable Care Act or ACA.

www.ache.org/books/OpsManagement2

This chapter outlines the purpose of the book, identifies challenges that current healthcare systems are facing, presents a systems view of healthcare, and provides a comprehensive framework for the use of operations tools and methods in healthcare. Finally, Vincent Valley Hospital and Health System (VVH), which is used in examples throughout the book, is described.

Purpose of This Book

Excellence in healthcare derives from three major areas of expertise: clinical care, leadership, and operations. Although clinical expertise and leadership are critical to an organization's success, this book focuses on operations—how to deliver high-quality care in a consistent, efficient manner.

Many books cover operational improvement tools, and some focus on using these tools in healthcare environments. So why have we devoted a book to the broad topic of healthcare operations? Because there is a real need for an *integrated* approach to operations improvement that puts all the tools in a logical context and provides a road map for their use. An integrated approach uses a clinical analogy—first find and diagnose an operations issue, then apply the appropriate treatment tool to solve the problem.

The field of operations research and management science is too deep to cover in one book. In *Healthcare Operations Management*, only tools and techniques that are currently being deployed in leading healthcare organizations are covered in enough detail to enable students and practitioners to use them in their work. Each chapter provides many references for deeper study. The authors have also included additional resources, exercises, and tools on the companion website that accompanies this book.

This book is organized so that each chapter builds on the previous one and is cross-referenced. However, each chapter also stands alone, so a reader interested in Six Sigma could start in Chapter 8 and then move back and forth into the other chapters.

This book does not specifically explore quality in healthcare as defined by the many agencies that have a mission to ensure healthcare quality, such as The Joint Commission, National Committee for Quality Assurance, National Quality Forum, or federally funded Quality Improvement Organizations. *The Healthcare Quality Book: Vision, Strategy, and Tools* (Ransom, Maulik, and Nash 2008) explores this perspective in depth and provides a useful companion to this book. However, the systems, tools, and techniques discussed here are essential to make the operational improvements needed to meet the expectations of these quality assurance organizations.

The Challenge

The United States spent more than $2.8 trillion on healthcare in 2011, 17.4 percent of the gross domestic product (GDP) and the most per capita in the world. National health expenditure as a share of GDP is expected to be 19.6 percent by 2019 (CMS 2010). At this level, one in every five dollars of the US economy will be devoted to healthcare.

Despite its high cost, the value delivered by the system has been questioned by many policymakers. Unexplained quality variations in healthcare were estimated in 1999 to result in 44,000 to 98,000 preventable deaths every year. Preventable healthcare-related injuries cost the economy between $17 billion and $29 billion annually, half of which represents direct healthcare costs (IOM 1999). The problems persist. A 2010 study of hospitals in North Carolina showed a high rate of adverse events that has not changed over time even though hospitals had sought to improve the safety of inpatient care (Landrigan et al. 2010).

These problems were studied in the landmark work of the **Institute of Medicine** (IOM 2001), *Crossing the Quality Chasm—A New Health System for the 21st Century*. The IOM panel concluded that the knowledge to improve patient care is available, but a gap—a chasm—separates that knowledge from everyday practice. The panel summarizes the goals of a new health system in six aims (Exhibit 1.1).

Institute of Medicine (IOM) The healthcare arm of the National Academy of Sciences; an independent, nonprofit organization providing unbiased and authoritative advice to decision makers and the public.

EXHIBIT 1.1
Six Aims of a New Health System

Patient care should be

1. *Safe*, avoiding injuries to patients from the care that is intended to help them;
2. *Effective*, providing services based on scientific knowledge to all who could benefit, and refraining from providing services to those not likely to benefit (avoiding underuse and overuse, respectively);
3. *Patient-centered*, providing care that is respectful of and responsive to individual patient preferences, needs, and values, and ensuring that patient values guide all clinical decisions;
4. *Timely*, reducing wait times and harmful delays for both those who receive and those who give care;
5. *Efficient*, avoiding waste of equipment, supplies, ideas, and energy; and
6. *Equitable*, providing care that does not vary in quality because of personal characteristics such as gender, ethnicity, geographic location, and socio-economic status.

SOURCE: Reprinted with permission from *Crossing the Quality Chasm—A New Health System for the 21st Century* © 2001 by the National Academy of Sciences, Courtesy of the National Academies Press, Washington, D.C.

The IOM panel recommended ten steps to close the gap between care with the above characteristics and current practice (Exhibit 1.2).

Many healthcare leaders have begun to address these issues and are capitalizing on proven tools employed by other industries to ensure high performance and quality outcomes. For major change to occur in the US health system, however, these strategies must be adopted by a broad spectrum of healthcare providers and implemented consistently throughout the continuum of care—ambulatory, inpatient, and acute settings and long-term care.

The payers for healthcare must engage with the delivery system to find new ways to partner for improvement. In addition, patients have to assume a stronger financial and self-care role in this new system. The ACA and subsequent health policy initiatives provide many new policies to support the achievement of these goals.

Although not all of the IOM goals can be accomplished through operational improvements, this book provides methods and tools to actively change the system to accomplish many aspects of them.

The Opportunity

Evidence-based medicine (EBM)
The conscientious and judicious use of the best current evidence in making decisions about the care of individual patients.

Although the current US health system presents numerous challenges, opportunities for improvement are emerging as well. Three major trends provide hope that significant change is possible.

Evidence-Based Medicine

The use of **evidence-based medicine (EBM)** for the delivery of healthcare is the result of 40 years of work by some of the most progressive and thoughtful practitioners in the nation. The movement has produced an array of care guidelines, care patterns, and new shared decision-making tools for both caregivers and patients. The effects of EBM can be powerful. Rotter and colleagues reviewed 27 studies worldwide with 11,938 patients and assessed the use of clinical pathways. They found that the cost of those patients who received care with the pathways was $4,919 per admission less than those who did not (Rotter et al. 2010).

Agency for Healthcare Research and Quality (AHRQ)
A federal agency that is part of the Department of Health and Human Services. It provides leadership and funding to identify and communicate the most effective methods to deliver high-quality healthcare in the United States.

Comprehensive resources are available to healthcare organizations that wish to emphasize EBM. For example, the National Guideline Clearinghouse (NGC 2011) is a comprehensive database of evidence-based clinical practice guidelines and related documents and contains more than 4,000 guidelines. NGC is an initiative of the **Agency for Healthcare Research and Quality (AHRQ)** of the US Department of Health and Human Services. NGC was originally created by AHRQ in partnership with the American Medical Association and American Association of Health Plans, now America's Health Insurance Plans (AHIP).

EXHIBIT 1.2
Ten Steps to
Close the Gap

The ten steps to close the gap are:

1. *Care based on continuous healing relationships.* Patients should receive care whenever they need it and in many forms, not just face-to-face visits. This rule implies that the healthcare system should be responsive at all times (24 hours a day, every day), and that access to care should be provided over the Internet, by telephone, and by other means in addition to face-to-face visits.

2. *Customization based on patient needs and values.* The system of care should be designed to meet the most common types of needs, but have the capability to respond to individual patient choices and preferences.

3. *The patient as the source of control.* Patients should be given all relevant information and the opportunity to exercise whatever degree of control they choose over healthcare decisions that affect them. The health system should be able to accommodate differences in patient preferences and encourage shared decision making.

4. *Shared knowledge and the free flow of information.* Patients should have unfettered access to their own medical information and to clinical knowledge. Clinicians and patients should communicate effectively and share information.

5. *Evidence-based decision making.* Patients should receive care based on the best available scientific knowledge. Care should not vary illogically from clinician to clinician or from place to place.

6. *Safety as a system property.* Patients should be safe from injury caused by the care system. Reducing risk and ensuring safety require greater attention to systems that help prevent and mitigate errors.

7. *The need for transparency.* The healthcare system should make available to patients and their families information that allows them to make informed decisions when selecting a health plan, hospital, or clinical practice, or when choosing among alternative treatments. This should include information describing the system's performance on safety, evidence-based practice, and patient satisfaction.

8. *Anticipation of needs.* The health system should anticipate patient needs rather than simply react to events.

9. *Continuous decrease in waste.* The health system should not waste resources or patient time.

10. *Cooperation among clinicians.* Clinicians and institutions should actively collaborate and communicate to ensure an appropriate exchange of information and coordination of care.

SOURCE: Reprinted with permission from *Crossing the Quality Chasm—A New Health System for the 21st Century* © 2001 by the National Academy of Sciences, Courtesy of the National Academies Press, Washington, D.C.

Knowledge-based management (KBM)
The use of data and information, rather than feelings or intuition, to support management decisions.

Health savings accounts (HSAs)
Personal accounts that can only be used for healthcare expenses. The funds are not taxed, and the balance can be rolled over from year to year. HSAs are normally used with high-deductible health insurance plans.

Consumer-directed healthcare
In general it means the consumer (patient) is well informed about healthcare prices and quality and makes personal buying decisions based on this information. The health savings account is frequently included as a key component of consumer-directed healthcare.

Knowledge-Based Management

Knowledge-based management (KBM) employs data and information, rather than feelings or intuition, to support management decisions. Practitioners of KBM use the tools contained in this book for cost reduction, increased safety, and improved clinical outcomes. The evidence for the efficacy of these techniques is contained in the operations research and management science literature. Although these tools have been taught in healthcare graduate programs for many years, they have not migrated widely into practice. The IOM has recognized the opportunities that KBM presents with its publication *Building a Better Delivery System: A New Engineering/Health Care Partnership* (Proctor et al. 2005).

Healthcare delivery has been slow to adopt information technologies, but many organizations are now beginning to aggressively implement electronic medical record systems and other automated tools. The Health Information Technology for Economic and Clinical Health (HITECH) Act supports the aggressive implementation of health information technology. Hillestad and colleagues (2005) have suggested that broad deployment of these systems could save up to $371 billion annually in the United States.

A More Active Role for the Consumer

Consumers are beginning to assume new roles in their own care through the use of health education and information and more effective partnering with their healthcare providers. Personal maintenance of wellness though a healthy lifestyle is one essential component. Understanding one's disease and treatment options and having an awareness of the cost of care are also important responsibilities of the consumer.

Patients will become good consumers of healthcare by finding and using price information in selecting providers and treatments. Many employers are now offering high-deductible health plans with accompanying **health savings accounts (HSAs)**. This type of **consumer-directed healthcare** is likely to grow and increase pressure on providers to deliver cost-effective, customer-sensitive, high-quality care. In addition, the ACA provides new tools for employers to incentivize their employees to engage in healthy lifestyles.

The healthcare delivery system of the future will support and empower active, informed consumers.

A Systems Look at Healthcare

The Clinical System

To improve healthcare operations, it is important to understand the series of interconnected systems that influence the delivery of clinical care (Exhibit 1.3).

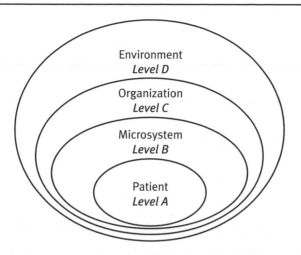

SOURCE: Ransom, Maulik, and Nash (2005). Based on Ferlie, E., and S. M. Shortell. 2001. "Improving the Quality of Healthcare in the United Kingdom and the United States: A Framework for Change." *The Milbank Quarterly* 79 (2): 281–316.

EXHIBIT 1.3
A Systems View of Healthcare

In the **patient care microsystem**, the *healthcare professional* provides hands-on care *to the patient*. Elements of the clinical microsystem include:

- The team of health professionals who provide clinical care to the patient
- The tools the team has to diagnose and treat the patient (e.g., imaging capabilities, lab tests, drugs)
- The logic for determining the appropriate treatments and the processes to deliver this care

Patient care microsystem
The level of healthcare delivery that includes providers, technology, and treatment processes.

Because common conditions (e.g., hypertension) affect a large number of patients, clinical research has determined the most effective way to treat these patients. Therefore, in many cases, the organization and functioning of the microsystem can be optimized.

Process improvements can be made at this level to ensure that the most effective, least costly care is delivered. In addition, the use of EBM guidelines can help ensure that the patient receives the correct treatment at the correct time.

The *organizational infrastructure* also influences the effective delivery of care to the patient. Ensuring that providers have the correct tools and skills is an important element of infrastructure. KBM optimizes the use of clinical tools.

The electronic health record is one of the most important advances in the clinical microsystem for both process improvement and the wider use of EBM.

Another key component of infrastructure is the leadership displayed by senior staff. Without leadership, effective progress or change will not occur.

Finally, the *environment* strongly influences the delivery of care. Key environmental factors include competition, government regulation, demographics, and payer policies. An organization's strategy is frequently influenced by such factors (e.g., a new regulation from Medicare, a new competitor).

Many of the systems concepts regarding healthcare delivery were initially developed by Avedis Donabedian. These fundamental contributions are discussed in depth in Chapter 2.

System Stability and Change

Elements in each layer of this system interact. Peter Senge (1990) provides a useful theory to understand the interaction of elements in a complex system such as healthcare. In his model, the structure of a system is the primary mechanism for producing an outcome. For example, an organized structure of facilities, trained professionals, supplies, equipment, and EBM care guidelines has a high probability of producing an expected clinical outcome.

No system is ever completely stable. Each system's performance is modified and controlled by feedback (Exhibit 1.4). Senge (1990, 75) defines *feedback* as "any reciprocal flow of influence. In systems thinking it is an axiom that every influence is both *cause* and *effect*." As shown in Exhibit 1.4, higher salaries provide an incentive for higher performance levels by employees. This, in turn, leads to better financial performance and profitability, and

EXHIBIT 1.4
Systems with Reinforcing and Balancing Feedback

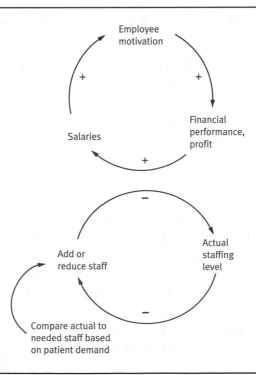

increased profits provide additional funds for higher salaries, and the cycle continues. Another frequent example in healthcare delivery is patient lab results that directly influence the medication ordered by a physician. A third example is a financial report that shows an overexpenditure in one category that will prompt a manager to reduce spending to meet budget goals.

A more formal systems definition with feedback includes a process, a sensor that monitors process output, a feedback loop, and a control that modifies how the process operates.

Feedback can be either reinforcing or balancing. *Reinforcing feedback* prompts change that builds on itself and amplifies the outcome of a process, taking the process further and further from its starting point. The effect of reinforcing feedback can be either positive or negative. For example, a reinforcing change of positive financial results for an organization could lead to higher salaries, which would then lead to even better financial performance because the employees were highly motivated. In contrast, a poor supervisor could lead to employee turnover, which could cause short staffing and could lead to even more turnover.

Balancing feedback prompts change that seeks stability. A balancing feedback loop attempts to return the system to its starting point. The human body provides a good example of a complex system that has many balancing feedback mechanisms. For example, an overheated body prompts perspiration until the body is cooled through evaporation. The clinical term for this type of balance is *homeostasis*. A clinical treatment process that controls drug dosing via real-time monitoring of the patient's physiological responses is an example of balancing feedback. Inpatient unit staffing levels that determine where in a hospital patients are admitted is another. All of these feedback mechanisms are designed to maintain balance in the system.

A confounding problem with feedback is delay. Delays occur when there are interruptions between actions and consequences. When this happens, systems tend to overshoot and perform poorly. For example, an emergency department might experience a surge in patients and call in additional staff. If the surge subsides, the added staff may not be needed and unnecessary expense will have been incurred.

As healthcare leaders focus on improving their operations, they must understand the systems in which change resides. Every change will be resisted and reinforced by feedback mechanisms, many of which are not clearly visible. Taking a broad systems view can improve the effectiveness of change.

Many subsystems in the total healthcare system are interconnected. These connections have feedback mechanisms that either reinforce or balance the subsystem's performance. Exhibit 1.5 shows a simple connection that originates in the environmental segment of the total health system. Each process has both reinforcing and balancing feedback.

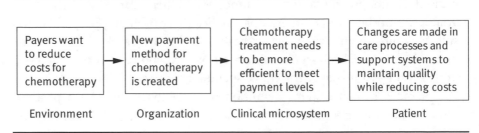

| Payers want to reduce costs for chemotherapy | New payment method for chemotherapy is created | Chemotherapy treatment needs to be more efficient to meet payment levels | Changes are made in care processes and support systems to maintain quality while reducing costs |

Environment   Organization   Clinical microsystem   Patient

An Integrating Framework for Operations Management in Healthcare

This book is divided into five major parts:

1. Introduction to Healthcare Operations
2. Setting Goals and Executing Strategy
3. Performance Improvement Tools, Techniques, and Programs
4. Applications to Contemporary Healthcare Operations Issues
5. Putting It All Together for Operational Excellence

This schema reflects our view that effective operations management in healthcare consists of highly focused strategy execution and organizational change accompanied by the disciplined use of analytical tools, techniques, and programs. The book includes examples of applications of this approach to common healthcare challenges.

Exhibit 1.6 illustrates this framework. An organization needs to understand the environment, develop a strategy, and implement a system to effectively deploy this strategy. At the same time, the organization must become adept at using all the tools of operations improvement contained in this book. These improvement tools can then be combined to attack the fundamental challenges of operating a complex healthcare delivery organization.

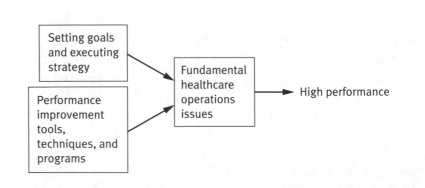

Introduction to Healthcare Operations

The introductory chapters provide an overview of the significant environmental trends healthcare delivery organizations face. Annual updates to industrywide trends can be found in *Futurescan: Healthcare Trends and Implications 2012–2017* (Society for Healthcare Strategy and Market Development and the Foundation of the American College of Healthcare Executives 2012). Progressive organizations will review these publications carefully. Then, using this information, they can respond to external forces by identifying either new strategies or current operating problems that must be addressed.

Business has been aggressively using operations improvement tools for the past 40 years, but the field of operations science actually began many centuries ago. Chapter 2 provides a brief history.

Healthcare operations are being strongly driven by the effects of EBM and pay-for-performance. Chapter 3 provides an overview of these trends and how organizations can effect change to meet current challenges and opportunities.

Setting Goals and Executing Strategy

A key component of effective operations is the ability to move strategy to action. Chapter 4 shows how the use of the balanced scorecard can accomplish this aim. Change in all organizations is challenging, and formal methods of project management (Chapter 5) can make effective, lasting improvements in an organization's operations.

Performance Improvement Tools, Techniques, and Programs

Once an organization has in place strategy implementation and change management processes, it needs to select the correct tools, techniques, and programs to analyze current operations and implement effective changes.

Chapter 6—Tools for Problem Solving and Decision Making—outlines the basic steps of problem solving, beginning with framing the question or problem and continuing through data collection and analyses to enable effective decision making. Chapter 7—Statistical Thinking and Statistical Problem Solving—provides a review of the building blocks for many of the more advanced tools used later in the book. (This chapter may serve as a review or reference for readers who already have good statistical skills.)

Some projects will require a focus on process improvement. Six Sigma tools (Chapter 8) can be used to reduce variability in the outcome of a process. Lean tools (Chapter 9) can be used to eliminate waste and increase speed. Many healthcare processes, such as patient flow, can be modeled and improved by using computer simulation (Chapter 10), which may also be used to evaluate project risks.

Applications to Contemporary Healthcare Operations Issues

This part of the book demonstrates how these concepts can be applied to some of today's fundamental healthcare challenges. Process improvement techniques are widely deployed in many organizations to significantly improve performance; Chapter 11 reviews the tools of process improvement and demonstrates their use in improving patient flow.

Scheduling and capacity management continue to be major concerns for many healthcare delivery organizations, particularly with the advent of advanced access. Chapter 12 demonstrates how simulation can be used to optimize scheduling. Chapter 13—Supply Chain Management—explores the optimal methods of acquiring supplies and maintaining appropriate inventory levels. Chapter 14 outlines a systems approach to improved financial results with a special emphasis on cost reductions. This is one of today's more important challenges.

In the end, any operations improvement will fail unless steps are taken to maintain the gains; Chapter 15—Holding the Gains—contains the necessary tools. The chapter also provides a more detailed algorithm that can help practitioners select the appropriate tools, methods, and techniques to make significant operational improvements. It includes an example of how Vincent Valley Hospital and Health System (VVH) uses all the tools in the book to achieve operational excellence.

Vincent Valley Hospital and Health System

Woven throughout the chapters are examples designed to consistently illustrate the tools discussed. A fictitious but realistic health system, VVH, is featured in these examples. (The companion website contains a more expansive description of VVH.)

www.ache.org/books/OpsManagement2

VVH is located in a Midwestern city of 1.5 million. VVH has 3,000 employees, operates 350 inpatient beds, and has a medical staff of 450 physicians. In addition, it operates nine clinics staffed by physicians who are employees of the system. VVH has two major competitor hospitals, and a number of surgeons from all three hospitals recently joined together to set up an independent ambulatory surgery center.

Three major health plans provide most of the private payment to VVH and, along with the state Medicaid system, have recently begun a pay-for-performance initiative. VVH has a strong balance sheet and a profit margin of approximately 2 percent, but it feels financially challenged.

The board of VVH includes many local industry leaders, who have asked the chief executive officer to focus on using the operational techniques that have led them to succeed in their businesses.

Conclusion

This book is an overview of operations management approaches and tools. It is expected that the successful reader will understand all the concepts in the book (and in current use in the field) and should be able to apply at the basic level some of the tools, techniques, and programs presented. It is not expected that the reader will be able to execute at the more advanced level (e.g., Six Sigma black belt, Project Management Professional). However, this book will prepare readers to work effectively with knowledgeable professionals and, most important, enable them to direct their work.

Discussion Questions

1. Review the ten action steps recommended by IOM to close the quality chasm. Rank them from easiest to most difficult to achieve, and give a rationale for your rankings.
2. Give three examples of possibilities for system improvement at the boundaries of the healthcare subsystems (patient, microsystem, organization, and environment).
3. Identify three systems in a healthcare organization (at any level) that have reinforcing feedback.
4. Identify three systems in a healthcare organization (at any level) that have balancing feedback.
5. Identify three systems in a healthcare organization (at any level) in which feedback delays affect the performance of the system.

HISTORY OF PERFORMANCE IMPROVEMENT

Operations Management in Action

During the Crimean War, reports of terrible conditions in military hospitals alarmed British citizens. In response to the outcry, Florence Nightingale was commissioned to oversee the introduction of nurses to military hospitals and to improve conditions in the hospitals. When Nightingale arrived in Scutari, Turkey, she found the hospital overcrowded and filthy. Nightingale instituted many changes to improve the sanitary conditions in the hospital, and many lives were saved as a result of these reforms.

Nightingale was one of the first people in healthcare to collect, tabulate, interpret, and graphically display data related to the effect of process changes on care outcomes. Today, this is called "evidence-based medicine." To quantify the overcrowding problem, she compared the amount of space per patient in London hospitals, 1,600 square feet, to the space in Scutari, about 400 square feet. She developed a standard Model Hospital Statistical Form to enable the collection of consistent data for analysis and comparison. In February 1855, the mortality rate of patients in Scutari was 42 percent. As a result of Nightingale's changes, by June the mortality rate decreased to 2.2 percent. To present these data in a persuasive manner, she developed a new type of graphic display, the polar area diagram.

After the war, Nightingale used the data she had collected to demonstrate that the mortality rate in Scutari, after her reforms, was significantly lower than in other British military hospitals. Although the British military hierarchy was resistant to her changes, the data were convincing and resulted in reforms to military hospitals and the establishment of the Royal Commission on the Health of the Army.

Florence Nightingale would recognize many of the philosophies, tools, and techniques outlined in this text as being essentially the same as those she effectively employed to achieve lasting reform in hospitals throughout the world.

SOURCES: Cohen (1984); Neuhauser (2003); and Nightingale (1858, 1999).

Overview

This chapter provides the background and historical context of performance improvement, which is not a new concept—many of the tools, techniques, and philosophies outlined in this text are based in the past. Although the terminology has changed, many of the core concepts remain the same.

The major topics in this chapter include:

- Systems thinking and knowledge-based management
- Scientific management and project management
- Quality experts
- Service typologies
- Philosophies of performance improvement, including Six Sigma, Lean, and supply chain management

Background

Operations management is the design, operation, and improvement of the processes and systems that create and deliver the organization's products and services. Operations managers plan and control delivery processes and systems within the organization. The goal of operations management is to produce and deliver the organization's products and services more effectively and efficiently. Healthcare professionals have realized that the theories, tools, and techniques of operations management, if properly applied, can enable their own organizations to become more efficient and effective. The operations management information presented in this book should enable healthcare professionals to design systems, processes, products, and services that meet the needs of their organizations' stakeholders. It should also enable the continuous improvement of these systems and services to meet the needs of a quickly changing environment.

The healthcare industry is facing many challenges. The costs of care and level of services delivered are increasing; more and more we are able to prolong lives as technology advances and the population ages. The need for quality care with zero defects, or failures in care, is being driven by government and other stakeholders. The need to produce more of a higher quality

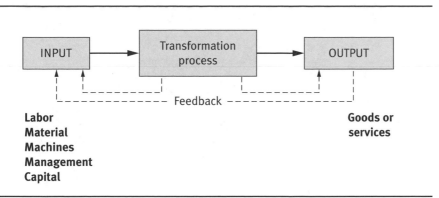

EXHIBIT 2.1
Systems View

product or service at a reduced cost can only be met through better utilization of resources.

The healthcare environment has recognized the need to control costs while increasing both the level and quality of service. These seemingly contradictory goals can only be reached if healthcare providers can offer their services more effectively and efficiently, better using limited resources that include financial assets, employees and staff, machines and facilities, and time. Healthcare providers have the need and opportunity to adopt many of the tools and techniques that have enabled other service industries and manufacturing to become more efficient and effective. Six Sigma and Lean are two of the philosophies that have been successfully implemented in the manufacturing sector to decrease costs, increase product quality, and improve timeliness of delivery (see Chapter 9 for full details on Six Sigma and Lean).

To improve systems and processes, one must first know the system or process and its desired inputs and outputs. This book takes a systems view of service provision and delivery, as illustrated in Exhibit 2.1.

Knowledge-Based Management

To design effective and efficient systems and processes or improve existing processes, knowledge of the systems and processes is needed. This book focuses on knowledge-based management (KBM)—using data and information to base management decisions on facts rather than feelings or intuition.

The **knowledge hierarchy,** as it is sometimes called in the literature, relates to the learning that ultimately underpins KBM and consists of the following five categories (Zeleny 1987) and is illustrated in Exhibit 2.2:

1. Data. Symbols or raw numbers that simply exist; they have no structure or organization. Organizations collect data with their computer systems; individuals collect data through their experiences. In short, know *nothing*.

Knowledge hierarchy
The foundation of knowledge-based management, comprising five categories of learning: data, information, knowledge, understanding, and wisdom.

EXHIBIT 2.2
Knowledge
Hierarchy

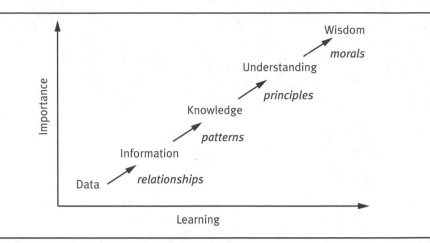

2. Information. Data that are organized or processed to have meaning. Information can be useful, but it is not *necessarily* useful. It can answer such questions as who, what, where, and when. Know *what*.
3. Knowledge. Information that is deliberately useful. Knowledge enables decision making. Know *how*.
4. Understanding. Allows use of what is known and enables the development of new knowledge. Understanding represents the difference between learning and memorizing. Know *why*.
5. Wisdom. Adds moral and ethical views to understanding. Wisdom answers questions to which there is no known correct answer and, in some cases, where there will never be a known correct answer. Know *right*.

Knowledge

A simple example may help explain this hierarchy. Your height is 67 inches, and your weight is 175 pounds (data). You have a body mass index (BMI) of 26.7 (information). A healthy BMI is 18.5 to 25.5 (knowledge). Your BMI is high, and to be healthy you should lower it (understanding). You begin a diet and exercise program and lower your BMI (wisdom).

Finnie (1997, 24) summarizes the relationships within the hierarchy, and our focus on its less important levels:

> Another aspect to learning relates to the five types of the content in the mind. We talk about the accumulation of information, but we fail to distinguish between data, information, knowledge, understanding, and wisdom. An ounce of information is worth a pound of data, an ounce of knowledge is worth a pound of information, an ounce of understanding is worth a pound of knowledge, an ounce of wisdom is worth a pound of understanding. In the past, our focus has been inversely related to

importance. We have focused mainly on data and information, a little bit on knowledge, nothing on understanding, and virtually less than nothing on wisdom.

The roots of the knowledge hierarchy can be traced even further back, to eighteenth-century philosopher Immanuel Kant, much of whose work attempted to address the questions of what and how we can know.

The two major philosophical movements that significantly influenced Kant were empiricism and rationalism (McCormick 2006). The empiricists, most notably John Locke, argued that human knowledge originates in one's experiences. According to Locke, the mind is a blank slate that fills with ideas through its interaction with the world; experience is where all knowledge originates. The rationalists, including Descartes and Galileo, on the other hand, argued that the world is knowable through an analysis of ideas and logical reasoning. Both the empiricists and rationalists viewed the mind as passive, either because it received ideas onto a blank slate or because it possessed innate ideas that could be logically analyzed.

Kant joined these philosophical ideologies and argued that experience leads to knowing only if the mind provides a structure for those experiences. Although the idea that the rational mind plays a role in defining reality is now common, in Kant's time this was a major insight into what and how we know. Knowledge does not flow from our experiences alone, nor from only our ability to reason; rather, knowledge flows from our ability to apply reasoning to our experiences. Relating Kant to the knowledge hierarchy, data are our experiences, information is obtained through logical reasoning, and knowledge is obtained when we take data and apply structured reasoning to that data to acquire knowledge (Ressler and Ahrens 2006).

The intent of this text is to enable readers to gain knowledge. We discuss tools and techniques that enable the application of logical reasoning to data in order to obtain knowledge and use it to make better decisions. This knowledge and understanding should enable the reader to provide healthcare in a more efficient and effective manner.

History of Scientific Management

Frederick Taylor originated the term **scientific management** in *The Principles of Scientific Management* (Taylor 1911). Scientific management methods called for eliminating the old rule-of-thumb, individual way of performing work and, through study and optimization of the work, replacing the varied methods with the one "best" way of performing the work to improve productivity and efficiency. Today, the term "scientific management" has been

Scientific management
A disciplined approach to studying a system or process and then using data to optimize it to be more efficient or effective.

replaced with *operations management*, but the intent is similar: study the process or system and determine ways to optimize it in order to make it more efficient and effective.

Mass Production

The Industrial Revolution and mass production set the stage for much of Taylor's work. Prior to the Industrial Revolution, individual craftsmen performed all tasks necessary to produce a good using their own tools and procedures. In the eighteenth century, Adam Smith advocated the division of labor—making work more efficient through specialization. To support a division of labor, a large number of workers are brought together, and each performs a specific task related to the production of a good. Thus, the factory system of mass production was born, and Henry Ford's assembly line eventually came into being, setting the stage for Taylor's scientific management.

Mass production allows for significant economies of scale, as predicted by Smith. Before Ford set up his moving assembly line, each car chassis was assembled by a single worker and took about 12½ hours to produce. After the introduction of the assembly line, this time was reduced to 93 minutes (Bellis 2006). The standardization of products and work allowed for a reduction in the time needed to produce cars and significantly reduced the costs of production. The selling price of the Model T fell from $1,000 to $360 between 1908 and 1916 (Simkin 2005), allowing Ford to capture a large portion of the market.

Although Ford is commonly credited with introducing the moving assembly line and mass production in modern times, they existed several hundred years earlier. The Venetian Arsenal of the 1500s produced nearly one ship every day and employed 16,000 people (NationMaster.com 2004). Ships were mass produced using premanufactured, standardized parts on a floating assembly line (Schmenner 2001).

One of the first examples of mass production in the healthcare industry is Shouldice Hospital (Heskett 2003). Much like Ford, who said people could have the Model T in any color, "so long as it's black," Shouldice performs just one type of surgery. The hospital performs only routine hernia operations, not more complicated hernia surgery or any other types of surgery.

There exists in healthcare growing evidence that experience in treating specific illnesses and conditions affects the outcome of that care. Higher volumes of cases often result in better outcomes (Halm, Lee, and Chassin 2002). Although higher volume alone does not produce better outcomes, the additional practice associated with higher volume results in better outcomes. The idea of "practice makes perfect," or learning-curve effects, has led organizations such as the Leapfrog Group (made up of organizations that provide healthcare benefits) to make patient volume one of its criteria for quality. The Agency for Healthcare Research and Quality (AHRQ) report "Making Health

Care Safer: A Critical Analysis of Patient Safety Practices" (Auerbach 2001) devotes an entire chapter to this issue and its effect on practice.

Frederick Taylor

Taylor began his work when mass production and the factory system were in their infancy. He believed that US industry was "wasting" human effort and that, as a result, national efficiency (now called productivity) was significantly lower than it could be. The introduction to *The Principles of Scientific Management* (Taylor 1911) illustrates his intent:

> But our larger wastes of human effort, which go on every day through such of our acts as are blundering, ill-directed, or inefficient, and which Mr. Roosevelt refers to as a lack of "national efficiency," are less visible, less tangible, and are but vaguely appreciated. . . . This paper has been written:
>
> *First.* To point out, through a series of simple illustrations, the great loss which the whole country is suffering through inefficiency in almost all of our daily acts.
>
> *Second.* To try to convince the reader that the remedy for this inefficiency lies in systematic management, rather than in searching for some unusual or extraordinary man.
>
> *Third.* To prove that the best management is a true science, resting upon clearly defined laws, rules, and principles, as a foundation. And further to show that the fundamental principles of scientific management are applicable to all kinds of human activities, from our simplest individual acts to the work of our great corporations, which call for the most elaborate cooperation. And, briefly, through a series of illustrations, to convince the reader that whenever these principles are correctly applied, results must follow which are truly astounding.

Note that Taylor specifically mentions systems management as opposed to the individual; this is a common theme that we revisit throughout this book. Rather than focusing on individuals as the cause of problems and the source of solutions, the focus is on systems and their optimization.

Taylor believed that much waste was the result of what he called "soldiering," which today might be called "slacking." He believed that the underlying causes of soldiering were as follows (Taylor 1911):

> *First.* The fallacy, which has from time immemorial been almost universal among workmen, that a material increase in the output of each man or each machine in the trade would result in the end in throwing a large number of men out of work.

Second. The defective systems of management which are in common use, and which make it necessary for each workman to soldier, or work slowly, in order that he may protect his own best interests.

Third. The inefficient rule-of-thumb methods, which are still almost universal in all trades, and in practicing which our workmen waste a large part of their effort.

To eliminate soldiering, Taylor proposed instituting incentive schemes. While at Midvale Steel Company, he used time studies to set daily production quotas. Incentives were paid to those workers reaching their daily goals, and those not reaching their goals were paid significantly less. Productivity at Midvale doubled. Not surprisingly, Taylor's ideas produced considerable backlash. The backlash against increasingly popular pay-for-performance programs in healthcare today is analogous to that experienced by Taylor.

Taylor believed there was "one best way" to perform a task and that careful study and analysis would lead to the discovery of that way. While at Bethlehem Steel Corporation, he studied the shoveling of coal. Using time studies and a careful analysis of how the work was done, he determined that the optimal amount per load was 21 pounds. Taylor then developed shovels that would hold exactly 21 pounds for each type of coal; workers had previously supplied their own shovels (NetMBA.com 2005). He also determined the ideal work rate and rest periods to ensure that workers could shovel all day without fatigue. As a result of Taylor's improved methods, Bethlehem Steel was able to reduce the number of workers shoveling coal from 500 to 140 (Nelson 1980).

Taylor's four principles of scientific management are to

1. develop and standardize work methods based on scientific study and use these to replace individual rule-of-thumb methods;
2. select, train, and develop workers rather than allowing them to choose their own tasks and train themselves;
3. develop a spirit of cooperation between management and workers to ensure that the scientifically developed work methods are both sustainable and implemented on a continuing basis; and
4. divide work between management and workers so that each does an equal share, where management plans the work and workers do the work.

Although some of Taylor's ideas would be problematic today—particularly the notion that workers are "machinelike" and motivated solely by money—many of his ideas can be seen in the foundations of newer initiatives such as Six Sigma and Lean.

Frank and Lillian Gilbreth

The Gilbreths were contemporaries of Frederick Taylor. Frank, who worked in the construction industry, noticed that no two bricklayers performed their tasks the same way. He believed that bricklaying could be standardized and the one best way determined. He studied the work of bricklaying and analyzed the workers' motions, finding much unnecessary stooping, walking, and reaching. He eliminated these motions by developing an adjustable scaffold designed to hold both bricks and mortar (Taylor 1911). As a result of this and other improvements, Frank Gilbreth reduced the number of motions in bricklaying from 18 to 5 (International Work Simplification Institute 1968) and raised output from 1,000 to 2,700 bricks a day (Perkins 1997). He applied what he had learned from his bricklaying experiments to other industries and work.

In his study of surgical operations, Frank Gilbreth found that doctors spent more time searching for instruments than performing the surgery. In response, he developed a technique still seen in operating rooms today: When the doctor needs an instrument, he extends his hand, palm up, and asks for the instrument, which is then placed in his hand. Not only does this eliminate searching for the instrument, but it allows the doctor to stay focused on the surgical area and therefore reduces surgical time (Perkins 1997).

Frank and Lillian Gilbreth may be more familiarly known as the parents in the book (Gilbreth and Carey 1948), movie (Lang 1950), and remake of the movie (Levy 2003) *Cheaper by the Dozen*. The Gilbreths incorporated many of their time-saving ideas in their family as well. For example, they only bought one type of sock for all 12 of their children, thus eliminating time-consuming sorting.

Scientific Management Today

Scientific management fell out of favor during the Depression, partly because of the belief that it dehumanized employees, but mainly because it was believed that productivity improvements resulted in downsizing and greater unemployment. Not until World War II was there a resurgence of interest in scientific management, or *operations research*, as it came to be called. Despite this period of disfavor, modern operations management has its roots in the theories of scientific management.

In healthcare today, standardized methods and procedures are used to reduce costs and increase the quality of outcomes. Specialized equipment has been developed to speed procedures and reduce labor costs. In some sense, we are still searching for the one best way. However, care must be taken to heed the lessons of the past. If the tools of operations management are perceived to be dehumanizing or to result in downsizing by healthcare organizations, their implementation will meet significant resistance.

Project Management

The discipline of project management began with the development of the Gantt chart in the early twentieth century. Henry Gantt worked closely with Frederick Taylor at Midvale Steel and in Navy ship construction during World War I. From this work, he developed Gantt charts—bar graphs that illustrate the duration of project tasks and visually display scheduled and actual progress. Gantt charts were used to help manage such large projects as the construction of the Hoover Dam and proved to be such a powerful tool that they are commonly used today.

Although Gantt charts were used in large projects, they are not ideal for large, complicated projects because they do not explicitly show precedence relationships, that is, what tasks need to be completed before other tasks can start. In the 1950s, two mathematic project scheduling techniques were developed: the **program evaluation and review technique (PERT)** and the **critical path method (CPM)**. Both techniques begin by developing a project network showing the precedence relationships among tasks and task duration.

PERT was developed by the US Navy in response to the desire to accelerate the Polaris missile program. This "need for speed" was precipitated by the Soviet launch of Sputnik, the first space satellite. PERT uses a probability distribution (the Beta distribution), rather than a point estimate, for the duration of each project task. The probability of completing the entire project in a given amount of time can then be determined. This technique is most useful for estimating project completion time when task times are uncertain and for evaluating risks to project completion prior to the start of a project.

The CPM technique was developed at the same time as PERT by the DuPont and Remington Rand corporations to manage plant maintenance projects. CPM uses the project network and point estimates of task duration times to determine the critical path through the network, or the sequence of activities that will take the longest to complete. If any one of the activities on the critical path is delayed, the entire project is delayed. This technique is most useful when task times can be estimated with certainty and is typically used in project management and control.

Although both of these techniques are powerful analytical tools for planning, implementing, controlling, and evaluating a project plan, performing the required calculations by hand is quite tedious, and their use was not widespread. With the advent of commercially available project management software for personal computers in the late 1960s, use of these techniques increased considerably. Today, numerous project management software packages are commercially available, and these techniques are used extensively in industry. Microsoft Project, for instance, can perform network analysis based on either PERT or CPM; however, the default is CPM, making this the more commonly used technique.

Program evaluation and review technique (PERT)
PERT is a graphic technique used to link and analyze all tasks within a project. This graph can then be used to optimize the project's schedule.

Critical path method (CPM)
The critical path is the longest path through a graph of linked tasks within a project. The critical path method is used to reduce the total time of a project by reducing the duration of tasks on the critical path.

Projects are an integral part of many of the process improvement initiatives found in the healthcare industry. Project management and its tools are needed to ensure that projects related to quality, Lean, and supply chain management are completed in the most effective and timely manner possible.

Quality

Walter Shewhart

Although W. Edwards Deming and Joseph Juran are sometimes referred to as the fathers of the quality movement, Walter Shewhart is its grandfather. Both Deming and Juran studied under Shewhart, and much of their work was influenced by his ideas.

Shewhart believed that managers needed certain information to enable them to make scientific, efficient, and economical decisions. He developed **statistical process control (SPC)** charts to supply that information (Shewhart 1931). He also believed that management and production practices need to be continuously evaluated and adopted or rejected based on this evaluation if an organization hopes to evolve and survive. The Deming cycle of improvement, or Deming wheel (**plan-do-check-act [PDCA]** or plan-do-study-act), was adapted from Shewhart's work (Shewhart and Deming 1939).

W. Edwards Deming

Deming was an employee of the US government in the 1930s and 1940s, working with statistical sampling techniques. He became a supporter and student of Shewhart, believing that his techniques could be useful in nonmanufacturing environments. Deming applied SPC methods to his work at the National Bureau of the Census to improve clerical operations in preparation for the 1940 population census. In some cases, productivity improved by a factor of six (Kansal and Rao 2006). Deming taught seminars to bring his and Shewhart's work to US and Canadian organizations, where major reductions in scrap and rework resulted. However, after the war Deming's ideas lost popularity in the United States, mainly because demand for all products was so great that quality became unimportant; any product was snapped up by hungry consumers.

After the war Deming went to Japan as an adviser for that country's census. While he was there, the Union of Japanese Scientists and Engineers invited him to lecture on quality control techniques, and Deming brought his message to Japanese executives: Improving quality will reduce expenses while increasing productivity and market share. During the 1950s and 1960s, Deming's ideas were widely known and implemented in Japan, but not in the United States.

Statistical process control (SPC)
A scientific approach to controlling the performance of a process by measuring the process outputs and then using statistical tools to determine whether this process is meeting expected performance.

Plan-do-check-act (PDCA)
A core process-improvement tool with four elements: Plan your change to a process; do the change; check to make sure it is working as expected; act to make sure this change is sustainable.

The energy crisis of the 1970s and resulting increase in popularity of Japanese automobiles and decline of the US auto industry set the stage for the return of Deming's ideas. The lower prices and higher quality of Japanese automobiles and electronic goods threatened US industries and the economy. The 1980 television documentary *If Japan Can, Why Can't We* (Mason 1980), investigating the increasing competition US industry was facing from Japan, made Deming and his quality ideas known to an even broader audience. Much like the Institute of Medicine report *To Err Is Human* (1999) increased awareness of the need for quality in healthcare, this documentary increased awareness of the need for quality in manufacturing.

Deming's quality ideas reflected his statistical background, but experience in their implementation caused him to broaden his approach. He believed that managers must understand the two types of variation. The first type, variation from special causes, is a result of a change in the system and can be identified or assigned and the problem fixed. The second type, variation from common causes, is a result of the natural differences in the system and cannot be eliminated without changing the system. Although it might be possible to identify the common causes of variation, they cannot be fixed without the authority and ability to improve the system, for which management is typically responsible.

Deming's quality ideas went far beyond SPC to include a systematic approach to problem solving and continuous process improvement with his PDCA cycle. He also believed that management is ultimately responsible for quality and must actively support and encourage quality "transformations" within organizations. In the preface to *Out of the Crisis*, Deming (1986) writes:

> Drastic changes are required. The first step in the transformation is to learn how to change. . . . Long term commitment to new learning and new philosophy is required of any management that seeks transformation. The timid and the faint-hearted, and people that expect quick results are doomed to disappointment. Whilst the introduction of statistical problem solving and quality techniques and computerization and robotization have a part to play, this is not the solution: Solving problems, big problems and little problems, will not halt the decline of American industry, nor will expansion in use of computers, gadgets, and robotic machinery.
>
> Benefits from massive expansion of new machinery also constitute a vain hope. Massive immediate expansion in the teaching of statistical methods to production workers is not the answer either, nor wholesale flashes of quality control circles. All these activities make their contribution, but they only prolong the life of the patient, they cannot halt the decline.

Only transformation of management and of Government's relations with industry can halt the decline.

Out of the Crisis contains Deming's famous 14 points for management (Deming 1986). Although not as well known, he also published an adaptation of the 14 points for medical service (Exhibit 2.3), which he attributed to Drs. Paul B. Batalden and Loren Vorlicky of the Health Services Research Center, Minneapolis.

The New Economics for Industry, Government, Education (Deming 1994) outlines the Deming System of Profound Knowledge. Deming believed that to transform organizations, the individuals in those organizations need to understand the four parts of his system of profound knowledge:

1. *Appreciation for a system*: everything is related to everything else, and those inside the system need to understand the relationships within it.
2. *Knowledge about variation*: this refers to what can and cannot be done to decrease either of the two types of variation.
3. *Theory of knowledge*: this refers to the need for understanding and knowledge rather than information.
4. *Knowledge of psychology*: people are intrinsically motivated and different from one another, and attempts to use extrinsic motivators can result in unwanted outcomes.

Deming's 14 points and system of profound knowledge still provide a road map for organizational transformation.

---

1. Establish constancy of purpose toward service.
   a. Define in operational terms what you mean by "service to patients."
   b. Specify standards of service for a year hence and for five years hence.
   c. Define the patients whom you are seeking to serve.
   d. Constancy of purpose brings innovation.
   e. Innovate for better service.
   f. Put resources into maintenance and new aids to production.
   g. Decide whom the administrators are responsible to and the means by which they will be held responsible.
   h. Translate this constancy of purpose to service to patients and the community.
   i. The board of directors must hold onto the purpose.

2. Adopt the new philosophy. We are in a new economic age. We can no longer live with commonly accepted levels of mistakes, materials not

(continued)

EXHIBIT 2.3
Deming's Adaptation of the 14 Points for Medical Service

EXHIBIT 2.3
Deming's
Adaptation of
the 14 Points for
Medical Service
(continued)

suited to the job, people on the job who do not know what the job is and are afraid to ask, failure of management to understand their job, antiquated methods of training on the job, and inadequate and ineffective supervision. The board must put resources into this new philosophy, with commitment to in-service training.

3. a. Require statistical evidence of quality of incoming materials, such as pharmaceuticals. Inspection is not the answer. Inspection is too late and is unreliable. Inspection does not produce quality. The quality is already built in and paid for. Require corrective action, where needed, for all tasks that are performed in the hospital.
   b. Institute a rigid program of feedback from patients in regard to their satisfaction with services.
   c. Look for evidence of rework or defects and the cost that may accrue.

4. Deal with vendors that can furnish statistical evidence of control. We must take a clear stand that price of services has no meaning without adequate measure of quality. Without such a stand for rigorous measures of quality, business drifts to the lowest bidder, low quality and high cost being the inevitable result.

   Requirement of suitable measures of quality will, in all likelihood, require us to reduce the number of vendors. We must work with vendors so that we understand the procedures that they use to achieve reduced numbers of defects.

5. Improve constantly and forever the system of production and service.

6. Restructure training.
   a. Develop the concept of tutors.
   b. Develop increased in-service education.
   c. Teach employees methods of statistical control on the job.
   d. Provide operational definitions of all jobs.
   e. Provide training until the learner's work reaches the state of statistical control.

7. Improve supervision. Supervision is the responsibility of the management.
   a. Supervisors need time to help people on the job.
   b. Supervisors need to find ways to translate the constancy of purpose to the individual employee.
   c. Supervisors must be trained in simple statistical methods with the aim to detect and eliminate special causes of mistakes and rework.
   d. Focus supervisory time on people who are out of statistical control and not those who are low performers. If the members of a group are in fact in statistical control, there will be some low performers and some high performers.

EXHIBIT 2.3
Deming's
Adaptation of
the 14 Points for
Medical Service
(continued)

   e. Teach supervisors how to use the results of surveys of patients.

8. Drive out fear. We must break down the class distinctions between types of workers within the organization—physicians, nonphysicians, clinical providers versus nonclinical providers, physician to physician. Discontinue gossip. Cease to blame employees for problems of the system. Management should be held responsible for faults of the system. People need to feel secure to make suggestions. Management must follow through on suggestions. People on the job cannot work effectively if they dare not offer suggestions for simplification and improvement of the system.

9. Break down barriers between departments. One way would be to encourage switches of personnel in related departments.

10. Eliminate numerical goals, slogans, and posters imploring people to do better. Instead, display accomplishments of the management in respect to helping employees improve their performance.

11. Eliminate work standards that set quotas. Work standards must produce quality, not mere quantity. It is better to take aim at rework, error, and defects.

12. Institute a massive training program in statistical techniques. Bring statistical techniques down to the level of the individual employee's job, and help him to gather information about the nature of his job in a systematic way.

13. Institute a vigorous program for retraining people in new skills. People must be secure about their jobs in the future and must know that acquiring new skills will facilitate security.

14. Create a structure in top management that will push every day on the previous 13 points. Top management may organize a task force with the authority and obligation to act. This task force will require guidance from an experienced consultant, but the consultant cannot take on obligations that only the management can carry out.

SOURCE: Deming, W. Edwards, *Out of the Crisis*, pp. 199–203, © 2000 Massachusetts Institute of Technology, by permission of The MIT Press.

Joseph M. Juran

Joseph Juran was a contemporary of Deming and a student of Shewhart. He began his career at the famous Western Electric Hawthorne Plant, site of the Hawthorne studies (Mayo 1933) related to worker motivation. Western Electric had close ties to Bell Telephone, Shewhart's employer, because the company was the sole supplier of telephone equipment to Bell.

During World War II, Juran served as assistant administrator for the Lend-Lease Administration. Juran's quality improvement techniques made

EXHIBIT 2.4
Juran's Quality
Trilogy

	Basic Quality Processes
Quality Planning	Identify the customers, both external and internal. Determine customer needs. Develop product features that respond to customer. Establish quality goals that meet the needs of customers and suppliers alike, and do so at a minimum combined cost. Develop a process that can produce the needed product features. Prove the process capability—prove that the process can meet quality goals under operating conditions.
Control	Choose control subjects—what to control. Choose units of measurement. Establish measurement. Establish standards of performance. Measure actual performance. Interpret the difference (actual versus standard). Take action on the difference.
Improvement	Prove the need for improvement. Identify specific projects for improvement. Organize to guide the projects. Organize for diagnosis—for discovery of causes. Diagnose to find the causes. Provide remedies. Prove that the remedies are effective under operating conditions. Provide for control to hold the gains.

SOURCE: Juran, J. M. 1986. "The Quality Trilogy." *Quality Progress* 19 (8): 19–24. Reprinted with permission from Juran Institute, Inc.

him instrumental in improving the efficiency of processes by eliminating unnecessary paperwork and ensuring the timely arrival of supplies to US allies.

Juran's Quality Handbook (Juran and Godfrey 1998) was first published in 1951 and remains a standard reference for quality. Juran was one of the first to define quality from the customer perspective as "fitness for use." He compared this definition with the alternative, and somewhat confusing, definition of quality as the number or type of features (Michael Porter's differentiation).

Juran's contributions to quality include the adaptation of the **Pareto principle** to the quality arena (see Chapter 8 for its application in quality improvement). According to this principle, 80 percent of defects are caused by 20 percent of problems, and quality improvement should therefore focus

Pareto principle
Developed by
Italian economist
Vilfredo Pareto
in 1906 based on
his observation
that 80 percent of
the wealth in Italy
was owned by
20 percent of the
population.

on the "vital few" to gain the most benefit. The roots of Six Sigma programs can be seen in Juran's (1986) **quality trilogy**, shown in Exhibit 2.4

Avedis Donabedian

Avedis Donabedian was born in 1919 in Beirut, Lebanon, and received a medical degree from the American University of Beirut. In 1955, he earned a master's degree in public health from Harvard University. While a student at Harvard, Donabedian wrote a paper on quality assessment that brought his work to the attention of various experts in the field of public health. He taught for a short period at New York Medical College before becoming a faculty member at the School of Public Health of the University of Michigan, where he stayed for the remainder of his career.

Shortly after Donabedian joined the University of Michigan faculty, the US Public Health Service began a project looking at the entire field of health services research. Donabedian was asked to review and evaluate the literature on quality assessment for this project. This work culminated in his famous article, "Evaluating the Quality of Medical Care" (Donabedian 1966). This was followed by a three-volume book set, *Exploration in Quality Assessment and Monitoring* (Donabedian 1980, 1982, 1985). Over the course of his career, Donabedian wrote 16 books and more than 100 articles focused on quality assessment and improvement in the healthcare sector on such topics as the definition of quality in healthcare, relationship between outcomes and process, effect of clinical decisions on quality, effectiveness of quality programs, and relationship between quality and cost (Sunol 2000).

Donabedian (1980) defined healthcare quality in terms of efficacy, efficiency, optimality, adaptability, legitimacy, equality, and cost. Donabedian (1966) was one of the first to view healthcare as a system composed of structure, process, and outcome, providing a framework for health services research still used today. He also highlighted many of the issues still faced in attempting to measure structures, processes, and outcomes.

Donabedian defined outcomes as recovery, restoration of function, and survival, but he also included less easily measured outcomes such as patient satisfaction. Process of care consists of the methods by which care is delivered, including gathering appropriate and necessary information, developing competence in diagnosis and therapy, and providing preventive care. Finally, structure is related to the environment in which care takes place, including facilities and equipment, medical staff qualifications, administrative structure, and programs. Donabedian (1966, 188) believed that quality of care is not only related to each of these elements individually, but also to the relationships among them:

> Clearly, the relationships between process and outcome, and between structure and both process and outcome, are not fully understood. With

Quality trilogy
A comprehensive quality improvement and management system with three key components: quality planning, control, and improvement.

regard to this, the requirements of validation are best expressed by the concept, already referred to, of a chain of events in which each event is an end to the one that comes before it and a necessary condition to the one that follows.

Similar to Deming and Juran, Donabedian advocated the continuous improvement of healthcare quality through structure and process changes supported by outcome assessment.

The influence of Donabedian's seminal work in healthcare can still be seen. Pay-for-performance programs (structure) reward providers for delivering care that meets evidence-based goals assessed in terms of process or outcomes. The 5 Million Lives Campaign (and its predecessor, the 100,000 Lives Campaign; IHI 2006) is a program (structure) designed to decrease mortality (outcome) through the use of evidence-based practices and procedures (process). Not only are assessments of process, structure, and outcome being developed, implemented, and reported, but the focus is shifting toward the more systematic view of healthcare advocated by Donabedian.

TQM and CQI, Leading to Six Sigma

The US Navy is credited with coining the term **total quality management (TQM)** in the 1980s to describe its approach, informed by Japanese models, to quality management and improvement (Hefkin 1993). TQM has come to mean a management philosophy or program aimed at ensuring quality (defined as customer satisfaction) by focusing on quality throughout the organization and product/service life cycle. All stakeholders in the organization participate in a continuous improvement cycle.

TQM (or **continuous quality improvement [CQI]**, as it is referred to in healthcare) is not defined by any one organization or individual and has come to encompass the theory and ideas of such quality experts as W. Edwards Deming, Joseph M. Juran, Philip B. Crosby, Armand V. Feigenbaum, Kaoru Ishikawa, and Avedis Donabedian. TQM may therefore mean different things to different people, and implementation and vocabulary vary from one organization to the next. Possibly as a result, TQM programs have become less popular in the United States and have been replaced with more codified programs such as Six Sigma, Lean, and the Baldrige criteria.

Six Sigma and TQM are both based on the teachings of Shewhart, Deming, Juran, and other quality experts. Both TQM and Six Sigma emphasize the importance of top management support and leadership, and both focus on continuous improvement as a means to ensure the long-term viability of an organization. The define-measure-analyze-improve-control cycle of Six Sigma has its roots in the PDCA cycle (see Chapter 8) of TQM. Six Sigma and TQM have been described as both philosophies and methodologies. Six Sigma can also be defined as a metric, or goal, of 3.4 defects per

Total quality management (TQM)
A management philosophy or program aimed at ensuring quality (defined as customer satisfaction) by focusing on quality throughout the organization and product/service life cycle.

Continuous quality improvement (CQI)
A comprehensive quality improvement and management system with three key components: quality planning, control, and improvement.

million opportunities, whereas TQM never had that specific goal. TQM was never as clearly defined as Six Sigma, nor are certification programs specifically associated with TQM.

TQM was defined mainly by academics and is more abstract and general, whereas Six Sigma has its base in industry—Motorola and GE were early developers—and is more specific, providing a clear framework for organizations to follow. Early TQM efforts focused on quality as the primary goal; improved business performance was thought to be a natural outcome of this goal. Quality departments were mainly responsible for TQM throughout the organization. While Six Sigma makes quality as defined by the customer a primary goal and focuses on tangible results, it also takes into account the effects on business performance. No longer is the focus on quality for quality's sake, but rather a quality focus is seen as a means to improve organizational performance. Six Sigma training in the use of specific tools and techniques provides common understanding and common vocabulary both throughout and across organizations; this method makes quality the goal of the entire organization, not just the quality department.

Basically, Six Sigma took the theory and tools of TQM and codified their implementation, providing a well-defined approach to quality so that organizations could more quickly and easily adopt Six Sigma.

ISO 9000

The **ISO 9000** series of standards are primarily concerned with quality management, or how the organization ensures that its products and services satisfy the customer's quality requirements and comply with applicable regulations. The five international ISO 9000 standards were first published in 1987 by the International Organization for Standardization (ISO). In 2002, the ISO 9000 standard was renamed ISO 9000:2000; the ISO 9001, 9002, and 9003 standards were consolidated into ISO 9001:2000. The standards are concerned with the processes of ensuring quality rather than the products or services themselves. These standards give organizations guidelines to develop and maintain effective quality systems.

ISO 9000
Standards developed by the International Organization for Standardization to give organizations guidelines to develop and maintain effective quality systems.

Many organizations require that their vendors be ISO certified. For an organization to be registered as an ISO 9001 supplier, it must demonstrate to an accredited registrar (third-party organizations who are themselves certified as registrars) compliance with the requirements specified in the standard(s). Organizations that are not required by their vendors to be certified can use the standards to ensure quality systems without attempting to be certified.

In the interest of improving the quality of healthcare and reducing or maintaining costs, many automotive manufacturers have begun to require that their healthcare providers be ISO 9001 certified. Driven by this, ISO developed guidelines for implementing ISO 9000 quality management systems in the healthcare sector, "IWA 1, Quality Management Systems—Guidelines for Process Improvements in Health Service Organizations" (ISO 2005).

Baldrige Award

Malcolm Baldrige National Quality Award
An annual award established by Congress in 1987 to recognize US organizations for their achievements in quality.

Japanese automobiles and electronics gained market share in the United States during the 1970s because of their higher quality and lower costs. In the early 1980s, both US government and industry believed that the only way for the country to stay competitive was to increase industry focus on quality. The **Malcolm Baldrige National Quality Award** was established by Congress in 1987 to recognize US organizations for their achievements in quality. It was hoped that the award would raise awareness about the importance of quality as a competitive priority and help disseminate best practices by providing examples of how to achieve quality and performance excellence. The award was originally given annually to a maximum of three organizations in each of three categories: manufacturing, service, and small business. In 1999 the categories of education and healthcare were added, and in 2002 the first Baldrige Award in healthcare was given. The healthcare category includes hospitals, health maintenance organizations, long-term care facilities, healthcare practitioner offices, home health agencies, health insurance companies, and medical and dental laboratories. By 2005, 83 applications had been submitted in the healthcare category. Two additional categories, nonprofit and government, were added in 2006.

The program is a cooperative effort of government and the private sector. The evaluations are performed by a board of examiners that includes experts from industry, academia, government, and nonprofits. The examiners volunteer their time to review applications, conduct site visits, and provide applicants with feedback on their strengths and opportunities for improvement in each of seven categories. Additionally, board members give presentations on quality management, performance improvement, and the Baldrige Award.

One of the main purposes of the award is the dissemination of best practices and strategies. Recipients are asked to participate in conferences, provide basic materials on their organizations' performance strategies and methods to interested parties, and answer inquiries from the media. Baldrige Award recipients have gone beyond these expectations to give thousands of presentations aimed at educating other organizations on the benefits of using the Baldrige framework and disseminating best practices. Since 2002 there has been a specific Baldrige award for healthcare, and many organizations now use the application process as a structure for their comprehensive quality improvement programs.

JIT, Leading to Lean and Agile

Just-in-time (JIT) is an inventory management strategy aimed at reducing or eliminating inventory. It is one part of Lean manufacturing, or the **Toyota Production System (TPS)**. The goal of Lean production is to eliminate waste, of which inventory is one form. JIT was the term originally used for Lean production in the United States, where industry leaders noted the success of the Japanese auto manufacturers and attempted to copy it by adopting Japanese practices. As academics and organizations realized that Lean production was more than JIT, inventory management terms such as *big JIT* and *little JIT* were employed, and JIT production became somewhat synonymous with Lean production. For clarity, the term "JIT" indicates the inventory management strategy in this text.

After World War II, Japanese industry needed to rebuild and grow, and its leaders wanted to copy the assembly line and mass production systems found in the United States. However, they had limited resources and limited storage space. At the Toyota Motor Corporation, Taiichi Ohno and Shigeo Shingo began to develop what has become known as the Toyota Production System, or TPS. They began by realizing that large amounts of capital dollars are tied up in inventory in the mass production system that was typical at that time.

Ohno and Shingo sought to reduce inventory by various means, most importantly by increasing the flow rate of product. Standardization reduced the number of parts in inventory and the number of tools and machines needed. Processes like single-minute exchange of die (SMED) allowed for quick changeovers of tooling, increasing the amount of time that could be used for production by reducing setup time. As in-process inventory was reduced, large amounts of capital were freed. Customer lead time and uncertainty about orders were reduced as the speed of product flow increased throughout the plant. Because inventory provides a buffer for poor quality, reducing inventory forced Toyota to pay extremely close attention to not only its own quality but suppliers' quality as well. To discover the best ways to fix the system to reduce inventory, management and line workers needed to cooperate, and teams became an integral part of Lean.

When the US auto industry began to be threatened by Japanese automobiles, management and scholars from the United States began to study this Japanese system. However, what they brought back were usually the most visible techniques of the program—JIT, kanbans, quality circles—rather than the underlying principles of Lean. Not surprisingly, many of the first US firms that attempted to copy this system failed; however, some were successful. *The Machine That Changed the World* (Womack, Jones, and Roos 1990), a study of Japanese, European, and American automobile manufacturing practices, first introduced the term *Lean manufacturing* and brought the theory, principles, and techniques of Lean to a broad audience.

Just-in-time (JIT)
An inventory management system designed to improve efficiency and reduce waste. Part of Lean manufacturing.

Toyota Production System (TPS)
A quality improvement system developed by Toyota for its auto manufacturing lines. TPS has broad applicability beyond auto manufacturing and is now commonly known as Lean manufacturing.

Lean is both a management philosophy and a strategy. Its goal is to eliminate all waste in the system. Although Lean production originated in manufacturing, the goal of eliminating waste is easily applied to the service sector. Many healthcare organizations are using the tools and techniques associated with Lean to improve efficiency and effectiveness.

Lean is sometimes seen as being broader than TQM or Six Sigma. In order to be truly Lean, an organization must have quality. In order to be a quality organization, it does not necessarily need to be Lean. On the other hand, if customers value speed of delivery and low cost, and quality is defined as customer satisfaction, a quality focus would cause an organization to strive to be Lean. Either program would result in the same outcome.

Baldrige, Six Sigma, Lean, and ISO 9000

All of these systems or frameworks are designed for performance improvement, and each differs in focus, tools, and techniques. However, all of these programs emphasize customer focus, process or system analysis, teamwork, and quality, and they are all compatible.

The importance of the organization's culture and management's ability to shape that culture cannot be overestimated. The successful implementation of any program or deployment of any technique requires a culture that supports those changes. The leading cause of failure of new initiatives is lack of top management support or lack of buy-in on the part of employees. Management must truly believe that a particular initiative will make the organization better and must demonstrate their support in that belief, both ideologically and financially, to ensure the success of the initiative. Employee buy-in and support will only happen when top management commitment is evident. Communication and training can aid this process, but only true management commitment will ensure success.

Service Typologies

Service typologies, or classification schemes, are primarily used to segment different types of services to gain strategic insight into the management and positioning of a particular service (Cook, Goh, and Chung 1999). The focus of these service typologies varies. A few are based on ownership type (e.g., nonprofit). A large number are based in a customer or marketing perspective with dimensions such as product tangibility or type of customer. Finally, some service typologies are more operational in nature. Here, the focus is on the more operational typologies, where typical dimensions include customer contact, capital intensity, customer involvement, and the service process.

Supply Chain Management

The term *supply chain management* (SCM) was first used in the early 1980s. In 2005, the Council of Supply Chain Management Professionals agreed on the following definition of SCM (Council of Supply Chain Management Professionals 2006):

> Supply Chain Management encompasses the planning and management of all activities involved in sourcing and procurement, conversion, and all Logistics Management activities. Importantly, it also includes coordination and collaboration with channel partners, which can be suppliers, intermediaries, third-party service providers, and customers. In essence, Supply Chain Management integrates supply and demand management within and across companies.

This definition makes it apparent that SCM is a broad discipline, encompassing activities outside as well as inside an organization.

SCM has its roots in **systems thinking**. Systems thinking is based on the idea that everything affects everything else. The need for systems thinking comes from the fact that it is possible, and even likely, to optimize one part of a system if the whole system is suboptimal. A current example of a suboptimal system in healthcare can be seen in prescription drugs. In the United States, the customer can optimize his drug purchases (minimize cost) by purchasing drugs from pharmacies located in foreign countries (e.g., Canada, Mexico). Often, these drugs are manufactured in the United States. While the customer has minimized his costs, the total supply chain has additional costs from the extra transportation incurred by shipping drugs to Canada or another foreign country and then back to the United States.

Systems thinking
A view of reality that emphasizes the relationships and interactions of each part of the system to all of the other parts.

SCM became increasingly important to manufacturing organizations in the late 1990s, driven by the need to decrease costs in response to competitive pressures and enabled by technological advances. As manufacturing became more automated, labor costs as a percentage of total costs decreased, and the percentage of material and supply costs increased. In 2006, 70 to 80 percent of the cost of a manufactured good was in purchased materials and services, and less than 25 percent was in labor (BEA 2006); this trend continues today. Consequently, there are fewer opportunities for reducing the cost of goods through decreasing labor and more opportunities associated with managing the supply chain. Additionally, advances in information technology allowed firms to collect and analyze the information needed to more efficiently manage their supply chains. SCM was enabled by technology, beginning with the inventory management systems of the 1970s, including materials requirements planning, followed by the enterprise resource planning systems of the 1990s. As industry moved to more sophisticated technological systems for managing

EXHIBIT 2.5   Important Events in Performance Improvement

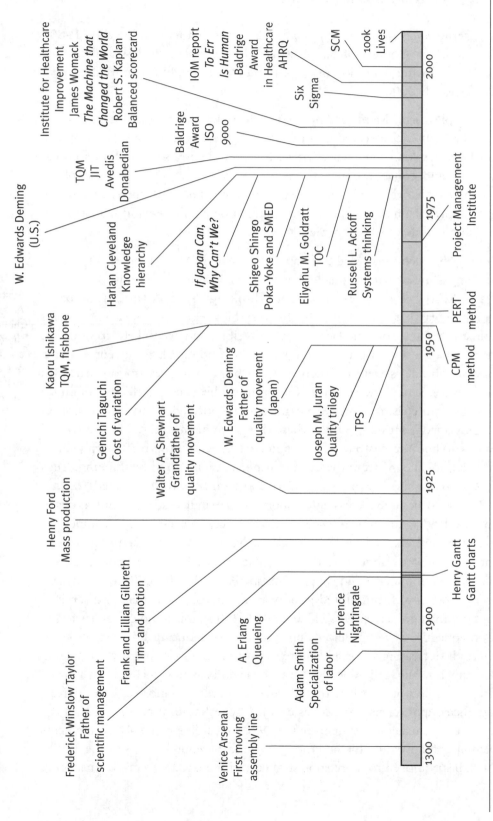

the flow of information and goods, the ability to collect and respond to information about the entire supply chain increased, and firms were able to actively manage their supply chains.

SCM is becoming increasingly important with the growing focus on reducing the costs of healthcare and the need to reduce those costs through the development of more efficient and effective supply chains.

Conclusion

Service organizations in general and healthcare organizations in particular have lagged in their adoption of process improvement philosophies, techniques, and tools of operations management, but they no longer have this option. Healthcare organizations are facing increasing pressures from consumers, industry, and governments to deliver their services in a more efficient and effective manner and need to adopt these "new" philosophies to remain competitive. In healthcare today, organizations such as the Institute for Healthcare Improvement (IHI) and AHRQ are leading the way in the development and dissemination of tools, techniques, and programs aimed at improving the quality, safety, efficiency, and effectiveness of the healthcare system. Although these tools and techniques have been adapted for contemporary healthcare, their roots are in the past, and an understanding of this history (Exhibit 2.5) can enable organizations to move successfully into the future.

Discussion Questions

1. What is the difference between data, information, knowledge, and wisdom? Give specific examples of each in your own organization.
2. How has operations management changed since its early days as scientific management?
3. What are the major factors leading to increased interest in the use of operations management tools and techniques in the healthcare sector?
4. Why has ISO 9000 certification become important to healthcare organizations?
5. Research firms that have won the Baldrige Award in the healthcare sector. What factors led to their success in winning the award?
6. What are some of the reasons for the success of Six Sigma?
7. What are some of the reasons for the success of Lean?
8. How are Lean initiatives similar to TQM and Six Sigma initiatives? How are they different?
9. Why is SCM becoming increasingly important to healthcare organizations?

EVIDENCE-BASED MEDICINE AND VALUE-BASED PURCHASING

Operations Management in Action

An alternative provider payment program in Massachusetts is showing promising results, giving hope that payment strategies outside traditional fee-for-service can work to reduce costs and increase quality.

Blue Cross and Blue Shield of Massachusetts launched its Alternative Quality Contract, AQC, in January 2009. The five-year contract is a modified global payment model where annual payments to medical groups are linked to monthly budgets for each patient with performance incentives.

In the first year, the 6,300 physicians working under AQCs improved care more than the 14,200 physicians working in the Blues' traditional HMO network, according to the report released by the Boston-based insurer.

The participating physicians have the opportunity to earn up to an additional 10 percent of their global budget by meeting 64 quality measures, including 32 hospital measures. These measure processes, outcomes, and patient-care experience. AQC participants did better than those physicians working under the traditional network agreement. For instance, the AQC groups' performance on preventative-care measures was three times that of non-AQC groups.

Reducing the rate of hospital readmissions and nonemergent emergency use are also goals of the program. The readmission rate averages 8 percent, but AQC groups in the program longest showed improvements, and a decrease equivalent to $1.8 million in avoided readmission costs. One AQC reduced its nonemergent ER visits by 22 percent, a $300,000 savings in annual ER costs, according to the report.

"When we launched the AQCs, we had the goals of improving quality and outcomes while significantly lowering the rate of growth in healthcare costs," said Dana Safran, vice president for performance measurement and improvement for the Massachusetts Blues. "We are strongly on track with both these goals."

SOURCE: Vesely (2011).

Overview

The science of medicine advanced rapidly through the latter half of the twentieth century with advances in pharmaceuticals, surgical techniques, laboratory and imaging technology, and the rapid subspecialization of medicine itself. This "age of miracles" improved health and lengthened life spans. In the mid-1960s, the federal government began the Medicare and Medicaid programs, and this new source of funding fueled the growth and expansion of the healthcare delivery system.

Unfortunately, because this growth was so explosive, many new tools and clinical approaches that had little scientific merit were initiated. As these clinical approaches were used broadly, they became community standards. In addition, many highly effective, simple clinical tools and techniques were not being used consistently.

In response to these problems, a number of courageous clinicians began the movement that has resulted in what is known today as evidence-based medicine (EBM). Evidence-based medicine is the conscientious and judicious use of the best current evidence in making decisions about the care of individual patients. In almost all cases, the broad application of EBM not only improves clinical outcomes for patients but reduces costs in the system as well.

This chapter reviews:

- The history, current status, and future of EBM
- Standard and custom care
- Public reporting and pay-for-performance (P4P)
- Issues in the use of P4P and public reporting for changing clinician behavior
- The Medicare value purchasing program

EBM is explored in depth, followed by an examination of how payers are using these principles to encourage the use of EBM by clinicians. The operations tools included in other chapters of this book are linked to achieving EBM goals. The chapter concludes with an illustration of the chartering of a project team to improve implementation of EBM at Vincent Valley Hospital and Health System (VVH).

The companion website contains many additional references and, because these topics are changing rapidly, will be updated frequently.

www.ache.org/books/OpsManagement2

Evidence-Based Medicine

The expansion of clinical knowledge has three major phases. First, basic research is done in the lab and with animal models. Second, carefully controlled clinical trials are conducted to demonstrate the efficacy of a new diagnostic or treatment methodology. Third, the clinical trial results are translated into clinical practice. The final phase of translation is where the system frequently breaks down. For example, in 2010 a survey of nearly 1,300 primary care physicians in the United States found that only about 20 percent of them recommend colorectal cancer screenings to their patients in accordance with current practice guidelines. About 40 percent of the doctors followed some of the practice guidelines, while the remaining 40 percent ignored practice guidelines (Yabroff et al. 2010).

The cure to this wide variation in practice is the *consistent application* of EBM. The major tool is the clinical guideline:

> Clinical practice guidelines are systematically developed statements to assist practitioner and patient decisions about appropriate healthcare for specific clinical circumstances. Evidence-based clinical guidance documents are heterogeneous, as is the terminology utilized to describe and/or label them. The phrases *guideline, protocol, practice parameter, pathway, standard,* etc., are used in many different contexts by different guideline developers (NCC 2012).

A comprehensive source for such information is the National Guideline Clearinghouse (2011), a database of evidence-based clinical practice guidelines and related documents that contains more than 4,000 guidelines. The Clearinghouse is a joint project of the Agency for Healthcare Research and Quality (AHRQ), the American Medical Association, and America's Health Insurance Plans. In addition, AHRQ provides easy-to-use resources for clinicians and patients though its Effective Health Care Program (AHRQ 2012).

What are the barriers to the wider application of EBM? Baiardini and colleagues (2009) reviewed the literature and identified 293 potential obstacles to the use of guidelines by physicians. They then grouped them into seven barriers:

1. Lack of knowledge that guidelines exist for a specific condition
2. Lack of familiarity with the details of specific guidelines
3. Disagreement with the guideline recommendations
4. Inability to effectively apply the guideline's recommendation due to lack of skill, resources, or training
5. Lack of trust in the effectiveness of the guideline to improve outcomes—particularly with an individual patient's condition
6. Resistance to change and reliance on habits
7. External factors (lack of resources, financial barriers or incentives, organizational factors)

The application of EBM is a two-way street that includes the physician and the patient. Baiardini and colleagues (2009) also identified barriers to patients' compliance with guidelines. These include the following:

- Patient characteristics, such as lack of social support or psychiatric or psychological comorbidity
- Patient difficulty in recognizing symptoms and adhering to therapies prescribed for the symptoms
- Complex therapeutic regimes
- Relationship and personal interactions between the patient and physician

Standard and Custom Patient Care

One historical criticism of EBM is that all patients are unique, and EBM is "cookbook" medicine that only applies to a few patients. EBM proponents counter this argument with simple examples of well-accepted and effective clinical practices that are inconsistently followed. A more productive view of the mix of the art and science in medicine is provided by Bohmer (2005), who suggests that all healthcare is a blend of custom and standard care. Exhibit 3.1 shows the four currently used models that blend these two approaches.

Model A (separate and select) provides an initial sorting by patients themselves. Those with standard problems are treated with standard care using EBM guidelines. Examples of this type of system are specialty hospitals for laser eye surgery or walk-in clinics operating in pharmacies and retail outlets. Patients who do not fit the provider's homogeneous clinical conditions are referred to other providers who can deliver customized care.

Model B (separate and accommodate) combines the two methods inside one provider organization. The Duke University Health System has developed standard protocols for its cardiac patients. Patients are initially sorted, and those who can be treated with the standard protocols are cared

EXHIBIT 3.1
Four
Approaches
to Blending
Custom and
Standard
Processes

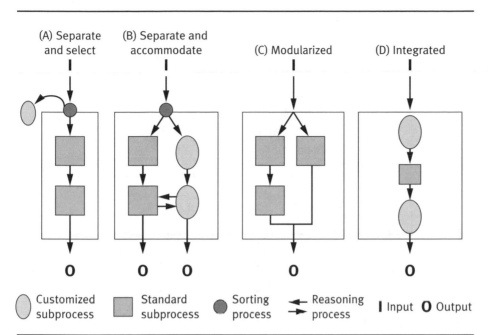

SOURCE: Bohmer, R. M. J. 2005. "Medicine's Service Challenge: Blending Custom and Standard Care." *Health Care Management Review* 30 (4): 322–30. Used with permission.

for by nurse practitioners using a standard care model. Cardiologists care for the remainder using custom care. However, on every fourth visit to the nurse practitioner, the cardiologist and nurse practitioner review the patient's case together to ensure that standard care is still the best treatment approach.

Model C (modularized) is used when the clinician moves from the role of care provider to that of architect of care design for the patient. In this case, a number of standard processes are assembled to treat the patient. The Andrews Air Force Base clinic uses this system to treat hypertension patients. "After an initial evaluation, treatment may include weight control, diet modification, drug therapy, stress control, and ongoing surveillance. Each component may be provided by a separate professional and sometimes a separate organization. What makes the care uniquely suited to each patient is the combination of components" (Bohmer 2005, 326).

Model D (integrated) combines both standard care and custom care in a single organization. In contrast to Model B, each patient receives a mix of both custom and standard care based on her condition. Intermountain Healthcare System (IHC) employs this model through the use of 62 standard care processes available as protocols in its electronic health record. These processes cover "the care of over 90 percent of patients admitted in IHC hospitals" (Bohmer 2005, 326). Clinicians are encouraged to override elements in these protocols when it is in the best interest of the patient. All of these

EXHIBIT 3.2
Prevention
Quality
Indicators

Number	Prevention Quality Indicator
1	Diabetes short-term complication admission rate
2	Perforated appendix admission rate
3	Diabetes long-term complication admission rate
4	Chronic obstructive pulmonary disease admission rate
5	Hypertension admission rate
6	Congestive heart failure admission rate
7	Low birth weight
8	Dehydration admission rate
9	Bacterial pneumonia admission rate
10	Urinary tract infection admission rate
11	Angina admission without procedure
12	Uncontrolled diabetes admission rate
13	Adult asthma admission rate
14	Rate of lower-extremity amputation among patients with diabetes
15	Adult asthma admission rate
16	Lower extremity amputation rate among diabetic patients

SOURCE: Agency for Healthcare Research and Quality (2006).

overrides are collected and analyzed, and changes are made to the protocol, which is an effective method to continuously improve clinical care.

All of the tools and techniques of operations improvement included in the remainder of this book can be used to make standard care processes operate effectively and efficiently.

Financial Gains from EBM

EBM has the potential to not only improve clinical outcomes but also to decrease total cost in the healthcare system. Potentially preventable hospitalizations, which might be avoided with high-quality outpatient treatment and disease management—provide a significant opportunity for financial savings in the delivery system.

Prevention quality indicator (PQI)
A set of measures that can be used with hospital discharge data to identify patients who may have hospitalizations or complications that could be avoided with the use of evidence-based ambulatory care.

AHRQ developed 16 **prevention quality indicators** (PQIs) to assist providers in reducing the number of potentially preventable hospitalizations for chronic and acute conditions throughout the United States (see Exhibit 3.2). A patient who is admitted to a hospital and has a PQI code is an individual whose hospitalization or other severe complication is potentially preventable when good, evidence-based outpatient care is delivered (AHRQ 2012c).

Investigators discovered that in 2007, potentially preventable conditions cost the United States $8.8 billion (Moy, Barrett, and Ho 2011).

At the health system level, financial gains can be significant if EBM is effectively executed. The Marshfield Clinic was a participant in the Medicare Physician Group Practice (PGP) Demonstration in 2009. The goal of the project was to reduce the total cost of care to Medicare beneficiaries while improving quality. Any savings gained (determined by comparison to other regional providers) would be shared by the clinic and Medicare. Marshfield was one of the most successful participants in the PGP demonstration and by the third year had met greater than 98 percent of the 32 quality measures (spread over diabetes, heart failure, coronary artery disease, hypertension, and preventive services) and received a performance payment of $13.8 million. Savings to Medicare that year totaled $23.49 million (Praxel 2009). The PGP demonstration provided the model for accountable care organizations that are part of the Patient Protection and Affordable Care Act (ACA). The accountable care organization (ACO) has become a key concept in healthcare delivery and is being used in both government and private sector delivery systems.

Chronic Disease Management

One of the most expensive aspects of all healthcare systems is the care of patients with chronic disease (e.g., diabetes, chronic obstructive pulmonary disease, congestive heart failure). Much of the variation in the outcomes of this care can be attributed to providers' and patients' lack of adherence to evidence-based medicine.

Fortunately many investigators have now looked beyond what clinical interventions provide good results (e.g., the use of statins) to identifying which systems of care produce superior results. (Chapter 8 provides more details and examples of the use of business process improvements to achieve higher quality care.)

Sochalski and colleagues (2009) studied approaches to managing patients with congestive heart failure. They looked at ten trials throughout the world, which included 2,028 patients. They measured approaches to care (team versus individual and methods of communication) and the outcomes of this care: readmissions to hospitals and the number of days between readmissions. The study found that patients who were enrolled in chronic care management programs that used a multidisciplinary team approach had fewer hospital readmissions and readmission days than routine care patients—a 2.9 percent reduction in readmissions per month and a 6.4 percent reduction in readmission days per month over routine care.

Another finding was that in-person communication led to significant reductions in both hospital readmissions (2.5 percent) and readmissions days per month (5.7 percent) over routine care. The combination of the team delivery and in-person communication yielded an almost threefold improvement in quality and cost reduction than patients in routine care.

The Chronic Care Model

Dr. Edward Wagner of the MacColl Institute for Healthcare Innovation, a leader in the improvement of chronic care, has developed one of the most widely accepted models for chronic disease management. The first important element of Wagner's model is population-based outreach, which ensures that all patients in need of chronic disease management receive it. Next, treatment plans are created that are sensitive to each patient's preferences. The most current evidence-based medicine is employed—this process is aided by clinical information systems with built-in decision support. The patient is encouraged to change risky behaviors and to manage himself better. The actual clinical visit changes in the Wagner model to allow more time for interaction between physicians and patients with complicated clinical issues. Visits for routine or specialized matters are handled by other healthcare professionals (e.g., nurses, pharmacists, dieticians, lay health workers). Close follow-up supported by clinical information system registries and patient reminders is also characteristic of effective chronic disease management (Wagner et al. 2001).

Healthcare Home

Healthcare home
Care that is accessible, continuous, comprehensive, family-centered, coordinated, compassionate, and culturally effective.

The **healthcare home** has emerged as an effective tool in the delivery of care to patients with chronic disease. The ACA supports this innovation with additional payment for Medicaid patients (§ 2703). The healthcare home has proven to be a valuable addition to the management of patients with chronic diseases and is now being funded by both government and private payers.

In 2008, the Institute for Clinical Systems Improvement convened a national group of 17 organizations that were implementing patient-centered healthcare homes. The organizations determined that an effective healthcare home must include these characteristics (ICSI 2010a):

1. Patients will identify a primary care practitioner and team.
2. Providers will routinely act from a patient-centered, whole-person orientation.
3. The team will aim for population health outcome improvement.
4. Care will be provided through a practice team tailored to the needs of each patient and situation.
5. The team will carry out practice-based care coordination.
6. The team will coordinate with the healthcare "neighborhood" of other teams and community.

7. Patients will actively participate in quality improvement and practice development.
8. The team will demonstrate a capacity for continuous learning and improvement.
9. The team will be supported by a sustainable business model and leadership alignment.
10. The team will be accountable for achieving a set of clinical, patient experience, and financial outcomes.

A study by Milstein and Gilbertson (2009) on the effectiveness of healthcare homes found three key components needed for success:

1. Individualized and intense caring for patients with chronic illness
2. Efficient service provision
3. Careful selection of specialists (taking into consideration quality and cost)

By carefully implementing these aspects of care, the healthcare homes studied reduced the total cost of care by 15 percent and improved quality, and providers reported a "less frenetic clinical pace" (Milstein and Gilbertson 2009).

Comparative Effective Research

The source for the evidence in EBM has been medical research that is published in respected and refereed journals. However, these studies have been initiated because of an investigator's interest, and therefore it is understandable that the efficacy of many common clinical approaches has never been adequately tested. This phenomenon can be attributed to the medical research community's historical and understandable bias toward developing leading-edge technologies that are designed to address intractable diseases and mysterious diagnostic challenges. Many aspects of routine healthcare have therefore never been sufficiently evaluated.

To address this problem, the ACA (and the American Recovery and Reinvestment Act) contained a new, significant policy direction with the establishment and funding of a nonprofit corporation, the Patient Centered Outcomes Research Institute. ACA Section 6301 states the mission of the institute as follows:

> The purpose of the institute is to assist patients, clinicians, purchasers, and policy-makers in making informed health decisions by advancing the quality and relevance of evidence concerning the manner in which diseases, disorders, and other health conditions can effectively and appropriately be prevented, diagnosed, treated, monitored, and managed through

research and evidence synthesis that considers variations in patient sub-populations, and the dissemination of research findings with respect to the relative health outcomes, clinical effectiveness, and appropriateness of the medical treatments, and services.

This institute complements the work of the National Institutes of Health and the AHRQ—both are part of the federal Department of Health and Human Services. One of AHRQ's responsibilities is to assist users of health information technology that is focused on clinical decision support to incorporate research findings into clinical practices and to promote the technology's ease of use. A major focus for the research topics addressed by the institute is related to chronic disease management.

Tools to Expand the Use of EBM

Value purchasing
A system using payment as a means to reward providers who publicly report results and achieve high levels of clinical care.

Organizations that are outside the healthcare delivery system itself have used the increased acceptance of EBM as the basis for new programs focused on encouraging increased implementation of EBM. These programs, sometimes called **value purchasing**, include both public reporting of clinical results and pay-for-performance (P4P).

Public Reporting

Public reporting
A statement of healthcare quality made by hospitals, long-term care facilities, and clinics. May also include patient satisfaction and provider charges.

Although strongly resisted by clinicians for many years, **public reporting** has come of age. The Centers for Medicare & Medicaid Services (CMS) now reports the performance of hospitals, long-term care facilities, and medical groups online (www.hospitalcompare.hhs.gov). Many health plans also report performance and the prices of providers in their networks to assist their plan members, particularly those with consumer-directed health insurance products.

In addition, community-based public reporting has risen with medical group reporting in a number of states. Leading examples include the following:

- California Cooperative Healthcare Reporting Initiative, San Francisco
- Massachusetts Health Quality Partners, Watertown
- Minnesota Community Measurement, St. Paul
- Wisconsin Collaborative for Healthcare Quality, Madison

Risk adjustment
Raising or lowering fees paid to providers on the basis of factors that may increase medical costs, such as age, sex, or illness.

Although it is a growing field, a number of issues surround public reporting. The first and most prominent is **risk adjustment**. Most clinicians feel their patients are "sicker" than average and that contemporary risk adjustment systems do not adequately account for this. Patient compliance is another challenging aspect of public reporting. If a doctor follows EBM guidelines for diagnosis and treatment, but the patient does not take her medication, should the doctor be given a poor grade?

One of the anticipated effects of public reporting is that patients will use the Internet to shop for quality healthcare products as they might for an automobile or a television. Currently, few patients use these public systems to guide their buying decisions. However, clinical leaders do review the public reports and target improvement efforts to areas where they have poor performance compared with their peers.

The Medicare public reporting system does appear to be affecting the quality of care. Werner and Bradlow (2010) examined whether hospital performance on key process indicators improved during the first three years that Medicare began to publicly report hospital quality. They also studied whether these changes improved patient outcomes or produced other quality improvements, such as reduced hospital readmission rates. For the 3,476 hospitals studied from 2004 to 2006, they found that hospital process performance improved and was associated with better patient outcomes and higher quality. For acute myocardial infarction (AMI) particularly, performance improvements were associated with declines in mortality rates, lengths of stay, and readmission rates (Werner and Bradlow 2010).

Pay-for-Performance and Payment Reform

Another logical tool to expand the use of EBM is the financing system. Many buyers of healthcare are now installing P4P systems to encourage providers to deliver EBM care.

P4P Methods

In general, P4P systems add payments to the amount that would otherwise be paid to a provider. To obtain these additional payments, the provider must demonstrate that he is delivering care that meets clinical EBM goals. These clinical measures can be either process or outcome measures.

Although many providers would prefer to be measured on outcomes, this approach is difficult to use as some outcomes need to be measured over many years. In addition, some providers have a small number of patients in a particular clinical group so outcome results can vary dramatically. Therefore, process measures are used for many conditions; these measures are backed by extensive EBM literature. For example, a patient with diabetes whose blood pressure is maintained in a normal range will experience fewer complications than one whose blood pressure is uncontrolled. Blood pressure can be measured and reported at every visit, whereas complications will occur infrequently.

In a study sponsored by the National Quality Forum, Schneider, Hussey, and Schnyer (2011) surveyed the breadth of payment reform meth-

EXHIBIT 3.3
General
Payment
Reform Model

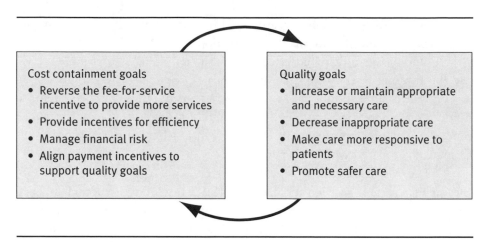

Cost containment goals
- Reverse the fee-for-service incentive to provide more services
- Provide incentives for efficiency
- Manage financial risk
- Align payment incentives to support quality goals

Quality goals
- Increase or maintain appropriate and necessary care
- Decrease inappropriate care
- Make care more responsive to patients
- Promote safer care

SOURCE: Schneider, Hussey, and Schnyer (2011).

ods and found nearly 100 implemented and proposed payment reform programs. They then classified these methods into 11 payment reform models. Many of these payment reform models are included in the ACA, and the goals for these reforms are illustrated by Exhibit 3.3.

Exhibit 3.4 provides a list and description of the models. Chapter 14 examines how organizations can apply the operations management tools contained throughout this book to succeed financially with each of these payment models.

Issues in P4P

P4P is a system that has breached the wall of professional autonomy to influence the day-to-day care of many patients. However, significant system changes frequently result in unintended consequences no matter how well they have been designed. Because P4P programs change behavior in providers, will payers cease to reward providers? How will P4P incentives be allocated from one disease to another? For example, will the P4P payments for patients with diabetes be higher than for patients with low back pain and, if so, by what rationale? Finally, where does the P4P funding come from—is it just another version of a discount or withhold?

Can P4P really motivate change? The potential impact of P4P on hospitals was modeled by Werner using the publicly reported Medicare quality measures (AMI, heart failure, and pneumonia) and the actual diagnosis-related group (DRG) payments to all US hospitals in 2004 and 2005 (Werner and Dudley 2009). The authors sought to determine if any P4P system could provide a bonus payment of 5 percent. The 5 percent level was chosen because the average hospital margin in 2004 was 4 percent; a 5 percent level was therefore assumed to be large enough to motivate a hospital's leader-

EXHIBIT 3.4
Payment
Reform Model
Details

	Model	Description
1.	Global payment	A single per-member per-month payment is made for services delivered to a patient, with payment adjustments based on measured performance and patient risk.
2.	ACO shared savings program	Groups of providers (known as accountable care organizations [ACOs]) that voluntarily assume responsibility for the care of a population of patients share payer savings if they meet quality and cost performance benchmarks.
3.	Medical home	A physician practice or other provider is eligible to receive additional payments if medical home criteria are met. Payment may include calculations based on quality and cost performance using a P4P-like mechanism.
4.	Bundled payment	A single bundled payment, which may include multiple providers in multiple care settings, is made for services delivered during an episode of care related to a medical condition or procedure.
5.	Hospital–physician gainsharing	Hospitals are permitted to provide payments to physicians that represent a share of savings resulting from collaborative efforts between the hospital and physicians to improve quality and efficiency.
6.	Payment for coordination	Payments are made to providers furnishing care coordination services that integrate care between providers.
7.	Hospital P4P	Hospitals receive differential payments for meeting or missing performance benchmarks.
8.	Payment adjustment for readmissions	Payments to hospitals are adjusted based on the rate of potentially avoidable readmissions.
9.	Payment adjustment for hospital-acquired conditions	Hospitals with high rates of hospital-acquired conditions are subject to a payment penalty, or treatment of hospital-acquired conditions or serious reportable events is not reimbursed.
10.	Physician P4P	Physicians receive differential payments for meeting or missing performance benchmarks.
11.	Payment for shared decision making	Payment is made for the provision of shared decision-making services.

SOURCE: Schneider, Hussey, and Schnyer (2011)

ship to make needed improvements. Hospitals were also grouped by their performance and the analysis of five P4P methods simulated. These methods are as follows:

1. Bonus payments to high-performing hospitals based on their relative rank
2. Bonus payments to high performers and penalties to low performers
3. Payment for achieving a target level of performance
4. Payment for target achievement and improvement
5. Payment of bonus if the percentage of patients recommended for care were given this care

The authors concluded:

With these advantages and disadvantages, it is evident that there is no perfect P4P payment strategy for every setting. The decision about which P4P strategy to use likely depends on the goal of P4P (to improve quality among low-performing providers or to maintain quality among high-performing providers); the distribution of performance within and across providers (whether it is highly variable or uniformly high); the percentage of payment available for P4P programs; and the overall level of performance (Werner and Dudley 2009).

The Medicare Value Purchasing Program

The ACA contains a new value purchasing program based on much of the research, practical experience, and analysis in both public reporting and P4P described in the previous section. If sections of the ACA are repealed or changed, value purchasing is likely to re-emerge in some form because it is so strongly supported by research.

"CMS views value-based purchasing as an important step to revamping how care and services are paid for, moving increasingly toward rewarding better value, outcomes, and innovations instead of merely volume. Their general goals include:

Use of Measures:

- Public reporting and value-based payment systems should rely on a mix of standards, process, outcomes, and patient experience measures, including measures of care transitions and changes in patient functional status. Across all programs, CMS seeks to move as quickly as possible to the use of primarily outcome and patient experience measures. To the extent practicable and appropriate, outcomes and patient experience measures should be adjusted for risk or other appropriate patient population or provider characteristics.
- Measures should be aligned across Medicare's and Medicaid's public reporting and payment systems. CMS seeks to evolve to a focused core set of measures appropriate to the specific provider category that reflects the level of care and the most important areas of service and measures for that provider.
- The collection of information should minimize the burden on providers to the extent possible. As part of that effort, CMS will continuously seek to align its measures with the adoption of meaningful use standards for health information technology (HIT), so the collection of performance information is part of care delivery.

- Measures used by CMS should be nationally endorsed by a multi-stakeholder organization. Measures should be aligned with best practices among other payers and the needs of the end users of the measures.

Scoring Methodology:

- Providers should be scored on their overall achievement relative to national or other appropriate benchmarks. In addition, scoring methodologies should consider improvement as an independent goal.
- Measures or measurement domains need not be given equal weight, but over time, scoring methodologies should be more weighted towards outcome, patient experience, and functional status measures.
- Scoring methodologies should be reliable, as straightforward as possible, and stable over time and should enable consumers, providers, and payers to make meaningful distinctions among providers" (CMS 2011).

Program Operation

The Medicare value purchasing program consists of a methodology for assessing the total performance of each hospital based on performance standards. CMS scores each hospital based on *achievement* and *improvement* for each applicable clinical process and patient experience measure. The measures used for this scoring are contained on the Hospital Compare website (www.hospitalcompare.hhs.gov).

CMS calculates a "total performance score for each hospital by combining the greater of the hospital's *achievement* or *improvement* points for each measure to determine a score for each domain. Each domain score is multiplied by a weight (clinical process of care: 70 percent, patient experience of care: 30 percent), and then added together for a weighted domain score. Each hospital's total performance score is converted into a value-based incentive payment utilizing a linear exchange function" (CMS 2011). P4P payments are then made.

CMS reduces every hospital's anticipated DRG payment by approximately 2 percent each year (the number varies based on past performance) and puts these funds into a pool. It then distributes these funds to each hospital based on their performance score. Some hospitals gain substantial revenue based on their attention to improving these aspects of the care they deliver.

The Medicare value purchasing program therefore meets its stated goals while rewarding both high achievement and improvement.

Clinical Decision Support

One development in the use of guidelines is the spread of clinical decision support systems, which are now becoming a standard part of electronic health records. As a clinician accesses a specific patient's medical record, the automated system provides advice on recommended treatments and needed follow up.

Marshfield Clinic PGP Demonstration

The electronic health record is particularly useful in chronic disease management and is well illustrated by the Marshfield Clinic's use of it and EBM as part of the Medicare PGP Demonstration Project, which resulted in both financial and quality gains (see page 49).

The *New York Times* reported in 2008:

"The Medicare pilot prompted Marshfield to take a fresh look at how it cares for various chronic conditions, including heart disease and hypertension. That led to a new software tool, called the iList, which has proved a big help, said Dr. Theodore A. Praxel, Marshfield's medical director of quality improvement and care management.

The iList (for *intervention list*) culls the patient records of a primary care physician, and ranks and flags patients by conditions not met, including uncontrolled blood pressure and cholesterol, overdue lab tests and vaccinations. Nurses and medical assistants then "work the iList," calling patients with reminders and scheduling them for exams and lab work.

In medicine, the computer is to memory what the X-ray machine is to vision—a technology that vastly surpasses human limitations. The benefits of a computer-helper, doctors say, become quickly evident in everyday practice" (Lohr 2008).

Institute for Clinical Systems Improvement—High-Tech Diagnostic Imaging

Clinical decision support can be applied across multiple electronic health record systems and need not be vendor specific. The Institute for Clinical Systems Improvement undertook a project to improve the appropriate utilization of CT, MRI, PET, and nuclear cardiology scans (ICSI 2012).

"Their approach consists of deploying a common set of appropriateness criteria that would be:

- available in the physician's office to provide clinical decision support at the time care is being discussed with the patient and prior to ordering HTDI tests

EXHIBIT 3.5
Decision
Support
Process
Embedded
in Electronic
Health Record

Provider sees appropriateness of test and higher utility options—opportunity to engage patient.

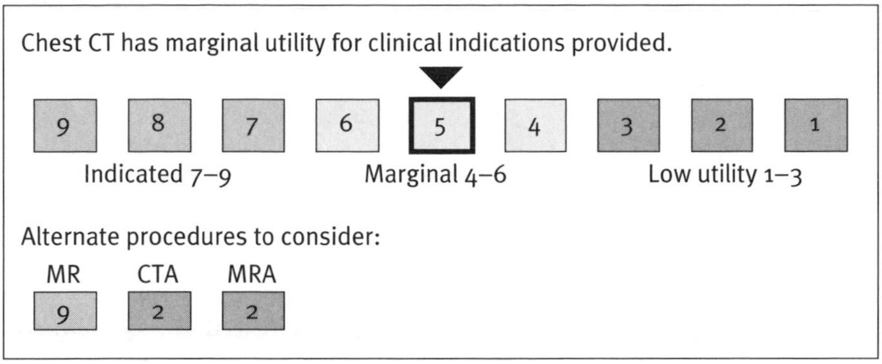

Chest CT has marginal utility for clinical indications provided.

▼

| 9 | 8 | 7 | 6 | 5 | 4 | 3 | 2 | 1 |

Indicated 7–9   Marginal 4–6   Low utility 1–3

Alternate procedures to consider:

MR   CTA   MRA

| 9 | 2 | 2 |

SOURCE: Copyright Institute for Clinical Systems Improvement 2011. Used with permission.

- embedded into an electronic medical record (EMR), or made available via a Web site
- continually enriched and expanded for improved outcomes" (ICSI 2009)

The ordering guidance screen is shown in Exhibit 3.5. The simple 1 through 9 rating on

"the level of diagnostic utility of the provider's selection carries multiple benefits, offering guidance to ordering providers and supporting shared decision making between providers and patients. For those organizations with full EHRs, the patient's clinical information is loaded automatically into this system which then makes its recommendation based on guidelines from the American College of Radiology and the American College of Cardiology.

When a test of a value that is below 6 is ordered, additional information is provided to the ordering physician, who may choose to continue and order the test or switch to another. All payers in the system have agreed to make payments no matter what level of test is ordered. In some cases the recommended test is, in fact, more expensive than the test originally ordered" (ICSI 2009).

The project has been successful in making appropriate recommendations to providers. Exhibit 3.6 shows the actual use of high-tech digital imaging (HTDI) versus the trend had the existing radiology management systems remained in place.

EXHIBIT 3.6
Utilization
of High-
Tech Digital
Imaging—
Actual vs. Trend

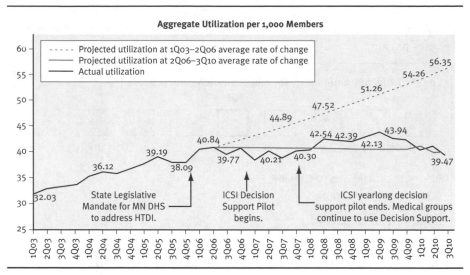

Aggregate Utilization per 1,000 Members

SOURCE: Copyright Institute for Clinical Systems Improvement 2011. Used with permission.

"The summary of the benefits of this system over three years among five large medical groups is:

- $84 million savings based on reduction of HTDI scans against projected trend line without decision-support
- 11,000 fewer administrative hours for just one medical group by having electronic decision support accepted versus calling the radiology benefits manager
- Decreased exposure to radiation—potentially preventing cancers" (ICSI 2010b).

The Future of Evidence-Based Medicine

One of the challenges of the more widespread use of EBM is the fact that it is based on clinical studies of many patients, which result in averaged results. However, no specific patient is every completely average, and therefore clinicians frequently vary from guidelines to compensate for this difference.

Archimedes model
A full-scale
mathematical
simulation of
human physiology
that can be used
to test the effect of
diseases and their
treatments.

The newest advances are being made in custom care. Perhaps the leading example of this approach is the **Archimedes model** originally developed by Kaiser Permanente. According to the company:

The Archimedes Model is a full-scale simulation model of human physiology, diseases, behaviors, interventions, and healthcare systems. By using advanced methods of mathematics, computing, and data systems, the model enables managers, administrators, and policymakers to be better informed and to make smarter decisions than has previously been possible.

The core of the model is hundreds of equations that represent human physiology and the effects of diseases. Attached to these are hundreds more equations and algorithms that realistically simulate the healthcare system, including processes such as tests, treatments, admissions, and physician behaviors. Together with population data, the equations are integrated into a single, large-scale simulation model that accurately represents what happens to real people in real healthcare systems (Archimedes Inc. 2012).

The model has been under construction since 1972 and now resides on a large server farm in California, where it is updated as new science is discovered and new clinical trials provide information on the treatment efficacy of new approaches. The Archimedes vModel is continuously tested against the results of clinical trials, and the correlation between the model and results is remarkably strong (Archimedes, Inc. 2012).

Because of its power, the model can be used to simulate an individual's physiology and her response to various treatments. This system will likely be integrated into clinical decision support tools in the future to provide a much higher level of recommendation to clinicians in unusual and unique circumstances.

Vincent Valley Hospital and Health System and P4P

The leadership of VVH felt it had a number of opportunities to succeed with the Medicare value purchasing program. It created a project team to improve the care of patients with pneumonia. The specific measures the team targeted for improvement were those in the Medicare program:

- Pneumonia patients assessed and given pneumococcal vaccination
- Pneumonia patients whose initial emergency room blood culture was performed prior to the administration of the first hospital dose of antibiotics
- Pneumonia patients given smoking cessation advice and counseling
- Pneumonia patients given initial antibiotic(s) within six hours after arrival
- Pneumonia patients given the most appropriate initial antibiotic(s)
- Pneumonia patients assessed and given influenza vaccination

The operations management tools and approaches detailed in the remainder of this book were used to improve performance for each of these measures. Chapter 15 describes how VVH accomplished this.

Conclusion

The use of EBM to develop systems of care is now becoming well accepted by most clinicians. Clinical results are being made transparent and becoming easily accessible to the general public. Payers are implementing systems that reward value, and providers are installing clinical decision support systems to help in their practice. The effective use of EBM will identify high-performance healthcare organizations, and its widespread use is a key to providing high-quality, cost-effective care throughout the world.

Discussion Questions

1. What are other examples of a care delivery setting with a mix of standard and custom care?
2. Select three PQIs from Exhibit 3.2 and go to the National Guideline Clearinghouse to find guidelines that would minimize hospital admissions for these conditions. What would be the challenges in implementing each of these guidelines?
3. Review the 11 payment reform methodologies (Exhibit 3.4) and rank them on two scales: ability to improve quality and ability to reduce healthcare inflation. Provide a rationale for your ranking.
4. What are three strategies to maximize P4P revenue?
5. Review the Archimedes website and develop a list of applications of the model beyond direct clinical care.

SETTING GOALS AND EXECUTING STRATEGY

STRATEGY AND THE BALANCED SCORECARD **4**

Operations Management in Action

The Malcolm Baldrige National Quality Award is the nation's highest honor for innovation and performance excellence. In 2008, the Poudre Valley Health System (PVHS) was one of three organizations to receive the award and the only healthcare recipient, making it one of the best hospitals in America. The Baldridge award (see Chapter 2) judges use a number of dimensions to evaluate each applicant's performance: leadership, strategic planning, customer focus, measurement and analysis, workforce focus, and process management.

PVHS is particularly strong in its use of the balanced scorecard to measure its performance and share best practices between departments. The metrics PVHS uses to track its performance are from the following areas:

- Employee culture
- Market share
- Physician engagement
- Clinical outcomes
- Customer service and patient satisfaction
- Financial performance

Winning the Baldrige Award brings an expectation to share an organization's journey with its greater community. PVHS established a Center for Performance Excellence to provide consulting, coaching, and presentation services to other organizations pursuing performance excellence. From the perspective of a Baldrige National Quality Award recipient, the center's consultants apply the lessons learned over the past decade.

SOURCE: Nuwash (2010).

Overview

Most healthcare organizations have good strategic plans; what frequently fails is their execution. This chapter demonstrates how the **balanced scorecard** can be an effective tool to consistently move strategy to execution. First, traditional management systems are examined and their failures explored. Next, the theory of the balanced scorecard and strategy mapping is reviewed and its application to healthcare organizations explained. Practical steps to implement and maintain a balanced scorecard system are provided. Detailed examples from Vincent Valley Hospital and Health System (VVH) will demonstrate the application of these tools. The companion website contains templates and explanatory videos that can be used for student exercises or to implement a balanced scorecard in an existing healthcare organization.

www.ache.org/books/OpsManagement2

In addition, a case study on the companion website includes data that can be used to develop a realistic dashboard.

This chapter gives readers a basic understanding of balanced scorecards to enable them to:

- explain how a balanced scorecard can be used to move strategy to action;
- explain how to monitor strategy from the four perspectives;
- identify key initiatives to achieve a strategic objective;
- develop a strategy map linking initiatives;
- identify and measure leading and lagging indicators for each initiative;
- understand the use of business intelligence tools to extract data for scorecards; and
- use Microsoft PowerPoint and Excel to create strategy maps and scorecards.

Moving Strategy to Execution

The Challenge of Execution

Environmental causes commonly cited for the failure of execution in healthcare organizations include intense financial pressures, complex operating structures, and cultures with multistakeholder leadership that resists change. New and redefined relationships of healthcare providers—particularly physicians, hospitals, and health plans—are being accompanied by a rapid growth of medical treatment knowledge and technology. Increased public scrutiny of how healthcare is delivered is leading to the associated rise of consumer-directed healthcare. The Patient Protection and Affordable Care Act (ACA) is also altering strategy significantly.

No matter how significant these external factors, most organizations founder on internal factors. Mankins and Steele (2005) studied strategy execution failures in all types of enterprises and identified nine key factors that contribute to poor performance:

1. Inadequate or unavailable resources
2. Poorly communicated strategy
3. Poorly defined actions required to execute the strategy
4. Unclear accountability for execution
5. Organizational silos
6. A culture that blocks execution
7. Inadequate performance monitoring
8. Inadequate consequences for failure or success
9. Poor, uncommitted senior leadership

These factors also plague healthcare organizations. To gain competitive advantage from its operations, an organization needs an effective system to move its strategies forward. The management systems of the past are poor tools for today's challenging environment.

The day-to-day world of a current healthcare leader is intense (Exhibit 4.1). Because of ever-present communications technologies (smartphones, e-mail, texts, blogs, social networks) managers float in a sea of inputs and daily challenges.

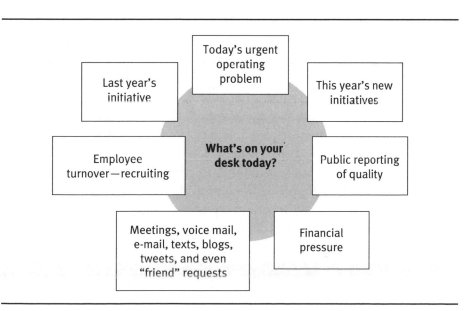

EXHIBIT 4.1
The Complex World of Today's Healthcare Leader

EXHIBIT 4.2
The Traditional
Theory of
Management

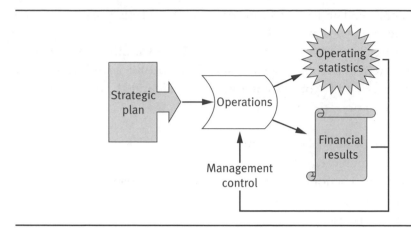

Healthcare leaders often focus on urgent issues rather than challenges of strategy execution. And although organizations can develop effective project managers (as discussed in Chapter 5), they will fail to compete successfully if they do not place these projects in a broader system of strategy implementation. Fortunately, the balanced scorecard provides a framework and sophisticated mechanisms to move from strategy to execution.

Why Do Today's Management Tools Fail?

Historically, most organizations have been managed with three primary tools: strategic plans, financial reports, and operational reports. Exhibit 4.2 shows the relationships among these tools. In this traditional system, the first step is to create a strategic plan, which is usually updated annually. Next, a budget and operations or project plan is created. The operations plan is sometimes referred to as the tactical plan; it provides a more detailed level of task descriptions with time lines and expected outcomes. The organization's performance is monitored by senior management through the financial and operational reports. Finally, if deviations from expected performance are encountered, managers take corrective action.

Although theoretically easy to grasp, this management system frequently fails for a number of common reasons. Organizations are awash in operating data, and there is no effort to identify key metrics. The strategic plans, financial reports, and operational reports are all created by different departments, and each report is reviewed in different time frames, often by different managers. Finally, none of the reports connects with each other.

These are the root causes of poor execution. If strategies are not linked to action items, operations will not change, nor will the financial results. In addition, strategic plans are frequently not linked to departmental or individual goals and, therefore, reside only on the shelf in the executive suite.

Many strategic plans contain a logic hole, meaning they lack an explanation of how accomplishing a strategic objective will provide a specific financial or operational outcome. For example:

- Strategic objective: increase the use of evidence-based medicine (EBM)
- Expected outcome: increased patient satisfaction

Although this proposition may seem correct on the surface, the logic to connect the use of EBM to patient satisfaction is unclear. In fact, patient satisfaction may decrease if providers consistently meet EBM guidelines by counseling patients on personal lifestyle issues (e.g., "Will you stop smoking?" or "You need to lose weight").

Frequently, the time frame of strategy execution is also problematic. Financial reports tend to be timely and accurate but only reflect the current reporting period. Unfortunately, the review of these reports does not encourage the long-term strategic allocation of resources (e.g., a major capital expenditure) that may require multiple-year investments. A good current-month financial outcome is probably due to an action that occurred many months in the past. The cumulative result of these problems is poor execution, leading to poor outcomes.

Robert Kaplan and David Norton

In the early 1990s, Kaplan and Norton (1996) undertook a study to examine how companies measure their performance. The growing sophistication of companywide information systems was beginning to provide senior management with executive information systems, which could provide sophisticated displays and dashboards of company performance. The original purpose of Kaplan and Norton's study was to understand and document this trend.

Their study uncovered a number of reporting practices that many leading companies were using to measure their performance. These firms looked at their operations from a number of perspectives that, in total, provided a balanced scorecard. The essential elements of this work were first reported in *The Balanced Scorecard: Translating Strategy into Action* (Kaplan and Norton 1996) and *The Strategy-Focused Organization* (Kaplan and Norton 2001). They have continued to write frequently to expand this concept (see Further Reading).

The key element of the balanced scorecard is, of course, balance. An organization can be viewed from many perspectives, but Kaplan and Norton identified four common perspectives from which an organization must examine its operations (Exhibit 4.3).

EXHIBIT 4.3
The Four
Perspectives in
the Balanced
Scorecard

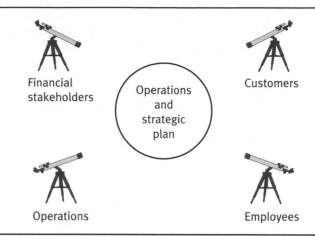

EXHIBIT 4.3
The Four
Perspectives in
the Balanced
Scorecard

1. Financial stakeholders
2. Customers
3. Internal process and innovation
4. Employee learning and growth

As an organization is viewed from each perspective, different measures of performance are important. Every perspective in a complete balanced scorecard contains a set of objectives, measures, targets, and actions. Each measure in each perspective must be linked to the organization's overall strategy.

The indicators of performance in each of the four perspectives must be both leading (predicting the future) and lagging (reporting on performance today). Indicators must also be obtained from inside the organization and from the external environment.

Although many think of the balanced scorecard as a reporting technique, its true power comes from its ability to link strategy to action. Balanced scorecard practitioners develop strategy maps that link projects and actions to outcomes in a series of maps. These maps display the "theory of the company" and can be evaluated and fine-tuned with many of the quantitative techniques described in Chapter 6. Kaplan and Norton (2001) have expanded their system of constructing strategy maps in *The Strategy-Focused Organization*.

The Balanced Scorecard in Healthcare

The balanced scorecard and its variations have been adopted by leading healthcare organizations.

In 2002 Inamdar and Kaplan (2002) reviewed the use of the balanced scorecard in healthcare and concluded that many healthcare organizations are effectively using scorecards to improve their competitive marketing position, financial results, and customer satisfaction.

Bloomquist and Yeager (2008) successfully implemented a balanced scorecard at Emory Healthcare as part of a major change from independent operating units to an integrated system. Their lessons learned include the following:

- *Be Flexible:* Not every measure will be correct the first time. Developing and implementing a balanced scorecard is an evolutionary process.
- *Be Consistent:* Create good documentation for each measure.
- *Be Clear:* Obtain leadership buy-in and understanding.
- *Be Open:* Frequent communication on multiple levels is key.
- *Be Thorough:* Use your existing infrastructure; do not create something new.
- *Be Efficient:* Ensure individual goal setting is not too cumbersome.
- *Be Inclusive:* Involve multiple departments even at the earliest stages.
- *Be Systematic:* Continuously improve the process.

The Balanced Scorecard as Part of a Strategic Management System

Although it does not substitute for a complete strategic management system, the balanced scorecard is a key element in such a system and provides an effective tool to move an organization's strategy and vision into action. The development of a balanced scorecard leads to the clarification of strategy and communicates and links strategic measures throughout an organization. Organizational leaders can plan projects, set targets, and align strategic initiatives during the creation of the balanced scorecard. If used properly, the balanced scorecard can also enhance strategic feedback and learning.

Elements of the Balanced Scorecard System

A complete balanced scorecard system will have the following elements, explained in detail in the next section:

- Organizational mission, vision, and strategy
- Perspectives
  - Financial
  - Customer
  - Internal business process
  - Learning and growing

- Strategy maps
- Strategic alignment—top to bottom
- Processes for identifying targets, resources, initiatives, and budgets
- Feedback and the strategic learning process

Mission and Vision

The balanced scorecard system presupposes that an organization has an effective mission, vision, and strategy in place. For example, the mission of VVH is "to provide high-quality, cost-effective healthcare to our community." Its vision: "Within five years, we will be financially sound and will be considered the place to receive high-quality care by the majority of the residents of our community." To accomplish this vision, VVH has identified six specific strategies:

1. Recruit five new primary care physicians
2. Implement the healthcare home model
3. Revise the VVH website to allow self-scheduling by patients
4. Increase the volume of obstetric care
5. Renegotiate health plan contracts to include performance incentives based on improved chronic disease management
6. Improve emergency department operations and patient satisfaction

The VVH example is used throughout this chapter to demonstrate the use of the balanced scorecard. The two strategies that will be examined in depth are increasing the volume of obstetric care and improving emergency department operations and patient satisfaction.

With an effective strategic plan in place, the next step is to evaluate its implementation as viewed from each of the four perspectives (financial, customer, operational, and learning and growing). Placing a perspective at the top of a balanced scorecard strategy map means that results in this perspective contain the final outcomes desired by an organization. In most organizations, the financial view is the top-most perspective. Therefore, the initiatives undertaken in the other three perspectives should result in positive financial performance for the organization.

"No margin, no mission" is still a true statement for nonprofit healthcare organizations. Nonprofit healthcare institutions need operating margins to provide financial stability and capital. However, some organizations prefer to position the customer (patient) as the top perspective. In that case, the initiatives undertaken in the other three perspectives will result in positive patient outcomes. (Modifications to the classic balanced scorecard are discussed at the end of this chapter.)

Financial Perspective

Although the other three perspectives and their associated areas of activity should lead to outstanding financial performance, some initiatives can be undertaken within the financial perspective by themselves. Although the focus of this book is not directly on healthcare finance, some general strategies should always be under consideration by an organization.

If an organization is in a growth mode, the focus should be on increasing revenue to accommodate this growth. If it is operating in a relatively stable environment, the organization may choose to emphasize profitability. If the organization is both stable and profitable, the focus can shift to investment—in both physical assets and human capital. Another major strategy in the financial domain is the diversification of both revenues and expenditures to minimize financial risk.

Revenue Growth

An organization that is in growth mode should be engaged in developing and deploying new products. Imaging centers are an example of the rapid introduction of ever more effective technologies. Another growth strategy is to find new uses for an existing technology. For example, VVH is planning to use its existing website to allow patients to schedule their own appointments, expecting that this will increase ambulatory care revenue.

A growing organization will seek new customers and markets. An example is placing primary care clinics where the population is experiencing rapid growth. Developing partnerships is another growth strategy. The accountable care organizational model provides a new vehicle for growth in Medicare and Medicaid markets and in new relationships with private health plans. Public reporting of costs and quality were explored in depth in Chapter 3, and as these data continue to expand, they will likely affect market share and revenue.

Cost Reduction—Productivity

In most cases, cost reductions improve financial performance. Chapters 6 through 13 provide tools for improving processes and reducing costs. However, other important strategies should also be evaluated.

The first is to redefine the channel mix; in other words, deliver services in another mode. The use of e-mail, telemedicine, and group visits are three examples redefining channel mix in primary care. The advanced use of new communication and health information technologies (HIT) will allow creative healthcare organizations to rethink the channels they use to deliver services.

A second, frequently overlooked, cost management strategy is to reduce overhead costs. All nonoperating costs should be scrutinized to ensure that they are contributing to the achievement of organizational outcomes.

Asset Utilization and Investment Strategy

Balance sheet management is also part of the financial perspective. Managing working capital assets, such as accounts payable, inventory, and accounts receivable, is part of this perspective. One of the most complex processes in healthcare is that of sending and collecting a bill. These systems are amenable to the process improvement tools in Chapters 6 through 11.

Another balance sheet strategy is to improve asset allocations. Does one invest more in buildings or equipment? Can an IT system be shared by more than one department? The analysis of these questions is well documented in *Healthcare Finance: An Introduction to Accounting and Financial Management* (Gapenski 2011); the initiatives and projects that surround such tradeoffs should be part of an organization's balanced scorecard.

Risk Management Through Diversity

The final key financial strategy is to minimize risk by increasing diversity. The more diverse an organization's revenue sources, the less likely it is that a significant change in any one source will have a major impact on the organization. Diversification of payers is difficult to achieve but should always be attempted. Product lines can be expanded in both clinical areas (e.g., emergency, birthing center, internal medicine) and delivery models (e.g., inpatient, ambulatory, standalone).

Geographic expansion is a classic diversification strategy. However, the greatest opportunity for diversification today may be innovative retail strategies to attract market share from the newly empowered consumer. Exhibit 4.4 lists many common metrics used to measure performance from the financial perspective.

Customer Perspective and Market Segmentation

The second perspective is to view an organization's operations from the customer's point of view. In most healthcare operations, the customer is the patient. Integrated health organizations, however, may operate insurance programs and health plans; their customers are then employers or the government. Health insurance exchanges are a new vehicle to connect directly with customers. Many hospitals and clinics also consider their community, in total, as the customer. The physician could also be seen as the customer in many hospital organizations.

Once the general customers are identified, it is helpful to segment them into smaller groups and determine the **value proposition** that will be

Value proposition
A marketing term summarizing the relative cost, features, and quality of a service or a good.

- Percent of budget—revenue
- Percent of budget—expense
- Days in accounts receivable
- Days of cash on hand
- Collection rate
- Return on assets
- Expense per relative value unit (RVU)
- Cost per surgical case
- Case-mix index
- Payer mix
- Growth, revenue, expense, and profit—product line
- Growth, revenue, expense, and profit—department
- Growth, revenue, and cost per adjusted patient day
- Growth, revenue, and cost per physician full-time equivalent (FTE)
- Price competitiveness on selected services
- Research grant revenue

EXHIBIT 4.4
Metrics to
Measure
Performance
from the
Financial
Perspective

delivered to each customer segment. Example market segments are patients with chronic illnesses (e.g., diabetes, congestive heart failure), obstetric care, sports medicine, cancer care, emergency care, Medicaid patients, small employers, and referring primary care physicians.

Customer Measures

Once market segments have been determined, a number of traditional measures of marketplace performance may be applied, the most prominent being market share. Customers should be individually tracked and measured in terms of both retention and acquisition, as it is always easier to retain an existing customer than to attract a new one. Customer satisfaction and prof itability are also useful measures. Exhibit 4.5 displays a number of common customer metrics.

Customers: The Value Proposition

Organizations create value to retain old customers and attract new ones. Each market segment may require products to have different attributes to maximize that segment's particular value proposition. For example, it may be important to be a price leader for outpatient imaging, as some patients will be paying for this service via a healthcare savings account. For another seg- ment emergency services, for example—speed of delivery may be critical. The personal relationship of provider to patient may be important in primary care but not as important in anesthesiology.

EXHIBIT 4.5
Metrics to
Measure
Performance
from the
Customer
Perspective

- Patient care volumes
  - By service, type, and physician
  - Turnover—new patients and those exiting the system
- Physician
  - Referral and admission rates
  - Satisfaction
  - Availability of resources (e.g., operating suite time)
- Market share by product line
- Clinical measures
  - Readmission rates
  - Complication rates
  - Compliance with evidence-based guidelines
  - Medical errors
- Customer service
  - Patient satisfaction
  - Waiting time
  - Cleanliness—ambience
  - Ease of navigation
  - Parking
  - Billing complaints
- Reputation
- Price comparisons relative to competitors

Image and reputation are particularly strong influences in consumer behavior and can be competitive advantages for specialty healthcare services. Careful understanding of the value proposition in an organization will lead to effective metrics and strategy maps in the balanced scorecard system.

Vincent Valley Hospital and Health System's Value Proposition

VVH has developed a value proposition for its obstetric services. Its market segment is pregnant women, aged 18 to 35. VVH believes the product attributes for this market should be

- quick access to care;
- warm and welcoming facilities;
- customer relations characterized by strong and personal relationships with nurses, midwives, and doctors; and
- an image of high-quality care that will be supported by an excellent system for referrals and air transport for high-risk deliveries.

VVH determined that the following metrics would be used to measure each of these attributes:

- The time from arrival to care in the obstetric suite
- A patient survey of facility attributes
- A patient survey of satisfaction with staff
- Percent of high-risk newborns referred and transported, and the clinical outcomes of these patients

The main value proposition for emergency care was identified as reduced waiting time. Following internal studies, competitive benchmarking, and patient focus groups, it was determined that VVH's goal would be to have fewer than 10 percent of its emergency department patients wait more than 30 minutes for care.

Internal Business Process Perspective

The third perspective in the balanced scorecard is that of internal business processes or operations—the primary focus of this book. According to Kaplan and Norton (1996), the internal business process perspective has three major components: innovation, ongoing process improvement, and post-sale service.

Innovation

A well-functioning healthcare organization will have a purposeful innovation process. Unfortunately, many health organizations today can only be characterized as reactionary. They respond to new reimbursement rules, government mandates, or technologies introduced through the medical staff. Bringing thoughtful innovation into the life cycle is one of the most pressing challenges contemporary organizations face.

The first step in an organized innovation process is to identify a potential market segment. Then, two primary questions need to be answered: (1) What benefits will customers value in tomorrow's market? and (2) How can the organization innovate to deliver those benefits? Once these questions have been researched and answered, product can be created.

Quality function deployment (Chapter 8) can be a useful tool for new product or service development. If a new service is on the clinical leading edge, it may require additional research and testing. A more mainstream service could require competitor research and review of the clinical literature. The principles of project management (Chapter 5) should be used throughout this process until the new service is operational and stable.

Standard innovation measures used in many industries outside health care include percent of total sales resulting from new products and from proprietary products, new product introductions per year, time to develop new products, and time to break even.

Healthcare operations tend toward stability (bordering on being rigid), and therefore, a major challenge is simply ensuring that all clinical staff use the latest and most effective diagnostic and treatment methodologies. However, with the passage of the ACA, those organizations with a well-functioning product development process will clearly have a competitive advantage.

Ongoing Process Improvement

The case for process improvement and operations excellence is made throughout this book. The project management system (Chapter 5) and process improvement tools (Chapters 6 through 11) are key to these activities. The strategic effect of process improvement and maintaining gains is discussed in Chapter 15.

Post-Sale Service

The final aspect of the operations perspective is the post-sales area, an area poorly executed in most healthcare delivery organizations. Sadly, the most common post-sale contact with a patient may be an undecipherable or incorrect bill.

Good post-service systems provide patients with follow-up information on the service they received. Patients with chronic diseases should be contacted periodically with reminders on diet, medication use, and the need to schedule follow-up visits. An outstanding post-sale system also finds opportunities for improvement in the service as well as possible innovations for the future. Open-ended survey questions, such as "From your perspective, how could our organization improve?" or "How else can we serve your healthcare needs?" can point to opportunities for improvement and innovation. Exhibit 4.6 lists common metrics used to measure operational performance.

Vincent Valley Hospital and Health System Internal Business Processes

VVH decided to execute four major projects to move its birthing center and emergency department strategies forward. The birthing center projects were to remodel and redecorate labor and delivery suites, contract with a regional health system for emergency transport of high-risk deliveries, and begin predelivery tours of labor and delivery facilities by nursing staff. The emergency department project was to execute a Lean analysis and kaizen event to improve patient flow.

Learning and Growing Perspective

The final perspective from which to view an organization is learning and growing. To effectively execute a strategy, employees must be motivated and

EXHIBIT 4.6
Metrics to
Measure
Performance
from the
Operational
Perspective

- Average length of stay—case-mix adjusted
- FTE/adjusted patient day
- FTE/diagnosis-related group (DRG)
- FTE/RVU
- FTE/clinic visit
- Waiting time inside clinical systems
- Access time to appointments
- Percent value-added time
- Utilization of resources (e.g., operating room, imaging suite)
- Patients leaving emergency department without being seen
- Operating room cancellations
- Admitting process performance
- Billing system performance
- Medication errors
- Nosocomial infections
- National Quality Forum (2002) "never events"

EXHIBIT 4.6
Metrics to
Measure
Performance
from the
Operational
Perspective

have the necessary tools to succeed. Therefore, a successful organization will make substantial investments in this aspect of its operations. Kaplan and Norton (1996) identified three critical aspects of learning and growing: employee skills and abilities, necessary IT, and employee motivation.

Employee Skills and Abilities

Although employees in healthcare usually come to their jobs with general training in their technical field, continuous updating of skills is necessary. Some healthcare organizations are effective in ensuring that clinical skills are updated but neglect training in other vital processes (e.g., purchasing systems, organization-wide strategies). A good measure of the attention paid to this area is the number of classes conducted by the organization or an outside contractor. Another important measure is the breadth of employee occupations attending these classes. For example, do all employees from doctors to housekeepers attend organization-wide training?

Necessary IT

Most healthcare workers are "knowledge workers." The more immediately and conveniently information is available to them, the more effectively they will be able to perform their jobs. Process redesign projects frequently use IT as a resource for automation and information retrieval. Measures of automation include number of employees having easy access to IT systems, percentage of individual jobs that have an automation component, and speed of installation of new IT capabilities.

Employee Motivation

A progressive culture and motivated employees are clearly competitive advantages; therefore, it is important to monitor these with some frequency. Measures of employee satisfaction include the following:

- Level of involvement with decisions
- Recognition for doing a good job
- Amount of access to information
- Level of encouragement of creativity and initiative
- Support for staff-level functions
- Overall satisfaction with the organization
- Turnover rate
- Absenteeism rate
- Training hours per employee

Data for many of these measures are typically collected with employee surveys.

These three aspects of learning and growing—employee skills, IT, and motivation—all contribute to employee satisfaction. A satisfied employee is also productive and will remain with the organization. Employee satisfaction, productivity, and loyalty make outstanding organizational performance possible.

Vincent Valley Hospital and Health System Learns and Grows

VVH realized its employees needed new skills to successfully execute some of its projects, so it engaged training firms to provide classes for all staff (Exhibit 4.7).

Linking Balanced Scorecard Measures to Strategy

Once expected objectives and their related measures are determined for each perspective, the initiatives to meet these goals must be developed. An initia-

EXHIBIT 4.7
VVH
Improvement
Projects and
Associated
Training

Project	Employees Involved	Training
Begin predelivery tours of labor and delivery facilities by nursing staff	Obstetric nursing and support staff	Customer service and sales
Execute a Lean analysis and kaizen event to improve patient flow in the emergency department	Managers and key clinicians in the emergency department	Lean tools (Chapter 9)

tive can be a simple action or a large project. However, it is important to logically link each initiative to the desired outcome through a series of cause-and-effect statements. These are usually constructed as "if-then" statements that tie each initiative together and contribute to the outcome; for example:

- If the wait time in the emergency department is decreased, then the patient will be more satisfied.
- If an admitting process is improved through the use of automation, then the final collection rate will improve.
- If an optically scanned wristband is used in conjunction with an electronic health record, then medication errors will decline.
- If a discharge summary is routinely dictated and transmitted to the primary care provider within 24 hours, then the number of readmissions within 30 days will decrease.

Each initiative should have measures associated with it, and every measure selected for a balanced scorecard should be an element in a chain of cause-effect relationships that communicate the organization's strategy.

Outcomes and Performance Drivers

Selecting appropriate measures for each initiative is critical. There are two basic types of indicators. Outcome indicators, familiar to most managers, are also termed **lagging indicators** because they result from earlier actions. Outcome indicators tend to be generic instead of tightly focused. Healthcare operations examples include profitability, market share, and patient satisfaction. The other type of indicator is a *performance driver,* or **leading indicator**. These indicators predict the future and are specific to an initiative and the organization's strategy. For example, a performance driver measure could be waiting time in the emergency department. A drop in waiting time should predict an improvement in the outcome indicator, patient satisfaction.

A common pitfall in developing indicators is the use of measures associated with the improvement project rather than with the process improvement. For example, the fact that a project to improve patient flow in a department is 88 percent complete is not as good an indicator as a measure of the actual change in patient flow, a 12 percent reduction in waiting time. Outcome measures are always preferred, but in some cases, they may be difficult or impossible to obtain.

Because the number of balanced scorecard measures should be limited, identifying measures that are indicators for a complex process is sometimes useful. For example, a seemingly simple indicator such as "time to next appointment" for patient scheduling will track many complex processes within an organization.

Lagging indicator
A performance measurement that assesses the outcome of existing actions.

Leading indicator
A performance measurement that predicts the future and is specific to an initiative or to organizational strategy. Also called a performance driver.

Strategy Maps

As discussed, a set of initiatives should be linked together by if-then statements to achieve a desired outcome. Both outcome and performance driver indicators should be determined for each initiative. These can be displayed graphically in a **strategy map**, which may be most helpfully organized into the four perspectives with learning and growing at the bottom and financial at the top. A general strategy map for any organization would include the following:

Strategy map
A set of initiatives that are graphically linked by if-then statements to describe an organization's strategy.

- If employees have skills, tools, and motivation, then they will improve operations.
- If operations are improved and marketing is also improved, then customers will buy more products and services.
- If customers buy more products and services and operations are run efficiently, then the organization's financial performance will improve.

Exhibit 4.8 shows a strategy map in which these general initiatives are indicated.

The strategy map is enhanced if each initiative also contains the strategic objective, measure used, and target results that the organization hopes to achieve. Each causal pathway from initiative to initiative needs to be as clear and quantitative as possible.

EXHIBIT 4.8
General
Strategy Map

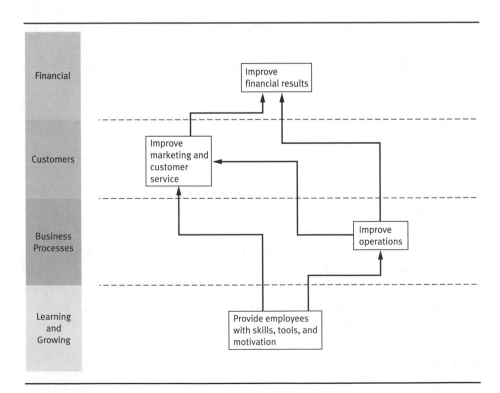

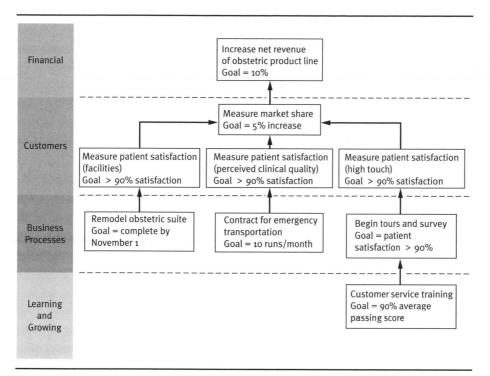

EXHIBIT 4.9
VVH Birthing
Center Strategy
Map

Vincent Valley Hospital and Health System Strategy Maps

VVH has two major areas of strategic focus—the birthing center and the emergency department. Exhibit 4.9 displays the strategy map for the birthing center.

Recall that VVH had decided to execute three major projects in this area. Other initiatives needed for the successful execution of each project are identified on the map. For instance, for nursing staff to successfully lead expectant mothers on tours of labor and delivery suites, they will need to participate in a customer service training program. After the tours begin, the birthing center will measure potential patients' satisfaction to ensure that the tours are being conducted effectively. Once patients deliver their babies in VVH's obstetric unit, they will again be surveyed on their experience with special questions on the effect of each of these major projects. These leading satisfaction indicators should predict the lagging indicators of increased market share and net revenue.

The second major strategy for VVH was to improve patient flow in the emergency department. Exhibit 4.10 shows the strategy map for the emergency department.

The first required steps in this strategy are forming a project team (Chapter 5) and learning how to use Lean process improvement tools (Chapter 9). Then the team can begin analyzing patient flow and implementing changes to improve flow. VVH has set a goal of reducing the amount of non-

EXHIBIT 4.10
VVH Emergency
Department
Strategy Map

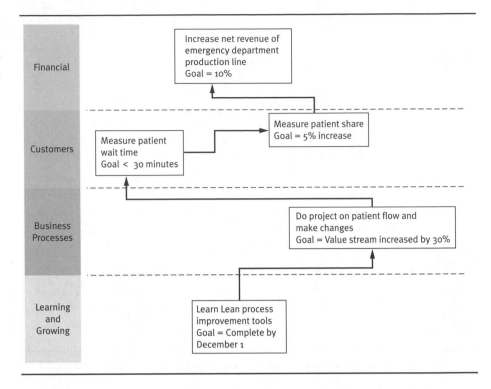

value-added time by 30 percent. Once this is accomplished, waiting time for 90 percent of patients should not exceed 30 minutes. A reduced waiting time should result in patients being more satisfied and, hence, a growth in market share and increased net revenue. Following are more formal cause-and-effect statements:

- If emergency department staff undertakes educational activities to learn project management and Lean, then they can effectively execute a patient flow improvement project.
- If a patient flow project is undertaken and non-value-added time is reduced by 30 percent, then the waiting time for 90 percent of the patients should never exceed 30 minutes.
- If the waiting time for most patients never exceeds 30 minutes, then they will be highly satisfied and this will increase the number of patients and VVH's market share.
- If the emergency department market share increases, then net revenue will increase.

The companion website contains a downloadable strategy map and linked scorecard. It also has a number of videos that demonstrate how to use and modify these tools for both student and practitioner use.

Implementation of the Balanced Scorecard

Linking and Communicating

The balanced scorecard can be used at many different levels in an organization. However, departmental scorecards should link to the divisional, and ultimately the corporate, level. Each scorecard should be linked upward and downward. For example, an obstetric initiative to increase revenue from normal childbirth will be linked to the corporate-level objective of overall increased revenue. Sometimes it is difficult to specifically link a departmental strategy map to corporate objectives. In this case, the department head must make a more general link by stating how a departmental initiative will influence a particular corporate goal. For example, improving the quality of the hospital laboratory testing system will generally influence the corporate objective that patients should perceive that the hospital provides the highest level of quality care.

The development and operation of scorecards at each level of an organization require disciplined communication, which can be an incentive for action. Balanced scorecards can also be used to communicate with an organization's external stakeholders. A well-implemented balanced scorecard system will be integrated with individual employee goals and the organization's performance management system.

Targets, Resources, Initiatives, and Budgets

A balanced scorecard strategy map consists of a series of linked initiatives. Each initiative should have a quantitative measure and a target. Initiatives can reside in one department, but they are frequently cross-departmental. Many initiatives are projects, and the process for successful project management (Chapter 5) should be followed. A well-implemented balanced scorecard will also link carefully to an organization's budget, particularly if initiatives and projects are expected to consume considerable operating or capital resources.

The use of the balanced scorecard does not obviate the use of additional operating statistics. Many other operating and financial measures still need to be collected and analyzed. If the performance of any of these measures deviates substantially from its expected target, a new strategy and initiative may be needed. For example, most healthcare organizations carefully track and monitor their accounts receivable. If this financial measure is within industry norms, it probably will not appear on an organization's balanced scorecard. However, if the accounts receivable balance drifts over time and begins to exceed expectations, a balanced scorecard initiative may be started to address the problem.

Displaying Results

The actual scorecard tracks and communicates the results of each initiative. (Chapter 7 provides many examples of visual displays.) A challenge for most organizations is to collect the data to display in the scorecard. Because the scorecard should have fewer than 20 measures, a simple solution is to assign this responsibility to one individual who develops efficient methods to collect the data and determines effective methods to display them. However, a more robust solution is the development of a data warehouse with associated analysis and reporting tools (see page 89).

www.ache.org/books/OpsManagement2

The companion website includes a straightforward balanced scorecard, built in Excel, that can store and display one year of data. Exhibit 4.11 shows the cover worksheet of this scorecard.

Ensuring That the Balanced Scorecard Works

Once a balanced scorecard system is created it must be monitored closely. Kaplan and Norton (2008) recommend that management teams divide their routine meetings into three types: operational reviews, strategy reviews, and strategy testing and adaptation. The operational meeting is held frequently (e.g., weekly) and is designed to respond to short-term problems and promote improvements. The strategy review meeting is held monthly and focuses on monitoring and fine-tuning the existing strategy map. The strategy testing and adaptation meeting should be held at least annually and more frequently if the environment is changing rapidly. These meetings are designed to improve or transform the existing strategy, develop new initiatives and revised maps, and authorize needed expenditures.

The explicit purpose of the balanced scorecard is to ensure the successful execution of an organization's strategy. But what if it does not achieve the desired results? There are two possible causes.

The first, most obvious, problem is that an initiative itself is not achieving its targeted results. For example, the emergency department's patient flow project may not be able to decrease non-valued-added time by 30 percent. In that case, the hospital may have to add an additional initiative, such as engaging a consultant. This measure will need to be carefully monitored and frequently posted on the scorecard.

The second, more complex, problem occurs when the successful execution of an initiative does not lead to achievement of the next linked target. For example, although waiting times in the emergency department are decreased, the emergency department may not gain market share. The solution to this problem is to reconsider the cause-and-effect relationships.

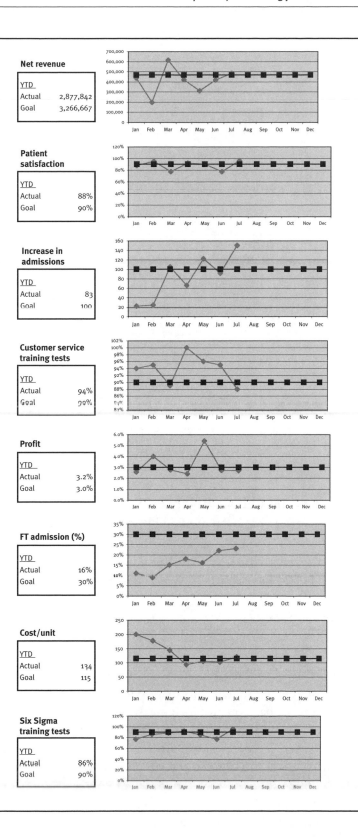

EXHIBIT 4.11
Balanced
Scorecard
Template
(Contained
on book
companion
website)

EXHIBIT 4.12
Rotated General
Strategy Map

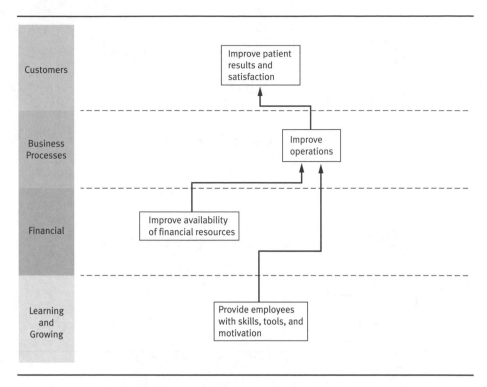

An organization should review its results and strategy map at least quarterly and revise its strategy annually, usually as part of the budgeting process.

Modifications of the Classic Balanced Scorecard

The balanced scorecard has been modified by many healthcare organizations, most commonly by placing the customer or patient at the top of the strategy map (Exhibit 4.12). Finance then becomes a means to achieve superior patient outcomes and satisfaction.

Implementation Issues

Two common challenges occur when implementing balanced scorecards: (1) determination and development of metrics, and (2) initiative prioritization.

The balanced scorecard is a quantitative tool and, therefore, requires data systems that generate timely information for inclusion. Each initiative on a strategy map should have quantitative measures, which should represent an even mix of leading and lagging measures. Each initiative should have a target as well. However, setting targets is an art: Too timid a goal will not move the organization forward, and too aggressive a goal will be discouraging.

Niven (2002) suggests that a number of sources should be used to construct targets. These include internal company operating data, executive interviews, internal and external strategic assessments, customer research, industry averages, and benchmarking data. Targets can be incremental based on current operating results (e.g., increase productivity in a nursing unit by 10 percent in the next 12 months), or they can be "stretch goals," which are possible but will require extraordinary effort to achieve (e.g., improve compliance with evidence-based guidelines for 98 percent of patients with diabetes). Too many measures and initiatives will confuse a scorecard; therefore, even the most sophisticated organizations limit their measures to 20 or fewer.

The second major implementation challenge is the prioritization of initiatives. Most organizations do not lack for current initiatives or projects, and influential leaders in the organization often propose many more. Niven (2002, 190) suggests a methodology to manage this phenomenon:

1. Inventory all current initiatives taking place within the organization.
2. Map those initiatives to the objectives of the balanced scorecard.
3. Consider eliminating nonstrategic initiatives, and develop missing initiatives.
4. Prioritize the remaining initiatives.

Most organizations will never be able to achieve perfect alignment with their balanced scorecard goals for all of their initiatives. However, the closer the alignment, the more likely the organization's strategic objectives will be achieved.

Business Intelligence

All contemporary organizations use automated systems to generate reports, and most information systems generate too many reports. This sea of data makes it challenging for the manager to find meaningful and actionable information. Fortunately, new tools have become available to effectively aggregate and analyze this information.

Data Warehousing

Organizational leaders frequently ask seemingly simple questions of their information technology departments that actually require complex processing to answer. Nothing is more frustrating than to go through the organizational pain and financial cost of installing a new electronic health record system and then find out you cannot retrieve what seems to be the most mundane data. Yet this frequently occurs. This conundrum is caused by the complex structure of today's operating systems, which are primarily designed to manage large data sets.

Data warehouse
A separate
but connected
computer
system designed
for accurate
data storage,
performance
reporting, and
data mining.

Data mining
An analytical
approach to
retrieving data
from data
warehouses to
discover new
patterns and
relationships
to support
management
decision making.

**Business
intelligence**
The combination
of data and
analytical tools to
find meaningful
and actionable
information. It
includes the
creation of data
warehouses in
order to support
data mining.

The solution to this problem is the **data warehouse**. A data warehouse is a separate but connected computer system designed for accurate data storage, performance reporting, and **data mining**. Data warehouses also usually contain data marts, which are smaller, subject-specific databases. Most database software allows all data marts in an organization to be combined into a data warehouse. Exhibit 4.13 shows the relationship of the operating systems, the data warehouse, and online analytical tools. The data warehouse should serve as the repository of data being reported on the balanced scorecard.

Data from operating systems are moved through a series of software programs known as ETL—extract, transform, and load. This process cleans the data and puts them into a form that is useful for analysis and reporting. Balanced scorecard data can usually be extracted and presented through performance reporting tools that are associated with the warehouse. However, data in warehouses can also be mined with sophisticated analytical tools to discover unexpected and interesting associations in operating data (e.g., which surgeons use which supplies). In addition, automated business rules software can also be used with the warehouse to improve operations (e.g., e-mailing a manager when a patient is readmitted within 30 days). The combination of the data warehouse and the analytical tools is called **business intelligence**.

Conclusion

This text is about how to get things done. The balanced scorecard provides a powerful tool to that end because it

- links strategy to action in the form of initiatives;
- provides a comprehensive communication tool inside and outside an organization; and
- is quantitatively based, providing a tool for ongoing strategy analysis and improvement.

Discussion Questions

1. What other indicators might be used in each of the four perspectives for public health agencies? For health plans?
2. If you were to add another perspective, what would it be? Draw a strategy map of a healthcare delivery organization and include this perspective.

Exhibit 4.13 Data Warehouse Environment

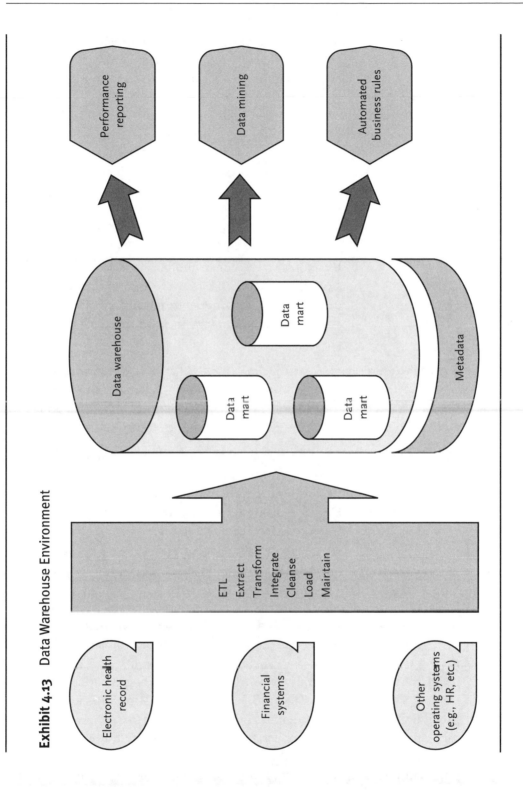

3. How do you manage the other operations of an organization, those that do not appear on a strategy map or balanced scorecard?
4. How would a department link its balanced scorecard to a corporate scorecard?
5. What methods could be used to involve the customer or patient in identifying the key elements of the balanced scorecard?

Chapter Exercises

1. View the web videos on www.ache.org/books/OpsManagement2 and download the PowerPoint strategy map and Excel worksheet.

   www.ache.org/books/OpsManagement2

   Develop a strategy map and balanced scorecard for a primary care dental clinic. Do Internet research to determine the challenges facing primary care dentistry, and develop a strategy map for success in this environment.

   Make sure that the strategy map includes at least eight initiatives and that they touch the four perspectives. Include targets, and be sure the metrics are a mix of leading and lagging indicators. Develop a plan to periodically review your map to ascertain its effectiveness.

2. Download the data for this chapter and develop a dashboard in Excel to identify readmissions within 30 days. A number of initiatives are described on the companion website that can be used to minimize readmissions. Do additional Internet research and then construct a strategy map to improve this readmission rate.

Case Study: St. Mary's/Duluth Clinic

St Mary's/Duluth Clinic (SMDC) Health System, a member of Essentia Health, serves a regional population of 460,000 in northeastern Minnesota, northwestern Wisconsin, and Michigan's Upper Peninsula. The integrated health system has four fully owned hospitals including St. Mary's Medical Center, SMDC Medical Center, St. Mary's Hospital of Superior, and Pine Medical Center. In addition, it has one integrated partner, Rainy Lake Medical Center, and works in cooperation with community hospitals across the region. SMDC also includes the Duluth Clinic, a nationally recognized 400+ physician multispecialty group, representing 55 medical specialties and providing care at 17 locations.

Exhibit 4.14 SMDC Strategy Map

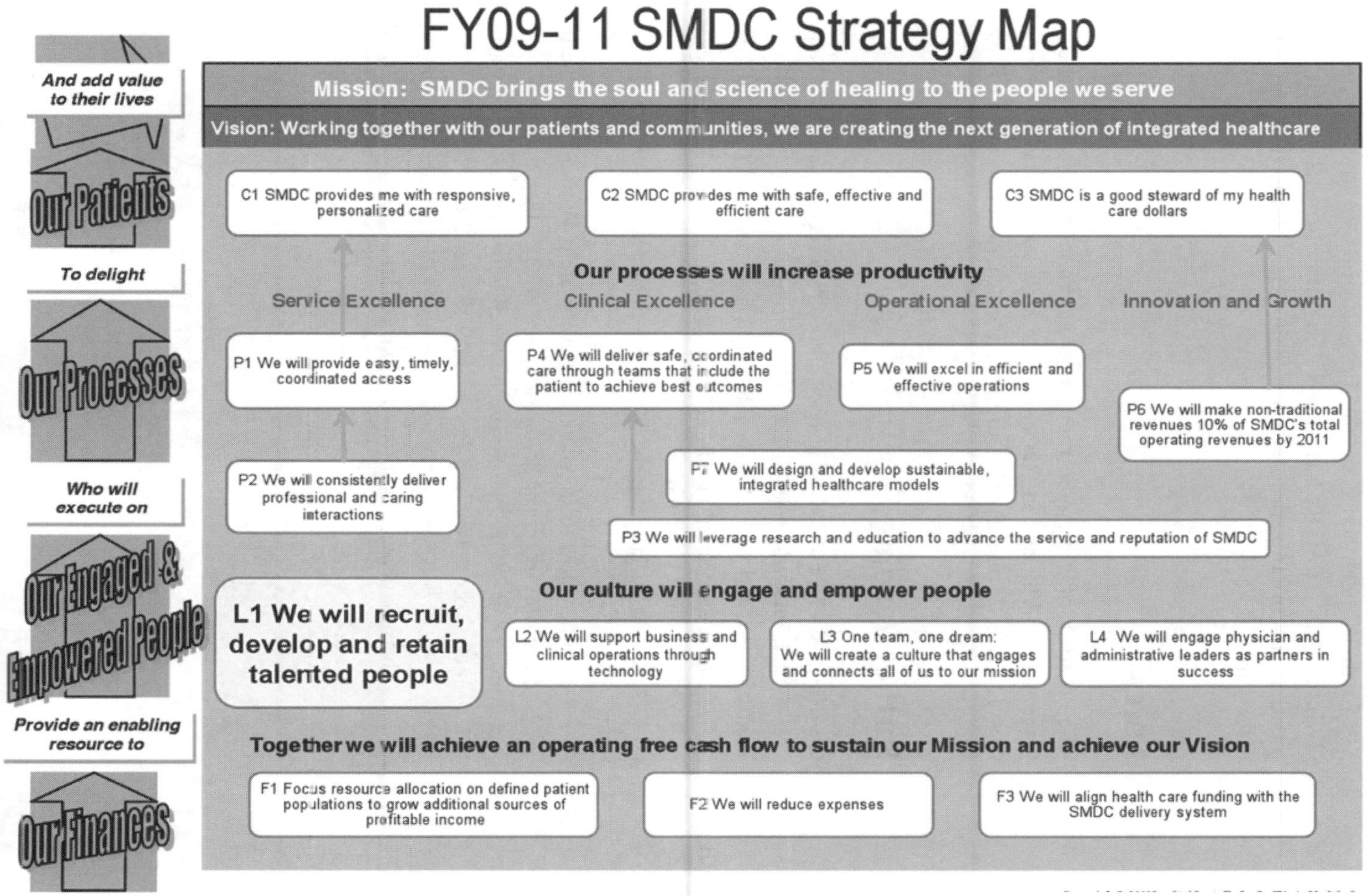

FY09–11 SMDC Strategy Map

Mission: SMDC brings the soul and science of healing to the people we serve

Vision: Working together with our patients and communities, we are creating the next generation of integrated healthcare

Service Excellence · Clinical Excellence · Operational Excellence · Innovation and Growth

And add value to their lives — Our Patients

C1 SMDC provides me with responsive, personalized care

C2 SMDC provides me with safe, effective and efficient care

C3 SMDC is a good steward of my health care dollars

Our processes will increase productivity

To delight — Our Processes

P1 We will provide easy, timely, coordinated access

P2 We will consistently deliver professional and caring interactions

P4 We will deliver safe, coordinated care through teams that include the patient to achieve best outcomes

P5 We will excel in efficient and effective operations

P6 We will make non-traditional revenues 10% of SMDC's total operating revenues by 2011

P₃ We will design and develop sustainable, integrated healthcare models

P3 We will leverage research and education to advance the service and reputation of SMDC

Our culture will engage and empower people

Who will execute on — Our Engaged & Empowered People

L1 We will recruit, develop and retain talented people

L2 We will support business and clinical operations through technology

L3 One team, one dream: We will create a culture that engages and connects all of us to our mission

L4 We will engage physician and administrative leaders as partners in success

Together we will achieve an operating free cash flow to sustain our Mission and achieve our Vision

Provide an enabling resource to — Our Finances

F1 Focus resource allocation on defined patient populations to grow additional sources of profitable income

F2 We will reduce expenses

F3 We will align health care funding with the SMDC delivery system

SOURCE: St. Mary's/Duluth Clinic Health System. Used with permission.

Examination of the strategy map shows that SMDC has rotated the financial perspective to the bottom and put the customer at the top (Exhibit 4.14). SMDC has only 17 initiatives on its strategy map, indicating that the organization is focused on those items that are key to moving it forward.

Notes

The creation of strategy in the new environment created by the Accountable Care Act is addressed in *Responding to Reform: A Strategy Guide for Healthcare Leaders*, Daniel B. McLaughlin, Health Administration Press.

Further Reading

Cleverley, W. O., and J. O. Cleverley. 2005. "Scorecards and Dashboards." *Healthcare Financial Management* 59 (7): 64–69.

Kaplan, R. S., and D. P. Norton. 2008a. *The Execution Premium: Linking Strategy to Operations for Competitive Advantage*. Boston: Harvard Business School Publishing Corporation.

———. 2008b. "Mastering the Management System." *Harvard Business Review* 86 (1): 62–77.

———. 2006. "How to Implement a New Strategy Without Disrupting Your Organization." *Harvard Business Review* 84 (3): 100–09.

Tarantino, D. P. 2003. "Using the Balanced Scorecard as a Performance Management Tool." *Physician Executive* 29 (5): 69–72.

Wyatt, J. 2004. "Scorecards, Dashboards, and KPIs: Keys to Integrated Performance Measurement." *Healthcare Financial Management* 58 (2): 76–80.

PROJECT MANAGEMENT

5

Operations Management in Action

Effective project management can be the basis for significant improvements in healthcare delivery. An excellent example is The Massachusetts Health Cooperative, which was initiated to "facilitate the ubiquitous adoption of electronic health records (EHR) in the Commonwealth of Massachusetts." The project team included

- senior managers who worked with community leaders and programs;
- practice consultants who worked with individual practices;
- project managers who used contemporary project management techniques to ensure that time, budget, and performance goals were met; and
- technical managers to ensure software and hardware performance.

Over 18 months, the project team installed EHRs into 97 percent of the target market (600 physicians). This project has now evolved into the Quality Data Center, which aggregates and analyzes clinical information from these EHRs for quality improvement and feedback to patients.

SOURCE: Mostashari, Tripathi, and Kendall (2009).

Overview

Everyone manages projects, whether painting a bedroom at home or adding a 100-bed wing to a hospital.

This chapter provides grounding in the science of project management. The major topics covered include

- selecting and chartering projects;
- using stakeholder analysis to set project requirements;
- developing a work breakdown structure and schedule;
- using Microsoft Project to develop project plans and monitor cost, schedule, and earned value;
- managing project communications, change control, and risk; and
- creating and leading project teams.

After reading this chapter and completing the associated exercises, readers should be able to

- create a project charter with a detailed plan for costs, schedule, scope, and performance;
- monitor the progress of a project, make changes as required, communicate to stakeholders, and manage risks; and
- develop the skills to successfully lead a project team.

If everyone manages projects, why is there a need to devote a chapter in a healthcare operations book to this topic? The answer lies in the question. Although everyone has life experiences in project management, few healthcare professionals take the time to understand and practice the science and discipline of project management. The ability to successfully move a project forward while meeting time and budget goals is a distinguishing characteristic of a high-quality, highly competitive healthcare organization.

Effective project management provides an opportunity for progressive healthcare organizations to quickly develop new clinical services, fix major operating problems, reduce expenses, and provide new consumer-directed products to their patients.

The problems with poor project management became apparent in the defense industry after World War II. Many new weapons systems were wildly over budget, were late, and did not perform as expected. The automated baggage conveyor system at Denver International Airport is another frequently cited example of poor project management. In 2005, after ten years of malfunctions and high maintenance costs, it was turned off and baggage is now handled manually.

Project management professional (PMP)
Professional certification of a project manager by the Project Management Institute.

A response to this problem was the gradual development of project management as a discipline, culminating in the establishment of the Project Management Institute (PMI) in 1969 (www.PMI.org). Today, PMI has more than 110,000 members, and more than 50,000 of those are certified as **project management professionals (PMPs)**.

PMI members have developed the **Project Management Body of Knowledge (PMBOK)** (PMI 2008), which details best practices for successful project management.

Carden and Egan (2008) undertook a comprehensive review of the scientific basis for project management. According to their study,

> . . . refereed research has indicated that project managers utilize tools and techniques along with people to ensure quality deliverables are on time, within scope, and within budget. Additionally, project leadership and a favorable development environment both are important to the successful delivery of projects. Therefore, the connection between knowledge and action can be used to frame behaviors by engaging in transactions to plan, organize, monitor, and report findings in order to maintain a dynamic balance with the organization, resources, tools, and the external environment.

Much as evidence-based medicine delineates the most effective methods to care for specific clinical conditions, the PMBOK provides science-based, field-tested guidelines for successful project management. This chapter is based on PMBOK principles as applied to healthcare. Healthcare professionals who spend much of their time leading projects should consider using resources available through PMI; for some, PMP certification may be appropriate.

Definition of a Project

A project is a one-time set of activities that culminates in a desired outcome. Therefore, activities that occur repeatedly, for example, making appointments for patients in a clinic, are not projects. However, the installation of new software to upgrade this capability would be a project. A major process improvement effort to reduce phone hold time for patients would also qualify as a project.

Slack (2005) provides a useful tool for determining the need for formal project management (Exhibit 5.1). Operating issues arise frequently; if they are simple, they can be fixed immediately by operating staff. More complicated problems can be addressed by using the tools detailed in Chapter 6. However, projects that are complex and have high organizational value need the discipline of formal project management. Many of the strategic initiatives on an organization's balanced scorecard should use the project management methodology.

A well-managed project will include a specified scope of work, expected outcomes and performance levels, a budget, and a detailed work breakdown tied to a schedule. It will also include a formal change procedure,

Project Management Body of Knowledge (PMBOK)
A book of science-based, field-tested guidelines for successful project management, developed by the Project Management Institute.

EXHIBIT 5.1
When to
Use Project
Management

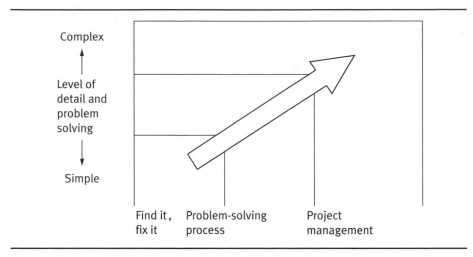

SOURCE: Slack (2005). Used with permission.

a communications plan, and a plan to deal with risk. Finally, all good projects will include a project conclusion process and a plan for redeployment of staff.

Many high-performing organizations will also have a formal executive-level chartering process for projects and a project management office to monitor enterprise-wide project activities. Some healthcare organizations (e.g., health plans) can have a substantial share of their operating resources invested in projects at any one time.

For effective execution of a project, PMI recommends that three elements must be present. A *project charter* begins the project and addresses stakeholder needs. A *project scope statement* identifies project outcomes, time lines, and budget in detail. Finally, to execute the project, a *project plan* must be developed; the plan includes scope management, work breakdown, schedule management, cost management, quality control, staffing management, communications, risk management, procurement, and the close-out process. Exhibit 5.2 displays the relationships among these elements.

Project Selection and Chartering

Project Selection

Most organizations have many projects vying for attention, funding, and senior executive support. The annual budget and strategic planning process serve as useful vehicles for prioritizing projects in many organizations. The balanced scorecard (Chapter 4) will help guide the identification of worthwhile strategic projects. Other external forces (e.g., new Medicare rules) or clinical innovations (e.g., new imaging technologies), however, will conspire

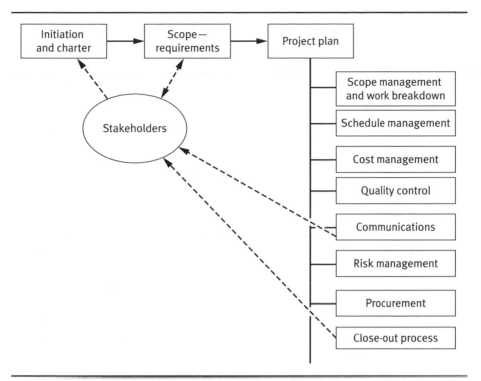

EXHIBIT 5.2
Complete
Project
Management
Process

to present an organization's leadership with a list of projects too long for successful implementation. It is helpful to use a quantitative approach, and Exhibit 5.3 provides an example. In this case, each possible project is scored on the four balanced scorecard perspectives with a predetermined weighting (Exhibit 5.3).

To use this tool, each potential project should be scored by a senior planning group based on how well it fits into the organization's strategy, its financial benefit, how it affects quality, its operational impact, the need for key personnel, and the costs and time required for the project itself. A scale of one (low) to ten (high) is usually used. Each criterion is also weighted; the scores are multiplied by their weight for each criterion and summed over all of the criteria. In Exhibit 5.3, Project A has a higher total score because of its importance to the organization's strategy. Such a ranking methodology helps organizations avoid committing resources to projects that may have a powerful internal champion but do not advance the organization's overall strategy. This matrix can be modified with other categories and weights based on an organization's current needs.

Project Charter

Once a project is identified for implementation, it needs to be chartered. Four factors interact to constrain the execution of a project charter: time,

EXHIBIT 5.3
Project
Management
Matrix

Criteria	Weight (%)	Project A Points	Project A Score	Project B Points	Project B Score
Overall linkage to strategy	45	7	3.15	1	0.45
Financial gain	15	5	0.75	10	1.5
Impact on clinical quality and patient satisfaction	10	5	0.50	10	1.0
Improvement in operational efficiency	10	8	0.80	10	1.0
Key staff available and effective project managers complete	10	8	0.80	10	1.0
Total cost and duration of the project	10	3	0.30	10	1.0
Total	·		6.30		5.95

SOURCE: Niven, P. R. 2002. *Balanced Scorecard Step by Step.* Figure 7.2: Prioritizing Balanced Scorecard Initiatives, page 194. Used with permission of John Wiley & Sons, Inc.

cost, scope, and performance. A successful project will have a scope that specifies the resulting performance level, how much time it will take, and its budgeted cost. A change in any one of these factors will affect the other three. This can be expressed mathematically as follows:

$$\text{Scope} = f(\text{Time, Cost, Performance})$$

Similarly,

$$\text{Time} = f(\text{Cost, Scope, Performance})$$

and so on.

Exhibit 5.4 demonstrates these relationships graphically. Here, the area of the triangle is a measure of the scope of the project. The length of each side of the triangle indicates the amount of time, money, or performance needed in the project. Because each side of the triangle is connected, changing any of these parameters affects the others. Exhibit 5.5 shows this same

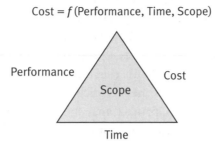

$$Cost = f(Performance, Time, Scope)$$

Performance

Cost

Scope

Time

EXHIBIT 5.4
Relationship of
Project Scope
to Performance
Level, Time, and
Cost

project with an increase in required performance level and shortened time lines. With the same scope, this "new" project will incur additional costs.

Although it is difficult to specifically and exactly determine the relationship between all four factors, the successful project manager understands this general relationship well and communicates it to project sponsors. A useful analogy is the balloon: If you push hard on part of it, a different part will bulge out. The classic project management dilemma is an increase in scope without additional time or funding (sometimes termed *scope creep*). Many project failures are directly attributable to ignoring this unyielding formula.

Stakeholder Identification and Dialogue

The first step in developing a project charter is to identify the **stakeholders**—in general, anyone who has an investment in the outcome of the project. Key stakeholders on a project include the project manager, customers, users, project team members, any contracted organizations involved, the project sponsor, those who can influence the project, and the project management office, if one exists in the organization.

The project manager is the individual held accountable for the project's success and, therefore, forms the core of the stakeholder group. The customer or user of the service or product is an important stakeholder who will influence and help determine the performance of the final product. Even if project team members serve on the project in a limited part-time

Stakeholder
Anyone who has a
vested interest in
the outcome of a
project, including
(but not limited
to) employees,
customers,
users, partner
organizations,
project sponsors,
and the project
manager.

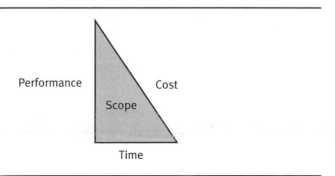

Performance

Cost

Scope

Time

EXHIBIT 5.5
Project with
Increased
Performance
Requirement
and Shortened
Schedule

role, the success of the project reflects on them and, therefore, they become stakeholders. A common contracting relationship in healthcare involves large information technology (IT) installations provided through an outside vendor, which would also be included as a project stakeholder. A project should always have a sponsor with enough executive-level influence to clear roadblocks as the project progresses; hence, such individuals need to be included in the stakeholder group. A project may be aided or hindered by many individuals or organizations that are not directly part of it; a global systems analysis should be performed (Chapter 1) to identify which of these should be included as stakeholders.

Once stakeholders have been identified, they need to be interviewed by the project manager to develop the project charter. If an important stakeholder is not available, the project manager should interview someone who represents her interests. At this point, it is important to differentiate between the needs and the wants of the stakeholders. Enough detail needs to be gathered to construct the project charter. When the project team is organized, it need not include all stakeholders, but the team should be vigilant in attempting to meet all stakeholder needs. The project team should also be cognizant of the culture of the organization, sometimes defined as "how things get done around here." Projects that challenge an organization's culture will encounter frequent difficulties.

"The project charter is the document that formally authorizes a project. The project charter provides the project manager with the authority to apply organizational resources to project activities" (PMI 2008). A project initiator, or sponsor external to the project, issues the charter and signs it to authorize the start of the project.

Feasibility Analysis

An important part of the project charter is determining the project's feasibility. Because the project should have already had an initial prioritization by the senior management team, the link to the organization's strategy has likely already been made. However, this link should be documented in the feasibility analysis. The operational and technical feasibility should also be examined. For example, if a new clinical project requires the construction of new facilities, this may impede its execution. An initial schedule should also be considered, as a needed completion date may be clearly impossible. Finally, both financial benefit and marketplace demand should be considered here. For details on conducting a financial feasibility analysis, see Gapenski (2011). All elements of the feasibility analysis should be included in the project charter document.

Project Charter Document

The project charter authorizes the project and serves as an executive summary. A formal charter document should be constructed with the following elements:

- Project mission statement
- Project purpose or justification and connection to strategic goals
- High-level requirements that satisfy customers, sponsors, and other stakeholders
- Assigned project manager and authority level
- Summary milestones
- Stakeholder influences
- Functional organizations and their participation
- Organizational, environmental, and external assumptions and constraints
- Financial business case, budget, and return on investment (ROI)
- Project sponsor with approval signature

A project charter template is contained on the companion website. The initial description of the project scope is found in the Requirements, Milestones, and Financial sections of the project charter.

www.ache.org/books/OpsManagement2

A project charter can be illustrated with an example from Vincent Valley Hospital and Health System (VVH). The hospital operates a primary care clinic (Riverview Clinic) in the south suburban area of Bakersville. Recently, the three largest health plans in the area instituted pay-for-performance programs in the areas of diabetes, asthma, congestive heart failure, and generic

---

Project Mission Statement

This project will increase the level of generic drug prescriptions to lower the costs to our patients and increase reimbursements to the clinic.

Project Purpose and Justification

Health plans in Bakersville have begun to provide additional funding to clinics that meet pay-for-performance guidelines. Although a number of chronic conditions are covered by these new payment systems, it is felt that generic drug use should be the first project executed because it is likely to be accomplished in a reasonable time frame with the maximum financial benefit to our patients and the clinic. Once this project has been executed, the clinic will move on to more complex clinical conditions. The team will be able to incorporate what they have learned about some of the barriers to success and methods to succeed on pay-for-performance projects. This project is a part of the larger VVH strategic initiative of maximizing pay-for-performance reimbursement.

EXHIBIT 5.6
Project Charter for VVH Generic Drug Project

(continued)

EXHIBIT 5.6
Project Charter
for VVH Generic
Drug Project
(continued)

High-Level Requirements

Once completed, a new prescribing process will

- continue to meet patients' clinical needs and provide high-quality care; and
- increase generic drug use by 4 percent from baseline within six months.

Assigned Project Manager and Authority Level

Sally Humphries, RN, will be the project manager.

Sally has authority to make changes in budget, time, scope, and performance by 10 percent. Any larger change requires approval from the clinic operating board.

Summary Milestones

- The project will commence on January 1.
- A system to identify approved generic drugs will be available on February 15.
- The system will go live on March 15.

Stakeholder Influences

The following stakeholders will influence the project:

- *Clinicians* will strive to provide the best care for their patients.
- *Patients* will need to understand the benefits of this new system.
- *Clinic staff* will need training and support tools.
- *Health plans* should be a partner in this project as part of the supply chain.
- *Pharmaceutical firms* should provide clinical information on the efficacy of certain generic drugs.

Functional Organizations and Their Participation

- Clinic management staff will lead.
- Compcare EHR vendor will perform software modifications.
- VVH IT department will support.
- VVH main pharmacy department will support.

Organizational, Environmental, and External Assumptions and Constraints

- Success depends on appropriate substitution of generic for brand-name drugs.
- Patients need to understand the benefits of this change.
- Health plans need to continue to fund this project over a number of years.
- IT modifications need to be approved rapidly by the VVH central IT department.

Financial Business Case—ROI

The project budget is $61,000 for personnel. Software modifications are included in the master VVH contract and, therefore, have no direct cost to this project. If the 4 percent increase in generic drug use is achieved, the two-year revenue increase should be approximately $75,000.

Project Sponsor with Approval Signature

Dr. Jim Anderson, Clinic President

James Anderson, MD

drug use. The health plans will pay primary care clinics bonuses if they achieve specific levels of performance in these areas. Riverview staff have decided to embark on a project to increase their use of generic drugs; their project charter is displayed in Exhibit 5.6.

Project Scope and Work Breakdown

Once a project has been chartered, the detailed work of planning can begin.

Tools

At this point, the project manager should consider acquiring two important tools. The first is the lowest of low tech, the humble three-ring binder. All projects need a continuous record of progress reports, team meetings, approved changes, and so on. A complex project will require many binders, but they will prove invaluable to the project manager. The classic organization of the binders is by date, so the first pages will be the project charter. Of course, if the organization has an effective imaging and document management system, this can substitute for the binders.

The second tool is project management software. Although many options are available, the market leader is Microsoft Project, which is referred to throughout the remainder of the chapter. Microsoft Project is part of the Microsoft Office suite and may already be on many computers in an organization. If not, a demonstration copy can be downloaded from Microsoft. The companion website for this book provides additional explanation and videos related to the use of Project, along with detailed illustrations of the software's use for the Riverview Clinic generic drug project. Go to the companion website, Chapter 5, to view a video on starting Project and setting its global parameters.

www.ache.org/books/OpsManagement2

Project management software is not essential for small projects, but it is helpful and almost required for any project that lasts longer than six months and involves a large team of individuals. Although the Riverview Clinic generic drug project is relatively small, Project software is used to manage it to provide an illustration of the program's applicability.

Scope

The project scope determines what falls inside and outside the scope of a project. The starting point for developing a scope document is the project charter, although the scope statement is much more detailed than the description contained in the project charter. The project manager will want to revisit many of the same stakeholders to acquire more detailed inputs and requirements. A simple methodology is to interview stakeholders and ask them to list the three most important outcomes of the project, which can be combined into project objectives. The objectives must be specific, achievable, measurable, and comprehensible to stakeholders. In addition, they should be stated in terms of time-limited "deliverables." The objective "improve the quality of care to patients with diabetes" is a poor one. "Improve the rate of foot exams by 25 percent in one year for patients with diabetes" is a much better objective.

In scope creation, it is important to avoid expanding the scope of the project: "While we are at it, we might as well ____." These ideas, sometimes called "gold plating," tend to be some of the most dangerous in the world of project management. The scope document should also provide detailed requirements and descriptions of expected outcomes. A good scope document is also specific about project boundaries. The Riverview Clinic project scope document might include a statement that the project does not include access to online pharmacological databases.

The scope document should specify deliverables such as implementation of a new process, installation of a new piece of equipment, or presentation of a paper report. The project organization is also specified in the scope document, including the project manager, team members, and specific relationships to all parts of the organization.

An initial evaluation of potential risks to the project should be enumerated in the scope document. The schedule length and milestones should be more detailed in the scope statement than in the charter. As discussed in the next section, however, the final schedule will be developed based on the work breakdown structure. Finally, the scope document should include methods to monitor progress and make changes where necessary, including the formal approvals required.

Work Breakdown Structure

Work breakdown structure (WBS)
A list of the tasks that need to be accomplished, their relationship to each other, and the resources required for a project to meet its goals.

The second major component of the scope document is the **work breakdown structure (WBS),** considered the engine of the project because it determines how its goals will be achieved. The WBS lists the tasks that need to be accomplished, including an estimate of the resources required (e.g., staff time, services, equipment). For complex projects, the WBS is a hierarchy of major tasks, subtasks, and work packages. Exhibit 5.7 demonstrates this graphically.

The size of each task should be constructed carefully. A task should not be so small that monitoring would consume a disproportionate share of the task itself. However, an overly large task cannot be effectively monitored and should be divided into subtasks and then work packages. The task should have enough detail associated with it that the individual responsible,

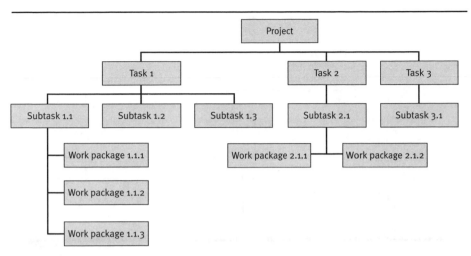

EXHIBIT 5.7
General Format for WBS

NOTE: This type of diagram can be easily generated in Microsoft Word and other Microsoft Office products by using the commands Insert → Picture → Organization Chart.

the cost, and the duration can be identified. A reasonable guideline is that a task should have a duration of one to three weeks to be effectively monitored. The completion of some tasks is critical to the success of the project. These tasks should be identified as *milestones*. The completion of milestones provides a convenient shorthand method to communicate overall project progress to stakeholders.

The WBS can be developed by the project team itself or with the help of outside experts who have executed similar projects. At this point in the project, the WBS is the best estimate of how the project will be executed. It is almost always inaccurate in some way, so the formal control and change procedures described in this section are essential to successful project management.

After the WBS has been constructed, the resources required and estimated time for each element must be determined. Estimating the time a task will require is an art. It is best done by a team of individuals. Any previous experiences and data can be helpful. One group process that has proved useful is the program evaluation and review technique (PERT) time estimation. Team members individually estimate the time a task will take as best, worst, and most likely. After averaging the team's response for each of the times, the final PERT time estimate is:

$$\text{Estimated task time} = \frac{\text{Best} + (4 \times \text{Most likely}) + \text{Worst}}{6}$$

After a number of meetings, the Riverview Clinic team determined that the generic drug project included three major tasks, each with two subtasks, that needed to be accomplished to meet the goals of the project. These subtasks are:

EXHIBIT 5.8
WBS for
Riverview Clinic
Generic Drug
Project

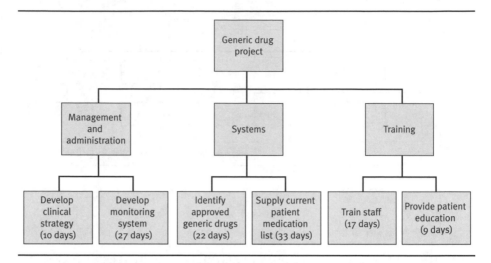

- Develop a clinical strategy that maintains quality care with the increased use of generics.
- Develop a system to inform clinicians of approved generics.
- Update systems to ensure that timely patient medication lists are available to clinicians.
- Develop and deploy a staff education plan.
- Develop a system to monitor performance.
- Develop and begin to use patient education materials.

The WBS is displayed in Exhibit 5.8. These actions represent the higher-level tasks for this project. For a project of this scope to proceed effectively, many more subtasks, perhaps 50 to 100, would be required; to illustrate the principles of project management, this WBS has been held to higher-level tasks.

It is important to note that the time estimate for each task is the total time needed to accomplish a task, not the calendar time it will take—a three-day task can be accomplished in three days by one person or in one day by three people.

The next step is to determine what resources are needed to accomplish these tasks. Riverview Clinic has decided that this project will be accomplished by four existing employees and the purchase of consulting time from VVH's IT supplier. The individuals involved are:

- Tom Simpson, clinic administrator
- Dr. Betsey Thompson, family physician
- Sally Humphries, RN, nursing supervisor
- Cindy Tang, billing manager
- Bill Onku, IT vendor support consultant

The Project software provides a convenient window to enter these individuals and their cost per hour. The program also provides higher levels of detail, such as the hours an individual can devote to the project and actual calendar days when they will be available. When using clinicians, the project manager should consider the revenue per hour from these individuals as opposed to their salaries and benefits, because most organizations will lose this revenue if the clinician has a busy practice. Exhibit 5.9 shows the Project window for the Riverview staff who will work on the generic drug project. A video at the companion website shows how to enter these data; find it in Chapter 5 on the site.

www.ache.org/books/OpsManagement?

Team members should be clear about their accountability for each task. A functional responsibility chart (sometimes called **RASIC**) is helpful; the Riverview project RASIC is displayed in Exhibit 5.10. The RASIC diagram is a matrix of team members and tasks from the WBS. For each task, one individual is responsible (R) for ensuring that the task is completed. Other team members may need to approve (A) the completion of the task. Additional team members may work on the task as well, so they are considered support (S). The obligation to inform (I) other team members helps a team communicate effectively. Finally, some team members need to be consulted (C) as a task is being implemented.

RASIC
A chart delineating all project team members' roles for each task in a project. The acronym comes from the members' roles: Responsible, Approval, Support, Informed, Consult.

Scheduling

Network Diagrams and Gantt Charts

Because the WBS was developed without a specific sequence, the next step is scheduling each task to accomplish the total project. First, the logical order of the tasks must be determined. For example, the Riverview project team determined that the system to identify appropriate generic drugs must be developed before the training of staff and patients can begin. Other con-

EXHIBIT 5.10
RASIC for
Riverview Clinic
Generic Drug
Project

WBS Task	Clinic Board of Directors	Lead M.D. Betsey Thompson	Administrator Tom Simpson	Project Manager Sally Humphries	Billing Cindy Tang	IT Bill Onku
Develop clinical strategy	A	R	C	C	I	I
System to identify approved generics		A	R	S	R	S
Updated medication lists		R	I	S	I	S
Patient education	A	S	S	R	I	I
Staff education		A	R	C	S	I
Monitoring system	A	C	R	C	S	C

NOTE: R = responsible; A = approval; S = support; I = inform; C = consult.

Network diagram
A scheduling tool that connects tasks in order of precedence.

straints must also be considered in the schedule, including required start or completion dates and resource availability.

Two tools are used to visually display the schedule. The first is a **network diagram** that connects each task in precedence order. This is essentially a process map (Chapter 6) where the process is performed only once. However, network diagrams never have paths that return to the beginning (as happens frequently in process maps). A practical way to develop an initial network diagram is to place each task on a sticky note and begin arranging them on a set of flip charts until they meet the logical and date constraints. The tasks can then be entered into a project management software system.

Exhibit 5.11 is the network diagram developed by the team for the Riverview Clinic generic drug project. This schedule can be entered into Project to generate a similar diagram. Another common scheduling tool is the **Gantt chart**, which lists each task on the left side of the page with a bar indicating the start and end times. The Gantt chart for the Riverview project, generated by Project, is shown in Exhibit 5.12. Each bar indicates the duration of the task, and the small arrows connecting the bars indicate the predecessor–successor relationship of the tasks. Chapter 5 on the companion website includes videos on how to enter tasks into Project and establish their precedence, which will generate the schedule. Also shown are the many ways in which the schedule and staff assignments can be viewed in Project.

Gantt chart
A scheduling tool that lists project tasks with bars indicating start and end dates for each task.

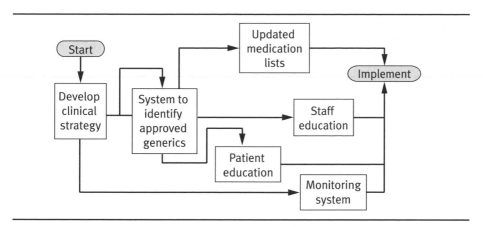

EXHIBIT 5.11
Network
Diagram for
Riverview
Generic Drug
Project

The next step is to assign resources to each task. Exhibit 5.13 shows how the resources are assigned for each day in the project. Care must be taken when assigning resources, as no person works 100 percent of the time. A practical limit is 80 percent, so it is helpful that Project generates a resource use graph (Exhibit 5.14) for each individual. If any single individual is allocated at more than 80 percent in any time period, the schedule may need to be adjusted to reduce this allocation. Adjusting the schedule to accommodate this constraint is known as "resource leveling." Go to the companion website, Chapter 5, to see a video on how to use Project to adjust staff time.

www.ache.org/books/OpsManagement2

A final review of this initial schedule is made to assess how many tasks are being performed in parallel (simultaneously). A project with few parallel tasks will take longer to accomplish than one with many parallel tasks. Another consideration may be date constraints. Examples include a task that cannot begin until a certain date because of staff availability, or a task that

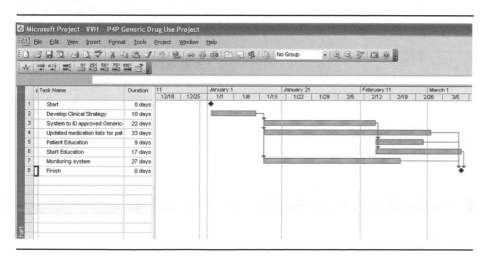

EXHIBIT 5.12
Riverview
Generic Drug
Project Gantt
Chart

EXHIBIT 5.13
Riverview
Generic Drug
Project, Tasks
with Resources
Assigned

●	Resource Name	Work	Details	M	T	W	T	F	S	S	M	T	W	T
	⊟ Unassigned	0 hrs	Work											
	Start	0 hrs	Work											
	Finish	0 hrs	Work											
1	⊟ Dr. Betsey Thompson	97.6 hrs	Work	0.8h	0.8h	0.8h	0.8h	0.8h			0.8h	0.8h	0.8h	0.8h
	Develop Clinical Strategy	40 hrs	Work											
	Patient Education	36 hrs	Work											
	Monitoring system	21.6 hrs	Work	0.8h	0.8h	0.8h	0.8h	0.8h			0.8h	0.8h	0.8h	0.8h
2	⊟ Sally Humphries RN	185.23 hrs	Work	4.63h	4.63h	4.63h	4.63h	4.63h			4.63h	4.63h	4.63h	4.63h
	Develop Clinical Strategy	40 hrs	Work											
	System to ID approved Gener	43.23 hrs	Work	2.63h	2.63h	2.63h	2.63h	2.63h			2.63h	2.63h	2.63h	2.63h
	Updated medication lists for p	66 hrs	Work	2h	2h	2h	2h	2h			2h	2h	2h	2h
	Patient Education	36 hrs	Work											
3	⊟ Tom Simpson	132.97 hrs	Work	1.6h	1.6h	1.6h	1.6h	1.6h			1.6h	1.6h	1.6h	1.6h
	Staff Education	89.77 hrs	Work											
	Monitoring system	43.2 hrs	Work	1.6h	1.6h	1.6h	1.6h	1.6h			1.6h	1.6h	1.6h	1.6h
4	⊟ Cindy Tang	156.78 hrs	Work	4.72h	4.72h	4.72h	4.72h	4.72h			4.72h	4.72h	4.72h	4.72h
	System to ID approved Gener	44.55 hrs	Work	2.72h	2.72h	2.72h	2.72h	2.72h			2.72h	2.72h	2.72h	2.72h
	Updated medication lists for p	66 hrs	Work	2h	2h	2h	2h	2h			2h	2h	2h	2h
	Staff Education	46.23 hrs	Work											
5	⊟ Bill Onku	190.08 hrs	Work	6.63h	6.63h	6.63h	6.63h	6.63h			6.63h	6.63h	6.63h	6.63h
	System to ID approved Gener	58.08 hrs	Work	2.63h	2.63h	2.63h	2.63h	2.63h			2.63h	2.63h	2.63h	2.63h
	Updated medication lists for p	132 hrs	Work	4h	4h	4h	4h	4h			4h	4h	4h	4h

must be complete by a certain date to meet an externally imposed deadline (e.g., new Medicare billing policy). The Project software provides tools to set these constraints inside the schedule.

Slack and the Critical Path

To optimize a schedule, the project manager must pay attention to slack in the schedule and to the critical path. If a task takes three days but does not

EXHIBIT 5.14
Resource Use
Graph for Tom
Simpson

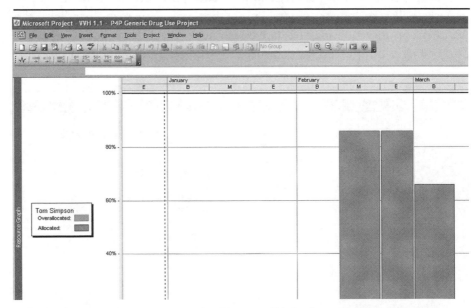

NOTE: As Tom's assignment represents more than 80 percent of his time for some weeks, the schedule or assignment should be revised.

need to be completed for five days, there would be two days of slack. The critical path is the longest sequence of tasks with no slack, or the shortest possible completion time of the project.

Slack is determined by the early finish and late finish dates. The *early finish date* is the earliest date that a task could possibly be completed, based on the early finish dates of predecessors. The *late finish date* is the latest date that a task can be completed without delaying the finish of the project; it is based on the late start and late finish dates of successor tasks. The difference between early finish and late finish dates determines the amount of slack. For critical path tasks (which have no slack), the early finish and late finish dates are identical. Tasks with slack can start later based on the amount of slack they have available. In other words, if a task takes three days and the earliest the task could be completed is day 18, based on its predecessors, and a late finish date of day 30, based on it successors, the slack for this task is 12 days; this task could start as late as day 27 without affecting the completion date of the project. The critical path, which determines the duration of a project, is the connected path through a project of critical tasks. Go to Chapter 5 on the website for a video that provides a simple way to understand this concept.

Calculating slack and the critical path can be complex and time consuming. Fortunately, Project does this automatically.

www.ache.org/books/OpsManagement2

In some cases (e.g., a basic clinical research project), it is difficult to estimate the duration of tasks. If a project has many tasks with high variability in their expected durations, the PERT estimating system should be used. PERT employs probabilistic task times to estimate slack and critical paths. PERT is good for time estimation prior to the start of the project, but the critical path method is better suited for project management once a project has begun. It is not particularly useful to have a range of start dates for a task—what is really important is when a task should have started and whether the project is ahead or behind.

Although Project provides a PERT scheduling function, the use of PERT is infrequent in healthcare and beyond the scope of this book. Exhibit 5.15 displays a Gantt chart for the Riverview generic drug project with both slack and critical path calculated.

Crashing the Project

Consider the following scenario. The clinic president has been notified by one health plan that if the Riverview generic drug project is implemented by March 1, the clinic will receive a $20,000 bonus. He asks the project manager to consider speeding up, or "crashing," the project.

The term *project crashing* has negative associations, as the thought of a computer crashing stirs up dire images. However, a crashed project is simply

EXHIBIT 5.15
Gantt Chart
for Riverview
Generic Drug
Project with
Slack and
Critical Path
Calculated

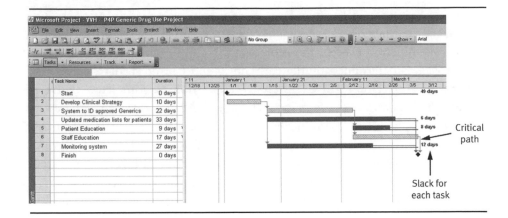

one that has been sped up. Crashing a project requires reducing the length of the critical path, which can be done by any of the following (Microsoft Corp. 2003):

• Shortening the duration of work on a task on the critical path
• Changing a task constraint to allow for more scheduling flexibility
• Breaking a critical task into smaller tasks that can be worked on simultaneously by different resources
• Revising task dependencies to allow more scheduling flexibility
• Setting lead time between dependent tasks where applicable
• Scheduling overtime
• Assigning additional resources to work on critical-path tasks
• Lowering performance goals (not recommended without strong stakeholder consultation)

The scope, time, duration, and performance relationships need to be considered in a crashed project. A crashed project has a high risk of costing more than the original schedule predicted, so the formal change procedure, discussed in the next section, should be used.

Project Control

It would be convenient if every project's schedule and costs occurred according to the initial project plan. However, because this is almost never the case, an effective project monitoring and change control system needs to be operating throughout the life of a project.

Monitoring Progress

The first important monitoring element is a system to measure schedule completion, cost, and expected performance against the initial plan. Micro-

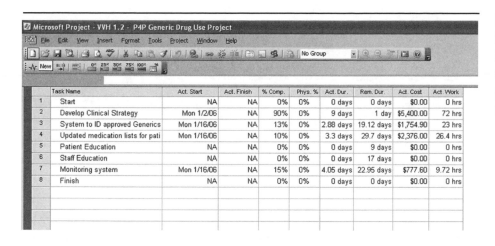

EXHIBIT 5.16
Status of
Riverview
Generic Drug
Project at Three
Weeks

soft Project provides a number of tools to assist the project manager. After the plan's initial scope document, WBS, staffing, and budget have been determined, they are saved as the "baseline plan." Any changes during the project can be compared to this initial baseline.

On a disciplined time basis (e.g., once per week), the project manager needs to receive a progress report from each task manager—the individual designated as responsible on the RASIC chart (Exhibit 5.10)—regarding schedule completion and cost. The enterprise version of Project contains some helpful tools to automate this sometimes tedious data-gathering task. Exhibit 5.16 shows a Project report on the progress of the generic drug project after three weeks. Go to Chapter 5 on the website for a video that shows how to generate progress reports.

www.ache.org/books/OpsManagement2

Earned Value Analysis

For large projects, **earned value analysis** provides a comprehensive vehicle to monitor progress. This tool provides a way to combine schedule and cost monitoring and is particularly useful in the early stages of a project.

The first step in an earned value analysis is to determine a status date, usually close to the project team's meeting date. Once the status date is determined, three fundamental values are calculated for each task. The first is the budgeted cost of tasks as scheduled in the project plan, based on the costs of resources that have been planned to complete the task. Called the *budgeted cost of work scheduled* (BCWS), this is the baseline expected cost up to the status date. The actual cost of completing all or some portion of the task, up to the status date, is the *actual cost of work performed* (ACWP).

The final variable is the value of the work performed by the status date, measured in currency. This is literally the value earned by the work

Earned value analysis
Provides one number that can be used to track the duration and cost of a project as compared to plan.

EXHIBIT 5.17
Riverview
Generic Drug
Project Earned
Value Analysis

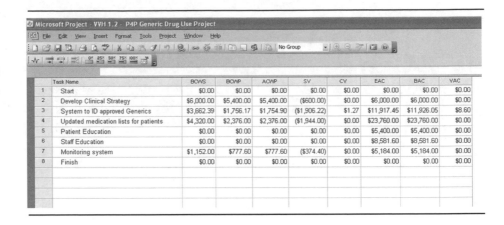

	Task Name	BCWS	BCWP	ACWP	SV	CV	EAC	BAC	VAC
1	Start	$0.00	$0.00	$0.00	$0.00	$0.00	$0.00	$0.00	$0.00
2	Develop Clinical Strategy	$6,000.00	$5,400.00	$5,400.00	($600.00)	$0.00	$6,000.00	$6,000.00	$0.00
3	System to ID approved Generics	$3,662.39	$1,756.17	$1,754.90	($1,906.22)	$1.27	$11,917.45	$11,926.05	$8.60
4	Updated medication lists for patients	$4,320.00	$2,376.00	$2,376.00	($1,944.00)	$0.00	$23,760.00	$23,760.00	$0.00
5	Patient Education	$0.00	$0.00	$0.00	$0.00	$0.00	$5,400.00	$5,400.00	$0.00
6	Staff Education	$0.00	$0.00	$0.00	$0.00	$0.00	$8,581.60	$8,581.60	$0.00
7	Monitoring system	$1,152.00	$777.60	$777.60	($374.40)	$0.00	$5,184.00	$5,184.00	$0.00
8	Finish	$0.00	$0.00	$0.00	$0.00	$0.00	$0.00	$0.00	$0.00

performed, called the *budgeted cost of work performed* (BCWP). BCWP is also called the earned value. For example, assume three people have been assigned to a task for a week, and all have been paid at $1,000 per week for a total of $3,000. However, one of the workers has only accomplished 50 percent of what he was assigned to do, so the *value* of his work is only $500. Therefore, $2,500 is the BCWP, or earned value. In this case, the ACWP is $3,000.

Project performance can be analyzed with earned value analysis. Assume a task has a budgeted cost (BCWS) of $1,000 and, by the status date, is 40 percent complete. The earned value (BCWP) is $400, but the scheduled value (BCWS) at the status date is $500. This indicates that the task is behind schedule—less value has been earned than was planned. Assume the task's actual cost (ACWP) at the status date is $600, perhaps because a more expensive resource was assigned to the task. Therefore, the task is also over budget—more cost has been incurred than was planned. The earlier in a project's life cycle discrepancies between ACWP, BCWP, and BCWS can be identified, the sooner steps can be taken to remedy the problem.

Earned value analysis is a powerful monitoring tool, especially for large and complex projects. The Project program can perform an earned value analysis like that displayed in Exhibit 5.17 for the Riverview generic drug project. The BCWP is less than the BCWS for three tasks, indicating that they are behind schedule. However, the AWCP is the same as the BWCP, so it does not appear that costs are currently a problem.

Three final columns are included in this report. The first is the projection for the *estimate at completion* (EAC), which is the expected total cost of a task or project based on performance as of the status date. EAC is also called forecast at completion, calculated as

$$EAC = ACWP + (BAC - BCWP)/CPI$$

The CPI is the **cost performance index**—the ratio of budgeted, or baseline, costs of work performed to actual costs of work performed (BCWP/ACWP). The *budget at completion* (BAC) shows an estimate of the total project cost. The *variance at completion* shows the difference between BAC and EAC. In Project, the EAC is the Total Cost field and the BAC is the Baseline Cost field from the associated baseline.

In addition to the CPI, a **schedule performance index** (SPI) can be calculated:

$$SPI = BCWP/BCWS$$

The two can be combined into one number—the **critical index** (CI)—which indicates the overall performance of a project:

$$CI = CPI \times SPI$$

If the CI dips below 0.8 or is above 1.2, the project may be in serious trouble, and active intervention is needed by the project team.

Change Control

The project manager should have a status meeting at least once a month, and preferably more frequently. At this meeting, the project team should review the actual status of the project based on task completion, expenses, personnel utilization, and progress toward expected project outcomes. The majority of time in these meetings should be devoted to problem solving, not reporting.

Once deviations are detected, their source and causes must be determined by the team. For major or complex deviations, diagnostic tools such as fishbone diagrams (Chapter 6) can be used. Three courses of action are now available: Ignore the deviation if it is small, take corrective action to remedy the problem, or modify the plan by using the formal change procedure developed in the project charter and scope document.

One major cause of deviations is an event that occurs outside the project. The environment will always be changing during a project's execution, and modifications of the project's scope or performance level may be necessary. For example, the application of a new clinical breakthrough may take priority over projects that improve support systems, or a competitor may initiate a new service that requires a response.

Using a formal change mechanism is one of the key characteristics of high-performing project managers. It is human nature to resist communicating a schedule or cost problem to project sponsors and stakeholders. However, the consequences of this inaction can be significant, if not fatal,

Cost performance index
The ratio of budgeted costs of work performed to actual costs of work performed.

Schedule performance index
The ratio of the budgeted cost of work performed to the budgeted cost of work scheduled.

Critical index
The product of the cost performance index and the schedule performance index.

to large projects. The change process also forces all parties involved in a project to subject themselves to disciplined analysis of options and creates disincentives for scope creep. Changes to the initial plan should be documented in writing and signed off on by the project sponsor as appropriate. They should be included in the project records (three-ring binders or equivalent).

The Riverview project charter (and subsequent scope document) states that changes in plan of less than 10 percent can be made by project manager Sally Humphries. Therefore, she could adjust the schedule by up to 4.9 days, the cost by up to $6,100, and the performance goal by 0.4 percent. For deviations greater than these amounts, Sally would need the clinic board to review and sign off. The companion website contains project change documentation and a sign-off template.

www.ache.org/books/OpsManagement2

Communications

A formal communication plan should be developed as part of scope creation. Communications to both internal and external stakeholders are critical to the success of a project. Many communications media can be used, including simple oral briefings, e-mails, and formal reports. A reasonable contemporary mix used by many organizations is a web-based intranet that contains detailed information on the project. An e-mail is sent to stakeholders periodically, with a summary progress report and links back to the website for more detailed information. A sophisticated communications plan will be fine-tuned to meet stakeholder needs and interests and will communicate only those issues of interest to each stakeholder. As part of the communications strategy, feedback from stakeholders should always be solicited, as changes in the project plan may affect the stakeholder in ways unknown to the project manager.

The project update communications should contain information gathered from quantitative reports. At a minimum, these communications should provide progress against baseline on schedule, cost, scope, and expected performance. Any changes to project baseline, as well as to the approval process, should be noted. Any issues that need resolution, or those that are being resolved, should also be noted. The expected completion date is always of interest to all stakeholders and should be a prominent part of any project plan communication.

Risk Management

Comprehensive prospective **risk management** is another characteristic of successful projects. Like many other aspects of project management, it takes discipline to develop a risk management plan at the beginning of a project and to update it continuously as the project progresses. A risk is an event that will cause the project to have a substantial deviation from planned schedule, cost, scope, or performance.

Risk management Within a project, the identification of possible risks that will affect the execution of the project and a plan to mitigate these risks.

The most direct way to develop a risk management plan is to begin with the WBS. Each task in the WBS should be assessed for risks, both known and unknown. Risks can occur for each task in its performance, duration, or cost; if a project has 50 tasks, it will have 150 potential risks.

A number of techniques can be used to identify risks, but the most straightforward is a brainstorming exercise by the project team. (Some of the tools found in Chapter 6—e.g., mind mapping, root cause analysis, force field analysis—could also be used in risk assessment.) Another useful technique is to interview stakeholders to identify risks to the project as viewed from the stakeholders' perspective. The organization's strategic plan is also a resource, as the plan will frequently contain a *strengths, weaknesses, opportunities, and threats (SWOT) analysis.* The weaknesses and threats sections may contain clues as to potential risks to a task within a project.

Once risks have been identified for each task in the WBS structure, the project team should also assign a risk probability to each. Those risks with the highest probability, or likelihood, of occurring during the project should be analyzed in depth and a risk management strategy devised. The failure mode and effects analysis method (Chapter 6) can also be used for a more rigorous risk analysis.

A quantitative analysis can also be conducted for tasks that have high risk or are critical to project execution. If data can be collected for similar tasks in multiple circumstances, probability distributions can be created and used for simulation and modeling. An example of this technique would be remodeling space in an older building. If an organization reviewed a number of recent remodeling projects, it might determine that the average cost per square foot of remodeled space is $200 with a normal distribution. This information could be used as the basis of a Monte Carlo simulation (Chapter 10) or as part of a decision tree (Chapter 6). The results of these simulations would provide the project manager with quantitative boundaries on the possible risks associated with the task and project and would be useful in constructing mitigation strategies.

Risk	Mitigation Plan
Generic drug use decreases quality	Assistance will be sought from • VVH hospital pharmacy • Pharmaceutical firms • Health plans
Computer systems do not work	• IT vendor has specialists on call who will be flown to Riverview Clinic • Assistance will be sought from VVH IT department
Software modifications are more expensive than budgeted	• Contingency funding has been earmarked in clinic budget

Tasks with the following characteristics should be looked at closely, as they may be high risk:

- A long duration
- Highly variable estimates of duration
- Dependence on external organizations
- Requirement of a unique resource (e.g., a physician who is on call)
- Likely to be affected by external government or payer policies

The management strategy for each identified risk should have three components. First, risk avoidance initiatives should be identified. It is always better to avoid an adverse event than to have to deal with its consequences. An example of a risk avoidance strategy is to provide mentoring to a young team member who has responsibility for key tasks in the project plan.

Mitigation plan
A set of tasks intended to reduce or eliminate the effect of risk in a project.

The second element of the risk management strategy is to develop a **mitigation plan**. An example of a mitigation response would be to bring additional people and financial resources to a task. Another might be to call on the project sponsor to help break an organizational logjam. Third, a project team may decide to transfer the risk to an insurance entity. This strategy is common in construction projects through the use of bonding for contractors.

All identified risks and their management plans should be outlined in a *risk register*, a listing of each task, identified risks, and prevention and mitigation plans. This risk management plan should be updated throughout the life of the project.

The Riverview project team identified three serious risks, which are listed in Exhibit 5.18 with their mitigation plans.

Quality Management, Procurement, the Project Management Office, and Project Closure

Quality Management

The majority of focus in this chapter has been on managing the scope, cost, and schedule of a project. The performance, or quality, of an operational project is the fourth key element in successful project management. In general, quality can be defined as meeting specified performance levels with minimal variation and waste.

The fundamental tools for accomplishing these goals are described in Chapters 6 and 8. More advanced techniques for reducing variation in outcomes can be found in Chapter 8 (quality and Six Sigma), and Chapter 9 discusses tools for waste reduction (Lean).

Throughout the life of a project, the project team should monitor the expected quality of the final product. Individual tasks that are part of a quality management function within a project should be created in the WBS. For example, one task in the Riverview generic drug project is to develop a monitoring system. This system will not only track the use of generic drugs but will also ascertain whether their use has any negative clinical effects.

Procurement

Many projects depend on outside vendors and contractors, so a procurement system integrated with an organization's project management system is essential. A purchasing or procurement department can be helpful in this process. Procurement staff will have developed templates for many of the processes described in the following sections. They will also have knowledge of the latest legal constraints an organization may face. However, the most useful attribute of the procurement department may be the frequency with which it executes the purchasing cycle. By performing this task frequently, its staff has developed expertise in the process and is aware of common pitfalls to avoid.

Contracting

Once an organization has decided to contract with a vendor for a portion of a project, three basic types of contracting are available. The *fixed price contract* is a lump sum for the performance of specified tasks. Fixed price contracts sometimes contain incentives for early delivery.

Cost reimbursement contracts provide payment to the vendor based on the vendor's direct and indirect costs of delivering the service for a specified task. Clearly documenting in advance how the vendor will calculate its costs is important.

The most open-ended type of contract is known as *time and materials.* Here, the task itself may be poorly defined, and the contractor is reimbursed for her actual time, materials, and overhead. A time and materials–type contract is commonly used for remodeling an older building, where the contractor is not certain of what she will find in the walls. Great caution and monitoring are needed when an organization uses this type of contracting.

Any contract should contain a **statement of work (SOW)**. The SOW contains a detailed scope statement, including WBS, for the work that will be performed by the contractor. It also includes expected quantity and quality levels, performance data, task durations, work locations, and other details that will be used to monitor the work of the contractor.

Statement of work (SOW)
A detailed set of tasks, expected outcomes, dates, and costs of a project undertaken by an external contractor.

Selecting a Vendor

Once a preliminary SOW has been developed, the organization will solicit proposals and select a vendor. A useful first step is to issue a *request for information (RFI)* to as many possible vendors as the project team can identify. The RFIs generate responses from vendors on their products and experience with similar organizations. Based on these responses, the number of feasible vendors can be reduced to a manageable set.

A more formal *request for proposal (RFP)* can then be issued. The RFP will ask for a detailed proposal, or bid. The following criteria should be considered in awarding the contract:

- Does the vendor clearly understand the organization's requirements?
- What is the total cost?
- Does the vendor have the capability and correct technical approach to deliver the requested service?
- Does the vendor have a management approach to monitor successful execution of the SOW?
- Can the vendor provide maintenance or meet future requirements and changes?
- Does the vendor provide references from clients that are similar to the contracting organization?
- Does the vendor assert intellectual or proprietary property rights in the products it supplies?

Payment Based on Earned Value

Vendor performance should be monitored and payments made based on the contract as described previously. The most sophisticated payment system for contractors employs earned value. This can be a useful tool in making payments, particularly to consultants or IT service vendors. Many of these vendors will initially request that customers pay them based on the hours their staff has worked; when using the earned value mechanism, the contractor is paid only for work actually accomplished.

The Riverview generic drug project task of providing updated patient medication lists is expected to require 132 hours of Bill Onku's time, at $130 per hour. Therefore, the BCWS of this task is $17,160. The project team initially determined that this task would require 48 modifications to the existing EHR system. At the three-week status meeting, project manager Sally Humphries reports that the task is 10 percent complete; however, Bill has only completed 2 of the 48 modifications, or 4.1 percent. Although Bill's employer sent Riverview Clinic an invoice for 10 percent of his time ($1,716), the clinic could reasonably make the case that it would pay only the BCWP, or earned value. The earned value here is 4.1 percent, or $703.56. Of course, payment based on earned value must be a part of the contract with the vendor.

The Project Management Office

Many organizations outside the healthcare industry (e.g., architects, consultants) are primarily project oriented. Such organizations have a centralized project management office (PMO) to oversee the work of their staff. Because healthcare delivery organizations are primarily operational, the majority do not use this structure.

However, departments within large hospitals and clinics, such as IT and quality, have begun to use a centralized project office approach. In addition, some organizations have designated and trained project leaders in Six Sigma or Lean techniques. These project leaders are assigned from a central PMO.

PMOs provide a central structure to monitor progress on all projects in an organization and reallocate resources as needed when projects encounter problems. They also provide a resource for the training and development of project managers. PMOs support the project manager in many ways, including but not limited to the following (PMI 2008):

- Managing shared resources across all projects administered by the PMO
- Identifying and developing project management methodology, best practices, and standards
- Coaching, mentoring, training, and oversight
- Monitoring compliance with project management standards, policies, procedures, and templates via project audits
- Developing and managing project policies, procedures, templates, and other shared documentation
- Coordinating communication across all projects

Another useful function for a PMO is to maintain an information system that can provide reports to project stakeholders and senior management. The contents of this information system can include the following:

- Progress reports on individual projects (schedule, cost, performance)
- Risk management (tasks with high risks and their current status)
- Performance failures and remediation steps
- A log of lessons learned

Project Closure

A successful project should have an organized closure process, which will include a formal stakeholder presentation and approval process. In addition, the project sponsor should sign off at project completion to signify that performance levels have been achieved and all deliverables have been received. During the close-out process, special attention should be paid to project staff, who will be interested in their next assignment. A disciplined handoff of staff from one project to the next will allow successful completion of the closure process.

All documents related to the project should be indexed and stored. This process can be helpful if outside vendors have participated in the project and a contract dispute arises in the future. Historical documents can also provide a good starting point for the next version of a project.

The project team should have a final session to identify lessons learned—good and bad—in the execution of the project. These lessons should be included in the project documentation and shared with other project managers within the organization.

Agile Project Management

In some situations, knowledge of the tasks necessary for project success is not available as the project is chartered and scheduled. In these cases, agile project management often works better than other methods. Agile project management is *adaptive*, in contrast to the *predictive* style of formal project management.

Characteristics of agile project management include the following:

- Customer satisfaction is achieved by rapid, continuous delivery of services or new processes.
- Newly prototyped services or processes are delivered frequently (weekly rather than monthly).

- The effectiveness and ease of use of these prototypes are the principal measures of progress.
- The project team can easily incorporate late changes.
- The project team and customer interact informally and frequently.
- The project team and the customer are co-located.
- Continuous attention is given to technical excellence and good design in the new services or processes.
- The project team regularly adapts to changing circumstances.

Exhibit 5.19 illustrates agile project management.

Agile project management is best used for "mysteries" to which there are no known answers (e.g., finding the best treatment for a new emerging disease) as opposed to "puzzles" to which the answer is known but complex (e.g., building a new clinic).

The Project Manager and Project Team

The project manager's role is pivotal to the success of any project. Selecting, developing, and nurturing high-functioning team members are also critical. The project manager's team skills include both running effective meetings and facilitating optimal dialogue within these meetings.

Team Skills

A project manager can take on many roles within a project. In many smaller healthcare projects, the project manager is actually the person who accomplishes many of the project tasks. In other projects, the project manager's job is solely leadership and the management of the many individuals performing

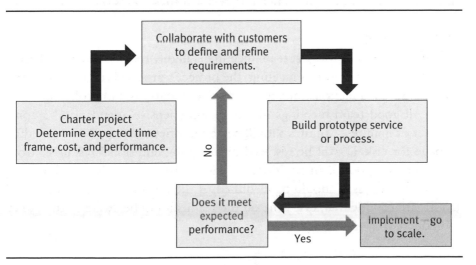

EXHIBIT 5.19
Agile Project
Management

EXHIBIT 5.20
Project
Manager's Role
Based on Effort
and Duration of
a Project

Variable	Small Project	Medium Project	Large Project
Effort range	40–360 hours	360–2,400 hours	2,400–10,000 hours
Duration	5 days–3 months	3–6 months	6–12+ months
Project leader role	"Doer" with some help	Manage and "do some"	Manage and lead

SOURCE: Slack (2005). Used with permission.

the tasks. Slack (2005) provides a useful matrix to determine what role a project manager should assume in projects of varying size (Exhibit 5.20).

Team Structure and Authority

The members and structure of a project team may be selected by the project manager but in many cases are outlined by the project sponsor and other members of senior management. Formally documenting the team makeup and how team members were assigned in the project charter and scope documents is important. Care should be taken to avoid overscheduling team members, as all members must have the needed time available to work on the project.

A number of key issues need to be addressed as the project team is formed. The most important is the project manager's level of authority to make decisions. Can the project manager commit resources, or must he ask senior management or department heads each time a new resource is needed? Is the budget controlled by the project manager, or does a central financial authority control it? Finally, is administrative support available to the team, or do the project team members need to perform these tasks themselves?

Team Meetings

A weekly or biweekly project team meeting is highly recommended to keep a project on schedule. At this meeting, the project's progress can be monitored and discussed and actions initiated to resolve deviations and problems.

All good team meetings include comprehensive agendas and a complete set of minutes. Minutes should be action oriented (e.g., "The schedule slippage for task 17 will be resolved by assigning additional resources from the temporary pool"). In addition, the individual accountable for following through on the issue should be identified. If the meeting's deliberations and actions are confidential, everyone on the team should be aware of the policy and adhere to it uniformly.

The decision-making process should be clear and understood by all team members. In some situations, all major decisions will be made by the project manager. In others, team members may have veto power if they represent a major department that may need to commit resources. Some major decisions may need to be reviewed and approved by individuals external to the project team. The use of data and analytical techniques is strongly encouraged as a part of the decision process.

Team members need to take responsibility for the success of the team. They can demonstrate this behavior by following through on commitments, contributing to the discussion, actively listening, and giving and accepting feedback. Everyone on a team should feel that she has a voice, and the project manager needs to lead the meeting in such a way as to balance the "air time" between team members. This means politely and artfully interrupting the wordy team member and summarizing his point; it also means calling on the silent team member to solicit input.

At the end of a meeting, it is useful to evaluate the meeting itself. The project manager and team can spend a few minutes reviewing questions such as:

- Did we accomplish our purpose?
- Did we take steps to maintain our gains?
- Did we document actions, results, and ideas?
- Did we work together successfully?
- Did we share our results with others?
- Did we recognize everyone's contribution and celebrate our achievements?

Leadership

Although this book is not primarily concerned with leadership, clearly the project manager must be able to lead a project forward. Effective project leadership requires the following skills:

- The ability to think critically using complex information
- The strategic capability to take a long-term view of the organization
- A systems view of the organization and its environment (Chapter 1)
- The ability to create and lead change
- An understanding of oneself to permit positive interactions, conflict resolution, and effective communication
- The ability to mentor and develop employees into high-performing teams
- The ability to develop a performance-based culture

Other resources on leadership are available from Health Administration Press at www.ache.org/pubs/topic.cfm#Leadership.

Conclusion

This chapter provides a basic introduction to the science and discipline of project management. The field is finding a home in healthcare IT departments and has a history in construction projects. Successful healthcare organizations of the future will use this rigorous methodology to make significant changes and improvements throughout their operations.

Discussion Questions

1. Who should be included as members of the project team, key stakeholders, and project sponsors in a clinical project in a physician's office? In a hospital? Support your choices.
2. Identify five common risks in healthcare clinical projects and develop contingency responses for each.

Chapter Exercises

1. Download the project charter and project schedule from the companion website. Complete the missing portions of the charter. Develop a risk assessment and mitigation plan. Add tasks to the schedule for those areas that require more specificity. Apply resources to each task, determine the critical path, and determine a method to crash the project to reduce its total duration by 20 percent.

   www.ache.org/books/OpsManagement2

2. Review the Institute for Healthcare Improvement website and identify and select a quality improvement project (www.ihi.org/knowledge/Pages/ImprovementStories/default.aspx). Although you will not know all the details of the organization that executed this project, create a charter document for your chosen project.
3. For the project identified above, create a feasible WBS and project schedule. Enter the schedule into Microsoft Project.

Further Reading

Bonabeau, E., N. Bodick, and R. W. Armstrong. 2008. "A More Rational Approach to New-Product Development." *Harvard Business Review* 86 (3): 96–102.

Chesbrough, H. W., and A. R. Garman. 2009. "How Open Innovation Can Help You Cope in Lean Times." *Harvard Business Review* 87 (12): 68–76.

Curlee, W., and R. L. Gordon. 2010. *Complexity Theory and Project Management*. Hoboken, NJ: Wiley.

Kendrick, T., Project Management Institute. 2010. *The Project Management Tool Kit*, 2nd ed. New York: AMACOM American Management Association.

Meredith, J. R., and S. J. Mantel. 2009. *Project Management: A Managerial Approach*, 7th ed. Hoboken, NJ: Wiley.

Meskendahl, S. 2010. "The Influence of Business Strategy on Project Portfolio Management and Its Success—A Conceptual Framework." *International Journal of Project Management* 28 (8): 807–17.

Project Management Institute. 2008. *A Guide to the Project Management Body of Knowledge (PMBOK® Guide)*, 4th ed. Newtown Square, PA: Project Management Institute, Inc.

Taylor, H. 2006. "Risk Management and Problem Resolution Strategies for IT Projects: Prescription and Practice." *Project Management Journal* 37 (5): 49–63.

Thamhain, H. J., and D. L. Wilemon. 1975. "Conflict Management in Project Life Cycles." *Sloan Management Review* 16 (3): 31.

Wheelwright, S. C., and K. B. Clark. 1992. "Creating Project Plans to Focus Product Development." *Harvard Business Review* 70 (2): 70–82.

Wills, K. R. 2010. *Essential Project Management Skills*. Boca Raton, FL: Taylor & Francis.

Young, T. L. 2010. *Successful Project Management*, 3rd ed. London; Philadelphia: Kogan Page.

PERFORMANCE IMPROVEMENT TOOLS, TECHNIQUES, AND PROGRAMS

TOOLS FOR PROBLEM SOLVING AND DECISION MAKING

Operations Management in Action

At Allegheny General Hospital in Pittsburgh, the two intensive care units had been averaging about 5.5 infections per 1,000 patient days, mostly bloodstream infections from catheters. That infection rate was a bit higher than the Pittsburgh average but a bit lower than the national average, says Dr. Richard Shannon, chairman of medicine at Allegheny General.

Over the prior 12 months, 37 patients, already some of the sickest people in the hospital, had 49 infections. Of those, 51 percent died. Dr. Shannon and the staff in the two units—doctors, residents, and nurses—applied the Toyota root-cause analysis system, investigating each new infection immediately.

Their main conclusion was that femoral intravenous lines, inserted into an artery near the groin, had a particularly high rate of infection. The team made an all-out effort to replace these lines with less risky ones in the arm or near the collarbone. Dr. Shannon, who oversees the two units, gave the directive to keep femoral lines to an absolute minimum. The result was a 90 percent decrease in the number of infections after just 90 days of using the new procedures.

SOURCE: Adapted from Wysocki (2004).

Overview

This chapter introduces the basic tools associated with problem solving and decision making. Much of the work of healthcare professionals is just that—making decisions and solving problems—and in an ever-changing world, that work must be accomplished well and quickly. A structured approach can enable efficient, effective problem solving and decision making. Major topics in this chapter include:

- The decision-making process, with a focus on framing the problem or issue
- Mapping techniques, including mind mapping, process mapping, activity mapping, and service blueprinting
- Problem identification tools, including root-cause analysis (RCA), failure mode and effects analysis (FMEA), and the theory of constraints (TOC)
- Analytical tools such as optimization using linear programming and decision analysis
- Force field analysis to address implementation issues

This chapter gives readers a basic understanding of various problem-solving tools and techniques to enable them to

- frame questions or problems,
- analyze the problem and various solutions to it, and
- implement those solutions.

The tools and techniques outlined in this chapter should provide a basis for tackling difficult, complicated problems.

Decision-Making Framework

A structured, rational approach to problem solving and decision making includes the following steps:

- Identifying and framing the issue or problem
- Generating or determining possible courses of action and evaluating those alternatives
- Choosing and implementing the best solution or alternative
- Reviewing and reflecting on the previous steps and outcomes

Decision Traps: The Ten Barriers to Brilliant Decision-Making and How to Overcome Them (Russo and Schoemaker 1989) outlines these steps (Exhibit 6.1) and the barriers encountered in decision making (Exhibit 6.2).

The plan-do-check-act process for continuous improvement (Chapters 8 and 9), the define-measure-analyze-improve-control process of Six Sigma (Chapter 8), and the outline for analysis (Chapter 11) all follow the same basic steps as outlined in the decision-making process. The tools and

Framing
 	
Typical amount
  of time: 5%
 	
Recommended amount
  of time: 20%
	Structuring the question. This means defining what must be decided and determining in a preliminary way what criteria would cause you to prefer one option over another. In framing, good decision makers think about the viewpoint from which they and others will look at the issue and decide which aspects they consider important and which they do not. Thus, they inevitably simplify the world.	**EXHIBIT 6.1**
		Decision Elements and Activities

Gathering intelligence
 	
Typical amount
  of time: 45%
 	
Recommended
  amount of time: 35%
	Seeking both the knowable facts and the reasonable estimates of "unknowables" that you will need to make the decision. Good decision makers manage intelligence gathering with deliberate effort to avoid such failings as overconfidence in what they currently believe and the tendency to seek information that confirms their biases.	

Coming to conclusions
 	
Typical amount
  of time: 40%
 	
Recommended
  amount of time: 25%
	Sound framing and good intelligence don't guarantee a wise decision. People cannot consistently make good decisions using seat-of-the-pants judgment alone, even with excellent data in front of them. A systematic approach forces you to examine many aspects and often leads to better decisions than hours of unorganized thinking would.	

Learning from feedback
 	
Typical amount
  of time: 10%
 	
Recommended
  amount of time: 20%
	Everyone needs to establish a system for learning from the results of past decisions. This usually means keeping track of what you expected would happen, systematically guarding against self-serving explanations, then making sure you review the lessons your feedback has produced the next time a similar decision comes along.	

SOURCE: *Decision Traps* by J. Edward Russo and Paul J. H. Schoemaker, copyright © 1989 by J. Edward Russo and Paul J. H. Schoemaker. Used by permission of Doubleday, a division of Random House, Inc.

techniques found in this book can be used to help in gathering the right information to make optimal decisions and learn from those decisions, as well as in the process of making those decisions. Often, the learning step in the decision-making process is neglected, but it should not be. It is important to evaluate and analyze both the decision made and the process(es) used in coming to the decision to ensure learning and enable continuous improvement.

EXHIBIT 6.2
The Ten Barriers
to Brilliant
Decision
Making and the
Key Elements
They Fall Into

Framing the Question

Plunging in—Beginning to gather information and reach conclusions without first taking a few minutes to think about the crux of the issue you're facing.

Frame blindness—Setting out to solve the wrong problem because you have created a mental framework for your decision with little thought, which causes you to overlook the best options or lose sight of important objectives.

Lack of frame control—Failing to consciously define the problem in more ways than one or being unduly influenced by the frames of others.

Gathering Intelligence

Overconfidence in your judgment—Failing to correct key factual information because you are too sure of your assumptions and opinions.

Shortsighted shortcuts—Relying inappropriately on "rules of thumb," such as implicitly trusting the most readily available information or anchoring too much on convenient facts.

Coming to Conclusions

Shooting from the hip—Believing you can keep straight in your head all the information you've discovered, and therefore you "wing it" rather than follow a systematic procedure.

Group failure—Assuming that with many smart people involved, good choices will follow automatically, and therefore you fail to manage the group decision process.

Learning/Failing to Learn from Feedback

Fooling yourself about feedback—Failing to interpret the evidence from past outcomes for what it really says, either because you're protecting your ego or because you are tricked by hindsight.

Not keeping track—Assuming that experience will make its lessons available automatically, and therefore you fail to keep systematic records to track results of your decisions and fail to analyze these results in ways that *will* reveal their true lessons.

Failure to audit your decision process—You fail to create an organized approach to understanding your own decision making, so you remain constantly exposed to all the aforementioned mistakes.

SOURCE: *Decision Traps* by J. Edward Russo and Paul J. H. Schoemaker, copyright © 1989 by J. Edward Russo and Paul J. H. Schoemaker. Used by permission of Doubleday, a division of Random House, Inc.

Framing

The frame of a problem or decision encompasses the assumptions, attitudes, and preconceived limits that an individual or a team brings to the analyses. These assumptions can limit the ability to solve the problem by reducing or eliminating creativity and causing the decision maker(s) to overlook possibilities. Alternatively, these assumptions can aid in problem solving by eliminating wildly improbable paths, but they usually hinder finding the best solution or finding a possible solution.

Millions of dollars and working hours are wasted in finding solutions to the wrong problems. An ill-defined problem or mistaken premise can eliminate promising solutions before they can even be considered. People tend to identify convenient problems and find solutions that are familiar to them rather than looking more deeply.

People also have a tendency to want to do something; quick and decisive action is seen as necessary in today's rapidly changing environment. Leaping to the solutions before taking the time to properly frame the problem will usually result in suboptimal solutions.

Potential solutions to any problem are directly related to, and limited by, the definition of the problem itself. However, framing the problem can be difficult, as it requires an understanding of the problem. If the problem is well understood, the solution is more likely to be obvious; when framing a problem, it is therefore important to be expansive, solicit many different viewpoints, and consider many possible scenarios, causes, and solutions. The tools outlined in this chapter are designed to help with this process.

Mapping Techniques

Mind Mapping

Tony Buzan is credited with developing the mind-mapping technique (Buzan 1991; Buzan and Buzan 1994). **Mind mapping** develops thoughts and ideas in a nonlinear fashion and typically uses pictures or phrases to organize and develop thoughts. In this structured brainstorming technique, ideas are organized on a "map" and the connections between them are made explicit. Mind mapping can be an effective technique for problem solving because it is not necessary to think linearly. Making connections that are not obvious or linear can lead to innovative solutions.

Mind mapping starts with the issue to be addressed placed in the center of the map. Ideas on causes, solutions, and so on radiate from the central theme. Questions such as who, what, where, why, when, and how are often helpful for problem solving. Exhibit 6.3 illustrates a mind map related to high accounts receivables.

Mind mapping
A nonlinear technique used to develop thoughts and ideas by placing pictures or phrases on a map to show logical connections.

EXHIBIT 6.3
Mind Map:
High Accounts
Receivables

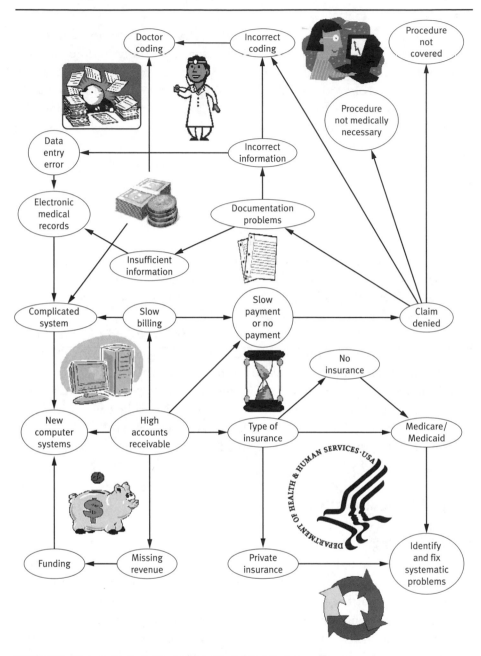

NOTE: Diagram created in Inspiration by Inspiration Software, Inc.

Process map
A graphic
depiction of a
process showing
the sequence of
events, including
tasks, decisions,
and other activities
from inputs to
outputs (i.e., a
flowchart).

Process Mapping

A **process map**, or flowchart, is a graphic depiction of a process showing inputs, outputs, and steps in the process. Depending on the purpose of the map, it can be high level or detailed. Exhibit 6.4 shows a high-level process map for the Riverview Clinic, and Exhibit 6.5 shows a more detailed map of

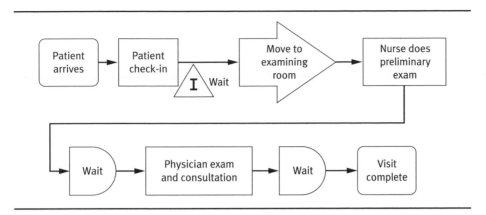

EXHIBIT 6.4
Riverview Clinic
High-Level
Process Map

the check-in process at the clinic. A process map gives a clear picture of what activities are carried out as part of the process, where the activity happens, and how activities are performed. Typically, process maps are used to understand and optimize a process. The process is commonly charted from the viewpoint of the material, information, or customer being processed (often the patient in healthcare) or the worker carrying out the work. Process mapping is one of the seven basic quality tools and an integral part of most improvement initiatives, including Six Sigma, Lean, balanced scorecard, RCA, and FMEA.

The steps for creating a process map or flowchart are:

1. *Assemble and train the team.* The team should consist of people from all areas and levels within the process of interest to ensure that the real process is captured.
2. *Determine the boundaries of the process (where it starts and ends?) and the level of detail desired.* The level of detail desired, or needed, will depend on the question or problem the team is addressing.

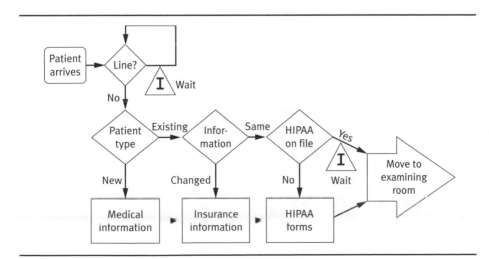

EXHIBIT 6.5
Riverview
Clinic Detailed
Process Map:
Patient Check-In

EXHIBIT 6.6
Standard
Flowchart
Symbols

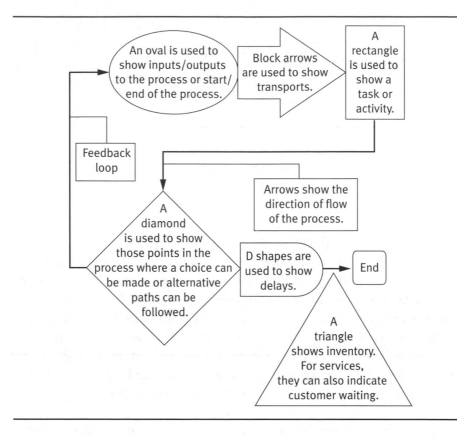

3. *Brainstorm the major process tasks and subtasks.* List them and arrange them in order. (Sticky notes are often helpful here.)

4. *Create a formal chart.* Once an initial flowchart has been generated, the chart can be formally drawn using standard symbols for process mapping (Exhibit 6.6). This can be done most efficiently using software such as Microsoft Visio. Note that when first developing a flowchart it is more important to obtain an accurate picture of the process than to worry about using the correct symbols.

5. *Make corrections.* The formal flowchart should be checked for accuracy by all relevant personnel. Often, inaccuracies will be found in the flowchart that need to be corrected in this step.

6. *Determine additional data needs.* Depending on the purpose of the flowchart, data may need to be collected, or more information may need to be added. Often, data on process performance are collected and added to the flowchart.

Measures of Process Performance

Measures of process performance include throughput time, cycle time, and percentage of value-added time (Chapter 9). Another important measure of process, subprocess, task, or resource performance is **capacity utilization**. Capacity is the maximum possible amount of output (goods or services) that a process or resource can produce or transform. Capacity measures can be based on outputs or on the availability of inputs. For example, if a hospital food service can provide, at most, 1,000 meals in one day, the food service has a capacity of 1,000 meals/day. If all magnetic resonance images (MRIs) take one hour to perform, the MRI machine would have a capacity of 24 MRIs/day. The choice of appropriate capacity measure varies with the situation.

> **Capacity utilization**
> The percentage of time that a resource (worker, equipment, space, etc.) or process is actually busy producing or transforming output.

Ideally, demand and capacity are perfectly matched. If demand is greater than capacity, some customers will not be served. If capacity is greater than demand, resources will be underutilized. In reality, perfectly matching demand and capacity can be difficult to accomplish because of fluctuations in demand. In a manufacturing environment, inventory can be used to compensate for demand fluctuations. In a service environment, this is not possible; therefore, excess capacity or a flexible workforce is often required to meet demand fluctuations. Advanced-access scheduling (Chapters 9 and 12) is one way for healthcare operations to more closely match capacity and demand.

Capacity utilization is the percentage of time that a resource (worker, equipment, space, etc.) or process is actually busy producing or transforming output. If the hospital food service only provides 800 meals/day, the capacity utilization is 80 percent. If the MRI machine only operates 18 hours/day, the capacity utilization is 75 percent ($18/24 \times 100$). Generally, higher capacity utilization is better, but caution must be used in evaluation. If the hospital food service had a goal of 95 percent capacity utilization, it could meet that goal by producing 950 meals/day, even if only 800 meals/day were actually consumed and 150 meals were discarded. Obviously, this would not be an effective use of resources, but food service would have met its goal.

Typically, the more costly the resource, the greater the importance of maximizing capacity utilization. For example, in a hospital emergency department the most costly resource is often the physician, and other resources (nurses, housekeeping, clerical staff, etc.) are less expensive. In this case, maximizing the utilization of the physicians is more important than maximizing the utilization of the other resources. It is often more economical to underutilize less expensive resources to maximize the utilization of more expensive resources. Simulation (Chapter 11) can be used to help determine the most effective use of various types of resources.

> **Cross-functional process map**
> A map that follows the flow of a process through the various departments of the organization using dashed lines to show the work being completed by a particular department or individual in the process. Also called a *swim lane process map*.

Cross-Functional (Swim Lane) Process Maps

The **cross-functional process map**, or "swim lane" map, is a specialized process map that follows the flow of a process through the various departments of the organization. The swim lanes indicated by the dashed lines between

Exhibit 6.7   Swim Lane Process Map

Detailed Process Map of Holding Room (part II)

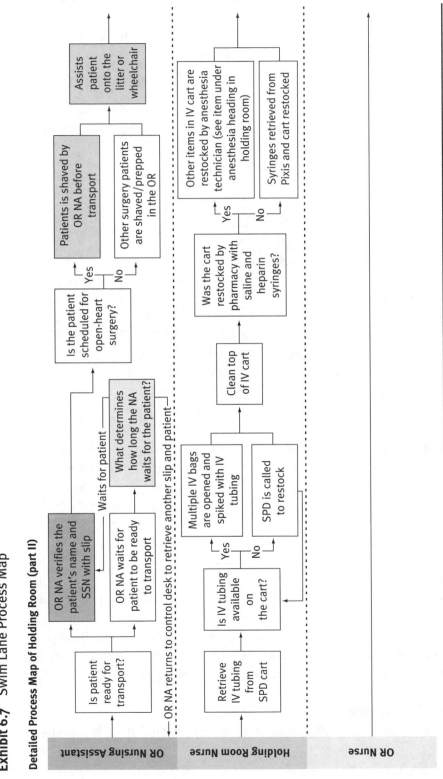

departments show the work being completed by a particular department or individual in the process. The swim lanes chart is useful for seeing the amount of times an item is handed off between departments and how many times the process is creating duplication and rework. Exhibit 6.7 is an example of the presurgery holding room for the Veterans Administration hospital.

Service Blueprinting

Service blueprinting (Shostack 1984) is a special form of process mapping (as is value stream mapping, covered in Chapter 9). Service blueprinting begins with mapping the process from the point of view of the customer. The typical purpose of a service blueprint is to identify points where the service might fail to satisfy the customer and then redesign or add controls to the system to reduce or eliminate the possibility of failure. The service blueprint separates onstage actions (those visible to the customer) and backstage actions and support processes (those not visible to the customer). A service blueprint specifies the line of interaction, where the customer and service provider come together, and the line of visibility, that is, what the customer sees or experiences, the tangible evidence that influences perceptions of the quality of service (Exhibit 6.8).

Service blueprinting
A process map that separates actions into onstage (visible to the customer) and backstage (not visible to the customer).

Problem Identification Tools

Root-Cause Analysis

Root-cause analysis (RCA) is a generic term used to describe structured, step-by-step techniques for problem solving. It aims to determine and correct the ultimate cause(s) of a problem, not just the visible symptoms, to ensure that the problem does not happen again. RCA consists of determining what happened, why it happened, and what can be done to prevent it from happening again.

Root-cause analysis (RCA)
A generic term describing structured, step-by-step techniques for problem solving.

EXHIBIT 6.8
Service Blueprint

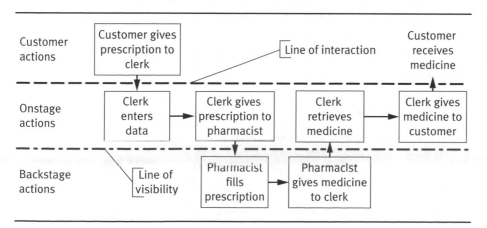

The Joint Commission (2005b) requires all accredited organizations to conduct an RCA of any sentinel event (an unexpected occurrence involving death or serious physical or psychological injury, or the risk thereof) and provides some tools (Joint Commission 2005a) to help an organization conduct that analysis. These tools are not only useful for sentinel events and Joint Commission requirements, but they also provide a framework for any RCA. A variety of commercial software is also available for RCAs.

Although an RCA can be done in many different ways, it is always based on asking why something happened, again and again, until the ultimate cause is found. Typically, something in the system or process, rather than human error, is found to be the ultimate cause. The five whys technique and cause-and-effect diagrams are examples of tools used in RCA.

Five Whys Technique

Five whys technique
A technique that uses a series of logical questions to find the root cause of a problem.

The **five whys technique** is simple but powerful. It consists of asking why the condition occurred, noting the answer, and then asking why for each answer over and over (five times is a good guide) until the "root" causes are identified. Often, the reason for a problem is only a symptom of the real cause—this technique can help eliminate the focus on symptoms, discover the root cause, and point the way to eliminating the root cause and ensuring that the problem does not occur again. For example:

1. A patient received the wrong medication. Why?
2. The doctor prescribed the wrong medication. Why?
3. There was information missing from the patient's chart. Why?
4. The patient's most recent lab test results had not been entered into the chart. Why?
5. The lab technician sent the results, but they were in transit and the patient's record had not been updated.

The root cause here is the time lag between the test and data entry. Identifying the root cause leads to different possible solutions to the problem than simply concluding that the doctor made a mistake. The system could be changed to increase the speed with which lab results are recorded or, at least, a note could be made on the chart that lab tests have been ordered but not yet recorded.

Cause-and-Effect Diagram

Using only the five whys technique for an RCA can be limiting because of the assumption that the effect is a result of a single cause at each level of why. Often, a set of causes is related to an effect. A cause-and-effect diagram can overcome these limits.

Service (Four Ps)	Manufacturing (Six Ms)
Policies	Machines
Procedures	Methods
People	Materials
Plant/technology	Measurements
	Mother nature (environment)
	Manpower (people)

EXHIBIT 6.9
Typical Cause-and-Effect Diagram Categories

Typically, a team uses a cause-and-effect diagram to investigate and eliminate a problem. The problem should be stated or framed as clearly as possible, including who is involved and where and when the problem occurs, to ensure that everyone on the team is attempting to solve the same problem.

One of the seven basic quality tools, this type of graphic is used to explore and display all of the potential causes of a problem. The cause-and-effect diagram is sometimes called an Ishikawa diagram (after its inventor, Kaoru Ishikawa [1985]) or a **fishbone diagram** (because it looks like the skeleton of a fish).

The problem, or outcome of interest, is the "head" of the fish. The rest of the diagram consists of a horizontal line leading to the problem statement and several branches, or "fishbones," vertical to the main line. The branches represent different categories of causes. The categories chosen may vary according to the problem, but there are some common choices (Exhibit 6.9).

Possible causes are attached to the appropriate branches. Each possible cause is examined to determine if there is a deeper cause behind it (Stage C in Exhibit 6.10); subcauses are attached as more bones. In the final diagram, causes are arranged according to relationships and distance from the effect. This can help in identifying areas to focus on and comparing the relative importance of different causes.

Cause-and-effect diagrams can also be drawn as tree diagrams. From a single outcome, or trunk, branches extend to represent major categories of inputs or causes that create that single outcome. These large branches then lead to smaller and smaller branches of causes all the way down to twigs at the ends. A process-type cause-and-effect diagram (Exhibit 6.11) can be used to investigate causes of problems at each step in a process. A process RCA is similar to a failure mode and effect analysis (FMEA), but less quantitative in nature.

An example from Vincent Valley Hospital and Health System (VVH) illustrates the cause-and-effect diagramming process. The hospital identified

Fishbone diagram
A graphical technique used to display the relationship between the potential causes of problems and the effect created by the problem. Sometimes called an *Ishikawa diagram.*

EXHIBIT 6.10
Cause-and-
Effect Example

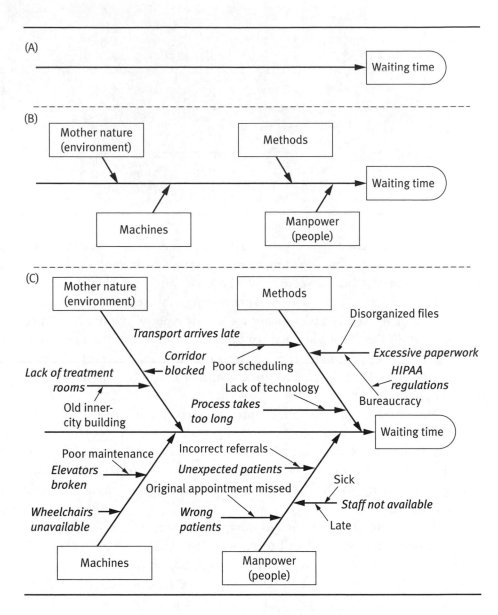

excessive waiting time as a problem, and a team was assembled to address the issue. The problem is placed in the head of the fish, as shown in Exhibit 6.10, Stage A. Next, branches are drawn off the large arrow representing the main categories of potential causes. Typical categories are shown in Exhibit 6.10, Stage B, but the chosen categories should suit the particular situation. Then, all of the possible causes inside each main category are identified. Each of these causes should be thoroughly explored to identify the causes of causes. This process continues, branching off into more and more causes of causes, until every possible cause has been identified (Stage C in Exhibit 6.10).

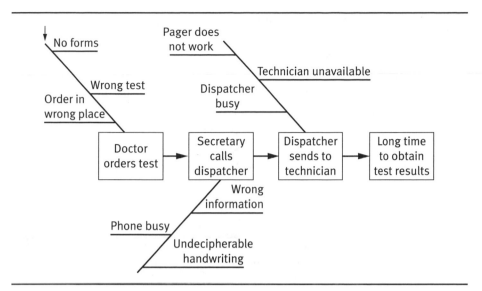

EXHIBIT 6.11
Process-Type
Cause-and-
Effect Diagram

Much of the value gained from building a cause-and-effect diagram comes from going through the exercise with a team of people. A common and deeper understanding of the problem develops, enabling ideas for further investigation.

Once the cause-and-effect diagram is complete, an assessment of the possible causes and their relative importance should be made. Obvious, easily fixable causes can be dealt with quickly. Data may need to be collected to assess the more complex possible causes and solutions. A Pareto analysis (Chapter 7) of the various causes is often used to separate the vital few from the trivial many. Building a cause-and-effect diagram is not necessarily a one-time exercise. The diagram can be used as a working document and updated as more data are collected and various solutions are tried.

Failure Mode and Effects Analysis

The **failure mode and effects analysis (FMEA)** process was developed by the US military in the late 1940s, originally aimed at equipment failure. More recently, FMEA has been adopted by many service industries, including healthcare, to evaluate process failure. Hospitals accredited by The Joint Commission are required to conduct at least one FMEA or similar proactive analysis annually (Joint Commission 2001). Where RCA is used to examine the underlying causes of a particular event or failure, FMEA is used to identify the ways in which a process (or piece of equipment) might potentially fail, and its goal is eliminating or reducing the severity of such a potential failure. By proactively looking at the potential causes of failure, risk of failure is either eliminated or reduced by using a FMEA.

Failure mode and effects analysis (FMEA)
A technique developed by the US military to identify the ways in which a process (or piece of equipment) might fail and to identify ways to mitigate those risks.

A typical FMEA consists of the following steps:

1. *Identify the process to be analyzed.* Typically, this is a principal process for the organization.
2. *Assemble and train the team.* Processes usually cross functional boundaries; therefore, the analysis should be performed by a team of relevant personnel. No one person or persons from a single functional area will have the knowledge needed to perform the analysis.
3. Develop a detailed process flowchart, including all steps in the process.
4. *Identify each step (or function) in the process.*
5. *Identify potential failures (or failure modes) at each step in the process.* Note that there may be more than one potential failure at each step.
6. Determine the worst potential consequence (or effect) of each possible failure.
7. *Identify the cause(s) (contributory factors) of each potential failure.* An RCA can be helpful in this step. Note that there may be more than one cause for each potential failure.
8. *Identify any failure "controls" that are currently present.* A control reduces the likelihood that causes or failures will occur, reduces the severity of an effect, or enables the occurrence of a cause or failure to be detected before it leads to the adverse effect.
9. *Rate the severity of each effect (on a scale of 1 to 10, with 10 being the most severe).* This rating should reflect the impact of any controls that reduce the severity of the effect.
10. *Rate the likelihood (occurrence score) that each cause will occur (on a scale of 1 to 10, with 10 being certain to occur).* This rating should reflect the impact of any controls that reduce the likelihood of occurrence.
11. Rate the effectiveness of each control (on a scale of 1 to 10, with 1 being an error-free detection system).
12. Multiply the three ratings by one another to obtain the risk priority number (RPN) for each cause or contributory factor.
13. *Use the RPNs to prioritize problems for corrective action.* All causes that result in an effect with a severity of 10 should be high on the priority list, regardless of RPN.
14. Develop an improvement plan to address the targeted causes (who, when, how assessed, etc.).

Exhibit 6.12 shows an example FMEA for patient falls from the Institute for Healthcare Improvement (IHI). IHI has an online interactive tool for FMEA and offers many real-world examples that can be used as a basis for FMEAs in other organizations (IHI 2005). The Veterans Affairs National

EXHIBIT 6.12
Patient Falls
FMEA

> fall prevention 3E

United States
Hospital-Community

Aim: Reduction of preventable falls by 50% for 2005

Process Data

Date: 03/28/2005

Step	Description
1	Fall assessment completed upon admission

Failure Mode	Causes	Effects	Occ	Det	Sev	RPN	Actions
Potential to fall	Effects of anesthesia, analgesia.	Potential injury	1	1	10	10	Patients are ambulated with assistance for first 24 hours per policy. Placed on fall risk precautions.
Patient is not assessed at time of admission.	Complete information not available regarding patient history. Patient may not be able or willing to cooperate with interview process	Inaccurate fall risk assigned to patient	2	2	8	32	24 hour chart audits to assure completion of admission evaluation

Step	Description
2	Inaccurate fall assessment

Failure Mode	Causes	Effects	Occ	Det	Sev	RPN	Actions
Potential to fall	Slip, trip, equipment, IV tubing, drains, drainge bags, liquid on floor, urinary urgency, diarrhea	No injury to severe injury	1	1	8	8	All patients are assigned fall risk category
Patient not identified as a fall risk through current process	Not using assessment tool(s) properly	Fall interventions are not implemented correctly.	2	2	7	28	Provide in orientation training on Fall prevention. Monitor Fall events for specific criteria.

Step	Description
3	Interventions not able to be implemented

Failure Mode	Causes	Effects	Occ	Det	Sev	RPN	Actions
Slip, trip fall	Tangled in tubing, trip on tubing, trip on drain bag, forget bag attached to bed, slip on drainage leaking form bag.	no injury to severe injury	1	10	3	30	Educate patient, monitor for leaking drains, assist patient to ambulate with IV and drain tubes.
Due to safety issues of a psychiatric unit, interventions may cause more harm than good.	Failure to implement safe alternatives for behavioral patients who are at risk of falls.	Patients are more unstable	2	2	8	32	Focused education with staff to review safe alternatives for fall prevention. Charge Nurse to include fall prevention in patient shift assessments

Step	Description
4	Medication Assessment/evaluations

Failure Mode	Causes	Effects	Occ	Det	Sev	RPN	Actions
Patients are overmedication -potential for falls	Patients are admitted agitated requiring stronger medication approach.	Patients become quickly drowsy and fall.	3	2	8	48	Medication training to identify sedative potentials. Post alerts on patients with high medication potential. Charge Nurse to include fall risk in shift assessment
Medications may slow judgement or increase ataxia	Medications that are being administered have sedating and ataxic effects	Slips, falls	8	2	9	144	Staff education regarding medications Charge Nurse to include fall risk in shift assessment

Calculated Totals

Total Risk Priority Number for the process	332

Occ: Likelihood of Occurrence (1-10)
Det: Likelihood of Detection (1-10)
    NOTE: 1 = Very likely it WILL be detected
            10 = Very likely it WILL NOT be detected
Sev: Severity (1-10)

SOURCE: IHI (2005). This material was accessed from the Institute for Healthcare Improvement's website, IHI.org. www.ihi.org/ihi/workspace/tools/fmea/ViewTool.aspx?ToolId=1248.

Center for Patient Safety (2006) has developed a less complex FMEA process based on rating only the severity and probability of occurrence and using the resulting number to prioritize problem areas.

Theory of Constraints

The **theory of constraints (TOC)** was first described in the business novel *The Goal* (Goldratt and Cox 1986). The TOC maintains that every organiza-

Theory of constraints (TOC)
The idea that every organization and process is subject to at least one constraint that limits it from moving toward or achieving its goal.

tion is subject to at least one constraint that limits it from moving toward or achieving its goal. For many organizations, the goal is to make money now as well as in the future. Some healthcare organizations may have a different, but still identifiable, goal. Eliminating or alleviating the constraint can enable the organization to come closer to its goal. Constraints can be physical (e.g., the capacity of a machine) or nonphysical (e.g., an organizational procedure). Five steps are involved in the TOC:

1. *Identify the constraint or bottleneck.* What is the limiting factor stopping the system or process from achieving the goal?
2. *Exploit the constraint.* Determine how to get the maximum performance out of the constraint without major system changes or capital improvements.
3. *Subordinate everything else to the constraint.* Other nonbottleneck resources (or steps in the process) should be synchronized to match the output of the constraint. Idleness at a nonbottleneck resource costs nothing, and nonbottlenecks should never produce more than can be consumed by the bottleneck resource. For example, if the operating room is a bottleneck and there is a surgical ward associated with it, a traditional view might encourage filling the ward. However, nothing would be gained (and operational losses would be incurred) by putting more patients on the ward than the operating room could process. Thus, the TOC solution is to lower ward occupancy to match the operating room's throughput, even if resources (heating, lighting, fixed staff costs, etc.) seem to be wasted.
4. *Elevate the constraint.* Do something (expend capital, hire more people, etc.) to increase the capacity of the constraining resource until it is no longer the constraint. Something else will be the new constraint.
5. Repeat the process for the new constraint.

The process must be reapplied, perhaps many times. It is important not to let inertia become a constraint. Many constraints are of an organization's own making—they are the entrenched rules, policies, and procedures that have developed over time.

TOC defines three operational measurements for organizations:

1. *Throughput:* the rate at which the system generates money. This is selling price minus the cost of raw materials. Labor costs are part of operating expense rather than throughput.
2. *Inventory:* the money the system invests in things it will sell. This includes inventories and buildings, land, and equipment.
3. *Operating expense:* the money the system spends turning inventory into throughput. This includes what would typically be called overhead.

The following four measurements are then used to identify results for the organization:

1. Net profit = Throughput – Operating expense
2. Return on investment (ROI) = (Throughput – Operating expense)/ Inventory
3. Productivity = Throughput/Operating expense
4. Turnover = Throughput/Inventory

These measurements can help employees make local decisions. A decision that results in increasing throughput, decreasing inventory, or decreasing the operating expense will generally be a good decision for the organization.

TOC has been used in healthcare at both a macro- and microlevel to analyze and improve systems. De Mast and colleagues (2011) developed a model that demonstrated a 37 percent increase of patients through a system, accounting for more than $300,000 in increased revenue. In a CT scanning department, the model was deployed to help improve the utilization of the scanning room that was identified as the constraint in the process. The model raised utilization of the bottleneck from 88 percent to more than 93 percent.

Stratton and Knight (2010) used TOC to help improve patient flow. The results of their study show a nearly 25 percent reduction in overall length of stay—from 8.6 to 6.3 days. In this instance a strategy of using buffers helped ensure the constraint was always working and processing patients. Because TOC focused on the entire hospital system, the researchers were able to demonstrate and improve systems by working on the discharge process. If a surgical suite or emergency department were able to process more people, it would need a hospital room for the patients to stay in; this model helped free up those rooms such that patients could move through the system more quickly.

Another way to manage constraints in a system is to acknowledge that there will always be a bottleneck and determine where it should be. Designing the system so that the bottleneck can be best managed or controlled can be a powerful way to deal with it.

Analytical Tools

Optimization

Optimization, or **mathematical programming**, is a technique used to determine the optimal allocation of limited resources given a desired goal. For example, the resources might be people, money, or equipment. Of all

Optimization
A technique used to determine the optimal allocation of limited resources (such as people, money, or equipment) given a desired goal. Also called mathematical programming.

EXHIBIT 6.13
DRG Linear
Programming
Problem Data

	Respiratory	Coronary Surgery	Birth/ Delivery	Alcohol/ Drug Abuse	Available
Resources					
Diagnostic services (hours)	7	10	2	1	325
ICU bed days	1	2.5	0.5	0	55
Routine bed days	5	7	2	7	420
Nursing care (hours)	50	88	27	50	3,800
Margin	$400.00	$2,500.00	$300.00	$50.00	
Minimum cases	15	10	20	10	

possible resource allocation(s), the goal or objective is to find the allocation(s) that maximizes or minimizes some numerical quantity such as profit or cost.

Optimization problems are classified as linear or nonlinear depending on whether the problem is linear with respect to the variables. In many cases, it is not practically possible to determine an exact solution for optimization problems; a variety of software packages offer algorithms to find good solutions.

EXHIBIT 6.14
Excel Solver
Setup for
DRG Linear
Programming
Problem

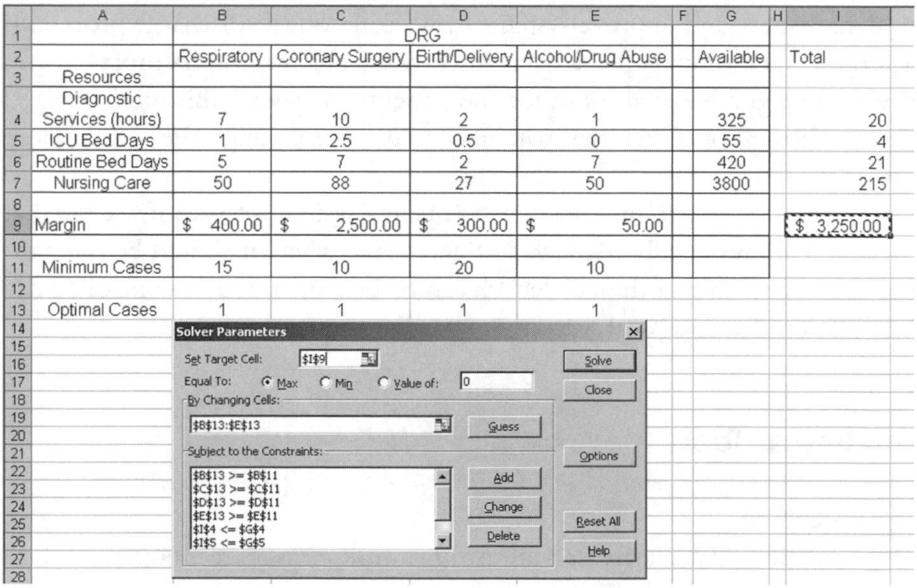

Optimization models have three basic elements:

1. An objective function—the quantity that needs to be minimized or maximized
2. The controllable inputs or decision variables that affect the value of the objective function
3. Constraints that limit the values that the decision variables can take on

A solution in which all of the constraints are satisfied is called a *feasible solution*. Most algorithms used to solve these types of problems begin by finding feasible solutions and trying to improve on them until a maximum or minimum is found.

Healthcare organizations need to maintain financial viability while working within various constraints on their resources. Optimization techniques can help these organizations make the best allocation decision. An example of how linear programming could be used in a healthcare organization using Microsoft Excel Solver follows.

Linear Programming

VVH wants to determine the optimal case mix for diagnosis-related groups (DRGs) that will maximize profits. Limited resources (e.g., space, qualified employees) are available to service the various DRGs, and minimum levels of service must be offered for each DRG (Exhibit 6.13).

Exhibit 6.14 shows that the respiratory DRG (DRGr) requires 7 hours of diagnostic services, 1 intensive care unit (ICU) bed day, 5 routine bed days, and 50 hours of nursing care. The profit for DRGr is $400, and the minimum service level is 15 cases.

The goal is to maximize profit, and the objective function is:

$$(\$400 \times DRGr) + (\$2{,}500 \times DRGcs) + (\$300 \times DRGbd) + (\$50 \times DRGada)$$

The constraints are as follows:
Diagnostic services:

$$(7 \times DRGr) + (10 \times DRGcs) + (2 \times DRGbd) + (1 \times DRGada) \leq 325 \quad (1)$$

ICU bed days:

$$(1 \times DRGr) + (2.5 \times DRGcs) + (0.5 \times DRGbd) \leq 55 \quad (2)$$

Routine bed days:

$$(5 \times DRGr) + (7 \times DRGcs) + (2 \times DRGbd) + (7 \times DRGada) \leq 420 \quad (3)$$

Nursing care:

$$(50 \times DRGr) + (88 \times DRGcs) + (27 \times DRGbd) + (50 \times DRGada) \leq 3,800 \quad (4)$$

Respiratory minimum case level:

$$DRGr \geq 15 \qquad\qquad (5)$$

Coronary surgery minimum case level:

$$DRGcs \geq 10 \qquad\qquad (6)$$

Birth/delivery minimum case level:

$$DRGbd \geq 20 \qquad\qquad (7)$$

Alcohol/drug abuse minimum case level:

$$DRGada \geq 10 \qquad\qquad (8)$$

Exhibit 6.15 shows the Excel Solver setup of this problem. Solver (Exhibit 6.14) finds that the hospital should service 15 DRGr cases, 12

EXHIBIT 6.15
Excel Solver
Solution for
DRG Linear
Programming
Problem

Target Cell (Max)

Cell	Name	Original Value	Final Value
$I$9	Margin Total	$ 3,250.00	$ 43,454.00

Adjustable Cells

Cell	Name	Original Value	Final Value
$B$13	Optimal Cases Respiratory	1	15
$C$13	Optimal Cases Coronary Surgery	1	12
$D$13	Optimal Cases Birth/Delivery	1	20
$E$13	Optimal Cases Alcohol/Drug Abuse	1	29.08

Constraints

Cell	Name	Cell Value	Formula	Status	Slack
$I$4	Diagnostic Services (hours) Total	294.08	$I$4 < =$G$4	Not Binding	30.92
$I$5	ICU Bed Days Total	55	$I$5 < =$G$5	Binding	0
$I$6	Routine Bed Days Total	402.56	$I$6 < =$G$6	Not Binding	17.44
$I$7	Nursing Care (hours) Total	3800	$I$7 < =$G$7	Binding	0
$E$13	Optimal Cases Alcohol/Drug Abuse	29.08	$E$13 > =$E$11	Not Binding	19.08
$D$13	Optimal Cases Birth/Delivery	20	$D$13 > =$D$11	Binding	0
$C$13	Optimal Cases Coronary Surgery	12	$C$13 > =$C$11	Not Binding	2
$B$13	Optimal Cases Respiratory	15	$B$13 > =$B$11	Binding	0

DRGcs cases, 20 DRGbd cases, and 29 DRGada cases. The total profit at the optimal case mix is:

$$(15 \times \$400) + (12 \times \$2,500) + (20 \times \$300) + (29 \times \$50) = \$43,450$$

Information relating to the resource constraints is found in the computer solution (Exhibit 6.15). The amounts reported as slack provide a measure of resource utilization. All available ICU bed days and hours of nursing care will be used. However, 17 routine bed days and almost 31 hours of diagnostic services will be unused. VVH may want to consider eliminating some hours of diagnostic services.

Constraints 5 through 8 relate to the minimum service level for each DRG category. Slack, or surplus, values represent services that should be provided in excess of a minimum level. Only the minimum levels for birth/delivery and respiratory care should be provided. However, 2 additional coronary surgery and 19 alcohol/drug abuse cases should be taken.

Sensitivity Analysis

Sensitivity analysis (Exhibit 6.16) examines the effect of varying the assumptions, or input variables, on the output of a model. Here, a sensitivity analysis is used to analyze the allocation and utilization of resources (diagnostic service hours, ICU bed days, routine bed days, nursing care) in relation to the objective function (total profit). Shadow prices (the Lagrange multiplier in Exhibit 6.16) show the dollar effect on total profit of adding or deleting one unit of the resource. This allows the organization to weigh the relative benefits of adding more resources. In this example, adding one ICU bed

Sensitivity analysis
A tool that examines the effect of independently changing input variables to see the impact on the output of a model.

Adjustable Cells

Cell	Name	Final Value	Reduced Gradient
$B$13	Optimal Cases Respiratory	15	−614.8
$C$13	Optimal Cases Coronary Surgery	12	0
$D$13	Optimal Cases Birth/Delivery	20	−209.4
$E$13	Optimal Cases Alcohol/Drug Abuse	29.08	0

Constraints

Cell	Name	Final Value	Lagrange Multiplier
$I$4	Diagnostic Services (hours) Total	294.08	0
$I$5	ICU Bed Days Total	55	964.8
$I$6	Routine Bed Days Total	402.56	0
$I$7	Nursing Care (hours) Total	3800	1

EXHIBIT 6.16
Sensitivity Analysis for DRG Linear Programming Problem

day would increase total profit by $964.80, and adding one hour of nursing care would increase total profit by $1. If the cost of either of these options is less than the additional profit, the hospital should increase those resources. Because there is slack in routine bed days and diagnostic services, adding more of either of these resources would not change the total profit; there is already an excess of these resources.

Shadow price information is also presented for the DRG minimum service-level requirements (the reduced gradient in Figure 6.16). The shadow price is a negative $614.80 for DRGr; total profit will decrease by $614.80 for each case taken above the minimum level required in the DRGr category. The DRGr category has a higher profit ($400) than the DRGada and, without this analysis, the hospital might have mistakenly tried to serve more DGRr cases to the detriment of DRGada cases.

Optimization can also allow organizations to run what-if analyses. For example, if a hospital wants to investigate the possibility of increasing beds in its ICU, perhaps by decreasing routine beds, it could use optimization to analyze the available choices.

Decision analysis
A structured process for examining and evaluating decisions.

Decision tree
A graphic representation of the order of future and current events of how decisions are made.

Decision Analysis

Decision analysis is a process for examining and evaluating decisions in a structured manner. A **decision tree** is a graphic representation of the order of events in a decision process. This structured process enables an evaluation of the risks and rewards of choosing a particular course of action.

In constructing a decision tree, events are linked from left to right in the order in which they would occur. Three types of events, represented by nodes, can occur: decision or choice events (squares), chance events (circles), and outcomes (triangles). Probabilities of chance events occurring and benefits or costs for event choices and outcomes are associated with each branch extending from a node. The result is a tree structure with branches for each event extending to the right.

A simple example will help to illustrate this process. A health maintenance organization (HMO) is considering the economic benefits of a preventive flu vaccination program. If the program is not offered, the estimated cost to the HMO if there is a flu outbreak is $8 million with a probability of 0.4 (40 percent) and $12 million with a probability of 0.6 (60 percent). The program is estimated to cost $7 million, and the probability of a flu outbreak occurring is 0.7 (70 percent). If a flu outbreak does occur and the HMO offers the program afterward, it will still cost the organization $7 million, but the resulting costs to the HMO would be reduced to $4 million with a probability of 0.4 (40 percent) or $6 million with a probability of 0.6 (60 percent). What should the HMO decide? The decision tree for the HMO vaccination program is shown in Exhibit 6.17.

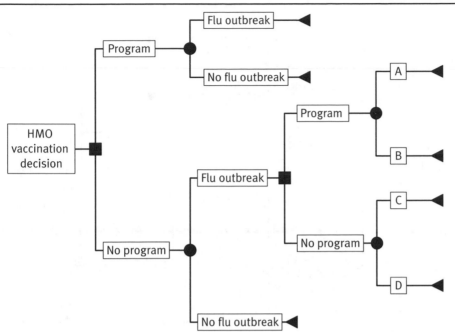

EXHIBIT 6.17
HMO
Vaccination
Program
Decision Tree 1

NOTE: The tree diagrams in Exhibits 6.17 to 6.21 were drawn with the help of PrecisionTree, a software product of Palisade Corp., Ithaca, NY: www.palisade.com.

The probability estimates for each of the chance nodes, benefits (in this case costs) of each decision branch, and outcome branch are added to the tree (Exhibit 6.18).

The value of a node can be calculated once the values for all subsequent nodes are found. The value of a decision node is the largest value of any branch out of that node. The assumption is that the decision that maximizes the benefits will be made. The value of a chance node is the expected value of the branches out of that node. Working from right to left, the value of all nodes in the tree can be calculated. The expected value of chance node 6 is $[0.6 \times (-12)] + [0.4 \times (-8)] = -10.4$. The expected value of chance node 5 is $[0.6 \times (-6)] + [0.4 \times (-4)] = -5.2$. The expected value of the secondary vaccination program is $-7 + (-5.2) = -12.2$, and the expected value of not implementing the secondary vaccination program is -10.4. Therefore, at decision node 4 the choice would be to not implement the secondary vaccination program.

At chance node 3 (no initial vaccination program), the expected value is $0.7 \times (-10.4) + 0.3 \times 0 = -7.28$. The expected value at chance node 2 is $0.7 \times 0 + 0.3 \times 0 = 0$, and the expected value of the initial vaccination program branch is $-7 + 0 = -7$. Therefore, at decision node 1 the choice would be to implement the initial vaccination program at a cost of $7 million. In contrast,

EXHIBIT 6.18
HMO
Vaccination
Program
Decision Tree 2

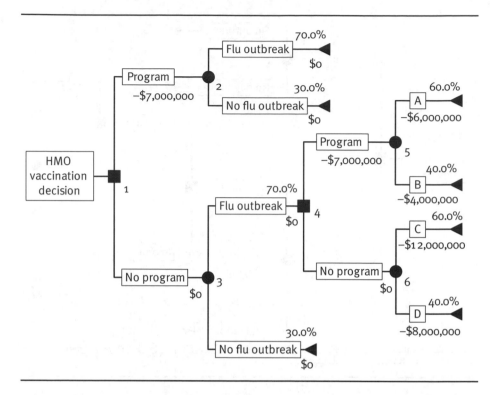

choosing not to implement the initial vaccination program has an expected cost of $7.28 million (Exhibit 6.19).

A risk analysis on this decision analysis can be conducted (Exhibit 6.20). Choosing to implement the vaccination program results in a cost of $7 million with a probability of 1. Choosing not to implement the initial vaccination program results in a cost of $12 million with a probability of 0.42, $8 million with a probability of 0.28, and no cost with a probability of 0.3. Choosing not to implement the vaccination program would be less costly 30 percent of the time, but 70 percent of the time it would be less costly to implement the vaccination program.

A sensitivity analysis might also be conducted to determine the effect of changing some or all of the parameters in the analysis. For example, if the risk of a flu outbreak was 0.6 rather than 0.7 (and all other parameters stayed the same), the optimal decision would be to not offer either vaccination program (Exhibit 6.21).

For this example, dollars were used to represent costs (or benefits), but any type of score could also be used. In the medical field, decision trees are often used in deciding among a variety of treatment options and cost models for medical applications (Freitas 2011; Ribas 2011).

Decision trees can be a powerful aid to evaluating and choosing the optimal course of action. However, care must be taken when using them.

EXHIBIT 6.19
HMO
Vaccination
Program
Decision Tree 3

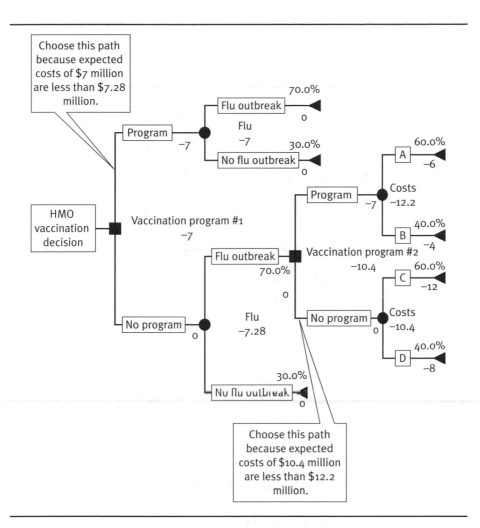

Choose this path because expected costs of $7 million are less than $7.28 million.

Choose this path because expected costs of $10.4 million are less than $12.2 million.

Possible outcomes and the probabilities and benefits associated with them are only estimates, and these estimates could differ greatly from the reality. Also, when using expected value (or expected utility) to choose the optimum path, the underlying assumption is that the decision will be made over and over.

EXHIBIT 6.20
Risk Analysis
for HMO
Vaccination
Program
Decision

| Number | *Initial Vaccination Program* | | *No Initial Vaccination Program* | |
	X	P	X	P
1	−7	1	−12	0.42
2			−8	0.28
3			0	0.3

X = Cost in millions of dollars; P = Probability

EXHIBIT 6.21
Decision
Analysis
Sensitivity to
Change in Risk
of Flu Outbreak

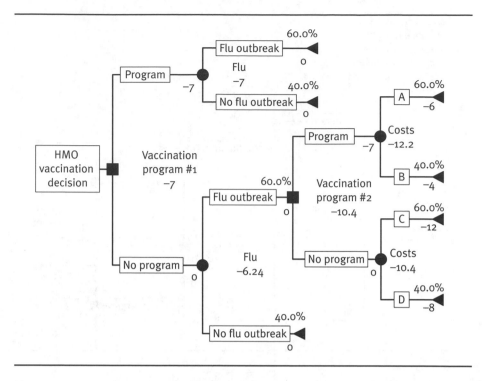

On average the expected payout is received, but in each individual situation different amounts are received.

Implementation: Force Field Analysis

Force field analysis
A graphical technique that demonstrates all the forces for and against making a key decision.

Derived from the work of Kurt Lewin (1951), **force field analysis** is a technique for evaluating all of the various forces for and against a proposed change. It can be used to decide if a proposed change can be successfully implemented. Alternatively, if a decision to change has already been made, force field analysis can be used to develop strategies that will enable the change to be implemented successfully.

In any situation, driving forces will help to achieve the change, and restraining forces will work against the change. Force field analysis identifies these forces and assigns relative scores to each. Exhibit 6.22 lists typical forces that should be considered. If the total score of the restraining forces is greater than the total score of the driving forces, the change may be doomed to failure. Force field analysis is typically used to determine how to strengthen or add driving forces or weaken the restraining forces to enable successful implementation of a change.

Patients at VVH believed that they were insufficiently involved in and informed about their care. After analyzing this problem, hospital staff

Available resources	Present or past practices
Costs	Institutional policies or norms
Vested interests	Personal or group attitudes and
Regulations	needs
Organizational	Social or organizational norms and
structures	values

EXHIBIT 6.22
Common Forces
to Consider
in Force Field
Analysis

believed that the problem could be solved (or lessened) by moving shift handover from the nurses' station to the patient's bedside. A force field analysis was conducted and is illustrated in Exhibit 6.23.

Although the restraining forces were greater than the driving forces in this example, a decision was made to implement the change in handover procedures. To improve the project's chances for success, a protocol was developed for the actual procedure, making explicit the following:

- Develop and disseminate the protocol (new driving force +2).
- Confidential information will be exchanged at the nurses' station, not at the bedside handover (decrease fear of disclosure by 2).
- Lateness was addressed and solutions were developed and incorporated into the protocol (decrease problems associated with late arrivals by 2).

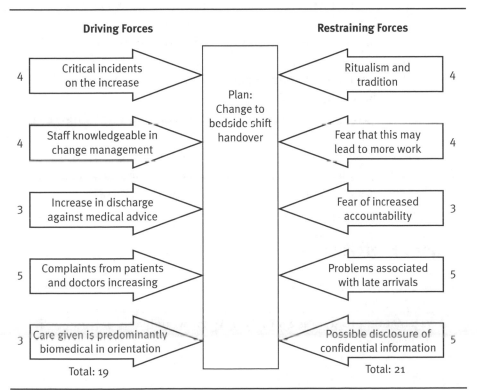

EXHIBIT 6.23
Force Field
Analysis

These changes increased the driving forces by 2, to 21, and decreased the restraining forces by 4, to 17. The change was successfully implemented; more important, patients felt more involved in their care and complaints were reduced.

Conclusion

The tools and techniques outlined in this chapter are intended to help organizations along the path of continuous improvement. The choice of tool and when to use that tool is dependent on the problem to be solved; in many situations, several tools from this and other chapters should be used to ensure that the best possible solution has been found.

Discussion Questions

1. Answer the following questions quickly for a fun illustration of some of the ten decision traps:
   • Can a person living in Milwaukee, Wisconsin, be buried west of the Mississippi?
   • If you had only one match and entered a room where there was a lamp, an oil heater, and some kindling wood, which would you light first?
   • How many animals of each species did Moses take along on the ark?
   • If a doctor gave you three pills and said to take one every half hour, how long would they last?
   • If you have two US coins totaling 55 cents and one of the coins is not a nickel, what are the two coins?
   What decision traps did you fall into when answering these questions?
2. Discuss a problem your organization has solved or a suboptimal decision the organization made because the frame was incorrect.

Chapter Exercises

1. In the HMO vaccination program example, analyze the situation if the probability of a flu outbreak is only 65 percent and the cost of the vaccination program is $8 million. What would your decision be in this case?

2. In the DRG case-mix problem, VVH has determined that it could convert 15 of its routine beds to ICU beds for a cost of $2,000. What should VVH do and why?

3. The high cost of medical care and insurance is a growing societal problem. Develop a mind map of this problem. (Advanced: Use Inspiration software.)

4. Individually or in teams, develop a map of a healthcare process or system with which you are familiar. Make sure that your process map has a start and an endpoint, all inputs and outputs are defined, and all key process steps are included. Explain your map to the rest of the class—this may help you to determine if anything is missing. (Advanced: Use Microsoft Visio.)

5. For this exercise, choose a service offered by a healthcare organization and create a service blueprint. You may have to imagine some of the systems and services that take place backstage if you are unfamiliar with them.

6. Think of a problem in your healthcare organization. Perform an RCA of the identified problem using the five whys technique and a fishbone diagram.

7. Pick one solution to the problem identified in Exercise 4 and do a force field analysis.

STATISTICAL THINKING AND STATISTICAL PROBLEM SOLVING

Operations Management in Action

In June 2009, the World Health Organization and the Centers for Disease Control and Prevention predicted the spread of a new influenza virus, H1N1, for the coming flu season. A resulting flood of media reports about the coming pandemic advised hand-washing as key to stopping the spread of the disease.

Sales of hand sanitizers rose from $69.4 million in 2008 to $118.4 million in 2009—a 70 percent jump. Bottles of the alcohol-based gel popped up everywhere from hospitals and classrooms to theme parks and offices. Some people kept spare bottles in their cars and purses so they could clean their hands dozens of times a day (De Nies, Pirone, and Santichen 2009).

This case illustrates how bias can influence actions. Sales of hand sanitizer were driven by the media bias toward the disease and not by the actual cases of reported influenza. Although the number of people who went to the hospital to be seen for "influenza" rose dramatically during this time, verified influenza cases decreased in the same period. The media had publicized H1N1 so heavily that people were going to the hospitals to be checked for the flu even though they had few or no actual flu symptoms.

According to the World Health Organization (2003), normal strains of influenza account for 250,000 to 500,000 deaths worldwide each year. The incidences of death are substantially lower in the United States than in most other countries. For those who contract the traditional strains of influenza, the mortality rate is less than 0.01 percent. The estimated mortality rate of the H1N1 strain of flu was even lower, at 0.007 to 0.045 percent (Fox 2009).

Later research showed that the global H1N1 influenza infection rate was far lower than the 50 percent that pandemic planners had envisioned as a possible worst case and was closer to 11 percent, which was on the low end of the initial models (Roos 2011).

Interestingly, research suggests that community-based hygiene efforts, such as using hand sanitizer, had no effect on reducing the spread of H1N1.

SOURCE: Aiello et al. (2010).

Statistical Thinking in Healthcare

What Is Statistical Thinking?

As presented by Dr. Kenneth Juran, statistical thinking is the collection, organization, analysis, interpretation, and presentation of data (Juran 2010). In most business systems in the healthcare industry, statistical thinking is lacking. Knowledge-based management and improvement require that decisions be based on facts rather than on feeling or intuition. Collecting the right data and analyzing them correctly enable fact-based decision making.

Variance
A statistical term that indicates how much a measurement varies around the mean.

Variance exists in all systems. Understanding and controlling variance distinguishes poor systems from high-performing systems. Hospitals often ignore the understanding of variance, and the erratic behavior manifests until there are major issues that often require system redesign (DeLia 2007). The importance of understanding statistical concepts in developing high-performing healthcare systems cannot be understated. The ability for our healthcare systems to sustain the delivery of high-quality healthcare depends on understanding and controlling variance. The irony of this is that many clinical quality and safety rules and regulations are designed and driven by the understanding of variance. However, the supporting business systems are often designed to meet regulatory agency requirements and not to manage the variance in the system. This situation provides the opportunity to make massive changes to both system performance and financial performance simply by understanding data and metrics.

Metrics and Key Process Indicators

The terms *metrics* and *key process indicators (KPIs)* have become more prevalent in recent years. Hospitals and healthcare systems are constantly searching to find better metrics that indicate the health of their overall system. For healthcare systems the term *metrics* can be difficult to grasp because it includes clinical metrics of safety and quality and well as business system metrics. Each of these two different systems has challenging aspects that make gathering and collecting data difficult.

To design effective and efficient systems or improve existing systems, knowledge of the system, including both inputs to the system and the desired output, is needed. The goal of data collection is to obtain valid information to better understand and improve the system being studied. Decisions or solutions based on invalid data are doomed to failure. Ensuring that the data obtained are valid is an important part of any study, and often the most problematic. What constitutes valid data in a healthcare system can often vary depending on which system is being analyzed.

Clinical systems are appropriately designed around patient safety and quality outcomes. These procedures are designed and tested under rigorous statistical guidelines. The outcome of these statistical procedures is that the delivery of care improves over time and patient safety and quality increase. Business systems, on the other hand, usually develop over time to meet the needs of the market and the technological needs of the institution. The net effect is that the system must be flexible to meet the ever-changing needs of the healthcare industry. These two systems are integral to any healthcare system but often conflict, which makes gathering good data for analysis challenging.

To change clinical processes the data must be perfect. The studies follow rigorous data collection procedures and include control groups and test groups, and results are compared under the most demanding statistical procedures. However, to change business systems, the data only need to be "good enough." The data should point to the major problems and provide a basis for how to change the system. The goal is continuous improvement, not perfection. Because both healthcare professionals and business developers work in the healthcare industry, they often argue about data and data integrity, which often leads to little or no analysis. Statistical thinking requires that our decisions be driven by data and not by individual preferences. However, ultimately the goal is continuous improvement, and the opposite of progress is doing nothing at all. The focus of this chapter is to provide a solid understanding of data collection, measurement, and analysis.

Foundations of Data Analysis

To become an effective practitioner of continuous improvement and an effective business analyst, it is essential to become adept at problem solving and data analysis, including the fundamental issues related to data collection, basic probability, and statistical analysis. For those readers with little or no background in statistics or probability, this chapter provides an introduction to the basic concepts used in fundamental problem solving, many of which are an integral part of the continuous improvement philosophy of quality.

For readers who wish to gain a greater understanding of statistics and probability, the companion website has in-depth coverage of many of statistical concepts and techniques. For purposes of this chapter we discuss the following topics:

- Data collection
- Graphic tools for data presentation and analysis
- Basic probability and conditional probability

At the end of this chapter, the reader should understand the fundamental tools of problem solving and quality.

Where to Start?

The critical error often made during problem solving is failing to understanding what data is needed to solve the problem or how the data will be acquired.

Why are the data needed, and what will they be used for? Will the patterns of the past be repeated in the future? If there is reason to believe that the future will look different from the past, data from the past will not help to answer the question and other, nonquantitative methods should be used. This is the logic phase of the data collection process, where the focus is on ensuring that the right question is being asked and that it is possible to answer that question.

Graphic Tools

A core technique of problem solving is to consider the data and problem visually prior to analyzing the data analytically. This section discusses graphic illustrations, including mapping, check sheets, histograms, Pareto charts, dot plots, and scatter plots.

Mapping

Graphic tools such as mind mapping can be employed to enable the collection of valid data. A mind map can be used to help frame the problem or question in an attempt to avoid logic errors (Exhibit 7.1 and Chapter 6).

Check Sheets

One of the critical tools used in problem solving is the check sheet. Check sheets are custom-designed forms that allow users to collect data on problems and defects. The form has checkboxes that describe typical problems in

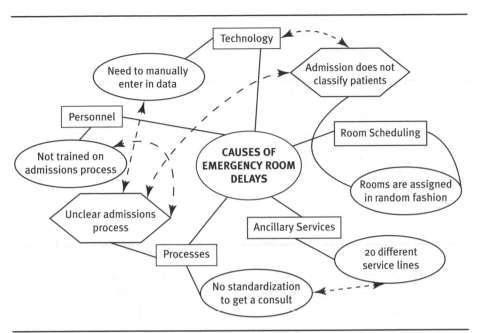

EXHIBIT 7.1
Causes of
Emergency
Room Delays

the system. When an employee uses a check sheet he checks the appropriate box every time an error occurs. These tools are designed to collect data in real time as it is being created. Check sheet data are an essential piece to collecting data prior to conducting effective analysis.

Effective check sheets may be simple to develop and comprehend, but they may be one of the most difficult tools to execute well. Effective check sheets have some of the following characteristics:

- Simple to use
- Data points at same level of analysis
- Few boxes for user to check
- Data collected as it occurs

When done correctly, a check sheet allows a data analyst to get current data that can be used to demonstrate the current state of a problem. However, many problems exist with check sheets, mostly related to the process of collecting the data. Many people will fill out check sheets incorrectly because they are not clear or they do not fill them out as the data is created.

Visual Representations of Data

Once valid data are collected, those data need to be analyzed to answer the original question or make a decision. The data need to be examined not only to determine their general characteristics, but also to look for interesting or unusual patterns. Subsequent sections of this chapter outline numeric tools that can be employed for this purpose.

EXHIBIT 7.2
Histogram
of Length of
Hospital Stay

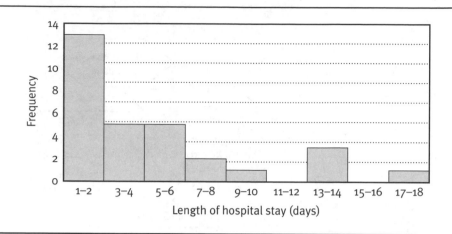

Visual representations of the data can be powerful in both answering questions and convincing others of the answers. Tufte (1997, 1990, 1983) provides guidance for visual presentation of data. The following sections present graphic analysis tools. The human mind is powerful and has the ability to discern patterns in data, which numeric methods can then be used to validate. The first step in data analysis is always to graph the data.

Histogram
A graph summarizing discrete or continuous data. Histograms visually display how much variation exists in the data.

www.ache.org/books/OpsManagement2

Histograms and Pareto Diagrams

Histograms and Pareto diagrams are two of the seven basic quality tools (Chapter 8). A **histogram** (Exhibit 7.2) is used to summarize discrete or continuous data. These graphs can be useful for investigating or illustrating important characteristics of the data, such as their overall shape, symmetry, location, spread, outliers, clusters, and gaps. However, for some distributions, a particular choice of bin width can distort the features of a data set. (For an example of this problem, see the Old Faithful Histogram applet linked from the companion website.)

To construct a histogram, the data are divided or grouped into classes. For each group, a rectangle is constructed with its base equal to the range of values in the group and its area proportional to the number of observations falling into the group. If the ranges are the same length, the height of the histogram will also be proportional to the number of observations falling into that group. Histograms are a useful tool that allows an analyst to see the shape of the distribution of the data. An analyst can quickly see if data points follow patterns of tight variation or wide variation or simply if some data points could be considered outliers to the overall data.

The histogram in Exhibit 7.2 demonstrates that the distribution is skewed to the right and that the majority of people stay between one and two days.

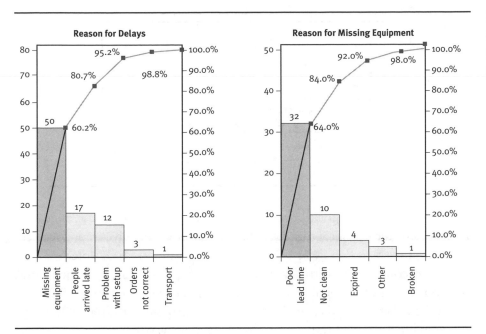

EXHIBIT 7.3
Causes for Delays in Surgery

Pareto diagrams are frequency diagrams that indicate the number of times a particular item occurs in a situation. The Pareto principle, or the 80/20 rule, indicates that 80 percent of costs, issues, or defects can be attributed to 20 percent of the items being measured. In Exhibit 7.3, a hospital collected data related to a high percentage of late starts for surgeries. In the first diagram, 80 percent of all issues are related to missing equipment at the start of surgery or to patients arriving late. Using another Pareto diagram to dissect the reasons for missing equipment demonstrated that 64 percent of those cases had insufficient lead time to clean, prepare, and load the surgery cart to arrive in time for the surgery. This analysis allowed a problem-solving team to focus its efforts on items that made an immediate impact on the situation.

Pareto diagram
A rank-ordered frequency chart that indicates the number of times a particular item occurs in a situation.

Dot Plots

A **dot plot** (Exhibit 7.4) is similar to a histogram, but the frequency of occurrence is represented by a dot. Dot plots are useful for displaying small data sets with positive values because they are quick and easy to construct by hand.

Dot plot
A chart in which frequency is represented by a dot. Useful for displaying small data sets with positive values.

Scatter Plots

Scatter plots are another of the seven basic quality tools (Chapter 8). A scatter plot graphically displays the relationship between a pair of variables and can give initial information on whether two variables are related, how strongly they are related, and the direction of the relationship. For example, is there a relationship between length of hospital stay and weight? Does length of stay increase (decrease) as weight increases? How strong is the relationship between

Scatter plot
A graph displaying two variables and whether they are related, how strongly they are related, and the direction of the relationship.

EXHIBIT 7.4
Dot Plot of
Length of
Hospital Stay

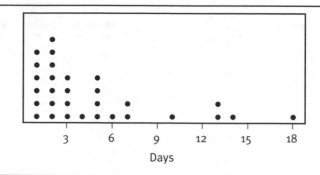

length of stay and weight? A scatter plot can help to answer these questions. Regression—the statistical tool related to scatter plots that gives more detailed, numeric answers to these questions—is discussed later in this chapter.

To construct a scatter plot related to the aforementioned questions, data on length of hospital stay and weight from the population of interest would be collected. Typically, the "cause," or independent variable, is on the horizontal (x) axis and the "effect," or dependent variable, is on the vertical (y) axis. Each pair of variables is plotted on this graph. A typical scatter plot is shown in Exhibit 7.5. Scatter plots are useful tools for determining what variables in the system need to be controlled to obtain desired outputs. Much like a Pareto diagram, the scatter plot helps narrow the amount of variables an analyst needs to understand how to solve the problem.

EXHIBIT 7.5
Scatter Plot
Between Wine
Consumption
and Vascular
Disease

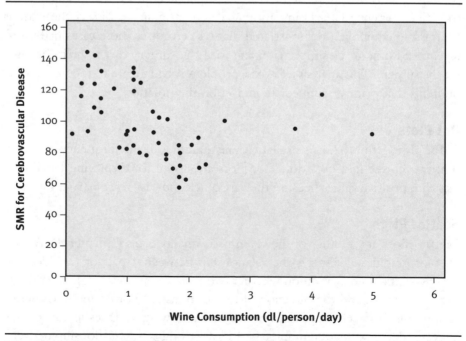

SOURCE: Truelsen and Grønbæk (1999).

Exhibit 7.5 clearly shows that the consumption of one to two glasses of wine per day will have a positive effect on reducing this form of vascular disease. This relationship would be negative because increased wine consumption leads to a reduction in disease.

Mathematic Descriptions

When describing or summarizing data, the three characteristics of interest for any analyst are central tendency, spread or variation, and the probability distribution. In this section, the following simple data set is used to illustrate some of these measures: 3, 6, 8, 3, 5.

Measures of Central Tendency

The three common measures of central tendency are mean, median, and mode.

Mean

The mean is the arithmetic average of the population:

$$\text{Population mean} = \mu = \frac{\sum x}{N},$$

where x = individual values and

N = number of values in the population.

The population mean can be estimated from a sample:

$$\text{Sample mean} = \bar{x} = \frac{\sum x}{n},$$

where n = number of values in the sample.

For our simple data set, $= \bar{x} = \dfrac{3 + 6 + 8 + 3 + 5}{5} = 5.$

Referring to the histogram in Exhibit 7.6, if the data shape looks like a bell curve the mean would be the point in the middle or the average of all data.

EXHIBIT 7.6
Histogram
of Summary
Quality Index

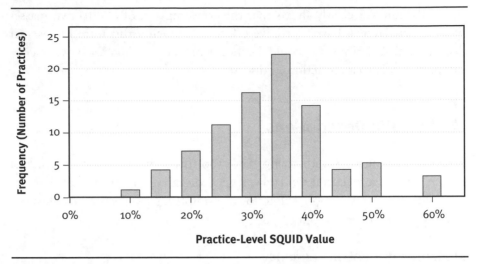

SOURCE: Truelsen and Grønbæk (1999).

Median

The median is the middle value of the sample or population. If the data are arranged into an array (an ordered data set),

$$3, 3, 5, 6, 8,$$
$$\uparrow$$

5 would be the middle value or median.

Mode

The mode is the most frequently occurring value. In the previous example, the value 3 occurs more often (two times) than any other value, so 3 would be the mode.

Measures of Variability

Several measures are commonly used to summarize the variability of the data, including range, mean absolute deviation (MAD), variance, and standard deviation.

Range

A simple way to capture the variability or spread in the data is to take the range, the difference between the high and low values. All of the information in the data is not being used with this measure, but it is simple to calculate:

$$\text{Range} = x_{high} - x_{low} = 8 - 3 - 5$$

Mean Absolute Deviation

Another possible measure of the variability or spread in the data is the average difference from the mean. However, for any data set this will equal zero, because the values above the mean will balance the values below the mean. One way to eliminate this problem is to take the absolute value of the differences from the mean. This measure is called the mean absolute deviation (MAD) and is commonly used in forecasting to measure variability. However, absolute values are difficult to work with mathematically:

$$\text{MAD} = \frac{\sum |x - \bar{x}|}{n} = \frac{2+1+3+2+0}{5} = \frac{8}{5} = 1.6$$

Variance

The average square difference from the mean—called the variance—provides another measure of the variability in the data. For a population, variance is a good estimator. However, for a sample it can be proven that variance is a biased estimator and needs to be adjusted; rather than dividing by n, the number of values in the sample, it must be divided by $n - 1$:

$$\text{Population variance} = \sigma^2 = \frac{\sum (x - \mu)^2}{N} = \frac{4+1+9+4+0}{5} = \frac{18}{5} = 3.6$$

$$\text{Sample variance} = s^2 = \frac{\sum (x - \bar{x})^2}{n-1} = \frac{4+1+9+4+0}{5-1} = \frac{18}{4} = 4.5$$

Standard Deviation

Taking the square root of the variance will result in the units of this measure being the same as the units of the mean, median, and mode. This measure, the **standard deviation**, is the most commonly used measure of variability.

Standard deviation
A measurement of variation around the mean.

$$\text{Population standard deviation} = \sqrt{\sigma^2}$$

$$= \sqrt{\frac{\sum (x - \mu)^2}{N}}$$

$$= \sqrt{\frac{4+4+0+1+9}{5}} = \sqrt{\frac{18}{5}} = \sqrt{3.6} = 1.9$$

$$\text{Sample standard deviation} = \sqrt{s^2}$$

$$= \sqrt{\frac{\sum (x - \bar{x})^2}{n}}$$

$$= \sqrt{\frac{4+4+0+1+9}{5-1}} = \sqrt{\frac{18}{4}} = \sqrt{4.5} = 2.1$$

Coefficient of variation
A measure of variation in the data relative to the measure of central tendency in the data.

Coefficient of Variation

Given another data set (data B) with a standard deviation of 5 and the sample data set (data A) with a standard deviation of 1.9 and a mean of 5, which data are more variable? This question cannot be answered without knowing the mean of data B. If the mean of data B is 5, then data B is more variable. However, if the mean of data B is 25, data B is less variable. The **coefficient of variation** (CV) is a measure of the relative variation in the data.

$$\text{Coefficient of variation} = \text{CV} = \frac{\sigma}{\mu} = 5$$

or

$$\frac{s}{\overline{x}} = \frac{1.9}{5} = 0.4$$

Shewhart's rule
An outlier exists in bell-shaped data if a data point is greater than three standard deviations from the mean.

Tukey's rule
An outlier exists in a skewed data set if a data point is greater than q1 – one step or q3 + one step.

Outliers

Outliers are observations that are far from the mean or median in the data set. An outlier is an important discovery because it represents opportunities for analysts. If data points are far from the mean or median, they present opportunities to improve.

If the histogram data are reasonably bell-shaped, we use **Shewhart's rule** to determine if outliers are present in the data.

Shewhart's rule indicates outliers are present if the data points are greater than the mean $\pm$ 3 $\times$ standard deviation.

If the histogram data are skewed (not bell-shaped), we use **Tukey's rule** to determine if outliers are present in the data:

$$Q1 - 1.5 \times IQR \text{ or } Q3 + 1.5 \times IQR$$

where Q1 and Q3 represent the first and third quartile of the data set and IQR is the interquartile range. The IQR is computed by taking Q3 – Q1.

Probability

A common belief in healthcare systems is that events related to illness are not predictable. In reality these types of events are more predictable than most people think. The laws of probability help explain the ability to predict the likelihood of events occurring. Many issues arise in healthcare systems because the impact of probability on the system is not understood. For example, not understanding the probability of increased admittance to the hospital could create a situation in which beds are not available to patients who need them.

Two types of models exist to explain what is seen in the world: deterministic and probabilistic. In a deterministic model, the given inputs *determine* the output with certainty. For example, given a person's date of birth and the current date, her age can be determined. The inputs determine the output.

Date of Birth
Current Date $\longrightarrow$ | Age Model | $\longrightarrow$ Person's Age

In a probabilistic model, the given inputs provide only an estimate of the output. For example, given a person's age, her remaining life span can only be *estimated*.

Age $\longrightarrow$ | Life Span Model | $\longrightarrow$ Person's Remaining Life Span

Determination of Probabilities

Probabilities can be determined through observation or experimentation; through applying theory or reason; or subjectively, through opinion.

Observed Probability

Observed probability is a summary of the observations or experiments and is referred to as *empirical probability* or *relative frequency*. Observed probability is the relative frequency of an event—the number of times the event occurred divided by the total number of trials.

> **Observed probability**
> The number of times an event occurred divided by the total number of trials.

$$P(A) = \frac{\text{Number of times A occurred}}{\text{Total number of observations, trials, or experiments}} = \frac{r}{n}$$

Drug or protocol effectiveness is often determined in this manner:

$$P(\text{Drug is effective}) = \frac{\text{Number of times patients cured}}{\text{Total number of patients given the drug}} = \frac{r}{n}$$

For business analysts, observed probability is the most common use of probability because it gives an accurate representation of how the system or processes are functioning.

Theoretical Probability

The second method of determining probability, the theoretical relative frequency of an event, is based on logic—it is the theoretical number of times an event will occur divided by the total number of possible outcomes.

$$P(A) = \frac{\text{Number of times A could occur}}{\text{Total number of possible outcomes}} = \frac{r}{n}$$

Casino revenues are based on this theoretical determination of probability. If a card is randomly selected from a common deck of 52, the probability that it will be a spade is determined as follows:

$$P(\text{Card is a spade}) = \frac{\text{Number of spades in the deck}}{\text{Total number of cards in the deck}} = \frac{13}{52} = 0.25$$

Theoretical probability is often used by health insurance companies to predict the number of times or occurrences of disease and illness to set premium rates.

Theoretical probability
The number of times an event will occur divided by the total number of possible outcomes.

Properties of Probabilities

Bounds on Probability

Probabilities are bounded. The least number of times an event could occur is zero; therefore, probabilities must always be greater than or equal to zero. An event that cannot occur will have a probability of zero. The largest number of times an event could occur is equal to the total possible number of outcomes—t cannot be any larger; therefore, probabilities must always be less than or equal to one:

$$0 \leq P(A) \leq 1$$

The sum of the probabilities of all possible outcomes is one. From this property, it follows that:

$$P(A) + P(A') = 1 \text{ and } 1 - P(A) = P(A)$$

where A' is not A. This property can be useful when determining probabilities: Often, it is easier to determine the probability of "not A" than the probability of A.

Multiplicative Property

Two events are independent if the outcome of one event does not affect the outcome of the other event. For two independent events, the probability of

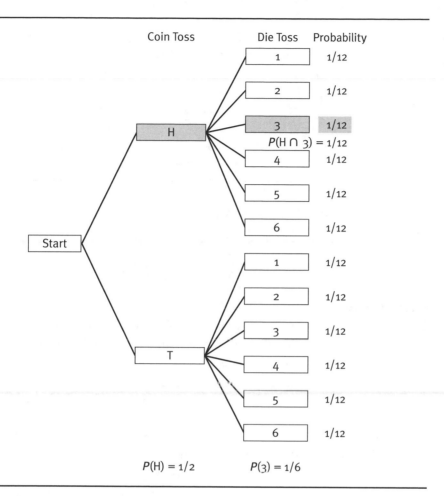

EXHIBIT 7.7
Tree Diagram—
Multiplicative
Property

both *A* **and** *B* occurring, or the intersection (∩) of *A* and *B*, is the probability of *A* occurring times the probability of *B* occurring:

$$P(A \text{ and } B \text{ occurring}) = P(A \cap B) = P(A) \times P(B)$$

Combining a coin toss with a die toss, what is the probability of obtaining both heads and a three?

$$P(H \cap 3) = P(H) \times P(3) = \frac{1}{2} \times \frac{1}{6} = \frac{1}{12}$$

A tree diagram (Exhibit 7.7) or a Venn diagram (Exhibit 7.8) can be used to illustrate this property. Note that decision trees (Chapter 6) are different from the tree diagrams presented here. Decision trees follow a time progression and analyses of the choices that can be made at particular points in time.

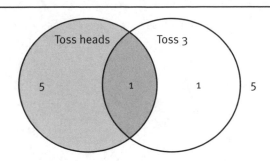

The multiplicative property provides a way to test whether events are independent. If they are not independent,

$$P(A \cap B) \neq P(A) \times P(B).$$

Additive Property

For two events, the probability of *A* **or** *B* occurring, the union ($\cup$) of *A* with *B*, is the probability of *A* occurring, plus the probability of *B* occurring, minus the probability of both *A* and *B* occurring:

$$P(A \text{ or } B \text{ occurring}) = P(A \cup B) = P(A) + P(B) + P(A \cap B)$$

Combining a coin toss with a die toss, what is the probability of obtaining heads or a three, but not both?

$$P(H \cup 3) = P(H) + P(3) - P(H \cap 3) = \frac{1}{2} + \frac{1}{6} - \frac{1}{12} = \frac{6}{12} + \frac{2}{12} - \frac{1}{12} = \frac{7}{12}$$

A tree diagram (Exhibit 7.9) or Venn diagram can be used to illustrate the additive property.

Conditional Probability

Conditional probability estimates how frequently events occur after a previous event has occurred. For example, suppose a patient usually waits in the emergency department for fewer than 30 minutes before being moved into an exam room. However, on Friday nights, when the department is busy, the wait is longer. Therefore, if it is a Friday night, the probability of waiting for 30 minutes or less is lower. This is the conditional probability of waiting less than 30 minutes given that it is a Friday night.

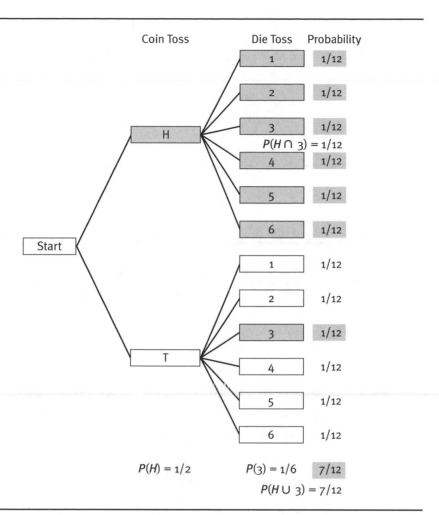

EXHIBIT 7.9
Tree Diagram—
Additive
Property

The conditional probability that A will occur given that B has occurred is as follows:

$$P(A\mid B) = \frac{P(A\cap B)}{P(B)}$$

Suppose a study was done of 100 emergency department patients; 50 patients were observed on a Friday night and 50 patients were observed at other times. On Friday night, 20 people waited less than 30 minutes, but 30 people waited longer than 30 minutes. At other times, 40 people waited less than 30 minutes, and only 10 people waited longer than 30 minutes. A contingency table (Exhibit 7.10) is used to summarize this information.

Contingency tables are used to examine the relationships between qualitative or categorical variables. A contingency table shows the frequency of one variable as a function of another variable. The column an observation

Contingency tables
A tool used to examine the relationships between qualitative or categorical variables.

EXHIBIT 7.10
Contingency
Table for
Emergency
Department
Wait Times

	≤ 30-Minute Wait	> 30-Minute Wait	
Friday night	20	30	50
Other times	40	10	50
Total	60	40	100

is in (≤ or > 30 minutes) is contingent upon (depends on) the row the subject is in (time of day).

For all patients, the probability of waiting longer than 30 minutes is:

$$P(\text{Wait} > 30 \text{ minutes}) = \frac{\text{Number of patients who wait} > 30}{\text{Total number of patients}}$$

$$= \frac{40}{100}$$

$$= 0.40$$

Furthermore, the (conditional) probability of waiting more than 30 minutes given that it is Friday night is:

$$P(A|\text{Friday night}) = \frac{P(\text{Wait} > 30 \text{ minutes and Friday night})}{P(\text{Friday night})}$$

$$\frac{\text{Number of patients who wait} > 30 \text{ minutes on Friday night}}{\text{Number of patients on Friday night}}$$

$$= \frac{30}{50}$$

$$= 0.60$$

A tree diagram for this example is shown in Exhibit 7.11.

Note that $P(A \cap B) = P(A \mid B) \times P(B) = P(B \mid A) \times P(A)$, and if one event has no effect on the other event (the events are independent), then $P(A \mid B) = P(A)$ and $P(A \cap B) = P(A) \times P(B)$. In the coin and die example, the coin toss and die toss are independent events, so the probability of tossing a six is the same no matter the outcome of the coin toss. For the emergency department wait time example, if night and wait time were independent, then the probability of waiting less than 30 minutes on a Friday night would be $0.5 \times 0.6 = 0.30$. But this is not true; wait time

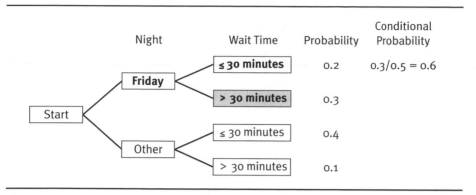

EXHIBIT 7.11

Tree Diagram—
Emergency
Department
Wait Time

and night are not independent—they are related. From this simple study, it could not be concluded that Friday night causes wait time.

Bayes' theorem allows the use of new information to update the conditional probability of an event. It is stated as follows:

Bayes' theorem
A formula used to revise the calculation of conditional probability as new information is obtained in the situation.

$$P(A|B) = \frac{P(A \cap B)}{P(B)} = \frac{P(B|A) \times P(A)}{P(B)} = \frac{P(B|A) \times P(A)}{P(B|A) \times P(A) + P(B|A') \times P(A')}$$

Bayes' theorem is often used to evaluate the probability of a false-positive test result. If a test for a particular disease is performed on a patient, there is a chance that the test will return a positive result even if the patient does not have the disease. Bayes' theorem allows the determination of the probability that a person who tests positive for a disease actually has the disease. For example, if a tested patient has the disease, the test reports that with 99 percent accuracy, and if the patient does not have the disease, the test reports that with 95 percent accuracy; also, suppose that the incidence of the disease is rare—only 0.1 percent of the population has the disease:

$$P(\text{No disease} \mid \text{Test positive}) =$$
$$\frac{P(\text{Test positive} \mid \text{No disease}) \times P(\text{No disease})}{P(\text{Test positive} \mid \text{No disease}) \times P(\text{No disease}) + P(\text{Test positive} \mid \text{Disease}) \times P(\text{Disease})}$$
$$\frac{0.050 \times 0.999}{0.050 \times 0.999 + 0.990 \times 0.001} = 0.981$$

A tree diagram (Exhibit 7.12) helps to illustrate this problem.

The test results are positive 0.00099 + 0.04995 = 0.05094 of the time; 0.04995 of that time, the person does not have the disease. Therefore, the

EXHIBIT 7.12
Tree Diagram—
Bayes' Theorem
Example

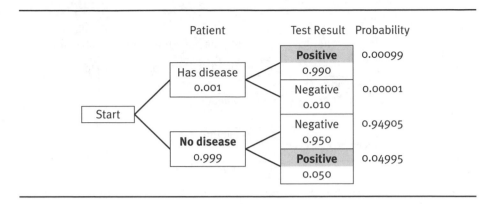

probability that a person does not have the disease, although the test for the disease was positive, is:

$$\frac{0.04995}{0.05094} = 0.981, \text{ or } 98.1 \text{ percent}$$

Conditional probability and Bayes' theorem are often used in healthcare in clinical studies to test drug interactions. In addition, conditional probability is useful in predicting outcomes based on demographics.

Confidence Intervals and Hypothesis Testing

Central Limit Theorem

Central limit theorem
A theory demonstrating that as the sample size from a population becomes sufficiently large, the sampling distribution of the means will approach normality, no matter the distribution of the original variable.

The **central limit theorem** states that as the sample size from a population becomes sufficiently large, the sampling distribution of the mean will approach normality, no matter the distribution of the original variable. Additionally, the mean of the sampling distribution is equal to the mean of the population and the standard deviation of the sampling distribution of the mean approaches $\sigma/\sqrt{n}$, where σ is the standard deviation of the population and n is the sample size. This means that if a sample is taken from *any* distribution, the mean of the sample will follow a normal distribution with mean $= \mu$ and standard deviation $\sigma/\sqrt{n}$, commonly called the standard error of the mean ($s_{\bar{x}}$ or SE). This is extremely valuable because data that follow the normal distribution have parameters that are easier to understand than those of data with non-normal distribution.

Confidence interval (CI)
The probability that a population parameter falls between two values.

The central limit theorem can be used to determine a **confidence interval (CI)** for the true mean of the population. If the standard deviation of the population is known, a CI for the mean would be:

$$\overline{x} - z_{\alpha/2} \times \sigma_{\overline{x}} \le \mu \le \overline{x} + z_{\alpha/2} \times \sigma_{\overline{x}}$$

$$\overline{x} - z_{\alpha/2} \times \frac{\sigma}{\sqrt{n}} \le \mu \le \overline{x} + z_{\alpha/2} \times \frac{\sigma}{\sqrt{n}}$$

where $z_{\alpha/2}$ is the z-value associated with an upper- or lower-tail probability of α. In other words, to obtain a 95 percent CI, the upper- and lower-tail probabilities would be 0.025 (2.5 percent in the upper tail and 2.5 percent in the lower tail, leaving 95 percent in the middle), and the associated z-value is 1.95 (2 is commonly used). Note that increasing the sample size will tighten the confidence limits.

If the population standard deviation (σ) is unknown, the sample standard deviation (s) is used to estimate the standard error of the mean:

$$\overline{x} - z_{\alpha/2} \times \sigma_{\overline{x}} \le \mu \le \overline{x} + z_{\alpha/2} \times \sigma_{\overline{x}}$$

$$\overline{x} - z_{\alpha/2} \times \frac{s}{\sqrt{n}} \le \mu \le \overline{x} + z_{\alpha/2} \times \frac{s}{\sqrt{n}}$$

Small samples (generally, $n < 30$) do not follow a z-distribution; they follow a t-distribution. The t distribution has greater probability in the tails of the distribution than a z-distribution and varies according to the degrees of freedom, $n - 1$, where n is the sample size. Therefore, for small samples, the following equation is used:

$$\overline{x} - t_{\alpha/2} \times \frac{s}{\sqrt{n}} \le \mu \le \overline{x} + t_{\alpha/2} \times \frac{s}{\sqrt{n}}$$

For example, if the waiting time for a random sample of 16 patients was measured and their mean wait time was found to be 10 minutes with a standard deviation of 2 minutes, a 95 percent CI for the true value of wait time would be:

$$\overline{x} - t_{\alpha/2} \times \frac{s}{\sqrt{n}} \le \mu \le \overline{x} + t_{\alpha/2} \times \frac{s}{\sqrt{n}}$$

$$10 - 2.13 \times \frac{2}{\sqrt{16}} \le \mu \le 10 + 2.13 \times \frac{2}{\sqrt{16}}$$

$$10 - 1.06 \le \mu \le 10 + 1.06$$

$$8.94 \le \mu \le 11.06$$

Because this is a 95 percent confidence interval, this means that 19 out of 20 times, if a similar sample is taken, the CI obtained would include the true value of the mean wait time. To an analyst, this would indicate that under similar situations, the expectation is that the mean value would be between 8.94 and 11.06.

If a larger sample of 49 patients had been taken and their mean wait time was found to be 10 minutes, with a standard deviation of 1 minute, a 95 percent CI for the true value of the mean would be:

$$\bar{x} - z_{\alpha/2} \times \frac{s}{\sqrt{n}} \leq \mu \leq \bar{x} + z_{\alpha/2} \times \frac{s}{\sqrt{n}}$$

$$10 - 2 \times \frac{1}{\sqrt{49}} \leq \mu \leq 10 + 2 \times \frac{1}{\sqrt{49}}$$

$$10 - 0.3 \leq \mu \leq 10 + 0.3$$

$$9.7 \leq \mu \leq 10.3$$

Hypothesis Testing

In the previous section, a range of likely values for the population parameter of interest could be obtained by computing a CI. This interval could be used to determine whether claims about the value were correct by determining whether the CI captured the claimed value. In the wait time example, if it was claimed that wait time for most patients was eight minutes, this claim would be rejected based on the information obtained. However, if it was claimed that the mean wait time was ten minutes, the study would support this claim. **Hypothesis testing** is a formal way of testing such claims and is closely related to CIs.

Hypothesis testing The process of testing a statistical distribution parameter against that of another distribution parameter to assess if statistical differences exist in the data.

In hypothesis testing there is a belief, called the null hypothesis; a competing belief, called the alternate hypothesis; and a decision rule for evaluating the beliefs. In the wait time example, these would be:

Belief, or H_o: $\mu = 8$ minutes

Alternative belief, or H_a: $\mu \neq 8$ minutes

Decision rule: If $t \geq t^*$, reject the null hypothesis, where $t = (\bar{x} - \mu)/\sigma_{\bar{x}}$, the number of standard errors away from the mean, and t^* is the test statistic based on the desired confidence level and the degrees of freedom. If t is greater than t^*, finding a sample mean that is different from the true value of the mean would be unlikely; therefore, the belief about the true value of the mean (H_o) would be rejected. In the wait time example, t^* for a 95 percent CI with 15 degrees of freedom (sample size of 16) is 2.13. Therefore, $t = (\bar{x} - \mu)/\sigma_{\bar{x}} = (10 - 8)/0.5$, and $t \geq t^*$. The belief (H_a) would be rejected.

More typically, hypothesis testing is used to determine whether an effect exists. For instance, a pharmaceutical company wants to evaluate a new headache remedy by administering it to a collection of subjects. If the new headache remedy appears to relieve headaches, it is important to be able to state with confidence that the effect was really due to the new remedy, not just chance. Most headaches eventually go away on their own, and some headaches (or some peoples' headaches) are difficult to relieve, so the company can make two kinds of mistakes: incorrectly concluding that the remedy works when in fact it does not, and failing to notice that an effective remedy works. The null hypothesis (H_0) is that the remedy does not relieve headaches; the alternative hypothesis (H_a) is that it does.

Type I and Type II Errors

A **Type I, or α, error** occurs if the company concludes that the remedy works when in fact it does not. A **Type II, or β, error** occurs if the remedy is effective but the company concludes that it is not.

Hypothesis testing is similar to determination of guilt within the US criminal court system. In a trial, it is assumed that the defendant is innocent (the null hypothesis) until proven guilty (the alternative hypothesis); evidence is presented (data), and the jury decides whether the defendant is guilty or not guilty based on proof (decision rule) that has to be beyond a reasonable doubt (level of confidence). A jury does not declare the defendant innocent, just not guilty.

If the defendant is really innocent but the jury decides that she is guilty, then it has sent an innocent person to jail (Type I error). If a defendant is really guilty, but the jury finds him not guilty, a criminal is free (Type II error). In the US criminal court system, a Type I error is considered more important than a Type II error, so a Type I error is protected against to the detriment of a Type II error. This is analogous to hypothesis testing (Kenney 1988), as illustrated in Exhibit 7.13.

Usually, the null hypothesis is that something is not present, that a treatment has no effect, or that no difference exists between the effects of different treatments. The alternative hypothesis is that some effect is present, that a treatment has an effect, or that there exists a difference in the effects of different treatments. Assuming the null hypothesis is true should make it possible to compute the probability that the test rejects the null hypothesis, given that it is true (Type I error.) The decision rule is based on the prob-

Type I, or α, error
The probability of rejecting the null hypothesis when it is true.

Type II, or β, error
The probability of accepting the null hypothesis when it is false.

Assessment or guess	Reality	
	Innocent	Guilty
Innocent	—	Type II error
Guilty	Type I error	—

EXHIBIT 7.13
Type I and Type II Error—Court System Example

EXHIBIT 7.14
Type I and
Type II Error—
Clinic Wait Time
Example

	Reality	
Assessment or guess	Wait times at the two clinics are the same ($\mu_1 = \mu_2$)	Wait times at the two clinics are **not** the same ($\mu_1 \neq \mu_2$)
Wait times at the two clinics are the same ($\mu_1 = \mu_2$)		Type II error
Wait times at the two clinics are **not** the same ($\mu_1 \neq \mu_2$)	Type I error	

ability of obtaining a sample mean (or other statistic) given the hypothesized mean (or other statistic).

A comparison of wait time at two different clinics, on two different days, or during two different periods would use the following hypothesis test:

$$H_o: \mu_1 - \mu_2$$
$$H_a: \mu_1 \neq \mu_2$$

Decision rule: If $t \geq t^*$, reject H_o

(Note that t^* is usually determined with statistical software using the Satherwaite approximation because the two-sample test statistic does not exactly follow a t-distribution.) Exhibit 7.14 illustrates the errors associated with this example.

Equal Variance t-Test

If the wait time at two different clinics were of interest, wait time for a random sample of patients from each clinic might be measured. If wait time for a sample of 10 patients (for explanatory purposes only) from each clinic were measured and it was determined that Clinic A had a mean wait time of 12 minutes, Clinic B had a mean wait time of 10 minutes, and both had a standard deviation of 1.5 minutes, the standard deviations could be pooled and the distribution *would* follow a t-distribution with ($n_1 + n_2 - 2$) degrees of freedom. At a 95 percent confidence level,

$$t = \frac{(\bar{x}_1 - \bar{x}_2) - (\mu_1 - \mu_2)}{s_p \sqrt{\frac{1}{n_1} + \frac{1}{n_2}}} \quad \text{where } s_p = \sqrt{\frac{(n_1 - 1)s_1^2 + (n_2 - 1)s_2^2}{n_1 + n_2 - 2}} = 1.5$$

$$\frac{(12 - 10) - (0)}{1.5\sqrt{\frac{1}{10} + \frac{1}{10}}} = \frac{2}{0.67} = 2.99 \geq t^* = 2.10$$

Therefore, this test would reject H_o, the belief that the mean wait time at the two clinics is the same.

Alternatively, a 95 percent CI for the difference in the two means could be found:

$$(\bar{x}_1 - \bar{x}_2) \pm t^* \times s_p \sqrt{\frac{1}{n_1} + \frac{1}{n_2}}$$
$$2 - (2.10 \times 0.67) \leq \mu_1 - \mu_2 \leq 2 + (2.10 \times 0.67)$$
$$0.6 \leq \mu_1 - \mu_2 \leq 3.4$$

Because the interval does not contain zero, the wait time for the two clinics is not the same.

Statistical software provides the *p*-value of this test. The *p*-value of a statistical significance test represents the probability of obtaining values of the test statistic that are equal to or greater than the observed test statistic. For the wait time example, the *p*-value is 0.015, meaning that H_o would be rejected with a confidence level of up to 98.5 percent, or that zero would not be contained in a 98.5 percent CI for the mean. Smaller *p*-values cause rejection of the null hypothesis. *T*-Tests can also be used to examine the mean difference between paired samples and can be performed when the standard deviations of the means differ. (See the companion website for more information on these types of *t*-tests.)

www.ache.org/books/OpsManagement2

Proportions

Recall the example in which staffing levels at two clinics were compared.

$$H_o: \pi_1 - \pi_2$$
$$H_a: \pi_1 \neq \pi_2$$
Decision rule: If $z \geq z^*$, reject H_o

The proportion of nurses at Clinic A was $12/20 = 0.60$, and the proportion of nurses at Clinic B was $10/20 = 0.50$. The standard error of the difference in sample proportions is

$$\sqrt{\frac{p(1-p)}{n_1} + \frac{p(1-p)}{n_2}}$$
$$\text{where } p = \frac{n_1 p_1 + n_2 p_2}{n_1 + n_2} = \frac{20(0.6) + (20)0.5}{40} = 0.55$$

At a 95 percent confidence level,

$$z = \frac{(p_1 - p_2) - (\pi_1 - \pi_2)}{\sqrt{\dfrac{p(1-p)}{n_1} + \dfrac{p(1-p)}{n_2}}} = \frac{(0.60 - 0.50) - (0)}{\sqrt{\dfrac{(0.55)(0.45)}{20} + \dfrac{(0.55)(0.45)}{20}}}$$

$$= \frac{0.10}{0.157} = 0.64 < t^* = 1.96$$

Therefore, H_o could not be rejected, and there could be no difference in the proportion of nurses at each clinic.

A CI for a proportion can be found from the following:

$$p - z_{\alpha/2} \times \sigma_p \le \pi \le p + z_{\alpha/2} \times \sigma_p \text{ where } \sigma_{\hat{p}} = \sqrt{\frac{p(1-p)}{n}}$$

$$p - z_{\alpha/2} \times \sqrt{\frac{p(1-p)}{n}} \le \pi \le p + z_{\alpha/2} \times \sqrt{\frac{p(1-p)}{n}}$$

A 95 percent CI for the difference in the two proportions of nurses is

$$(p_1 - p_2) \pm z \times \sqrt{\frac{p(1-p)}{n_1} + \frac{p(1-p)}{n_2}}$$

$$0.10 - (1.96 \times 0.157) \le \pi_1 - \pi_2 \le 0.10 + (1.96 \times 0.157)$$

$$-0.2 \le \pi_1 - \pi_2 \le 0.41$$

Statistical significance
The differences in two parameters of two data sets are large enough to reject the null hypothesis using hypothesis testing.

Practical significance
The differences in the parameters of two data sets are large enough to be meaningful for the person or organization studying the situation whether or not it is statistically significant.

Because the interval contains zero, the proportion of nurses at the two clinics may not be different. The p-value for this test is 0.53; therefore, H_o would not be rejected.

Practical Versus Statistical Significance

Distinguishing between **statistical significance** and **practical significance** is important. Statistical significance is related to the ability of the test to reject the null hypothesis, whereas practical significance looks at whether the difference is large enough to be of value in a practical sense. If the sample size is large enough, statistical significance can be found for small differences when there is limited or no practical importance associated with the finding.

For instance, in the clinic wait time example, if the mean wait time at Clinic A was 10.1 minutes, the mean wait time at Clinic B was 10.0 minutes, and the standard deviation for both was 1 minute, the difference would not be significant if the sample size at both clinics was 10; if, however, the sample size was 1,000, the difference would be statistically significant. The statistical results from Minitab (a statistical software package) for this example are shown

EXHIBIT 7.15
Statistical
Significance of
Differences—
Minitab Output
for Clinic Wait
Time Example

Two-Sample *T*-Test and CI

Sample	N	Mean	SD	SEM
1	10	10.10	1.00	0.32
2	10	10.00	1.00	0.32

Difference = $\mu_1 - \mu_2$
Estimate for difference: 0.100000
95% CI for difference: (−0.839561, 1.039561)
T-test of difference = 0 (vs not =): *T*-value = 0.22
P-value = 0.826 df = 18
Both use Pooled SD = 1.0000

Two-Sample *T*-Test and CI

Sample	N	Mean	SD	SEM
1	1000	10.10	1.00	0.032
2	1000	10.00	1.00	0.032

Difference = $\mu_1 - \mu_2$
Estimate for difference: 0.100000
95% CI for difference: (0.012295, 0.187705)
T-test of difference = 0 (vs not =): *T*-value = 2.24
P-value = 0.025 df = 1998
Both use Pooled SD = 1.0000

in Exhibit 7.15. Tests for statistical significance should not be applied blindly—the practical significance of a difference of 0.1 minute is a judgment call.

Simple Linear Regression

Regression is a statistical tool used to model the association of a variable with one or more explanatory variables. The variables are typically metric, although there are ways to analyze categorical variables using regression. The relationship(s) can be described using an equation.

Simple linear regression is the simplest type of regression. The equation representing the relationship between two variables is $Y = \beta X + \alpha + \varepsilon$. Most everyone will remember $Y = mX + b$ from high school. In statistics, α is used for the intercept (the b from high school), β signifies the slope (the

Simple linear regression
An equation that relates two variables using a slope and an intercept in a linear fashion.

EXHIBIT 7.16
Data for
Regression
Example:
Relationship
Between
Number of
Dependents
and Yearly
Healthcare
Expense

Number of Dependents	Annual Healthcare Expense ($1,000)
0	3
1	2
2	6
3	7
4	7

m from high school; in statistics *m* or *μ* represents the mean, so a different variable name is used), and *ε* is the error.

A simple example will help to illustrate the concept of regression. Assume that the relationship between number of dependents and yearly healthcare expense was of interest and the data in Exhibit 7.16 were collected (for explanatory purposes only, as a larger data set would be needed for a true regression analysis).

First, to visually examine the nature of the relationship between the variables, a scatter plot of the data (Exhibit 7.17) would be produced. From the scatter plot, it appears that a linear relationship exists—a line could be drawn that best represents the relationship between the two variables.

The best model would have the smallest total absolute error. Because absolute values are mathematically intractable, the errors are squared instead. The best-fitting line has a minimum sum of squared error.

EXHIBIT 7.17
Scatter Plot—
Number of
Dependents
vs. Annual
Healthcare
Costs

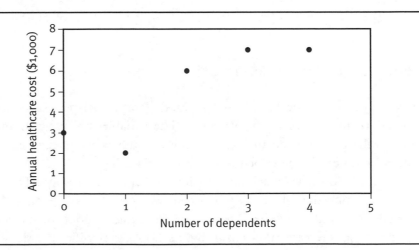

X	Y	$\hat{Y} = 1(X) + 3$	e^2	$\hat{Y} = 1.3(X) + 3$	e^2	$\hat{Y} = 0(X) + 5$	e^2
0	3	3	0	2.4	0.36	5	4
1	2	4	4	3.7	2.89	5	9
2	6	5	1	5.0	1.00	5	1
3	7	6	1	6.3	0.49	5	4
4	7	7	0	7.6	0.36	5	4
Σ			6		5.10		22

EXHIBIT 7.18
Sum of Squared Errors Associated with the Various Linear Models

The line $\hat{Y} = 1.3(X) + 2.4$ has the lowest squared error for the data (Exhibit 7.18).

Interpretation

The earlier linear model is interpreted as follows. The slope of the line indicates that with each additional dependent the annual cost of healthcare rises by $1,300 on average; according to the intercept, when there are no dependents the annual cost of healthcare is $2,400. If there were no information, where $X = 0$ (no data), the intercept would not be a meaningful number.

Coefficient of Determination and Correlation Coefficient

The next question is, How good is the model? This measure of how well the model fits the data is called the **coefficient of determination** (r^2). Note that this is not a statistical test, but rather a measure of the percentage of error explained by the model. The square root of this number is called the **correlation coefficient** (r). A negative correlation coefficient indicates a negative slope, and a positive correlation coefficient indicates a positive slope. The correlation coefficient is a measure of the linear relationship between two variables, with a value of one indicating perfect correlation and a value of zero indicating no relationship. (Refer to Exhibit 7.19 for some scatter plots and their correlation coefficients.)

Coefficient of determination
The measure of how well a model fits the data.

Correlation coefficient
A measure of the linear relationship between two variables.

The coefficient of determination (r^2) measures the percentage of variance explained in (Y) using the (X) variable. Examining Exhibit 7.20, the $r^2 = 0.768$, which could be interpreted as 77 percent of the variance in Annual Healthcare Expense (Y variable), can be explained using Number of Dependents (X variable). The "best" value a model can achieve is 100 percent of the variance explained. But is 77 percent a "good" value? The answer depends on many factors. A number closer to 100 percent is ideal, but if your sample size is sufficiently large, finding a variable that explains 25 percent of the variance could be helpful.

EXHIBIT 7.19
Scatter Plot
with Possible
Relationship
Lines

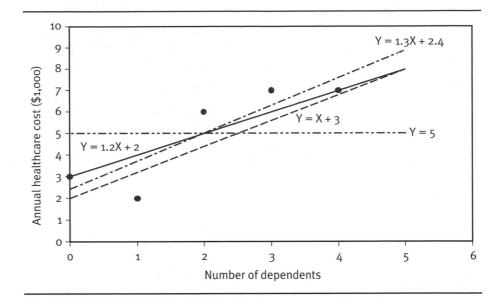

Problems with Correlation Coefficients

The coefficient of determination and the correlation coefficient are both measures of the *linear relationship* between two variables. A scatter plot of the two variables should always be examined when initially evaluating the appropriateness of a model. Statistical techniques for judging the appropriateness of the model are discussed later in this chapter.

Does a low r^2 mean there is no relationship between two variables? No. Exhibit 7.21 illustrates two cases (1 and 2) in which r^2 and r are both zero. In case 1, there is no relationship; in case 2, there is a relationship, just not a *linear* relationship. The relationship can be perfectly captured with the equation $Y = \alpha + \beta_1 X + \beta_2 X_2$, a curve or quadratic relationship. Later in the chapter, curve-type relationships are discussed. A low r^2 may also mean that other variables needed to explain the outcome variable are "missing" from the model.

Does a reasonable or high r^2 mean the model is a good fit to the data? No. Exhibit 7.21 illustrates several cases in which the model is not a good fit to the data. The r^2 and r can be heavily influenced by outliers, as in cases 4 and 6. In case 5, a better model would be a curve. Always look at the scatter plot of the data.

EXHIBIT 7.20
Regression
Output for
Healthcare
Expense
Example

SUMMARY OUTPUT

Regression Statistics	
Multiple R	0.8765
R Square	0.7682
Adjusted R Square	0.6909
Standard Error	0.8790
Observations	5

	Coefficients
Intercept	−0.9545
Y—$1000 Annual Health care Expense	0.5909

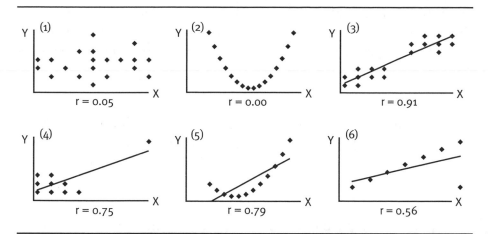

EXHIBIT 7.21
Low and High r and r^2 Example Plots

Does a high r^2 mean that *useful* predictions will be obtained with the model? No. Remember the previous discussion of practical and statistical significance. Finally, does a high r^2 mean that there is a causal relationship between the variables? No—correlation is not causation. The observed correlation between two variables might be due to the action of a third, unobserved variable. For example, Yule (1926) found a high positive correlation between yearly suicides and membership in the Church of England. However, membership in the Church of England did not *cause* suicides.

Statistical Measures of Model Fit

If there is no linear relationship between the two variables, the slope of the best-fitting line will be zero. This idea underlies the statistical tests for the "goodness of fit" of the model.

F-test

The F-test is a hypothesis test of whether all β values in the model $Y = \alpha + \beta X + \varepsilon$ are equal to zero. In the case of simple linear regression, there is only one β, and this is a test of whether β is zero.

$$H_0: \text{all } \beta \text{ values} = 0$$
$$H_a: \text{all } \beta \text{ values} \neq 0$$

Decision rule: If $F^* \geq F_{(1-\alpha;\ 1;\ n-2)}$, reject H_0

$$F^* = \frac{\text{Mean square regression}}{\text{Mean square error}} = \frac{MSR}{MSE} = \frac{SSR/1}{SSE/n-2}$$

If the two variables are related, the regression line will explain most of the variance, and SSR will be large in comparison to SSE. Therefore, large values of F^* imply that there is a relationship and the slope of the line is not equal to zero.

t-Test

For simple linear regression, the t-test will give the same answer as the F-test. The t-test is a hypothesis test of whether a particular $\beta = 0$.

$$H_o: \beta = 0$$
$$H_a: \beta \neq 0$$

Decision rule: If $t^* \geq F_{(1-\alpha;\, 1;\, n-2)}$, reject H_o
$$t^* = b/s_b$$

Alternatively, a CI for β would be:

$$b - t_{(1-\alpha;\, n-2)}s_b \leq \beta \leq b - t_{(1-\alpha;\, n-2)}s_b$$

If the interval contains zero, H_o can be rejected. Statistical software will provide these tests for linear regression as well as r and R^2.

Assumptions of Linear Regression

Linear regression is based on several principal assumptions:

- The dependent and independent variables are linearly related.
- The errors associated with the model are not serially correlated.
- The errors are normally distributed and have constant variance.

If these assumptions are violated, the resulting model will be misleading.

Various plots (and statistical tests) can be used to detect such problems. These plots are usually provided by the software and should be examined for evidence of violations of the assumptions of regression. A scatter plot of the observed versus predicted value should be symmetrically distributed around a diagonal line. A scatter plot of residuals versus predicted value should be symmetrically distributed around a horizontal line. A normal probability plot of the residuals should fall closely around a diagonal line.

If there is evidence that the assumptions of linear regression are being violated, a transformation of the dependent or independent variables may fix the problem. Alternatively, one or two extreme values may be causing the problems. Such values should be scrutinized closely: Are they *genuine* (i.e., not the result of data entry errors), are they *explainable*, are *similar events* likely to occur again in the future, and how *influential* are they in the model-fitting results? If the values are merely errors, or if they can be explained as unique events not likely to be repeated, there may be cause to remove them. In some cases, however, the extreme values in the data may provide the most useful information about values of some of the coefficients or provide the most realistic guide to the magnitudes of prediction errors.

Transformations

If the variables are not linearly related or the assumptions of regression are violated, the variables can be transformed to possibly produce a better model. **Transformations** are applied to ensure that the model is accurate and reliable. If a person jogged to her doctor's appointment, she would need to wait before having her blood pressure measured if a high reading would result in a diagnosis of hypertension. Blood pressure values obtained immediately after exercising are unsuitable for detecting hypertension; the reason for waiting is not to avoid the diagnosis of hypertension but to ensure that a high reading can be believed. It is the same with transformations.

Transformation
The process of converting a variable by linear regression into a format that is more readily usable.

Deciding which transformation is best is often an exercise in trial and error in which several transformations are tried to see which one provides the best model. Possible transformations include square root, square, cube, log, and inverse. If the data are transformed, this needs to be accounted for when interpreting the findings. For example, imagine that the original variable was measured in days but, to improve the model, an inverse transformation was applied. Here, it would be important to remember that the lower the value for this transformed variable (1/days), the higher the value of the original variable (days). If the dependent variable is binary (0/1), the assumptions of regression are violated. The logit transformation of the variable, $\ln[p/(1-p)]$, is used in this case.

Conclusion

An outline for analysis is shown in Exhibit 7.22, with its relationships to the plan-do-check-act (PDCA) process for continuous improvement (Chapters 8 and 9), the define-measure-analyze-improve-control (DMAIC) process of Six Sigma (Chapter 8), and the key elements of decision making (Chapter 6).

Which Technique to Use

The statistical tool or technique chosen to analyze the data depends on the type of data collected. Many statistical tests are not included in this chapter but are included in the supplemental section on our companion website.

www.ache.org/books/UpsManagement2

EXHIBIT 7.22
Outline for
Analysis

	PDCA	DMAIC	Key Element
1. Define the problem/question.	Plan	Define	Frame
2. Determine what data will be needed to address the problem/question.	Plan	Define	Frame
3. Collect the data.	Do	Measure	Gather
4. Graph the data.	Do	Analyze	Gather
5. Analyze the data using the appropriate tool.	Do	Analyze	Conclude
6. Fix the problem.	Do	Improve	Conclude
7. Evaluate the effectiveness of the solution.	Check	Control	Learn
8. Start again.	Plan	Define	Frame

Discussion Questions

1. Discuss a situation from your personal experience in which a study had bad data. What were the problems with data collection and accuracy? How were the data collected, and what were the reported problems with data collection?
2. John Allen Paulos (http://abcnews.go.com/Technology/WhosCounting/) and Jordan Ellenberg (www.slate.com/authors .jordan_ellenberg.html) both write on numbers, statistics, and probability. Read an article of interest to you and discuss.
3. Discuss how you would redesign a report you receive at work to make it more useful for you. Would a visual presentation of the data be helpful? How would you present the data?
4. Discuss the difference between correlation and causation.
5. Discuss the difference between statistical and practical significance.
6. The balanced scorecard, Six Sigma, Lean, and simulation employ many of the tools, techniques, and tests found in this chapter. Discuss how, where, and why a particular tool would be used for each.

Chapter Exercises

The following problems use data from three data sets available on the companion website. Each data set contains the raw data as well as reduced or reorganized data for ease of analysis.

1. Think of a question, problem, or issue in your organization. Design a study to address the issue. Be sure to discuss how you would address all aspects of data collection. How would you collect the data? How could you make sure that the data are representative of the actual situation?

2. Using the data in Health Insurance Coverage.xls, compare insurance coverage in Minnesota to coverage in Texas.
   a. Analyze the validity of the data.
   b. Produce a histogram to compare the two states. Do Minnesota and Texas appear to have similar coverage types?
   c. Produce a Pareto chart for the two states. What does this chart indicate?
   d. What is the probability that a resident of Minnesota or Texas will be uninsured? Insured? Insured by Medicare or Medicaid?
   e. What is the 95 percent CI for the proportion of uninsured in Texas? In Minnesota? What is the 99 percent CI?
   f. What is the 99 percent CI for the difference in the two proportions?
   g. Set up and perform a hypothesis test to determine if the proportion of uninsured differs at a 95 percent confidence level between the two states.
   h. Comment on the statement, "Living in Texas causes more people to be uninsured." What other information might be helpful here?

3. Use the data in the World Health.xls to analyze worldwide life expectancy. Answer the following questions:
   a. Construct a histogram, dot plot, and normal probability plot of CIA life expectancy at birth (years), total for 2006. What do these graphs indicate? Is this random variable normally distributed?
   b. Construct a graph of CIA life expectancy—total, male, and female. What do these graphs show?
   c. Determine the mean, median, mode, range, variance, and standard deviation for CIA life expectancy—total, male, and female. What do these numbers show?
   d. What is the 95 percent CI for mean life expectancy of males and females? The 99 percent CI?
   e. What is the 99 percent CI for the difference in the two means?
   f. Set up and perform a hypothesis test to determine if life expectancy for males and females differs at a 95 percent confidence level.
   g. Construct histogram and normal probability plots for CIA gross domestic product, televisions, and hospital beds. Do these random variables appear normally distributed?

h. Perform three separate simple linear regression analyses for CIA gross domestic product, televisions, and hospital beds with CIA life expectancy total. Interpret your results. (Note: Excel will not perform a regression analysis when data are missing. The workbook "World Health Regression" has eliminated countries for which there are no data on life expectancy. You may need to sort the data and run the analysis only on complete data.)

i. Discuss the following statement: "World life expectancy could be increased if everyone in the world owned a television."

j. Look at *x-y* scatter plots for each pair of variables in (h). Do the relationships appear to be linear? Would a transformation of the *x* variable improve the regression?

QUALITY MANAGEMENT: FOCUS ON SIX SIGMA

Operations Management in Action

In late 2008, The Joint Commission initiated the Center for Transforming Healthcare to help hospitals learn how to correctly apply quality tools, such as Six Sigma, to improve overall quality and safety. Eight hospitals agreed to be part of the project. According to the findings:

> Teams from The Joint Commission and the eight hospitals first agreed how to measure hand hygiene, developed the measurement system, and proved its reliability. Applying the measurement system produced the first discovery: Baseline hand hygiene performance at the hospitals in April 2009 was a disappointingly low 48 percent.

> The next crucial step was to understand the exact causes of poor hand hygiene. Each hospital team used tools used in Six Sigma programs to find every important cause of failure and validated its importance statistically. This led to the second discovery: There were 15 different causes of poor hand hygiene. Some of the most frequent causes were misleading data suggesting that performance was much better than it actually was; inconvenient placement of dispensers for alcohol hand rub; gaps in training of healthcare workers in hand hygiene; and a poorly developed safety culture, which did not support people who attempted to prevent others from failing to wash their hands. Each cause requires a different, specific intervention to improve hand hygiene.

> The third discovery came when the teams examined the distribution of the causes whose significance they had validated across the eight hospitals: Each

hospital had a different set of important causes. The implications of this finding are important. A time-honored method of improving healthcare is the replication of "best practices."

Using this approach, the eight hospitals reported in August 2010 that their aggregate performance for hand hygiene had risen to 81 percent.

This case highlights several important concepts that are critical to the Six Sigma and quality management approach. Effective quality management systems use data to make decisions about improving quality. Evidence-based medicine uses the best available clinical research to help medical practitioners make effective decisions.

In this operations management case, several factors were found to be important to hand hygiene; however, the causes of the problems varied by hospital. The evidence indicated that the problems are not universal, and blindly applying the data from one hospital to another may not improve the situation at all. In addition, several of the beliefs about the causes of poor hand hygiene and level of effectiveness of the hand hygiene program were dispelled by the data. The data demonstrated the actual level of hygiene was much lower than the perceived level of hand hygiene. Finally, by using the data to support the action plan, the hospitals were able to demonstrate a significant improvement. The remainder of this chapter will highlight these elements of Six Sigma in greater detail.

SOURCE: Copyrighted and published by Project HOPE/Health Affairs as Mark R. Chassin and Jerod M. Loeb, "The Ongoing Quality Improvement Journey: Next Stop, High Reliability," 2011. *Health Affairs 30* (4): 559–68. The published article is archived and available online at www.healthaffairs.org.

Overview

Quality management became imperative for the manufacturing sector in the 1970s and 1980s, for service organizations in the 1980s and 1990s, and, finally, for the healthcare industry in the 1990s, culminating with a 1999 Institute of Medicine (IOM) report, *To Err Is Human*, that detailed alarming statistics on the number of people harmed by the healthcare system and recommended major improvements in quality as related to patient safety. The report recognized the need for systemic changes and called for innovative solutions to ensure improvement in the quality of healthcare.

The healthcare industry is facing increasing pressure not only to increase quality but also to reduce costs. This chapter provides an introduction to quality management tools and techniques that are being successfully used by healthcare organizations. The major topics covered include

- defining quality;
- the costs of quality;
- quality programs, including ISO 9000, the Baldrige criteria, and Six Sigma (note that Six Sigma programs are different from Six Sigma tools);
- Six Sigma tools and techniques, including the define-measure-analyze-improve-control (DMAIC) process, seven basic quality tools, statistical process control (SPC), and process capability; and
- other quality tools and techniques, including quality function deployment (QFD), Taguchi methods, and poka-yoke.

After completing this chapter, readers should have a basic understanding of quality, quality programs, and quality tools, enabling application of the tools and techniques to begin improving quality in their organizations.

Defining Quality

Although most people would agree that ensuring quality in healthcare is of the utmost importance, many would disagree on exactly what "quality" means. The supplying organization's perspective includes performance (or design) quality and conformance quality. Performance quality includes the features and attributes designed into the product or service. Conformance quality is concerned with how well the product or service conforms to desired goals or specifications.

Garvin (1987) defines eight dimensions of product quality from the customer's perspective:

1. *Performance*: operating characteristics
2. *Features*: supplements to the basic characteristics of the product
3. *Reliability*: the probability that the product will work over time
4. *Conformance*: product conformance to established standards
5. *Durability*: length of time that the product will continue to operate
6. *Serviceability*: ease of repair
7. *Esthetics*: beauty related to the look or feel of the product
8. *Perceived value*: perceptions of the product

Parasuraman, Zeithaml, and Berry (1988) define five dimensions of service quality:

1. *Tangibles*: physical facilities, equipment, and appearance of personnel
2. *Reliability*: ability to perform promised service dependably and accurately

3. *Responsiveness*: willingness to help customers and provide prompt service
4. *Assurance*: knowledge and courtesy of employees and their ability to inspire trust and confidence
5. *Empathy*: care and individualized attention

From the healthcare perspective, most would agree that the elements of quality surround the patient. The 2001 IOM report *Crossing the Quality Chasm* outlines six dimensions of quality in healthcare: safe, effective, patient-centered, timely, efficient, and equitable. The Quality Assurance Project (2003) outlines nine dimensions of quality in healthcare: technical performance, access to services, effectiveness of care, efficiency of service delivery, interpersonal relations, continuity of services, safety, physical infrastructure and comfort, and choice.

Obviously, quality and its various dimensions may be viewed in many ways. The dimensions relevant to one organization or project may not be relevant to a different organization.

Cost of Quality

The costs of quality—or the costs of poor quality, according to Juran and Godfrey (1998)—are the costs associated with providing a poor-quality product or service. Crosby (1979) says that the **cost of quality** is "the expense of nonconformance—the cost of doing things wrong."

Cost of quality
The costs associated with producing poor-quality goods and services, including tangible costs, such as scrap and rejects, and intangible costs, such as lost customer goodwill.

Quality improvement initiatives and projects cannot be justified simply because "everyone is doing it," but rather must be justified on the basis of financial or societal benefits. Goldstein and Iossifova (2011) demonstrated that hospitals with significant financial resources were able to benefit greatly from the use of quality management practices. Fineberg (2012) notes that the potential annual excess cost from systemic waste in the United States healthcare system is more than $765 billion, including $210 billion in unnecessary services, $130 billion in inefficiently delivered services, $190 billion in excess administrative costs, $105 billion in excessively high prices, $55 billion in missed opportunities for disease prevention, and $75 billion in fraud. In all, these costs amount to approximately 30 percent of total health expenditures in the system. Problems such as poor quality of care, overtreatment, and administrative waste could account for as much as $1 trillion annually in costs that do not contribute to improving the health of the population.

According to Juran, the cost of quality is usually separated into four parts:

1. *External failure*: costs associated with failure after the customer receives the product or service (e.g., sentinel events, incorrect billing)
2. *Internal failure*: costs associated with failure before the customer receives the product or service (e.g., overtime for nurses because of treatment errors, re-inserting an IV several times)
3. *Appraisal*: costs associated with inspecting and evaluating the quality of supplies or the final product/service (e.g., X-ray costs associated with ensuring no surgical equipment was left inside patients, hiring a person to inspect supply cabinets to make sure the right equipment is in place)
4. *Prevention*: costs incurred to eliminate or minimize appraisal and failure costs (e.g., Six Sigma training costs, automated equipment for lab testing)

Often, the costs of prevention are seen as expenses while the other, less apparent costs of appraisal and failure are hidden in the system (Suver, Neumann, and Boles 1992). However, preventing quality problems is usually less costly than fixing quality failures. Striving for continuous improvement in quality can not only improve quality, it can also improve an organization's financial situation.

While many companies have used the costs of quality as a mechanism to categorize their overall quality costs, most companies use the costs of quality as a way of thinking about quality in the system. Particularly in healthcare, where providers are taught to save the patient at all costs, the costs related to that mentality can be extreme. For example, suppose a hospital has a sentinel event of a scope not being cleaned prior to surgery. As a result of this history, one of the MDs starts to clean his own scopes to make sure they are sterile prior to surgery. What are the costs associated with that doctor cleaning his own scope? While it may seem that the doctor is doing the right thing by cleaning the scope to ensure the quality of the surgery, how much of this expensive resource's time was spent on this activity? How many surgeries does the hospital lose as a result of the doctor not being available? In addition, the doctor may not be qualified to clean scopes; a lower-cost technician is often trained to do this job. The hospital administrator may say the budget has no room to hire a new technician to perform this task. These are all costs of poor quality. If the system had been designed correctly to begin with, the scopes would already be clean.

Changing employees' mindset to see the cost of poor quality can be a difficult task. However, it is essential if a continuous improvement program is going to survive in healthcare. Sometimes doing whatever it takes leads to workarounds and lower overall system quality.

Quality Programs

This book focuses on the Six Sigma methodology because of its popularity and demonstrated effectiveness, but there are other, equally valid programs for quality management and continuous improvement. ISO 9000 certification and the Baldrige criteria can provide a framework for organizational improvement. Although each of these programs or methodologies has a slightly different focus, their underlying principles are basically the same.

ISO 9000

The International Organization for Standardization (ISO) 9000 series (2006) is primarily concerned with ensuring that organizations maintain consistently high levels of quality. The ISO standards are process oriented and require evidence of outcome achievement. Many organizations require that their vendors be ISO certified, meaning that they have demonstrated to an accredited registrar (a certified third-party organization) compliance with the requirements specified in the standard(s). Organizations seeking certification must implement formal policies, processes, and procedures to ensure that the needs of their customers are being met. To do this, all aspects of their quality systems need to be documented, monitored (or audited), and controlled so that continuous improvements can be made.

ISO 9000:2000 provides a quality management system that takes into account the measures, settings, services, and functions of both clinical and administrative activities within the healthcare industry. ISO 9000-IWA1 provides basic definitions and guidelines that can help healthcare providers select and use the appropriate standard. ISO 9001:2000 standards are system requirements, whereas ISO 9004:2000 is a guideline that goes beyond the other standards to help organizations improve the efficiency of their operations.

The five sections of the ISO 9001:2000 standard are based on quality management principles and define what should be done to consistently provide products and services that meet customer requirements. Organizations must demonstrate appropriate application of the standards through extensive documentation. The five sections of the ISO 9001:2000 standard are:

1. *Quality management system.* The establishment and documentation of a quality management system, including quality policy, quality goals, and a system of control.
2. *Management responsibility.* Management must continually analyze, review, and improve the quality management system.

3. *Resource management.* Employees must be qualified and trained for the job they are doing. Other resources (facilities, equipment, support services) must be sufficient to produce quality products and services.

4. *Measurement, analysis, and improvement.* The organization will carry out inspection, testing, measurement, analysis, and improvement processes.

5. *Product realization.* The processes that produce the organization's product or service must be well controlled.

ISO 9000 provides a methodology and framework for ensuring that an organization has efficiently and effectively defined, organized, integrated, and synchronized its quality management system to optimize performance and ensure customer satisfaction. Dr. Paul M. Schyve (2000), senior vice president of The Joint Commission, believes that accreditation, ISO 9000, and the Baldrige criteria can complement and augment one another as part of a healthcare organization's overall efforts to achieve performance excellence.

Baldrige Criteria

The Malcolm Baldrige National Quality Award was established to recognize US organizations for their achievements in quality. The award has raised awareness about the importance of quality as a competitive priority and helped to disseminate best practices in achieving world-class quality by providing examples of how to achieve quality and performance excellence.

The Baldrige system (Baldrige National Quality Program 2005) focuses on continual improvement of key processes to deliver exceptional customer value. Customers are key to the Baldrige concept; however, employees are the ones who deliver that exceptional value to the customer, and the Baldrige system also places significant emphasis on building and retaining a skilled, motivated, and satisfied workforce. Finally, quality is not desired for quality's sake, but rather it is needed to drive business performance; the Baldrige criteria place almost 50 percent of their weight on outcomes. These outcomes include strategies that lead to improved market performance, increased market share, customer retention, and satisfaction. Organizations are encouraged to use financial information such as profit trends to analyze the connections to overall performance.

The Baldrige criteria consist of seven categories of excellence (Exhibit 8.1) and have been used by thousands of organizations as a self-assessment and improvement tool. Many organizations do not even apply for the award, but still use the framework as an internal assessment and improvement tool. Healthcare organizations that have received the award include the following (Baldrige Performance Excellence Program 2011).

EXHIBIT 8.1
Baldrige Criteria
for Performance
Excellence
Framework:
A Systems
Perspective

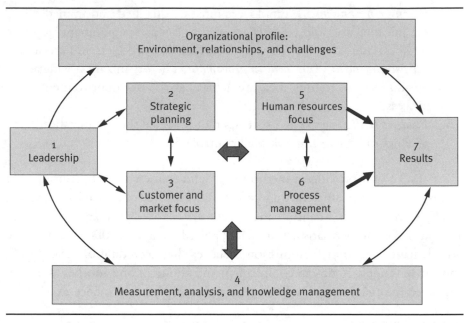

SOURCE: Baldrige National Quality Program (2006b).

- Henry Ford Health System, Detroit (2011)
- Schneck Medical Center, Indiana (2011)
- Advocate Good Samaritan Hospital, Illinois (2010)
- Heartland Health, Missouri (2009)

Six Sigma

Six Sigma began in the 1980s at Motorola as the organization's in-house quality improvement program. Six Sigma has since become the defining quality strategy for many organizations. GE has been widely seen as the company that has had the greatest success with Six Sigma programs. GE used Six Sigma as a mechanism to gain strategic advantages through quality.

Six Sigma has been defined as a philosophy, a methodology, a set of tools, and a goal. Critical to the success of Six Sigma is the focus of the program on business strategy with an emphasis on eliminating defects through removal of variance in business systems. The Six Sigma philosophy transforms the culture of the organization, and its methodology employs a project team–based approach to process improvement using the define-measure-analyze-improve-control (DMAIC) cycle. Six Sigma is composed of a set of quantitative and qualitative statistically based tools used to provide management with facts to allow improvement of an organization's performance. Finally, Six Sigma also represents a goal of no more than 3.4 defects per million opportunities (DPMOs).

Six Sigma programs can take many forms, depending on the organization, but the successful ones all share some common themes:

- Top management support for Six Sigma as a business strategy
- Extensive change management training to pave the way for a new way of conducting business
- Team-based projects for improvement that directly affect the organization's strategic success and financial health
- Extensive training at all levels of the organization in the methodology and use of tools and techniques
- Emphasis on the DMAIC approach and use of quantitative measures of project success

Strategy and Measurement

The success of Six Sigma programs hinges on the organization's ability to use the program as a technique for achieving strategic goals. When properly executed, Six Sigma uses a series of projects to help propel the organization's strategy forward. These projects are often internally focused, such as reducing overall patient length of stay, reducing the cost of inventory, and increasing accuracy and quality of various procedures. Many of these initiatives originate from the strategic dashboard and balanced scorecard discussed in Chapter 4. The balanced scorecard provides the measurement system that is used when choosing Six Sigma projects and assigning resources.

Culture

Six Sigma, like all other successful change initiatives, requires and supports cultural change within the organization. The culture of the organization can be thought of as its personality, made up of the assumptions, values, norms, and beliefs of the whole of the organization's members. It is evidenced by how tasks are performed, how problems are solved, and how employees interact with one another and the outside world. Leaders and employees of organizations both shape and are shaped by the culture of the organization. For any organization to achieve Six Sigma or 3.4 defects per million, the entire organization must create a mindset of continuous improvement. This mindset is the culture of the organization. Organizations that attempt to use Six Sigma but do not embrace the culture necessary to achieve it struggle in achieving long-term, sustainable results.

Leadership

To lead true change in any organization, top executives must have a sense of purpose for the organization and what it must achieve to be successful. However, there is a big difference between truly supporting a major organizational initiative and only vocally supporting the effort. The organization's leaders must provide human and financial resources to get the program launched to "hardwire" or embed the gains into the culture of the organization made during the continuous improvement journey. Perhaps the most critical element of the top leadership is to set targets for department supervisors, such as the chief of surgery and the director of primary care, and then hold those leaders accountable for achieving those targets. Without a core set of metrics for the organization, any Six Sigma effort will be limited in its ability to achieve success since the metrics provide the baseline from which comparison is made.

Organizational Infrastructure and Training

Successful Six Sigma initiatives require a high level of proficiency in the application of the method's qualitative and quantitative tools and techniques. To achieve this, Six Sigma initiatives involve an extensive amount of training at all levels of the organization.

As shown in Exhibit 8.2, the Six Sigma infrastructure is hierarchical. As with any other pyramid, the base provides a broad foundation for the structure. Without the involvement of all employees in the continuous improvement efforts, the structure would collapse. Moving up the pyramid, the technical and project management skills of the workers involved are increased. As employees receive more training and become more proficient, they are designated as *yellow belts, green belts, black belts,* and *master black belts.* At the top of the pyramid is the *deployment champion.*

Yellow belts. Yellow belts are given training on basic quality management and problem-solving techniques. Training on the fundamental

EXHIBIT 8.2
Six Sigma
Infrastructure

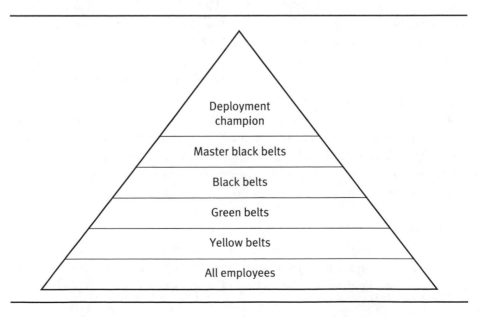

problem-solving techniques can last a half day or a full day. Yellow belts help collect, collate, and analyze data related to projects that affect their workflow.

Green belts. Green belts organize projects and solve problems at the front lines of the organization. In healthcare Six Sigma programs, the green belts help solve the immediate problems when patients receive care. Most green belts spend between 10 and 25 percent of their total time running projects, which usually accounts for two to three projects per year. In great Six Sigma systems the green belts are effective project managers and tend to be influential people from various departments within the organization.

Green belts receive training covering quality management and control, problem solving, data analysis, group facilitation, and project management. To obtain certification, they must usually pass a written exam and successfully complete and defend a Six Sigma project. Green belts continue to perform their usual jobs in addition to Six Sigma projects. Many organizations have a goal of training all their employees to the green-belt level.

Black belts. If green belts are project managers, black belts are portfolio managers. The black belt oversees large organization projects that are usually composed of many smaller green belt projects. For example, a project to increase throughput in an operating room could consist of several smaller projects involving room turnover, staff scheduling, equipment accuracy, and many other tasks. An organization's black belts should focus on achieving significant improvement to measurements that organization deems important.

Black belts have more Six Sigma project leadership experience than green belts. They have more training in higher-level statistical methods, and they mentor green belts. Black belts are dedicated full-time to the Six Sigma efforts of the organization. Their primary responsibility is to ensure that the major projects selected are successful.

Master black belts. Master black belts are qualified to train and mentor green belts and black belts and therefore given more extensive training in statistical methods as well as communication and teaching skills. Master black belts are often seen as the oracles of the Six Sigma programs and treated as internal consultants who make sure all of the project management systems are moving along.

Deployment champion. At the top of the pyramid is the deployment champion, who is responsible for the progress of the Six Sigma program and making sure it is hitting the targets set in the strategic plan. The deployment champion serves a vital role as the liaison between top management, key process owners, and the various black and green belts in the organization. She coordinates all of the major initiatives, allocates resources, and manages expectations for the major projects in the organization.

EXHIBIT 8.3
DMAIC Process

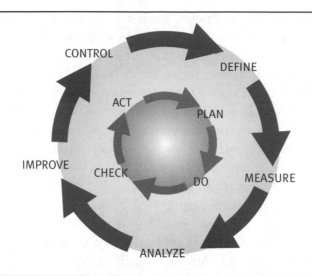

This infrastructure serves several purposes: It provides the organization with in-house experts; enables everyone in the organization to speak the same language, to understand exactly what Six Sigma and Six Sigma projects are all about; and, by using black belts for a limited amount of time and then returning them to their usual positions within the organization, seeds the organization with Six Sigma disciples. In addition, the hierarchy ensures that the organizational goals and objectives are being met.

Define-Measure-Analyze-Improve-Control

DMAIC is the acronym for the five phases of a Six Sigma project: define, measure, analyze, improve, and control. The DMAIC framework, or improvement cycle (Exhibit 8.3), is used almost universally to guide Six Sigma process improvement projects. DMAIC is based on the plan-do-check-act continuous improvement cycle developed by Shewart and Deming but is much more specific.

The definition of *insanity* is "doing the same thing over and over again and expecting different results." Six Sigma uses this definition as a core tenet of its philosophy. At the core of this definition we can assume that if we do the same things over and over again the system will produce the same results. The DMAIC process is designed to help develop consistently repeatable processes that deliver value to the end customer or patient in the healthcare system.

Define

In the definition phase, the Six Sigma team chooses a project based on the strategic objectives of the business and the needs or requirements of the customers of the process. The problem to be solved (or process to be improved) is operationally defined in terms of measurable results. "Good" Six Sigma projects typically have the following attributes:

- The project will save or make money for the organization.
- The desired process outcomes are measurable.
- The problem is important to the business, has a clear relationship to organizational strategy, and is (or will be) supported by the organization.

A benchmarking study of project selection (iSixSigma 2005) found that most organizations (89 percent of respondents) prioritize Six Sigma projects on the basis of financial savings. The survey also found that the existence of formal project selection processes, process documentation, and rigorous requirements for project approval were all important to the success of Six Sigma projects.

In the definition phase, internal and external customers of the process are identified and their "critical to quality" (CTQ) characteristics are determined. CTQs are the key measurable characteristics of a product or process for which minimum performance standards desired by the customer can be determined. Often, CTQs must be translated from a qualitative customer statement to a quantitative specification. In this phase, the team also defines project boundaries and maps the process (Chapters 5 and 6).

Measure

In the measurement phase, team members must understand how well the process they are analyzing meets the requirements set by the customer. To do this, the team determines the current capability and stability of the process. Using the function $Y = f(x)$ as a mechanism to understand how process outputs (Y) are affected by (x), the team begins by collecting data on the key process output variables. Once the key variables are identified, reliable metrics are determined for them (see Exhibit 8.4). The inputs to the process are identified and prioritized. Root-cause analysis (RCA) or failure mode and effects analysis (FMEA) is sometimes used here to determine the key process input variables. Valid, reliable metrics are determined for the input variables as well. A data collection plan for the process is determined and implemented

EXHIBIT 8.4
Six Sigma
Process Metrics

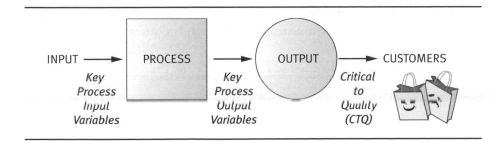

INPUT → PROCESS → OUTPUT → CUSTOMERS

Key Process Input Variables   Key Process Output Variables   Critical to Quality (CTQ)

related to the input and output variables. The purpose of this phase of the project is to establish the current state of the process to evaluate the effect of any changes to it.

Analyze

In the analysis phase, the team analyzes the data that have been collected to determine true root causes, or which of the many input variables can be best utilized to eliminate variation or failure in the process and improve the outcomes.

Improve

In the improvement phase, the team identifies, evaluates, and implements the improvement solutions. Possible solutions are identified and evaluated in terms of their probability of successful implementation. A plan for deployment of solutions is developed, and the solutions are implemented. Here, actual results should be measured to quantify the effect of the project.

Critical to the improvement phase is ensuring that the solutions that are tested and implemented address the problems identified in the project. People on Six Sigma teams often arrive with preconceived notions on how to solve problems and manipulate the data results to justify their solution (Bednarz 2012). For example, a director may want to hire a new doctor, and he may look at the results and point to a lack of capacity in the system as justification to request a new doctor. However, this solution may not be the constraint to the system and would increase and not reduce spending. The solutions that are implemented should address the issues uncovered in the data analysis phase of the project. When team members push solutions that do not address the issues uncovered by the data, inferior solutions may reduce performance and increase costs. Over time if inferior solutions are implemented, the organization will cease using programs like Six Sigma because of lack of results from the program. The implementation and control phases of any project are the most difficult in which to achieve success.

Control

In the control phase, controls are put in place to ensure that process improvement gains are maintained and the process does not revert to the "old way." The improvements are institutionalized through modification of structures and systems (training, incentives, monitoring). This "hardwiring" of the change will eventually become the new baseline for the system.

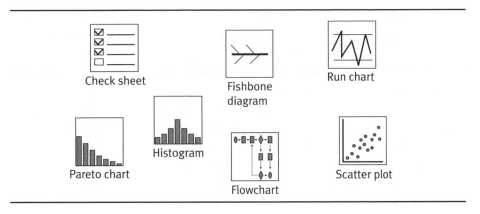

EXHIBIT 8.5
Seven Quality
Tools

Seven Basic Quality Tools

The seven fundamental tools used in quality management and Six Sigma were first popularized by Kauro Ishikawa (1985), who believed that up to 95 percent of quality-related problems could be solved with these fundamental tools (see Exhibit 8.5):

- *Fishbone diagram*: tool for analyzing and illustrating the root causes of an effect (Chapter 6)
- *Check sheet*: simple form used to collect data. Hatch marks are used to record frequency of occurrence for various categories. Frequently, check sheet data are used to produce histograms and Pareto charts.
- *Histogram*: graph used to show frequency distributions (Chapter 7)
- *Pareto chart*: sorted histogram. Pareto charts are used to separate the vital few from the trivial many, based on the idea that 80 percent of quality problems are due to 20 percent of causes (Chapter 7).
- *Flowchart*: process map (Chapter 6)
- *Scatter plot*: graphical technique to analyze the relationship between two variables (Chapter 7)
- *Run chart*: plot of a process characteristic, in chronologic sequence, used to examine trends. A control chart, discussed in the next section, is a type of run chart.

Statistical Process Control

Statistical process control (SPC) is a statistics-based methodology for determining when a process is moving out of control. All processes have variation in output, some of it caused by factors that can be identified and managed (assignable or special) and some of it inherent in the process (common). SPC is aimed at discovering variation due to assignable causes so that adjustments can be made and "bad" output is not produced.

In SPC, samples of process output are taken over time, measured, and plotted on a control chart. From statistics theory, the sample means will follow a normal distribution. From the central limit theorem, 99.7 percent of sample means will have a sample mean within ±3 standard errors of the overall mean and 0.3 percent will have a sample mean outside those limits. If the process is working as it should, only three times out of 1,000 would a sample mean outside the three standard error limits be obtained. These three standard error limits $(s_{\bar{x}})$ are the **control limits** on a control chart.

If the sample means fall outside the control limits (or follow statistically unusual patterns), the process is likely experiencing variation due to assignable or special causes and is out of control. The special causes should be found and corrected. After the process is fixed, the sample means should fall within the control limits, and the process should again be "in control."

Some statistically unusual patterns that indicate that a process is out of control are shown in Exhibit 8.6. A more complete list can be found in Sytsma (1997).

Often, the sample mean ($\bar{X}$, called X-bar) or **X-bar chart** t-chart is used in conjunction with a **range (R) chart**. R-charts follow many of the same rules as X-bar charts and can be used as an additional check on the status of a process. There are also c-charts, used when the measured process output is the count of discrete events (e.g., number of occurrences in a day), and p-charts, used when the output is a proportion. There are also more sophisticated types of control charts that can be used in healthcare organizations (Lim 2003).

A control chart could also be set up using individual values rather than sample means. However, this is not often done for two reasons. First, the individual values must be normally distributed. Second, data collection can be expensive. It usually costs less to collect samples of the data than to collect all of the data.

Riverview Clinic SPC

The Riverview Clinic of Vincent Valley Hospital and Health System (VVH) is undertaking a Six Sigma project to reduce its waiting times. In the measurement phase of the project, data were collected on waiting time, and Riverview decided that a control chart would be helpful for understanding the current situation. Six observations of waiting time were made over 20 days. At randomly chosen times throughout each of 20 days, the next patient to enter the clinic was chosen. The time from when this patient entered the clinic until he exited was recorded (Exhibit 8.7).

Riverview used the standard deviation of all of the observations to estimate the standard deviation of the population. The three-sigma control limits for the X-bar chart are:

Control limits
Common variation limits that are ±3 standard deviations from the mean.

X-bar chart
Measures process performance of sample means for continuous data.

Range (R) chart
Measures process performance of sample ranges for continuous data.

One sample more than ±3 standard errors from mean

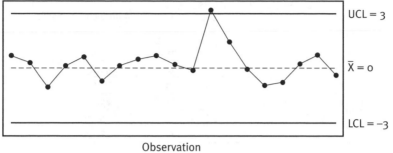

8 or more samples above (or below) mean

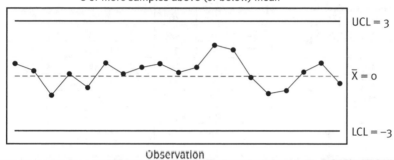

14 or more samples oscillating

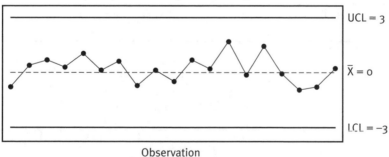

6 or more samples increasing (or decreasing)

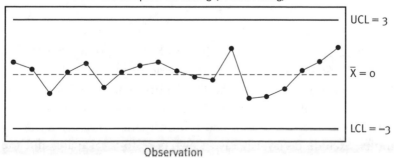

EXHIBIT 8.6
Out-of-Control
Patterns

EXHIBIT 8.7
Riverview Clinic
Wait Times, in
Minutes

| Day | Observations of Wait Times (minutes) Observation | | | | | | Sample Mean | Sample Range |
	1	2	3	4	5	6		
1	29	29	22	31	29	31	28.50	9
2	24	29	40	26	36	30	30.83	16
3	28	33	25	26	28	33	28.83	8
4	26	31	38	30	23	28	29.33	15
5	36	29	24	29	26	32	29.33	12
6	26	27	32	25	30	29	28.17	7
7	22	33	30	31	37	34	31.17	15
8	40	29	26	29	32	30	31.00	14
9	32	32	21	34	28	29	29.33	13
10	34	26	35	27	31	26	29.83	9
11	35	30	29	30	31	27	30.33	8
12	31	39	32	32	30	31	32.50	9
13	36	24	30	29	31	26	29.33	12
14	25	23	29	31	25	23	26.00	8
15	38	43	37	35	38	32	37.17	11
16	35	29	30	25	28	30	29.50	10
17	26	29	20	33	30	28	27.67	13
18	22	29	26	30	36	28	28.50	14
19	33	33	34	37	28	30	32.50	9
20	26	26	34	34	25	36	30.17	11

Standard Deviation = 4.42   Overall Mean = 30.00

$$\bar{x} - z_{\alpha/2} \times \sigma_{\bar{x}} \leq \mu \leq \bar{x} + z_{\alpha/2} \times \sigma_{\bar{x}}$$

$$\bar{x} - z_{\alpha/2} \times \frac{s}{\sqrt{n}} \leq \mu \leq \bar{x} + z_{\alpha/2} \times \frac{s}{\sqrt{n}}$$

$$30 - 3 \times \frac{4.4}{\sqrt{6}} \leq \mu \leq 30 + 3 \times \frac{4.4}{\sqrt{6}}$$

$$30 - 5.4 \leq \mu \leq 30 + 5.4$$

$$24.6 \leq \mu \leq 35.4$$

Looking at the control chart (Exhibit 8.8), it appears that Day 15 was out of control. An investigation found that on Day 15 the clinic was short-staffed because of a school holiday. The control chart cannot be used as is because of the out-of-control point. Riverview could choose to continue to collect data until all points are in control, or it could recalculate the control chart limits, excluding Day 15. Riverview chose to recalculate, and the new three-sigma limits are:

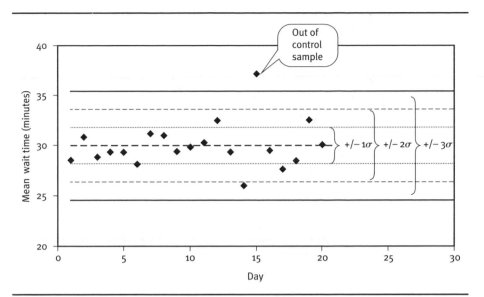

EXHIBIT 8.8
Riverview Clinic
Wait Times:
X-Bar Control
Chart

$$\bar{x} - z_{\alpha/2} \times \sigma_{\bar{x}} \leq \mu \leq \bar{x} + z_{\alpha/2} \times \sigma_{\bar{x}}$$

$$\bar{x} - z_{\alpha/2} \times \frac{s}{\sqrt{n}} \leq \mu \leq \bar{x} + z_{\alpha/2} \times \frac{s}{\sqrt{n}}$$

$$30 - 3 \times \frac{4.1}{\sqrt{6}} \leq \mu \leq 30 + 3 \times \frac{4.1}{\sqrt{6}}$$

$$30 - 5.0 \leq \mu \leq 30 + 5.0$$

$$25.0 \leq \mu \leq 35.0$$

Unless the system is changed, 50 percent of Riverview patients will experience a wait time longer than 30 minutes (50 percent will experience a wait time of less than 30 minutes), and 10 percent of Riverview patients will experience a wait time of greater than 35.3 minutes (90 percent will experience a wait time of less than 35.3 minutes).

$$\mu \leq \bar{x} + z_{\alpha} \times \sigma_{x}$$

$$\mu \leq \bar{x} + z\alpha \times s; \ z_{0.9} = 1.3$$

$$\mu \leq 30 + (1.3 \times 4.1)$$

$$\mu \leq 30 + 5.3$$

$$\mu \leq 35.3$$

If Riverview's goal for its Six Sigma project is to ensure that 90 percent of patients experience a wait time of no more than 30 minutes, the clinic needs to improve the system. The Six Sigma team would need to reduce mean wait time to 24.7 minutes if the process variation remains the same (Exhibit 8.9).

EXHIBIT 8.9
Riverview Clinic
Wait Time

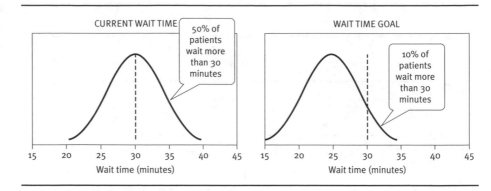

$$\mu \le \bar{x} + z_\alpha \times \sigma_x$$
$$\mu \le \bar{x} + z_\alpha \times s;\ z_{0.9} = 1.3$$
$$\mu \le 30$$
$$\mu \le 24.7 + 5.3;\ \bar{x} = 24.7$$

Process Capability and Six Sigma Quality

Process capability
A measure of how
well a process can
produce output
that meets desired
standards or
specifications.

Process capability measures how well a process can produce output that meets desired standards or specifications. This critical measurement in Six Sigma systems determines how well the internal processes are conforming to customer requirements. This is done by comparing the natural (or common) variability of an in-control process, the process width, to the specification width. Specifications are determined by outside forces (such as customers or management), but process variability is not determined—it is simply a natural part of any process. A capable process is a process that produces few defects, where a defect is defined as an output outside specification limits.

The two common measures of process capability are C_p and C_{pk}. C_p is used when the process is centered on the specification limits; the mean of the process is the same as the mean of the specification limits. C_{pk} is used when the process is not centered. A capable process will have a C_p or C_{pk} greater than 1. At a C_p of 1, the process will produce about three defects per 1,000.

$$C_p = \frac{USL - LSL}{6\sigma} \text{ and is estimated by } \hat{C}_p = \frac{USL - LSL}{6s}$$

$$C_{pk} = \min\left[\frac{\bar{x} - LSL}{3\sigma} \text{ or } \frac{USL - \bar{x}}{3\sigma}\right]$$

$$\text{and is estimated by } \hat{C}_{pk} = \min\left[\frac{\bar{x} - LSL}{3s} \text{ or } \frac{USL - \bar{x}}{3s}\right]$$

NOTE: USL = upper specification limit and LSL = lower specification limit

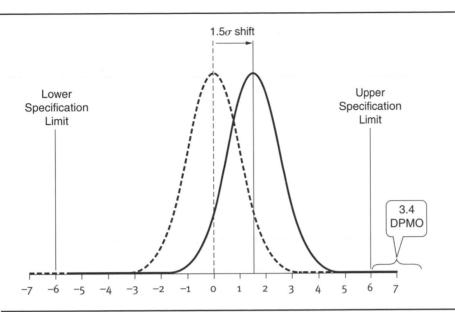

EXHIBIT 8.10
Six Sigma
Process
Capability
Limits

Six Sigma quality is defined as fewer than 3.4 defects per million opportunities (DPMO). This definition can be somewhat confusing, as it corresponds to the 4.5 sigma one tail probability limit for the normal distribution. Six Sigma allows for a 1.5-sigma shift in the mean of the process and $C_{pk} = 1.5$ (Exhibit 8.10).

Riverview Clinic Process Capability

Riverview Clinic management has decided that no patient should wait more than 40 minutes, a waiting time upper specification limit (USL) of 40 minutes. The Six Sigma team wants to determine if the process is capable. Note that because there is no lower specification limit (waiting time less than some lower limit would not be a "defect"), C_{pk} is the correct measure of process capability.

$$\hat{C}_{pk} = \left[\frac{USL - \bar{x}}{3s}\right] = \frac{40 - 30}{3 \times 4.1} = \frac{10}{12.3} = 0.81$$

The C_{pk} is less than 1. Therefore, the process is not capable, and 7,000 DPMOs are expected [$x \sim N(30, 16.8)$, $P(x > 40) = 0.007$].

The team determines that to ensure Six Sigma quality, the specification limit would need to be 48.8 minutes:

$$\hat{C}_{pk} = 1.5 = \left[\frac{USL - \bar{x}}{3s}\right] = \frac{USL - 30}{12.3} = \frac{48.8 - 30}{12.3} \quad \therefore \quad USL = 48.8$$

EXHIBIT 8.11
Rolled
Throughput
Yield

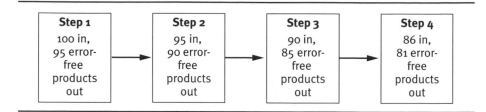

If the Riverview Six Sigma team determined that Six Sigma quality with a specification limit of 40 minutes was a reasonable goal, it could reduce average wait time, reduce the variation in the process, or do some combination of both.

$$\hat{C}_{pk} = \left[\frac{USL - \bar{x}}{3s}\right] = \frac{USL - \bar{x}}{12.3} = \frac{40 - 21}{12.3} \quad \therefore \ \bar{x} = 21$$

$$\hat{C}_{pk} = 1.5 = \left[\frac{USL - \bar{x}}{3s}\right] = \frac{40 - 30}{3s} = \frac{10}{3 \times 2.2} \quad \therefore \ s = 2.2$$

Average wait time would need to be reduced to 21 minutes, or the standard deviation of the process would need to be reduced to 2.2 minutes to reach the goal.

Rolled Throughput Yield

**Rolled throughput
yield**
The probability
that a unit (of
product or service)
will pass through
all process steps
free of defects.

Rolled throughput yield (RTY) measures overall process performance. It is the probability that a unit (of product or service) will pass through all process steps free of defects. For example, consider a process comprising four steps or subprocesses. If each step has a 5 percent probability of producing an error or defect (95 percent probability of an error-free outcome), the RTY of the overall process is 81 percent—considerably lower than that in the individual steps (Exhibit 8.11).

Additional Quality Tools

**Quality function
deployment (QFD)**
A technique
that translates
customer
requirements
into specific
product or process
requirements.

In addition to the quality tools and techniques commonly associated with Six Sigma, many other tools can be used in process improvement. **Quality function deployment (QFD)** and Taguchi methods are often used in the development of new products or processes to ensure quality outcomes. However, they can also be used to improve existing products and processes. Benchmarking is used to help to determine best practices and adapt them to the organization to achieve superior performance. Mistake-proofing, or poka-yoke, is used to minimize the possibility of an error occurring. All of these tools are an essential part of an organization's quality toolbox.

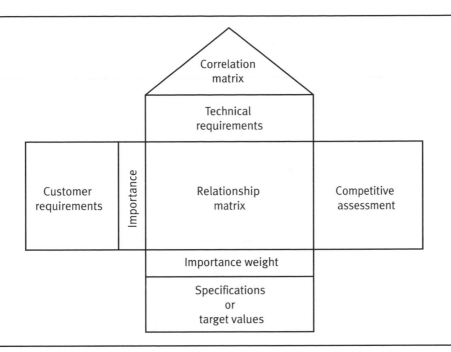

EXHIBIT 8.12
House of
Quality

Quality Function Deployment

QFD is a structured process for identifying customer needs and wants and translating them into a product or process that meets those needs. This tool is most often used in the development phase of a new product or process, but it can also be used to redesign an existing product or process. Typically, QFD is found in a Design for Six Sigma (DFSS) project, where the goal is to design the process to meet Six Sigma goals. The QFD process uses a matrix called the house of quality (Exhibit 8.12) to organize data in a usable fashion.

The first step in QFD is to determine customer requirements. Customer requirements represent the voice of the customer (VOC) and are often stated in customer terms, not technical terms. A particular product or service can have many customers, and the VOC of all must be heard.

Market research tools are used to capture the VOC. The many customer needs found are organized into a few key customer requirements, which are weighted based on their relative importance to the customer. Typically, a scale of 1 to 5 is used, with 5 representing the most important. The customer requirements and their related importance are listed on the left side of the QFD diagram.

A competitive analysis based on the identified customer needs is also performed. The question here is how well competitors meet customer needs. Typically, a scale of 1 to 5 is used here as well, with 5 indicating that the competitor completely meets this need. The competitive analysis is used to focus the development of the service or product to determine where there are opportunities to gain competitive advantage and where the organization is at a competitive disadvantage. This can help the development team to focus on important strategic characteristics of the product or service. The competitors' scores on each of the customer requirements are listed on the right side of the QFD diagram.

Technical requirements of the product or process that relate to customer requirements are determined. For example, if customers want speedy service time, a related technical requirement might be 90 percent of all service times be less than 20 minutes. The technical requirements are listed horizontally across the top of the QFD diagram. The relationship between the customer requirements and technical requirements is evaluated. Usually, the relationships are evaluated as strong, medium, or weak, and symbols are used to represent these relationships in the relationship matrix. Numeric values are assigned to the relative weights (5 = strong, 3 = medium, 1 = weak), and these values are placed in the matrix.

Positive and negative interactions among the technical requirements are evaluated as strongly positive, positive, strongly negative, and negative. Symbols are used to represent these relationships in the "roof," or correlation matrix, of the house of quality. This makes clear the trade-offs involved in product and process design.

Customer importance weights are multiplied by relationship weights and summed for each technical requirement to determine the importance weights. Target values are developed based on the house of quality.

Historically, QFD was a phased process. The aforementioned is the planning phase; for product development, planning is followed by additional houses of quality related to parts, process, and production. For service development and improvement, using only the first house of quality or the first house of quality followed by the process house is often sufficient. For examples of QFD applications in healthcare environments, see Sarker and colleagues (2010), and for a complete review of QFD applications in healthcare and other industries, see Sharma and Rawani (2010).

Riverview Clinic QFD

Many diabetes patients at the Riverview Clinic were not returning for routine preventive exams. The team formed to address this problem decided to use QFD to improve the process and began by soliciting the VOC via focus groups. The team found the following patient needs and wants:

- To know (or be reminded) that they need to schedule a preventive exam
- To know why an office visit is needed
- A convenient means to schedule their appointments

EXHIBIT 8.13
Riverview Clinic House of Quality for Patients with Diabetes

		Initial notification	Subsequent notification	Information on need	Time to schedule	Appointment length range	On-time appointment	Our service	Competitor A	Competitor B
Time knowledge	5	5	3					3	5	3
Why knowledge	3			5				3	5	3
Convenient	4				5			3	3	3
Appointment length	3					5	3	2	3	3
Appointment time	4					3	5	2	4	3
		25	15	15	20	27	29			
		Yes	3	3 channels	8 minutes	8 minutes	90%			

- That their appointments be on time
- To know that their appointments will last a certain length of time

Patient rankings of the importance of these needs and wants were determined via patient surveys.

A competitive analysis of Riverview Clinic's two main competitors was conducted based on the determined needs and wants of Riverview's patients with diabetes. The team developed related technical requirements and evaluated the interactions between them. The house of quality developed is shown in Exhibit 8.13. On-time appointments have the highest importance ranking because they affect both appointment time and appointment length.

The team then evaluated various process changes and improvements related to the determined technical requirements. To meet these technical requirements, they decided to notify patients via postcard and follow this with e-mail and phone notification if needed. The postcard and e-mail contained information related to the need for an office visit and directed patients to the clinic's website for more information. Appointment scheduling was made available via the Internet as well as by phone. Staffing levels and appointment times were adjusted to ensure that appointments were on time and approximately the same length. Training was conducted to help physicians and nurses understand the need to maintain constant appointment lengths and provide them with tools to ensure consistent length.

EXHIBIT 8.14
Riverview
QFD Technical
Requirements
and Related
Process Change

Technical Requirement	Process Change
Initial notification	Postcard mailed
Subsequent notifications	E-mail and/or phone call
Information on need	Website
Time to schedule	Website and phone
Appointment length range	Staff levels adjusted
On-time appointment	Staff training

Exhibit 8.14 outlines these process changes and related technical requirements. After the changes were implemented, the team checked to ensure that the technical requirements determined with the house of quality were being met.

Taguchi Methods

Taguchi methods
The idea that product development should focus on "perfect" rather than on conformance to specifications.

Taguchi methods refer to two related ideas first introduced by Genichi Taguchi. Rather than the quality of a product or service being good or bad, in which good is within some specified tolerance limits and bad is outside those limits, quality is related to the distance from some target value; further from the target is worse. Taguchi developed experimental design techniques where the target value and the associated variation are important. The optimal process design is not necessarily where the target value is maximized but where variation is minimal in relation to the target. In other words, the process is robust and will perform well under less-than-ideal conditions.

Taguchi methods are often used in DFSS where the product or service is designed to be error free while meeting or exceeding the needs of the customer. Rather than fixing an existing product or service, the design process of the product or service should ensure quality from the start.

Benchmarking

According to the American Productivity and Quality Center (2005), benchmarking is "the process of identifying, understanding, and adapting outstanding practices and processes from organizations anywhere in the world to help your organization improve its performance." Benchmarking is focused on how to improve any given process by finding, studying, and implementing best practices. These best practices may be found within the organization, in competitor organizations, and even in organizations outside the particular market or industry. Best practices are everywhere—the challenge is to find them and adapt them to the organization.

The benchmarking process consists of deciding what to benchmark, determining how to measure it, gathering information and data, and then implementing the best practice within the organization. Benchmarking can be an important part of a quality improvement initiative, and many health-care organizations are involved in benchmarking (Olson et al. 2008). The journal *Healthcare Benchmarks and Quality Improvement* has information on many of these initiatives.

Poka-Yoke

Poka-yoke (a Japanese phrase meaning to avoid inadvertent errors), or mistake-proofing, is a way to prevent errors from happening. A poka-yoke is a mechanism that either prevents a mistake from being made or makes the mistake immediately obvious so that no adverse outcomes are experienced. For example, all of the instruments required in a surgical procedure are found on an instrument tray with indentations for each instrument. After the procedure is complete, the instruments are replaced in the tray. This process provides a quick visual check to ensure that all instruments are removed before closing the patient's incision. Locating the controls for a mammography machine so that the technician cannot start the machine unless she is shielded from radiation via a wall provides another example of mistake-proofing a process. In FMEA, identified fail points are good candidates for poka-yoke.

Poka-yoke
A mechanism that prevents mistakes or makes them immediately obvious to prevent adverse outcomes.

Technology can often enable poka-yoke. When patient data are put into a system, the software is often programmed to provide an error message if the data are incorrect. For example, a Social Security number is nine digits long; no more than nine digits can be entered into the Social Security field, and an error message appears if fewer than nine digits are entered. In the past, surgical sponges were counted before and after a procedure to ensure that none were left in a patient. Now, the sponges can be radio frequency identification tagged, eliminating the error-prone counting process, and a simple scan can be used to determine if any sponges remain in the patient.

Riverview Clinic Six Sigma Generic Drug Project

Management determined that a strategic objective for Riverview Clinic was meeting pay-for-performance goals related to prescribing generic drugs, and a project team was organized to meet this goal. Benchmarking was done to help the team determine which pay-for-performance measure to focus on and to define reasonable goals for the project. The team found that 10 percent of nongeneric prescription drugs could be replaced with generic drugs and that other clinics had successfully met this goal.

EXHIBIT 8.15
Riverview Clinic
Prescription
Process

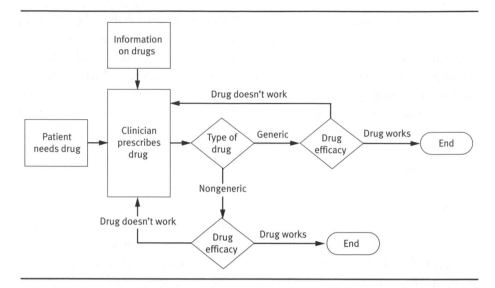

Define

In the definition phase, the team articulated the project goals, scope, and business case. This included developing the project charter, determining customer requirements, and diagramming a process map. The charter for this project is found in Chapter 5; it defines the project's goals, scope, and business case.

The team identified the health plans and patients as being customers of the process. The outputs of the process were identified as prescriptions and the efficacy of those prescriptions. The process inputs were physician judgment and the information technology (IT) system for drug lists. Additionally, pharmaceutical firms provide input on drug efficacy. The process map developed by the team is shown in Exhibit 8.15.

Measure

The team determined that the percentage of generic (versus nongeneric) drugs prescribed and the percentage of prescription changes after prescription of a generic drug would be used to quantify the outcomes. Additionally, the team decided that it would need to track and record data on all nongeneric drugs prescribed by each individual clinician for one month.

Analyze

After one month, the team analyzed the data and found that, overall, clinicians prescribed 65 percent generic drugs (Exhibit 8.16), and prescription changes were needed for 3 percent of all prescriptions. An example of the data collected is shown in Exhibit 8.17. The team generated a Pareto analysis by clinician and drug to determine if particular drugs or clinicians were more

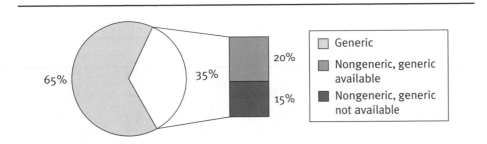

EXHIBIT 8.16
Riverview
Generic Drug
Project: Drug
Type and
Availability

problematic. The analysis showed that some drugs were more problematic but that all clinicians were about the same (Exhibit 8.18.)

The team reexamined its stated goal of increasing generic drug prescriptions by 4 percent in light of the data collected. If all prescriptions for the top four nongeneric drugs for which a generic drug is available could be changed to generics, Riverview would increase generic prescriptions by 5 percent. Therefore, they decided that the original goal was still reasonable.

EXHIBIT 8.17
Riverview Clinic
Generic Drug
Project Example
Data

Date	Clinician	Drug	Drug Type	Generic Available	Represcribe
1-Jan	Smith	F	Nongeneric	Yes	No
1-Jan	Davis	G	Generic	Yes	No
1-Jan	Jones	L	Generic	Yes	No
1-Jan	Anderson	F	Nongeneric	No	No
1-Jan	Swanson	R	Generic	Yes	Yes
1-Jan	Smith	S	Nongeneric	Yes	No
1-Jan	Swanson	U	Generic	Yes	No
1-Jan	Jones	P	Generic	Yes	No
1-Jan	Jones	S	Nongeneric	No	No
1 Jan	Swanson	A	Generic	Yes	No
.	.	.	.	.	.
.	.	.	.	.	.
.	.	.	.	.	.
31-Jan	Anderson	F	Nongeneric	Yes	No
31-Jan	Anderson	E	Nongeneric	No	No
31-Jan	Davis	T	Generic	Yes	No
31-Jan	Smith	Y	Generic	Yes	No
31-Jan	Jones	D	Generic	Yes	No
31-Jan	Swanson	J	Generic	Yes	No
31-Jan	Swanson	I	Nongeneric	Yes	No
31-Jan	Smith	T	Generic	Yes	No
31-Jan	Davis	G	Generic	Yes	No
31-Jan	Anderson	H	Generic	Yes	No

EXHIBIT 8.18
Riverview Clinic
Generic Drug
Project: Pareto
Diagrams

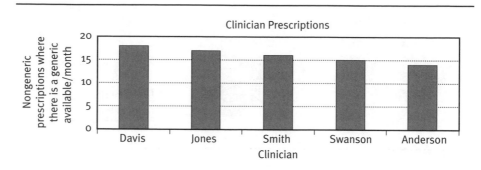

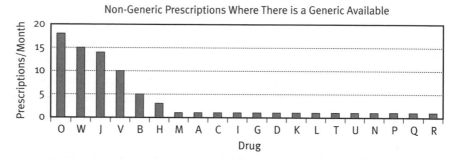

Improve

The team conducted an RCA of the reasons for prescribing nongeneric drugs and determined that the major cause was the clinician's lack of awareness of a generic replacement for the prescribed drug. In addition to the IT system that will identify approved generic drugs, the team decided to publish, based on data from the previous month, a monthly top five list of nongeneric drugs for which an approved generic exists. The team continued to collect and analyze data after these changes were implemented and found that prescriptions for generic drugs had risen by 4.5 percent after six months.

Control

To measure progress and ensure continued compliance, the team set up a weekly control chart for generic prescriptions and continued to monitor and publish the top five list. The team conducted an end-of-project evaluation to document the steps taken and results achieved, and to ensure that learning from the project was retained in the organization.

Conclusion

The Six Sigma DMAIC process is a framework for improvement. At any point in the process, it may be necessary to backtrack to ensure improvement.

EXHIBIT 8.19

Quality Tools and Techniques Selector Chart

Tool or Technique	Define	Measure	Analyze	Improve	Control
7 Quality control tools					
Cause-and-effect diagram			X		
Run chart		X	X		
Check sheet					
Histogram		X	X		
Pareto chart		X	X	X	
Scatter plot			X		X
Flowchart	X	X			
Other tools and techniques					
Mind-mapping/ brainstorming	X		X	X	
5 Whys/RCA			X		
FMEA			X	X	
Pie chart			X		
Hypothesis testing			X		
Control chart		X		X	X
Process capability		X		X	X
QFD		X	X	X	
Benchmarking	X	X	X	X	
Poka-yoke				X	
Gantt chart				X	
Project planning	X			X	X
Charters	X				
Tree diagram				X	
Force field analysis				X	X
Balanced scorecard	X	X	X	X	X

For example, what the team thought was the root cause of the problem may be found not to be the true root cause. Or, when attempting to analyze the data, it may be that insufficient data, or the wrong data, were taken. In both cases, it may be necessary to go back in the DMAIC process to ensure a successful project.

At each stop in the DMAIC process, various tools could be used. The choice of tool is related to the problem and possible solutions. Exhibit 8.19 outlines suggestions for when to choose a particular tool or technique. This is only a guideline—use whatever tool is most appropriate for the situation.

Discussion Questions

1. Read the Executive Summary of the IOM report *To Err Is Human* (www.nap.edu/openbook.php?isbn=0309068371) and answer the following questions: Why did this report spur an interest in quality management in the healthcare industry? What does IOM recommend to address these problems? How much has been done since 1999?

2. What does quality in healthcare mean to your organization? To you personally?

3. Discuss a real example of each of the four costs of quality in a healthcare organization.

4. Compare and contrast ISO 9000, the Baldrige criteria, and Six Sigma. (More information on each of these programs is linked from the companion website.) Which would you find most appropriate to your organization? Why?

www.ache.org/books/OpsManagement2

5. Think of at least three poka-yokes currently used in the healthcare industry. Can you think of a new one for your organization?

Chapter Exercises

1. Clinicians at VVH have been complaining about the turnaround time for blood work. The laboratory manager decides to investigate the problem and collects turnaround time data on five randomly selected requests every day for one month.

	Observation						Observation				
Day	1	2	3	4	5	Day	1	2	3	4	5
1	44	41	80	51	25	16	14	44	35	52	76
2	28	32	58	42	18	17	52	84	55	63	15
3	54	83	59	50	46	18	28	20	67	76	69
4	57	53	63	15	52	19	25	23	35	21	23
5	30	50	62	68	42	20	46	74	24	10	47
6	42	40	50	49	73	21	33	54	62	40	27
7	26	17	50	47	91	22	64	55	62	14	72
8	54	39	39	82	28	23	53	49	72	49	61
9	46	62	53	64	57	24	15	16	18	35	78
10	49	71	34	42	43	25	64	9	51	47	70
11	53	64	12	35	43	26	36	21	51	40	57
12	75	43	43	50	64	27	24	58	19	88	16
13	74	19	52	55	59	28	75	66	34	27	71
14	91	40	66	15	73	29	60	42	20	59	60
15	59	32	59	49	71	30	52	28	85	39	67

a. Construct an X-bar chart using the standard deviation of the observations to estimate the population standard deviation. Construct an X-bar chart and r-chart using the range to calculate the control limits. (The Excel template on the companion website will do this for you.)

www.ache.org/books/OpsManagement2

b. Is the process in control? Explain.

c. If the clinicians feel that any time over 100 minutes is unacceptable, what are the C_p and C_{pk} of this process?

d. What are the next steps for the laboratory manager?

2. Riverview Clinic has started a customer satisfaction program. In addition to other questions, each patient is asked if he is satisfied with his overall experience at the clinic. Patients can respond "yes," if they were satisfied, or "no," if they were not satisfied. Typically, 200 patients are seen at the clinic each day. The data collected for two months are shown below.

Day	Proportion of patients who were unsatisfied	Day	Proportion of patients who were unsatisfied	Day	Proportion of patients who were unsatisfied
1	0.17	15	0.15	28	0.18
2	0.13	16	0.14	29	0.19
3	0.15	17	0.13	30	0.14
4	0.22	18	0.15	31	0.19
5	0.16	19	0.15	31	0.10
6	0.13	20	0.22	33	0.17
7	0.17	21	0.19	34	0.15
8	0.17	22	0.15	35	0.17
9	0.11	23	0.12	36	0.15
10	0.16	24	0.16	37	0.15
11	0.15	25	0.18	38	0.15
12	0.17	26	0.14	39	0.14
13	0.17	27	0.17	40	0.19
14	0.12				

a. Construct a p-chart using the collected data.

b. Is the process in control?

c. On average, how many patients are satisfied with Riverview Clinic's service? If Riverview wants 90 percent (on average) of patients to be satisfied, what should the clinic do next?

3. Think of a problem in your organization that Six Sigma could help to solve. Map the process and determine the key process input variables, the key process output variables, the CTQs, and exactly *how* you could measure them.

www.ache.org/books/OpsManagement2

4. Use QFD to develop a house of quality for the VVH emergency department (you may need to guess the numbers you do not know). An Excel template (QFD.xls) available on the companion website may be helpful for this problem.

THE LEAN ENTERPRISE

9

Operations Management in Action

Park Nicollet (PN), a healthcare system in Minnesota, has been using Lean tools to help improve the flow of its processes since 2003. In 2009, PN used Lean tools integrated with clinician guidance to design a new care model to manage patients on anticoagulants.

Anticoagulants, such as warfarin, can be extremely dangerous medications. Warfarin is often prescribed to cardiac patients to prevent blood clots and is also used to treat or prevent venous thrombosis and pulmonary embolism. However, the drug can cause severe bleeding that can be life threatening. As a result, most hospitals have specialized units that specifically deal with the dangers of warfarin.

PN used the Lean tools to help alleviate issues with the delivery of the anticoagulants. The primary metric that PN focused on was "INR time in desired range." INR (international normalized ratio) is a measurement established by the World Health Organization (WHO) for reporting the results of blood coagulation tests. PN's tests were hitting the desired range 38 percent of the time.

To improve the system, PN standardized several policies related to the administration of warfarin. First, it initiated centralized dosing models using nurse clinicians. This step ensured that only certain people had the authority to administer the medications, which greatly improved PN's ability to track the amount of warfarin given to patients.

Next, PN decentralized management of each patient to his local clinic. This step ensured that each patient was getting personalized care and attention because the drug orders were given by his primary doctor.

Specific Lean tools used in the improvement include visual management and standardization for orders, poka-yoke to limit errors, standard work for the triage of phone calls, and kaizen to improve processes in the system. In addition, a consistent formal education system was deployed to help reduce the issues in the future.

These improvements helped PN increase the INR percentage to an "in range" of more than 70 percent. The average cost to administer the medication per patient/per year reduced from a baseline measure of $1,300 to an average $442 per patient/per year. Finally, the hospital admission rate of patients using warfarin reduced from 15.9 percent to 11.2 percent.

SOURCE: Trajano, Mattson, and Sanford (2011).

Overview

Lean tools and techniques have been employed extensively in manufacturing organizations since the 1990s to improve the efficiency and effectiveness of those organizations. More recently, many healthcare organizations have begun to realize the transformative potential of Lean (Panchak 2003; Womack et al. 2005).

The healthcare industry is facing increasing pressure to employ resources in an effective manner to reduce costs and increase patient satisfaction. This chapter provides an introduction to the Lean philosophy as well as the various Lean tools and techniques used by many healthcare organizations today. The major topics covered include:

- The Lean philosophy
- Defining waste
- Kaizen
- Value stream mapping
- Other Lean tools, techniques, and ideas, including the five Ss, spaghetti diagrams, kaizen events, takt time, kanbans, single-minute exchange of die, heijunka, jidoka, andon, standardized work, and pull

After completing this chapter, readers should have a basic understanding of Lean tools, techniques, and philosophy. This should help them understand how Lean could be used in their organizations and enable them to employ its tools and techniques to facilitate continuous improvement.

What Is Lean?

As described in Chapter 2, Lean production was developed by Taiichi Ohno, Toyota's chief of production after World War II. The Toyota Production System (TPS) was studied by researchers at MIT and documented in the book *The Machine That Changed the World* (Womack, Jones, and Roos 1990). The Lean system originated from just-in-time (JIT) production and became widely adapted in many manufacturing operations. Lean spread quickly to healthcare organizations because the removal of waste in the system will improve the clinical measure of safety (Caldwell, Brexler, and Gillem 2005; Chalice 2005; Spear 2005).

Where Six Sigma, total quality management (TQM), and continuous quality improvement create customer value by eliminating defects, Lean creates seamless flow to the customer by eliminating waste. Although Six Sigma and Lean are different, their methodologies, tools, and outcomes are similar. Both programs have Japanese roots, as evidenced by the terminology associated with them, and they use many of the same tools and techniques.

The TPS or Lean Production House (Exhibit 9.1) is based on a foundation of stability and standardization. The pillars of the house represent the systems that create value for the customer (the roof of the house). The left side of the structure represents producing what you need just-in-time for

EXHIBIT 9.1
Lean Production House

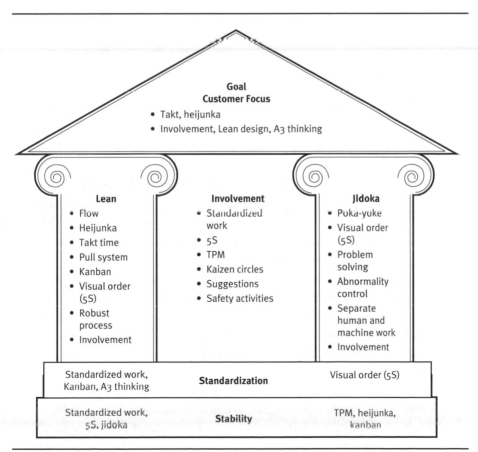

SOURCE: Pascal (2007).

the customer. To execute this correctly the system must remove waste. The right side of the structure represents automation, or designing the system to stop when defects are produced and remove them. The middle section is the human factor that links the two systems together. The ultimate goal is to produce as much value to the customer as possible.

A Lean organization is focused on eliminating all types of waste. Like Six Sigma, Lean has been defined as a philosophy, methodology, and set of tools. The Lean philosophy is to produce only what is needed, when it is needed, and with no waste. The Lean methodology begins by examining the system or process to determine where value is added and where it is not; steps in the process that do not add value are eliminated, and those that do add value are optimized. Lean tools include value stream mapping, the five Ss, spaghetti diagrams, kaizen events, kanbans, single-minute exchange of die, heijunka, jidoka, and standardized work.

Types of Waste

In Lean, waste is called *muda*, which comes from the Japanese term for waste. Many types of waste are found in organizations. Ohno defined seven categories of waste related to manufacturing, and they can be reinterpreted for services and healthcare:

1. *Overproduction*: producing more than is demanded or producing before the product is needed to meet demand. Printing reports and labels and preparing meals when they are not needed are examples of overproduction in healthcare.
2. *Waiting*: time during which value is not being added to the product or service. Waiting can refer to either the patient waiting in healthcare or the provider waiting for a patient. Anytime waiting occurs, the resources in the system are not being productive or adding value to the end customer in the system.
3. *Transportation*: unnecessary travel of the primary product in the system. In healthcare, transport is so common the name describes an entire department, which is often called to move patients in clinics and hospitals to different areas of the facility. Other forms of transportation include bringing equipment and supplies to various places in a facility.
4. *Inventory*: holding or purchasing raw materials, work-in-process (WIP), and finished goods that are not immediately needed. In healthcare, wasted inventory includes supplies and pharmaceuticals. Too much inventory costs money and limits the organization's ability

to be profitable. In addition, the probability of having outdated drugs on-site increases, creating a greater risk to patients.

5. *Motion*: actions of providers or operators that do not add value to the product. This could also include repetitive-type motion that causes injury. In healthcare, wasted motion includes unnecessary travel of the service provider to obtain supplies or information.

6. *Overprocessing*: unnecessary processing or steps and procedures that do not add value to the product or service. Numerous examples of overprocessing in healthcare relate to recordkeeping and documentation. Many of the computerized order entry systems (CPOE) also require overprocessing to work effectively.

7. *Defects*: production of a part or service that is scrapped or requires rework. In healthcare, defect waste includes mundane errors, such as misfiling documents, and serious errors resulting in the death of a patient. The Joint Commission (2012) classifies catastrophic defects resulting in death or serious injury as a result of mistakes as sentinel events.

Effective Lean systems focus on eliminating all waste through continuous improvement.

Kaizen

Kaizen is the Japanese term for "change for the better," or continuous improvement. Kaizen has become the vehicle in which Lean systems make changes and improve. The philosophy of kaizen involves all employees in making suggestions for improvement, then implementing those suggestions quickly. Kaizen is based on the assumption that everything can be improved and that many small incremental changes will result in a better system. Prior to adopting a kaizen philosophy organizations used to believe, "If it isn't broken, leave it alone"; with a kaizen philosophy, organizations believe, "Even if it isn't broken, it can be improved." An organization that does not focus on continuous improvement will not be able to compete with other organizations that are continuously improving. Because Lean systems target removing waste, opportunity to improve should occur immediately and continuously.

Kaizen can be both a general philosophy of improvement centering on the entire system or value stream and a specific improvement technique for a particular process. The kaizen philosophy of continuous improvement consists of five basic steps:

Kaizen
Continuous improvement based on the belief that everything can be improved and that incremental changes result in a better system.

1. *Specify value*: Identify activities that provide value from the customer's perspective.
2. *Map and improve the value stream*: Determine the sequence of activities or current state of the process and the desired future state. Eliminate non-value-added steps and other waste.
3. *Flow*: Enable the process to flow as smoothly and quickly as possible.
4. *Pull*: Enable the customer to drive products or services.
5. *Perfection*: Repeat the process to ensure a focus on continuous improvement.

The kaizen philosophy is enabled by the various tools and techniques of Lean.

Value Stream Mapping

Value stream map
An overview of how a system transforms supplies into finished goods for the customer.

A **value stream map** is a big-picture view of how a system transforms supplies into finished goods for the customer. Effective value stream maps include all of the steps in the process—both the value-adding and the non-value-adding steps—and their related measurements in producing and delivering a product or service. Both information processing and transformational processing steps are included in a value stream map.

The value stream map shows process flow from a systems perspective and can help in determining how to measure and improve the system or process of interest. The value stream map can enable the organization to focus on the entire value stream rather than just a specific step or piece of the stream. Without a view of the entire stream, it is possible, even likely, that individual parts of the system will be optimized according to the needs of those parts, but the resulting system will be suboptimal. This occurs frequently in healthcare organizations that are separated by departments. One department, such as labs or X-ray—may make a decision to help its own processes, but that decision may have an adverse impact on other areas of the organization, such as the operation rooms or emergency department.

Value stream mapping in healthcare is typically done from the perspective of the patient, where the goal is to optimize her journey through the system. Information, material, and patient flows are captured in the value stream map. Each step in the process is classified as value-added or non-value-added. Value-added activities are those that change the item being worked on in some way that the customer desires. Using the value stream methodology, value is classified into three elements:

1. Does the patient care about the activity?
2. Does the activity transform the end product in some way?
3. Is the activity done right the first time?

If all three questions cannot be answered in the affirmative, the activity would be considered non-value-added and should be removed from the system.

Non-value-added activities can be further classified as necessary or unnecessary. An example of a necessary non-value-added activity that organizations must perform is payroll. Payroll activities do not add value for customers, but employees must be paid. Activities that are classified as non-value-added and unnecessary should be eliminated. Activities that are necessary but non-value-added should be examined to determine if they can be made unnecessary and eliminated. Value-added and necessary but non-value-added activities are candidates for improvement and waste reduction. The value stream map enables organizations to see all of the activities in a value stream and focus their improvement efforts (Womack and Jones 1999).

A common measurement for the progress of Lean initiatives is percent value added. The total time for the process to be completed is also measured. This can be accomplished by measuring the time a single item, customer, or patient spends to complete the entire process. At each step in the process, the value-added time is measured:

$$\% \text{ Value added} = \frac{\text{Value-added time}}{\text{Total time in system}} \times 100$$

The goal of Lean is to increase percent value added by increasing this ratio. Many processes have a percent value added of 5 percent or less. Best-in-class value-added time is often 20 percent or less. Value streams help organizations to focus on flow and not on waiting. Value streams with low value-added percentages are often full of wait times. Traditional healthcare processes involving several departments having less than 1 percent total value-added time are not uncommon.

Once the value stream map has been generated, kaizen activities can be identified that will allow the organization to increase the percent-value-added time and employ resources in the most effective manner possible.

Vincent Valley Hospital and Health System Value Stream Mapping

Vincent Valley Hospital and Health System (VVH) identified its birthing center as an area in need of improvement and decided to use Lean tools and techniques to accomplish its objectives. The goals for the Lean initiative were to decrease costs and increase patient satisfaction. Project management tools (Chapter 5) were used to ensure success.

Initially, a team was formed to improve the operations of the birthing center. The team consisted of the manager of the birthing unit (the project manager), two physicians, three nurses (one from triage, one from labor and delivery, and one from postpartum), and the manager of admissions. All team members were trained in Lean tools and techniques and started the project by developing a high-level value stream map over the course of several weeks (Exhibit 9.2). The team mapped patient and information flows in the birthing center and collected data related to staffing type and level as well as length of time for the various process steps. The high-level value stream map was used to help the team decide where to focus its efforts. The team then developed a plan for the coming year based on the opportunities identified.

Measures and Tools

Takt Time

Takt time
The speed with which customers must be served to satisfy demand for the service.

Takt is a German word meaning rhythm or beat. It is often associated with the rhythm set by a conductor to ensure that the orchestra plays in unison. **Takt time** determines the speed with which customers must be served to satisfy demand for the service. The calculation is as follows:

$$\text{Takt time} = \frac{\text{Available work time/Day}}{\text{Customer demand/Day}}$$

Cycle time
The time it takes to accomplish a task in a system.

Cycle time is the time it takes for a system to accomplish a task in a system. Cycle time for a system will be equal to the longest task-cycle time in that system. Cycle time is often referred to as the "drip rate" of the system. If you picture a leaky faucet, the cycle time would be the rate at which water drips from the faucet. In a perfect Lean system, cycle time and takt time are equal. If cycle time is greater than takt time, demand will not be satisfied and customers or patients will wait. If cycle time is less than takt time in a manufacturing environment, inventory is generated; in a service environment, resources are underutilized. In a Lean system, the rate at which a product or service can be produced is set by customer demand, not by the organization's ability (or inability) to supply the product or service.

Throughput time
The time for an item to complete the entire process, including waiting time and transport time.

Throughput Time

Throughput time is the time for an item to complete the entire process. It includes waiting time and transport time as well as actual processing time. In a healthcare clinic, for example, throughput time would be the total time

EXHIBIT 9.2   VVH Birthing Center Value Stream Map

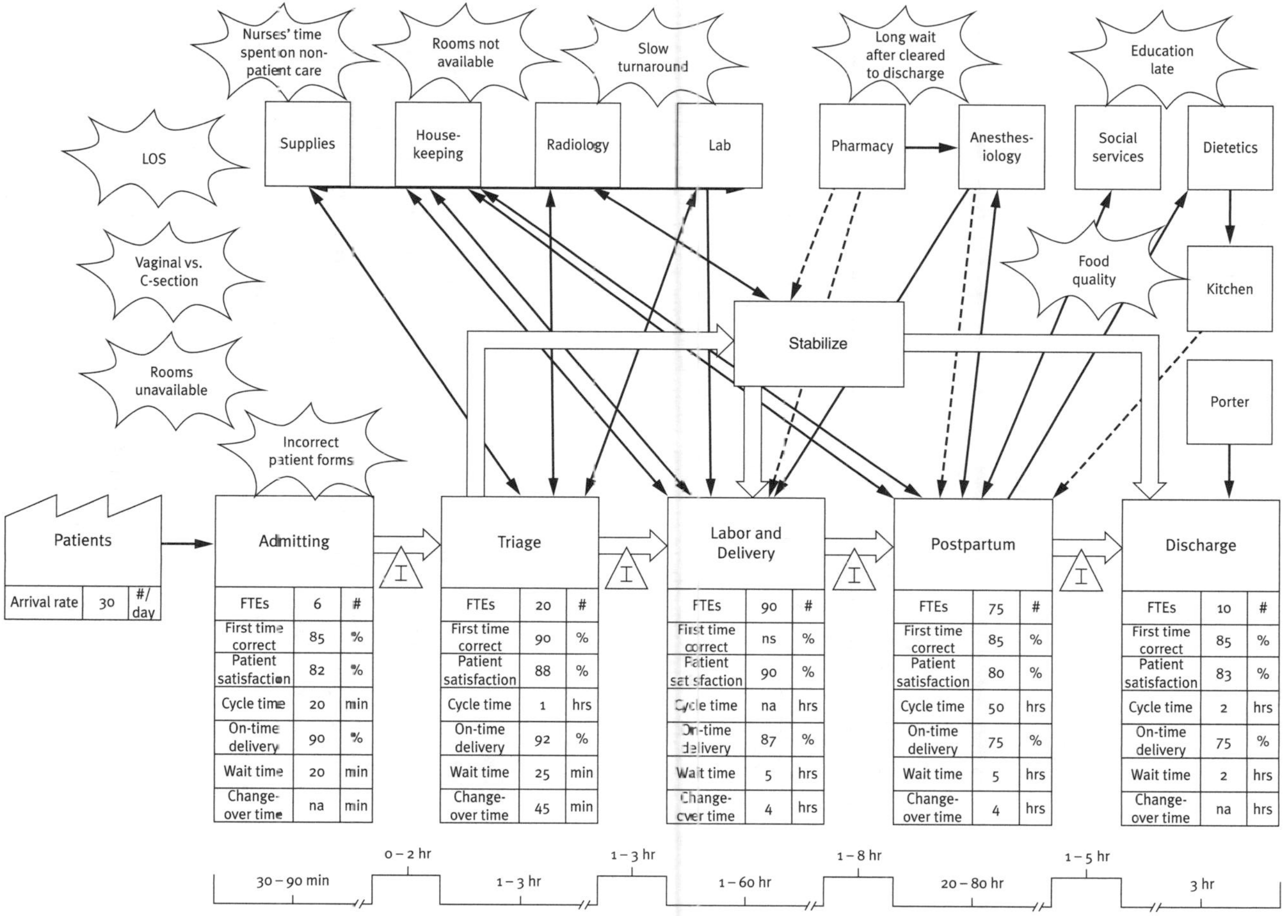

Kaizen bursts: Education late · Food quality · Long wait after cleared to discharge · Slow turnaround · Rooms not available · Nurses' time spent on non-patient care · Incorrect patient forms · LOS · Vaginal vs. C-section · Rooms unavailable

Support boxes: Dietetics · Kitchen · Porter · Social services · Anesthesiology · Pharmacy · Lab · Radiology · Housekeeping · Supplies · Stabilize

Patients — Arrival rate 30 #/day

Admitting

FTEs	6	#
First time correct	85	%
Patient satisfaction	82	%
Cycle time	20	min
On-time delivery	90	%
Wait time	20	min
Change-over time	na	min

Triage

FTEs	20	#
First time correct	90	%
Patient satisfaction	88	%
Cycle time	1	hr
On-time delivery	92	%
Wait time	25	min
Change-over time	45	min

Labor and Delivery

FTEs	90	#
First time correct	ns	%
Patient satisfaction	90	%
Cycle time	na	hrs
On-time delivery	87	%
Wait time	5	hrs
Change-over time	4	hrs

Postpartum

FTEs	75	#
First time correct	85	%
Patient satisfaction	80	%
Cycle time	50	hrs
On-time delivery	75	%
Wait time	5	hrs
Change-over time	4	hrs

Discharge

FTEs	10	#
First time correct	85	%
Patient satisfaction	83	%
Cycle time	2	hrs
On-time delivery	75	%
Wait time	2	hrs
Change-over time	na	hrs

Timeline: 30–90 min · 0–2 hr · 1–3 hr · 1–3 hr · 1–60 hr · 1–8 hr · 20–80 hr · 1–5 hr · 3 hr

NOTE: Created with eVSM software from GumshoeKI, Inc., a Microsoft Visio add-on.

EXHIBIT 9.3
Riverview
Clinic Cycle,
Throughput,
and Takt Times

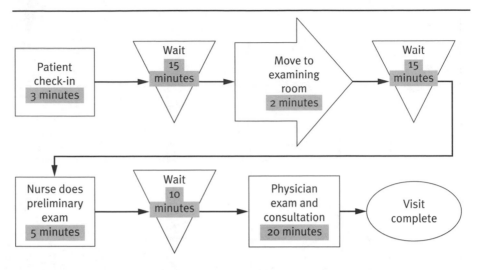

NOTE: Created with Microsoft Visio®.

the patient spends at the clinic, starting when he walks through the door and ending when he walks out; this includes not only the time the patient is interacting with a clinician, but also time spent waiting in the waiting room and examining room. In a perfectly Lean system, there would be no waiting time, and throughput time would be minimized. In most instances throughput time is driven by the non-value-added activities and not the provider–patient interaction.

Riverview Clinic

VVH's Riverview Clinic collected the data shown in Exhibit 9.3 for a typical patient visit. Here, the physician exam and consultation has the longest task time, 20 minutes; therefore, the cycle time for this process is 20 minutes. Assuming that physician time is not constrained, every physician could output one patient from this process every 20 minutes. However, the throughput time is equal to the total amount of time a patient spends in the system. Here, it is:

$$3 + 15 + 2 + 15 + 5 + 10 + 20 = 70 \text{ minutes}$$

The available work time per physician day is 5 hours (physicians work 10 hours per day, but only 50 percent of that time is spent with patients), the clinic has 8 physicians, and 100 patients are expected at the clinic every day.

$$\text{Takt time} = \frac{8 \text{ Physicians} \times 5 \text{ Hours/Day}}{100 \text{ Patients/Day}} = 0.4 \text{ Physician hours/Patient}$$

$$= 24 \text{ Physician minutes/Patient}$$

Therefore, to meet demand, the clinic needs to serve one patient every 24 minutes. Because cycle time (20 minutes) is less than takt time (24 minutes), the clinic can meet demand.

Assuming that patient check-in is necessary but non-value-added and that both the nurse preliminary exam and the physician exam and consultation are value-added tasks, the value-added time for this process is:

$$5 \text{ Minutes (Nurse preliminary exam)}$$
$$+ \text{ } 20 \text{ Minutes (Physician exam and consultation)} = 25 \text{ Minutes}$$

and the percent value-added time is:

$$25 \text{ Minutes}/70 \text{ Minutes} = 36\%$$

This example assumes all of the steps in check-in are value-added. The reality is that many of the steps we perform in any given activity in a process are non-value-added. A Lean system works toward decreasing throughput time and increasing percent value-added time. The tools discussed in the following sections can aid in achieving these goals as building blocks to the overall Lean system.

Five Ss

The five Ss are workplace practices that constitute the foundation of other Lean activities; the Japanese words for these practices all begin with S. The five Ss are essentially ways to ensure a clean and organized workplace. Often, they are seen as obvious and self-evident; a clean and organized workplace will be more efficient. However, without a continuing focus on these five practices, workplaces often become disorganized and inefficient.

The five practices, with their Japanese names and the English terms typically used to describe them, are:

1. *Seiri (sort)*: Separate necessary from unnecessary items, including tools, parts, materials, and paperwork, and remove the unnecessary items.
2. *Seiton (set in order)*: Arrange the necessary items neatly, providing visual cues to where items should be placed.
3. *Seiso (shine)*: Clean the work area.
4. *Seiketsu (standardize)*: Standardize the first three Ss so that cleanliness is maintained.
5. *Shitsuke (sustain)*: Ensure that the first four Ss continue to be performed on a regular basis.

Many hospitals and healthcare organizations have adopted a sixth S in the system, safety. Many organizations now adopt the six S process, where safety is considered paramount in the design of the sustainable process (EPA 2011).

The five Ss or six Ss are often the first step an organization takes in its Lean journey because so much waste can be eliminated by ensuring an organized and efficient workplace. Effective five S requires that the organization build discipline to continue the efforts in the long term. If an organization cannot sustain a simple mechanism to keep an area clean and organized, it will struggle with more complex systems. Five-S systems can be easy to build but are difficult to maintain. Exhibit 9.4 displays an audit form for scheduling regular audits to make sure the system is sustainable.

Spaghetti Diagram

Spaghetti diagram
A visual representation of the movement or travel of materials, employees, or customers.

A **spaghetti diagram** is a visual representation of the movement or travel of materials, employees, or customers. In healthcare, a spaghetti diagram is often used to document or investigate the movements of caregivers or patients. Typically, the patient or caregiver spends a significant amount of time moving from place to place and often backtracks. A spaghetti diagram (Exhibit 9.5) can help to find and eliminate wasted movement in the system.

Kaizen Event or Blitz

Kaizen event
A focused, short-term project aimed at improving a particular process.

A **kaizen event** or blitz (sometimes referred to as a rapid process improvement workshop) is a focused, short-term project aimed at improving a particular process. A kaizen event is usually performed by a cross-functional team of eight to ten people, always including at least one person who works with or in the process. The rest of the team should include personnel from other functional areas and even nonemployees with an interest in improving the process. In healthcare organizations, staff, nurses, doctors, and other professionals, as well as management personnel from across departments, should be represented.

Typically, a kaizen event consists of the following steps, based on the plan-do-check-act (PDCA) improvement cycle of Deming and Juran:

1. Determine and define the objective(s).
2. Determine the current state of the process by mapping and measuring the process. Measurements will be related to the desired objectives but often include such things as cycle time, waiting time, WIP, throughput time, and travel distance.
3. Determine the requirements of the process (takt time), develop target goals, and design the future state or ideal state of the process.

EXHIBIT 9.4

Sample 5S Audit Form, Veterans Administration, Minneapolis

5S AUDIT FORM				
Area:			Date:	
	Yes	No	Date corrected	Comments:
Sort				
Only required items for the work area are present				
High use items are readily available				
Appropriate items are grouped together				
1S				
Set in order				Comments:
Materials properly stored so they can be used and returned easily				
All floor locations and work areas clearly marked with tape or paint				
Cabinets, shelves and containers are labeled and organized				
2S				
Shine				Comments:
Floors and entire area are clean and free of clutter				
All equipment is clean, free from leaks, chips and soiled spots				
All work surfaces, cabinets and shelves are clean and free from clutter				
3S				
Standardize				Comments:
Appropriate inventory on hand				
Appropriate number of each type of equipment present				
Pictures and/or labels are standardized and visible				
4S				
Sustain				Comments:
Life Safety Code requirements compliant				
Labels, signals and area demarcations are maintained				
5S corrective actions completed from last audit				
5S				
Immediate Corrective Action(s):				

EXHIBIT 9.5
Spaghetti Map
for Setting up
Education Room

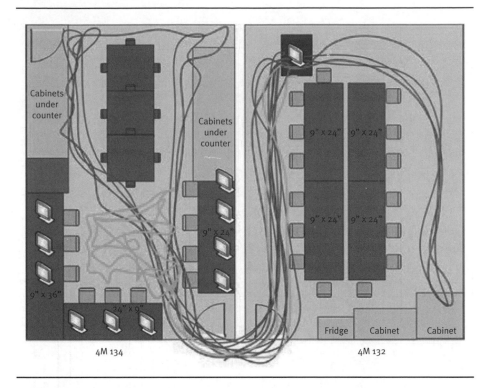

Cabinets under counter

Cabinets under counter

9" x 24"

9" x 24"   9" x 24"

9" x 24"   9" x 24"

9" x 24"

9" x 36"

24" x 9"

Fridge   Cabinet   Cabinet

4M 134

4M 132

4. Create a plan for implementation, including who, what, when, and so on.
5. Implement the improvements.
6. Check the effectiveness of the improvements.
7. Document and standardize the improved process.
8. Report the results of the event on an A3 reporting form.
9. Continue the cycle.

The kaizen event is based on the notion that most processes can be quickly (and relatively inexpensively) improved, in which case it makes sense to "just do it" rather than be paralyzed by resistance to change. A kaizen event is typically one week long and begins with training in the tools of Lean, followed by analysis and measurement of the current process and generation of possible ideas for improvement. By midweek, a proposal for changes to improve the process should be ready. The proposal should include the improved process flow and metrics for determining the effects of the changes. The proposed changes are implemented and tested during the remainder of the week. At the end of the week, a team is expected to report the results on an A3 reporting form. The A3 is a summary of the project results presented on a one-page, standard letter size A3 sheet of paper. By the following week, the new process should be in place.

A kaizen event can be a powerful way to quickly and inexpensively improve processes. The results are usually a significantly improved process and increased employee pride and satisfaction.

VVH Kaizen Event

The value stream map developed for the VVH birthing center highlighted the fact that nursing staff was spending a significant amount of time on activities not related to actual patient care. This not only resulted in dissatisfied patients, physicians, and nurses, it also increased staffing costs to the hospital. A kaizen blitz was planned to address this problem in the postpartum area of the birthing center.

The nursing administrator was charged with leading the kaizen event. She put together a team consisting of a physician, a housekeeper, two nurses' assistants, and two nurses. On Monday morning, the team began the kaizen event with four hours of Lean training. On Monday afternoon, they developed a spaghetti diagram for a typical nurse and began collecting data related to the amount of time nursing staff spent on various activities. They also collected historical data on patient load and staffing levels.

On Tuesday morning, the team continued to collect data. On Tuesday afternoon, they analyzed the data and found that nursing staff spent only 50 percent of their time in actual patient care. A significant amount of time— one hour per eight-hour shift—was spent locating equipment, supplies, and information. The team decided that a 50 percent reduction in this time was a reasonable goal for the kaizen event.

On Wednesday morning, the team used root-cause analysis to determine the reasons nursing staff spent so much time locating and moving equipment and supplies. They determined that one of the major causes was general disorder in the supply/equipment room and patient rooms.

On Wednesday afternoon, the team organized the supply/equipment room. They began by determining what supplies and equipment were necessary and removing those that were unnecessary. Next, they organized the supply/equipment room by determining which items were often needed together and locating those items close to one another. All storage areas were labeled, and specific locations for equipment were designated visually. White boards were installed to enable the tracking and location of equipment. The team also developed and posted a map of the room so that the location of equipment and supplies could be easily determined.

On Thursday, the team worked on reorganizing all of the patient rooms, standardizing the layout and location of items in each one. First, the team observed one of the patient rooms and determined the equipment and supply needs of physicians and nurses. All nonessential items were removed, creating more space. Additionally, rooms were stocked with supplies used on a routine basis to reduce trips to the central supply room. A procedure was also established to restock supplies on a daily basis.

On Friday morning, the kaizen team again collected data on the amount of time nursing staff spent on various activities. They found that after implementing the changes, the time nursing staff spent locating and moving supplies and equipment was reduced to approximately 20 minutes in an eight-hour shift, a 66 percent reduction. Friday afternoon was spent documenting the kaizen event and putting systems in place to ensure that the new procedures and organization would be maintained.

Standardized Work

Standardized work
Documentation of the precise way in which every step in a process should be completed.

Standardized work is an essential part of Lean and provides the baseline for continuous improvement. Standardized work refers to the methods of how a process is executed. All effective standardized work procedures include written documentation of the precise way in which every step in a process should be performed. It should not be seen as a rigid system of compliance, but rather as a means of communicating and codifying current best practices within the organization to provide a baseline from which improvements can be made to the process. Standardized work is critical in developing an effective Lean system as it represents the baseline against which all future improvements will be measured.

All relevant stakeholders of the process should be involved in establishing standard work. Standardizing work in this way assumes that the people most intimately involved with the process have the most knowledge of how to best perform the work. It can promote employee buy-in and ownership of the process and responsibility for improvement. Clear documentation and specific work instructions ensure that variation and waste are minimized. Standardized work should be seen as a step on the road to improvement. It allows doctors and nurses to perform at their licensure level more often because basic business processes run more effectively using standardized work (Lowe et al. 2012). This then leads to standardized measures that provide cost effectiveness and improve patient outcomes.

Care path
A sequence of best practices for healthcare staff to follow for a diagnosis or procedure, designed to minimize waste and maximize quality of care.

In the healthcare industry, examples of standardized work include treatment protocols and the establishment of **care paths**. (Care paths are also examples of evidence-based medicine, which is explored in more depth in Chapter 3.) Massachusetts General Hospital developed and implemented a care path for coronary artery bypass graft (CABG) surgery that resulted in an average length of stay reduction of 1.5 days; significant cost savings were associated with that reduction (Wheelwright and Weber 2004).

As part of an overall program to improve practices and reduce costs, Massachusetts General identified the establishment of a care path for CABG surgery. A care path is "an optimal sequencing and timing of interventions by physicians, nurses, and other staff for a particular diagnosis or procedure, designed to minimize delays and resource utilization and at the same time maximize the quality of care" (Wheelwright and Weber 2004). A care path defines and documents specifically what should happen to a patient the day before surgery, the day after surgery, and on postsurgical days. The care path was not intended to dictate medical treatment, but to standardize procedures as much as possible to reduce variability and improve the quality of outcomes.

The team that developed the care path included 25 participants representing the various areas involved in treatment. The team took more than a year to develop the initial care path, but because of its breadth of inclusion and applicability, resistance to implementation was minimal. After the successful implementation of the CABG surgical care path, Massachusetts General Hospital developed and implemented more than 50 care paths related to surgical procedures and medical treatments (Wheelwright and Weber 2004).

Standard work processes can be used in clinical, support, and administrative operations of healthcare organizations. The development and documentation of standardized processes and procedures can be a powerful tool for engaging and involving everyone in the organization in continuous improvement.

Jidoka and Andon

In Lean systems, **jidoka** refers to the ability to stop the process in the event of a problem. The term stems from the weaving loom invented by Sakichi Toyoda, founder of the Toyota Group. The loom stopped itself if a thread broke, eliminating the possibility that defective cloth would be produced.

Jidoka prevents defects from being passed from one step in the system to the next and enables the swift detection and correction of errors. If the system or process is stopped when a problem is found, everyone in the process works quickly to identify and eliminate the source of the error. In ancient Japan, an **andon** was a paper lantern used as a signal; in a Lean system, an andon is a visual or audible signaling device used to indicate a problem in the process. Andons are typically used in conjunction with jidoka.

In his book, *The Checklist Manifesto*, Atul Gawande (2009) highlights the benefits that hospitals gain by using simple checklists prior to inducing a patient in surgery. These checklists are a mechanism to make sure everyone in the surgical suite is on the same page, and they also give the surgical team a chance to stop the line if protocol has not been properly followed.

Virginia Mason Medical Center implemented a jidoka-andon system called the Patient Safety Alert System (Womack et al. 2005). If a caregiver believes that something is not right in the care process, she not only can, but must, stop the process. The person who has noticed the problem calls (or alerts, via the Internet) the patient safety department. The appropriate process

Jidoka
The ability to prevent defects by stopping a process when an error occurs.

Andon
A visual or audible signaling device used to indicate a problem in the process, typically used in conjunction with jidoka.

EXHIBIT 9.6
Kanban System

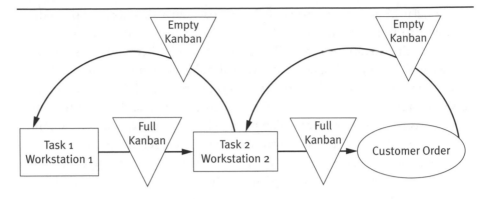

NOTE: Created with Microsoft Visio®.

stakeholders or relevant managers immediately come to determine and correct the root cause of the problem. After two years, the number of alerts per month rose from 3 to 17, enabling Virginia Mason to correct most problems in the process before they become more serious. The alerts are primarily related to systems issues, medication errors, and problems with equipment or facilities.

Kanban

Kanban is a Japanese term meaning signal. A kanban uses containers of a certain size to signal the need for more production or the movement of product. The customer indicates that he wants product, a kanban is released to the last operation in the system to signal the customer demand, and that station begins to produce product in response. As incoming material is consumed at the last workstation, another kanban will be emptied and sent to the previous workstation to signal that production should begin at that station. The empty kanbans go backward through the production system to signal the need to produce in response to customer demand (see Exhibit 9.6). This ensures that production is only done in response to customer demand, not simply because production capacity exists.

Kanban
A visual signal that triggers the movement of inventory or product in a system.

In a healthcare environment, kanbans can be used for supplies or pharmaceuticals to signal the need to order more. For example, a pharmacy would have two kanbans; when the first kanban is emptied, this signals the need to order more and an order is placed. The second kanban is emptied while waiting for the order to arrive. Ideally, the first kanban is received from the supplier at the point that the second kanban is empty and the cycle continues. The size of the kanbans is related to demand for the pharmaceutical during lead time for the order. The number and size of the kanbans determine the amount of inventory in the system.

In a healthcare environment, kanbans could also be used to control the flow of patients, ensuring continuous flow. For example, for patients

EXHIBIT 9.7
Kanban for
Echo/CT Scan

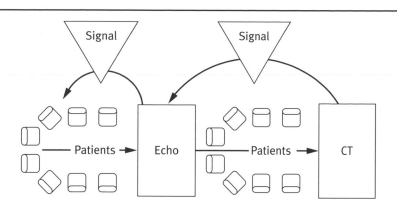

NOTE: Created with Microsoft Visio®.

needing both an echocardiography (echo) procedure and a computed tomography (CT) scan, where the echo procedure is to be performed before the CT scan, the CT scan could pull patients through the process. When a CT is performed, a patient is taken from the pool of patients between CT and echo. A kanban (signal) is sent to the echo station to indicate that another patient should receive an echo (see Exhibit 9.7). This ensures that a constant pool of patients is kept between the two processes. The patient pool should be large enough to ensure that the CT is busy even when disturbances in the echo process occur. However, this must be balanced with the need to keep patients from waiting for long periods. Eventually, in a Lean system, the pool size would be reduced to one.

Rapid Changeover

The rapid changeover, or single-minute exchange of die (SMED), system was developed by Shigeo Shingo (1985) of Toyota. Originally, it was used by manufacturing organizations to reduce changeover or setup time, the time between producing the last good part of one product and the first good part of a different product. Currently, the technique is used to reduce setup time for both manufacturing and services. In healthcare, the SMED system translates better as *rapid changeover*. In healthcare environments, setup is the time needed, or taken, between the completion of one procedure and the start of the next. In addition, setup time is needed when a patient checks out of a hospital to prepare a room for a new patient.

The rapid changeover technique consists of three steps:

1. Separating internal activities from external activities
2. Converting internal setup activities to external activities
3. Streamlining all setup activities

Internal activities are those activities that must be done in the system; they could not be done offline. For example, cleaning an operating room (OR) prior to the next surgery is an internal setup activity; it could not be completed outside the OR. However, organizing the surgical instruments for the next surgery is an external setup, as this could be done outside the OR to allow for speedier changeover of the OR.

Setup includes finding and organizing instruments, getting supplies, cleaning rooms, and obtaining paperwork. In the healthcare environment, rapid changeover can help alleviate surgery suite backlogs and cancellations because the room can be turned over quickly and the surgery teams can maximize the amount of time they are in surgery (AHRQ 2007).

To streamline activities, Lean teams must look for opportunities to do tasks in parallel and find ways to automate the process. For example, many manufacturers have helped the turnover of surgery rooms by manufacturing disposable sleeves that cover all of the lights and fixtures in the room. Instead of having to scrub all of those fixtures, a team simply has to replace the sleeves.

Heijunka and Advanced Access

Heijunka
The process of eliminating variations in volume and variety of production to reduce waste.

Heijunka is a Japanese term meaning "make flat and level." It refers to eliminating variations in volume and variety of production to reduce waste. In healthcare environments, this often means determining how to level patient demand. Producing goods or services at a level rate allows organizations to be more responsive to customers and better use their own resources. In healthcare, advanced access provides a good example of the benefits of heijunka.

Several studies have shown that many people are unable to obtain timely primary care appointments (Murray and Berwick 2003). Advanced access scheduling reduces the time between scheduling an appointment for care and the actual appointment. It is based on the principles of Lean and aims for swift, even patient flow through the system. In clinical settings, reducing the wait time for appointments has been shown to decrease no-show rates (Kennedy and Hsu 2003) and improve both patient and staff satisfaction (Radel et al. 2001). Revenues are increased (O'Hare and Corlett 2004) as a result of higher patient volumes and increased staff and clinician productivity. Additionally, greater continuity of care (Belardi, Weir, and Craig 2004) should increase the quality of care and result in more positive outcomes for patients.

Although the benefits of advanced access are great, implementation can be difficult because the concept challenges established practices and beliefs. However, if the delay between making an appointment and the actual appointment is relatively constant, implementing advanced access should be possible.

Centra, a multisite primary care clinic located in Chicago, began advanced access scheduling in 2001. The organization was able to reduce access time to 3 days or less, patient satisfaction increased from 72 percent to 85 percent, and continuity of care was significantly increased (75 percent of visits occurred with a patient's primary physician, compared with 40 percent prior to advanced access). The biggest issue encountered was the greater demand for popular clinicians and the need to address this inequity on an ongoing basis (Murray et al. 2003).

Successful implementation of advanced access requires that supply and demand be balanced. To do this, accurate estimates of both supply and demand are needed, backlog must be reduced or eliminated, and the variety of appointment types needs to be minimized. Once supply and demand are known, demand profiles may need to be adjusted and the availability of bottleneck resources increased (Murray and Berwick 2003). IHI (2006b) offers extensive online resources to aid healthcare organizations in implementing advanced access, and Chapter 12 discusses the concept in more detail.

The Merger of Lean and Six Sigma Programs

Many organizations have begun combining the philosophies and tools of both Lean and Six Sigma into Lean Sigma (George 2002). Although proponents of Lean or Six Sigma might say that these initiatives are quite different and champion one or the other, the two methods are complementary, and combining them can be effective for many organizations.

Exhibit 9.8 provides a classic illustration of how the two unique continuous improvement programs should be used together. In this illustration the water represents waste in the system. The water hides the rocks so the boat can move downstream without any issues. In healthcare systems, this waste often shows up in one of two forms: excess supplies and inventory or too much demand on the system. Once the water is removed the rocks become exposed, thus making it dangerous for the boat to sail downstream. The rocks represent major issues in our systems, such as sentinel events and excessive overtime paid to nurses and other staff. To sail the boat without issues, the problems must be reduced by removing variance in the system. For example, perhaps too much overtime is being paid to the staff in the surgical suite of a hospital. Further analysis finds that staff is spending excess time looking for equipment, which delays surgeries and forces the overtime. To get the boat to sail smoothly, the problems of looking for equipment must be reduced and removed.

The Lean system focuses on eliminating waste and streamlining flow. In the previous example the waste in the system was identified as excessive

EXHIBIT 9.8
Lean and Six
Sigma

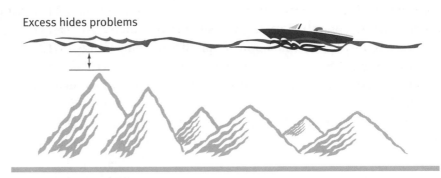

Lean Six Sigma Approach

Excess hides problems

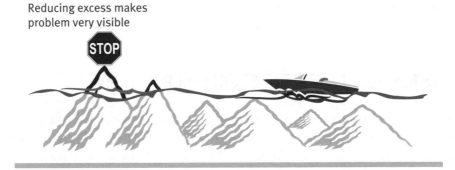

Lean Six Sigma Approach

Reducing excess makes
problem very visible

Lean Six Sigma Approach

Reduce problems/
Remove variation

waiting as a result of waiting for the equipment. The excessive waste in this situation may even lead to the hiring of extra people to make sure the equipment reaches the OR suite on time. The Six Sigma program focuses on creating value to the customer, eliminating defects, and reducing variation. The Six Sigma approach would identify the reasons why the equipment arrived late to the OR and systematically reduce and remove those sources of variance. Both Lean and Six Sigma are ultimately focused on continuous improvement of any system. The Six Sigma process using the DMAIC structure always begins with defining the issues or problems as they relate to the customer. The focus on reducing variance in the eyes of the customer allows Six Sigma programs to create customer value. The kaizen philosophy of Lean begins with determining what customers value, followed by mapping and improving the process to achieve flow and pull. Lean thinking enables identification of the areas causing inefficiencies. However, to truly achieve Lean, variation in the processes must be eliminated—Six Sigma will help to do this. Focusing on the customer and eliminating waste will not only result in increased customer satisfaction, it will also reduce costs and increase the profitability of the organization. Together, Lean and Six Sigma can provide the philosophies and tools needed to ensure that the organization is continuously improving. Recent research supports the idea that the implementation of continuous improvement is a gradual addition of skill sets and not choosing a specific system like Lean or Six Sigma (Belohlav et al. 2010).

Discussion Questions

1. What are the drivers behind the healthcare industry's focus on employing resources in an effective manner and on patient satisfaction?
2. What are the differences between Lean and Six Sigma? The similarities? Would you like to see both in your organization? Why or why not?
3. From your own experiences, discuss a specific example of each of the seven types of waste.
4. From your own experiences, describe a specific instance in which standardized work, kanban, jidoka and andon, and rapid changeover would enable an organization to become more effective or efficient.
5. Does your primary care clinic have advanced access scheduling? Should it? To determine supply and demand and track progress, what measures would you recommend to your clinic?
6. Are there any drawbacks to Lean Sigma? Explain.

Chapter Exercises

1. A simple value stream map for patients requiring a colonoscopy at an endoscopy clinic is shown in Exhibit 9.9. Assume that patients recover in the same room where the colonoscopy is performed and the clinic has two colonoscopy rooms. What is the cycle time for the process? What is the throughput time? What is the percent value

EXHIBIT 9.9
Value Stream
Map for
Colonoscopies

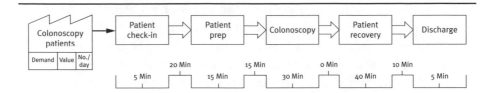

NOTE: Created with eVSM™ software from GumshoeKI, Inc., a Microsoft Visio® add-on.

added in this process? If the clinic operates 10 hours a day and demand is 12 patients per day, what is the takt time? If demand is 20 patients per day, what is the takt time? What would you do in the second situation?

2. Draw a high-level value stream map for your organization (or a part of your organization). Pick a part of this map and draw a more detailed value stream map for it. On each map, be sure to identify the information you would need to complete the map and exactly how you might obtain it. What are the takt and throughput times of your process? Identify at least three kaizen opportunities on your map.

3. For one of your kaizen opportunities described above, describe the kaizen event you would plan if you were the kaizen leader.

SIMULATION

10

Operations Management in Action

Surgeons at BC Children's Hospital have a way to shorten wait lists and get their patients through the hospital system more efficiently and with less stress.

Drs. Geoff Blair and Jacques Leblanc, head and assistant head of surgery, respectively, have created a simulation model, not unlike those used by airlines and the military during wartime, that allows for the movement of large numbers of people.

Using a branch of mathematical analysis known as the "science of decision making," including game theory and queuing theory, Drs. Blair and Leblanc believed it was possible to simulate and test how changes to patient flow and surgical scheduling would affect throughput, patient waiting times, and budgets, without adversely affecting ongoing operations.

They created a model to simulate the processes from the moment a patient enters BC Children's for surgery to the time they leave. This includes OR prep time, how long each procedure takes per surgeon, how patients are moved from the ICU to the appropriate unit, available bed space, and actual recovery times.

Programmers added random factors provided by hospital staff, such as unscheduled emergency cases, unplanned fluctuations in staff levels due to illness, equipment breakdowns, and clerical problems. They also came up with a block schedule analysis tool the hospital could use to test various schedule changes and assess their impact on future wait times, staffing, and costs.

The team used aliases of more than 30,000 actual patient files from the previous three years to ensure confidentiality was maintained during the simulation process. They checked the accuracy of the program by running a one-year simulation of patient flow, and the results compared to what actually transpired during that period.

The value of the simulation is that it can effectively get past the what-if? while staff try to come up with ways to deal with growing wait lists and escalating costs, says Dr. Blair.

"In healthcare, we've been relying on our puny human minds to try to deal with all these systems of queues and decision-making. And the interaction of everything has to be brought to bear to get a kid at Children's Hospital who needs surgery into the operating room, with everybody who needs to be there, with all the equipment that needs to be there, on time, at an appropriate time that reflects the child's medical condition. It's not unlike the same complexity airlines face when faced with ticketing, boarding passes, security, baggage handling, runway availability, 747s unloading their passengers while another 747 is boarding passengers. So why not use the same sort of approach?" he asked.

The model has been a boon for block scheduling, he says. OR times have been set since the hospital opened in 1982, but with the aid of the simulation tool, those surgeries with the longest wait lists can be reallocated without causing a logjam.

"The human tendency is to avoid changing, because we don't know what's going to happen," said Blair. "There's a real inertia in healthcare. And governments are increasingly demanding more proof that we deserve more money, to prove that we are being as efficient as possible. What we can do with this block scheduler [is] simulate what will happen because we have all the data entered in real time—every patient who is waiting is now in the system—and we can then take time away from orthopedics, cardiac surgery and give it to ophthalmology, say, and then we just run it. Within minutes, we can see graphically exactly what will happen to the waiting lists in cardiac surgery, orthopedics, and ophthalmology. It allows us to tweak time in areas that are not in bad shape and not inconvenience anybody; we can predict scientifically, in a valid way, what will happen if we make this change. This removes the fear of change."

The Simulation Tool, as it's called, will also be used to better manage outpatient clinics as well as OR time. It's also going to be applied to better management of beds.

In one striking scenario used by the programmers, Wednesday morning rounds with surgeons and nurses were changed to the afternoon and resulted in an additional 54 surgeries being performed over the course of a year.

"This isn't a cure for cancer," said Blair. "But it could go a long way to 'curing' some of the major problems that affect us every day in our attempts to deliver care to our kids here."

SOURCE: Haley, L. 2005. "Simulation Aims to Speed Patients Through Surgeries." *Medical Post* 41 (1): 2–3. Reprinted with permission.

Overview

Simulation is the process of modeling reality to gain a better understanding of the phenomena or system being studied. Simulation allows the user to ask and answer what-if questions in an environment that is more cost-effective, less dangerous, faster, or more practical than the real world.

Although the simulation techniques outlined in this chapter are computer-based mathematic models, simulation does not require mathematic models or computer analysis. A fire drill, for example, is a simulation of what would or could happen in the event of a real fire. The drill is run to address any problems that might arise if there were a real fire, without the danger associated with a real fire. Different types of simulations are appropriate for many different contexts.

The report *Building a Better Delivery System: A New Engineering/ Health Care Partnership*, a joint effort between the National Academy of Engineering and the Institute of Medicine (2005), identifies engineering tools and technologies that could be employed to help to overcome the current safety, quality, cost, and access crises faced by the healthcare industry. This report specifically cites systems modeling and simulation as tools that have the power to enable healthcare organizations to improve quality, efficiency, and safety.

This chapter provides an introduction to simulation and the theories underlying it. The major topics covered include:

- How, where, and why simulation can be used
- The simulation process
- Monte Carlo simulation
- Queuing theory
- Discrete event simulation

After completing this chapter, readers should have a basic understanding of simulation. This should help them recognize how simulation could be used in their organizations to evaluate choices and optimize processes and systems.

Uses of Simulation

Simulation can be used for many different purposes, including performance, proof, discovery, entertainment, training, education, and prediction (Axelrod 2006).

Performance simulation can actually carry out some task for an organization or entity. It is related to artificial intelligence and usually simulates a human behavior. Voice recognition and robotic-assisted surgery are examples of performance simulation.

Simulation can be used to discover new relationships and principles and to provide proof of a theory. For example, Conway's Game of Life (Berlekamp, Conway, and Guy 2003) is used to discover and prove that simple rules can result in complex behavior. Simulations can also be used to entertain, as with virtual reality video games.

Simulation is often used for education and training purposes. Increasingly, simulators are being used to educate healthcare professionals in medical concepts and decision making as well as to train them in therapeutic and diagnostic procedures. For example, the mannequin simulator Resusci-Anne has been used for CPR training since the 1960s (Grenvik and Schaefer 2004). Since then, simulations related to medical training and education have become increasingly sophisticated. Training simulations allow users to practice decisions and techniques in a safe environment where an incorrect decision does not have serious consequences.

Predictive simulation can be used to evaluate the design of new products, systems, or procedures as well as to analyze and improve existing products, systems, or procedures. This chapter focuses on predictive simulation—specifically, Monte Carlo simulation and discrete event simulation.

The Simulation Process

Simulation begins with development of a model. Once the model has been built and validated, the output of the simulation is analyzed to address the original question or problem (Exhibit 10.1).

EXHIBIT 10.1
Simulation
Process

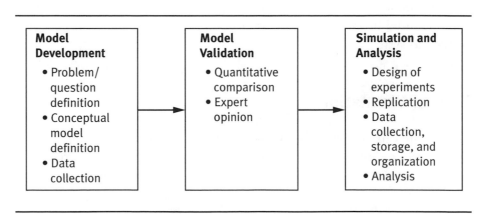

Model Development	Model Validation	Simulation and Analysis
• Problem/ question definition • Conceptual model definition • Data collection	• Quantitative comparison • Expert opinion	• Design of experiments • Replication • Data collection, storage, and organization • Analysis

Model Development

The first step in model development is to define the problem or question to be answered with the simulation. The usefulness of the simulation will be driven by the accuracy of the problem definition.

The next step in developing a simulation model is defining the conceptual model. Here, the system is described analytically or mathematically; inputs and outputs are determined, and relationships are defined. Because real-world systems are complex and difficult to represent analytically, assumptions about the system must be made. A perfect model of the system is seldom possible, and approximations appropriate for the study must be made. There is usually a trade-off between model validity and model complexity; all things being equal, however, a simpler model is better.

Once the conceptual model has been defined, information required for the simulation must be collected. Data related to the probability distributions of random variables in the system, data defining the relationships in the simulation, and data related to the output behavior of existing systems are collected. These data will be used in running and validating the simulation.

The final step in model development is actually building the computer model. In the past, this meant coding the software for the model. Today, many commercially available software packages make this step relatively simple.

Model Validation

The validity of a simulation is related to how closely the simulation mirrors reality and answers the question that was asked. Simulations can be developed that are technically correct but do not accurately reflect reality or do not address the intended question or problem. Therefore, assessing the validity of the simulation is an essential, but often difficult, step.

Ideally, the simulation is run and quantitative output data of the simulation are compared to output data from the real system to determine whether they are similar. Alternatively, experts are asked to determine if the design and output of the simulation make sense to them. If the simulation is not deemed valid, the model must be redeveloped.

Simulation and Output Analysis

Here, the simulation model is actually run and output data are collected. If a number of different variables and variable states are of interest, experimental design can be used to determine the specifications of those variables so that the experiments can be optimally run in a timely, cost-effective manner. Ensuring reliable results may require many replications of the simulation. The results of the simulations must be collected, organized, and stored. Finally, the output data must be analyzed to determine the "answer" to the original question or problem.

Monte Carlo Simulation

Monte Carlo simulation
A mathematical technique that allows a modeler to enter input variables as probability distributions that will create output variables with probabilistic outcomes.

Monte Carlo simulation was pioneered by John von Nuemann, Stanislaw Ulam, and Nicholas Metropolis in the 1940s while they were working on the Manhattan Project to develop the first atomic bomb (Metropolis 1987). This group conceived of the idea of modeling the output of a system by using input variables that could not be known exactly but could be represented with probability distributions. Many repetitions of the model were run, and the behavior of the real system could be estimated based on the outcomes of the many replications. This technique came to be known as Monte Carlo simulation because of its use of probability distributions (discussed in Chapter 7) and their relationship to the games of chance found in the famous casino.

The Monte Carlo method consists of defining the relationships in a system mathematically. The random variables in the model (those that are uncertain and have a range of possible values) are not characterized by a single number but by a probability distribution. The probability distribution used to characterize the random variable is chosen based on historical data or expert knowledge of the situation. Many solutions to the model are determined, each one found by sampling from the probability distributions associated with the random variables. The solution is not a single number but a distribution of possible outcomes that can be characterized statistically.

A simple, non-computer-based example of Monte Carlo simulation is provided here to aid in understanding. A clinic wishes to estimate the amount of revenue that will be collected from each patient. Fifty percent of the clinic's patients do not pay for their services, and it is equally likely that they will pay or not pay. The clinic has collected information on charges incurred by the most recent 360 patients (Exhibit 10.2).

EXHIBIT 10.2
Payment Information for Monte Carlo Simulation

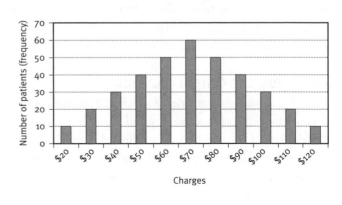

Number of patients (frequency)	Charges ($)
10	$ 20
20	$ 30
30	$ 40
40	$ 50
50	$ 60
60	$ 70
50	$ 80
40	$ 90
30	$ 100
20	$ 110
10	$ 120
Total 360	
Average	$ 70

The payment per patient is modeled by:

Probability of payment × Charges/Patient = Payment/Patient

A deterministic solution to this problem would be:

0.50 × $70/Patient = $35 per Patient

A Monte Carlo simulation of this problem is based on calculating the payment from many individual simulated patients. The probability of payment can be simulated by flipping a coin to represent the probability that a patient will pay, where heads represents payment and equals 1, and tails represents nonpayment and equals 0. The charges incurred can be simulated by rolling two six-sided dice and multiplying their total by $10. The payment for the simulated patient is calculated as 0 or 1 times the dice total times $10. This process is repeated many times to determine the payment per patient. For example, in the first trial a heads is rolled and the dice total is 7. The patient payment is:

1 × 7 × $10 = $70

The first ten trials of this simulation are shown in Exhibit 10.3, and a frequency diagram of the output of 100 trials is shown in Exhibit 10.4. Although on average each patient pays $35, 50 percent of the patients pay nothing, a small percentage pay as much as $120, and no individual patient pays $35. Using averages or most likely values can mask a significant amount of information. Just as a person can easily drown in a river that is, on

EXHIBIT 10.3
Simulation Trials

Trial No.	Coin Flip	Payment	Dice Total	Charges	Patient Payment
1	H	1	7	$70.00	$70.00
2	T	0	10	$100.00	$—
3	H	1	8	$80.00	$80.00
4	T	0	8	$80.00	$—
5	H	1	9	$90.00	$90.00
6	T	0	8	$80.00	$—
7	H	1	7	$70.00	$70.00
8	T	0	10	$100.00	$—
9	H	1	9	$90.00	$90.00
10	T	0	10	$100.00	$—

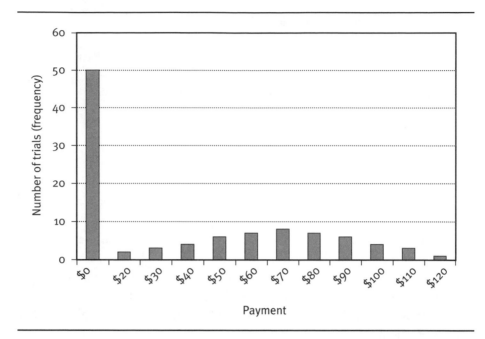

average, only three feet deep, decisions based on averages are often flawed (Savage 2002). Monte Carlo simulation can reveal hidden information and is often used in business and economics to gain a clearer understanding of the risks and rewards of a situation or decision.

Flipping coins, rolling dice, and calculating output for thousands of trials would be tedious; however, a computer can accomplish these tasks quickly and easily. There are many commercially available software packages for Monte Carlo simulation; Crystal Ball (Oracle Corporation 2012) and @Risk (Palisade Corporation 2012) are two of the more popular Microsoft Excel–based packages.

Vincent Valley Hospital and Health System Example

Vincent Valley Hospital and Health System (VVH) is trying to decide if it should participate in a new pay-for-performance (Chapter 3) incentive program offered by the three largest health plans in the area. This program focuses on community-acquired pneumonia (CAP), and hospital performance is evaluated based on composite measures of quality related to this condition. Incentives are based on performance: Hospitals scoring above 0.90 will receive a 2 percent bonus payment on top of the standard diagnosis-related group (DRG) payment; hospitals scoring above 0.85 will receive a 1 percent bonus; hospitals scoring below 0.70 will incur a 1 percent reduction in the standard DRG payment; and hospitals scoring below 0.65 will incur a 2 percent reduction.

EXHIBIT 10.5
CAP Payment
Data

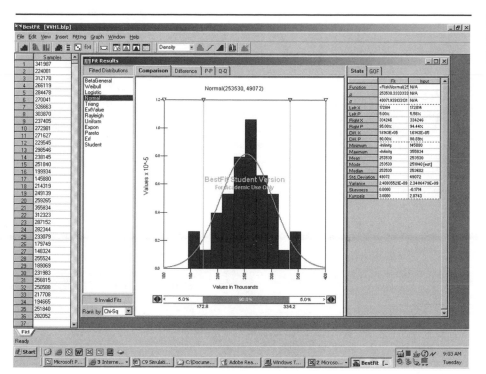

NOTE: Created with BestFit 4.5.

VVH has collected payment data related to this condition for the previous 36 months. The organization used BestFit to find the probability distribution that will best represent these data and determined that the data can be represented fairly well by a normal distribution (Exhibit 10.5) with mean (μ) = \$250,000/month and standard deviation (σ) = \$50,000/month.

Because VVH has no historical data related to the success or cost of a program to increase quality scores related to CAP, expert opinion must be used to estimate them. After discussions with experts, the VVH team believes that reaching a score of greater than 0.90 will cost the organization between \$10,000 and \$50,000, with any cost in the range being equally likely (i.e., a uniform distribution).

VVH also needs to estimate the probability of receiving various quality scores. A triangular distribution is fairly easy to estimate from expert opinion. All that is needed to define this distribution are high, low, and most likely values. Again, after talking with various internal and external experts, VVH believes that the most likely score it will receive will be 0.88, but that score could be as high as 0.95 or as low as 0.60.

A deterministic evaluation of this situation, using point estimates for all values, results in the following analysis:

EXHIBIT 10.6
Monte Carlo
Simulation of
CAP Pay-for-
Performance
Program

Point Estimate	
CAP Quality Score	Pay for Performance Factor
0.00	−0.02
0.65	−0.01
0.70	0.00
0.85	0.01
0.90	0.02

Revenue/ Month	Revenue/ Year	Quality Score	Payment or Penalty	Bonus Payment	Costs/ Year	Profit = Revenue − Costs
$ 250,000.00	$ 3,000,000.00	0.88	0.01	$ 30,000.00	$ 30,000.00	$ -

Simulation Using @Risk						
Revenue/ Month	Revenue/ Year	Quality Score	Payment or Penalty Factor	Bonus Payment or Penalty Charge	Costs/ Year	Profit = Revenue − Costs
$ 250,000.00	$ 3,000,000.00	0.81	0.00	0	$ 30,000.00	$ (30,000.00)
"= RiskNormal (250,000, 50,000)"	"= Revenue/ Month * 12"	"= RiskTriang (0.6, 0.88, 0.95)"	"= VLOOKUP (D15,B4:C8,2, TRUE)"	"= Revenue/ Year * Payment or Penalty Factor"	"= RiskUniform (10,000, 50,000)"	"= RiskOutput() Revenue − Cost"

NOTE: Created with @Risk 4.5.

$$\text{Profit} = \text{Revenue} - \text{Cost}$$
$$\text{Revenue} = (\text{Revenue/Month} \times 12 \text{ Months/Year}) \times \text{Quality bonus or penalty}$$
$$= (\$250{,}000/\text{Month} \times 12 \text{ Months/Year}) \times 0.01$$
$$= \$30{,}000/\text{year}$$
$$\text{Cost} = \$30{,}000/\text{year}$$
$$\text{Profit} = \$30{,}000/\text{year} - \$30{,}000/\text{year} = \$0$$

From this analysis, it appears that there will be no net gain or loss should VVH decide to participate in the pay-for-performance program. However, a Monte Carlo simulation of the situation reveals some additional information. The Excel spreadsheet for this scenario is shown in Exhibit 10.6, and the results of the first few simulation trials are shown in Exhibit 10.7.

On the first trial, @Risk randomly selects from a normal distribution with mean of $250,000 and standard deviation of $50,000 and finds that the first month's revenue is $155,687 for CAP-related conditions. @Risk repeats this process for the remaining 11 months and sums those months to obtain a total of $2,699,013 for the year. Random selection from a uniform distribution of costs finds a cost of $17,032, and random selection from a triangular distribution of quality scores determines a score of 0.84. In this trial VVH would not be charged a penalty, nor would it receive a bonus. Therefore, VVH would experience a total loss (negative profit) of $17,032, equal to the cost of the program.

EXHIBIT 10.7
Monte Carlo
Simulation of
CAP Pay-for-
Performance
Program

Output Simulation	Revenue/ Month 1	Revenue/ Year 1	Quality Score 1	Costs/ Year 1	Profit = Revenue − Costs 1
Iteration/Cell	$B$14	$C$14	$D$14	$G$14	$H$14
1	155,687.1563	$2,699,013.25	0.840952277	17,032.68359	$ (17,032.68)
2	244,965.375	$2,903,593.00	0.764673352	15,443.74902	$ (15,443.75)
3	257,408.3125	$2,924,186.25	0.785211325	26,655.60938	$ (26,655.61)
4	335,716.8438	$3,441,799.25	0.652704477	31,370.79883	$ (65,788.80)
5	232,497.8281	$2,857,697.00	0.823849738	46,067.85156	$ (46,067.85)

NOTE: Created with @Risk 4.5.

@Risk performs many of these trials, collects output data, and provides statistics and graphs that can be used to analyze this situation. Exhibit 10.8 shows the distribution of profits for this situation. In contrast to the point estimate obtained in the deterministic analysis, this analysis shows that if

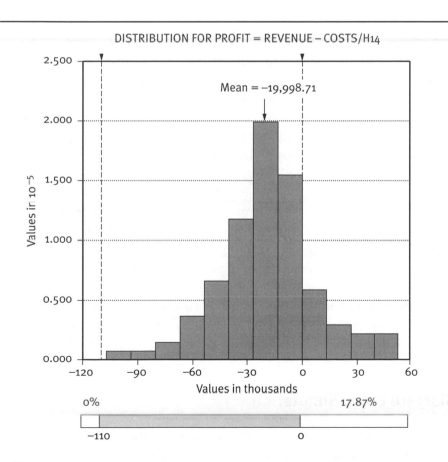

EXHIBIT 10.8
Simulated
Distribution
of Profits for
CAP Pay-for-
Performance
Program

DISTRIBUTION FOR PROFIT = REVENUE − COSTS/H14

Mean = −19,998.71

Values in 10⁻⁵

Values in thousands

0%   17.87%

−110   0

NOTE: Created with @Risk 4.5.

EXHIBIT 10.9
Tornado Graph
for CAP Pay-for-
Performance
Program

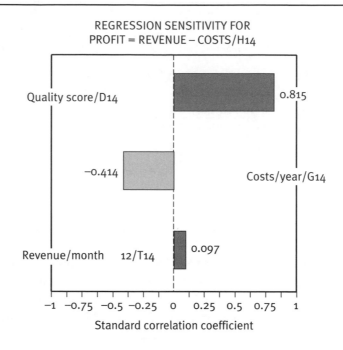

REGRESSION SENSITIVITY FOR
PROFIT = REVENUE − COSTS/H14

Quality score/D14 — 0.815

−0.414 — Costs/year/G14

Revenue/month 12/T14 — 0.097

Standard correlation coefficient
(axis: −1 −0.75 −0.5 −0.25 0 0.25 0.5 0.75 1)

NOTE: Created with @Risk 4.5.

VVH chooses to participate in the pay-for-performance program, it will break even or make a profit less than 20 percent of the time. More than 80 percent of the time, VVH will incur a loss that could be as large as $108,000.

Tornado graph
A sensitivity graph used to display relative strength of variables in a simulation model.

A **tornado graph** showing the correlation between each input and the output can be a useful analytic tool (Exhibit 10.9). Here, the quality score received has the most important relationship to profit (or loss). In this case, it highlights the importance of VVH's investment resulting in the achievement of a high quality score. If VVH believes that a $30,000 investment will result in the quality scores indicated, it may not want to participate in the pay-for-performance program. Alternatively, if VVH decides to participate, it is imperative that the investment results in high quality scores. The VVH team may want to evaluate different types of programs or strategies to increase the probability of achieving a high quality score.

Monte Carlo analyses are particularly useful in enabling organizations to evaluate the probable outcomes of decisions, evaluate the risks involved with those decisions, and develop strategies to mitigate those risks.

Discrete event simulation (DES)
A simulation technique that uses probability distributions to represent random variables.

Discrete Event Simulation

Like Monte Carlo simulation, **discrete event simulation (DES)** is based on using probability distributions to represent random variables. DES, however, has its roots in queuing, or waiting line, theory.

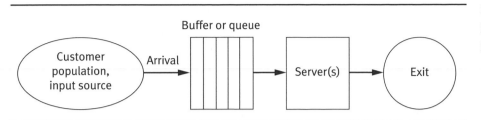

EXHIBIT 10.10
Simple Queuing
System

Buffer or queue

Customer population, input source

Arrival

Server(s)

Exit

Queuing (Waiting Line) Theory

Although most people are familiar with waiting in line, few are familiar with, or even aware of, **queuing theory** or the theory of waiting lines. Most people's experience with waiting lines is when they are actually part of those lines, for example, when waiting to check out in a retail environment. In a manufacturing environment, items wait in line to be worked on. In a service environment, customers wait for a service to be performed.

Queuing theory
The mathematical study of wait lines.

Queues, or lines, form because the resources needed to serve them (servers) are limited—it is economically unfeasible to have unlimited resources. Queuing theory is used to study systems to determine the best balance between service to customers (short or no waiting lines, implying many resources or servers) and economic considerations (few servers, implying long lines). A simple queuing system is illustrated in Exhibit 10.10.

Customers (often referred to as entities) arrive and are either served (if there is no line) or enter the queue (if others are waiting to be served). Once they are served, customers exit the system.

The customer population, or input source, can be either finite or infinite. If the source is effectively infinite, the analysis of the system is easier because simplifying assumptions can be made.

The arrival process is characterized by the arrival pattern, the rate at which customers arrive (number of customers/unit of time), or interarrival time (time between arrivals) and the distribution in time of those arrivals. The distribution of arrivals can be constant or variable. A constant arrival distribution would have a fixed interarrival time. A variable, or random, arrival pattern is described by a probability distribution. The **queue discipline** is the method by which customers are selected from the queue to be served. Often, customers are served in the order in which they arrived—first come, first served. However, many other queue disciplines are possible, and choice of a particular discipline can greatly affect system performance. For example, choosing the customer whose service can be completed most quickly (shortest processing time) usually minimizes the average time customers spend waiting in line. This is one reason urgent care centers are often located near an emergency department—urgent issues can usually be handled more quickly than true emergencies.

Queue discipline
In queuing theory, the method by which customers are selected from the queue to be served.

The service process is characterized by the number of servers and service time. Like arrivals, the distribution of service times can be constant or variable. Often, the exponential distribution (Chapter 7) is used to model variable service times, and μ is the mean service rate.

Queuing Notation

The type of queuing system is identified with specific notation of the form A/B/c/D/E. The A represents the interarrival time distribution, and B represents the service time distribution. A and B would be represented with a D for deterministic, or constant, rates. The c represents the number of servers, D represents the maximum queue size, and E is the size of the input population. When both queue and input population are assumed to be infinite, D and E are typically omitted. An M/M/1 queuing system, therefore, has an exponential service time distribution, single server, infinite possible queue length, and infinite input population, and it is assumed that only one queue exists.

Queuing Solutions

Analytic solutions for some simple queuing systems at equilibrium, or steady state (after the system has been running for some time and is unchanging, often referred to as a stable system), have been determined. The derivation of these results is outside the scope of this text; see Cooper (1981) for a complete derivation and results for many other types of queuing systems.

Here, the results for an M/M/1 queuing system with $\lambda < \mu$—the arrival rate less than the service rate—are presented. Note that if $\lambda \geq \mu$ (customers arrive faster than they are served), the queue will become infinitely long, the number of customers in the system will become infinite, waiting time will become infinite, and the server will experience 100 percent capacity utilization. The following formulas can be used to determine some characteristics of the queuing system at steady state:

Capacity utilization = Percentage of time the server is busy =

$$\rho = \frac{\lambda}{\mu} = \frac{\text{Mean arrival rate}}{\text{Mean service rate}} = \frac{1/\text{Mean time between arrivals}}{1/\text{Mean service time}}$$

$$= \frac{\text{Mean service time}}{\text{Mean time between arrivals}}$$

Average waiting time in queue $= W_q = \dfrac{\lambda}{\mu(\mu - \lambda)}$

Average time in the system =
Average waiting time in queue + average service time =

$$W_s = W_q + \frac{1}{\mu} = \frac{1}{\mu - \lambda}$$

Average length of queue (or Average number in queue) =

$$L_q = \frac{\lambda^2}{\mu(\mu - \lambda)} = \left(\frac{\lambda}{\mu}\right)\left(\frac{\lambda}{\mu - \lambda}\right)$$

Average total number of customers in the system =

$$L_s = \frac{\lambda}{\mu - \lambda} = \lambda W_s = \text{Arrival rate} \times \text{Time in the system}$$

This last result is called **Little's law** and applies to all types of queuing systems and subsystems. To summarize this result in plain language, in a stable system or process, the number of things in the system is equal to the rate at which things arrive to the system multiplied by the time they spend in the system. In a stable system, the average rate at which things arrive to the system is equal to the average rate at which things leave the system. If this were not true, the system would not be stable.

Little's law can also be restated using other terminology:

Inventory (Things in the system)
= Arrival rate (or Departure rate) × Throughput time (Flow time)
and
Throughput time = Inventory/Arrival rate

Knowledge of two of the variables in Little's law allows calculation of the third variable. Consider a clinic that services 200 patients in an eight-hour day, or an average of 25 patients an hour (λ). The average number of patients in the clinic (waiting room, exams rooms, etc.) is 15 (I). Therefore, the average throughput time is:

$$T = I/\lambda$$

$$= \frac{15 \text{ Patients}}{25 \text{ Patients/Hour}}$$

$$= 0.6 \text{ Hour}$$

Hence, each patient spends an average of 36 minutes in the clinic.

Little's law
The relationship between arrival rate to a system, the time a patient spends in the system, and the number of items in a system.

Little's law has important implications for process improvement and can be seen as the basis of many improvement techniques. Throughput time can be decreased by decreasing inventory or increasing departure rate. Lean initiatives often focus on decreasing throughput time (or increasing throughput rate) by decreasing inventory. The theory of constraints (Chapter 6) focuses on identifying and eliminating system bottlenecks. The departure rate in any system will be equal to 1/task cycle time of the slowest task in the system or process (the bottleneck). Decreasing the amount of time an object spends at the bottleneck task therefore increases the departure rate of the system and decreases throughput time.

VVH M/M/1 Queue

VVH had been receiving complaints from patients related to crowded conditions in the waiting area for magnetic resonance imaging (MRI) procedures. VVH wanted an average of only one patient waiting in line for the MRI. The organization collected data on arrival and service rates and found that for MRI the mean service rate (μ) was four patients per hour, exponentially distributed. VVH also found that the mean arrival rate was three patients per hour (λ).

Capacity utilization of MRI = Percentage of time the MRI is busy =

$$\rho = \frac{\lambda}{\mu} = \frac{3}{4} = 75\% \text{ or } \rho = \frac{1/\mu}{1/\lambda} = \frac{15 \text{ Minutes}}{20 \text{ Minutes}} = 75\%$$

If one customer arrives every 20 minutes, and it takes 15 minutes to perform the MRI, the MRI will be busy 75 percent of the time.

Average time waiting in line =

$$W_q = \frac{\lambda}{\mu(\mu - \lambda)} = \frac{3}{4(4-3)} = \frac{3}{4} = 0.75 \text{ Hour}$$

Average time in the system =

$$W_s = \frac{1}{\mu - \lambda} = \frac{1}{4-3} = 1 \text{ Hour}$$

Average total number of patients in the system =

$$L_s = \frac{\lambda}{\mu - \lambda} = \frac{3}{4 - 3} = 3 \text{ Patients or}$$

$$L_s = \lambda W_s = \text{Arrival rate} \times \text{Time in the system} =$$
$$3 \text{ Patients/Hour} \times 1 \text{ Hour} = 3 \text{ Patients}$$

Average number of patients in waiting line =

$$L_q = \frac{\lambda^2}{\mu(\mu - \lambda)} = \left(\frac{\lambda}{\mu}\right)\left(\frac{\lambda}{\mu - \lambda}\right) = \left(\frac{3}{4}\right)\left(\frac{3}{4 - 3}\right)$$

$$= \frac{3^2}{4(4 - 3)} = \frac{9}{4} = 2.25 \text{ Patients}$$

To decrease the average number of patients waiting, VVH needs to decrease the utilization, $\rho = \lambda/\mu$, of the MRI process. In other words, the service rate must be increased or the arrival rate decreased. VVH could increase the service rate by making the MRI process more efficient so that the average time to perform the procedure is decreased, and MRIs can be performed on a greater number of patients in an hour. Alternatively, VVH could decrease the arrival rate by scheduling fewer patients per hour.

To achieve its goal (assuming that the service rate is not increased), VVH needs to decrease the arrival rate to:

$$L_q = \frac{\lambda^2}{\mu(\mu - \lambda)} = \frac{\lambda^2}{4(4 - \lambda)} = 1$$
$$\lambda^2 = 4 \times (4 - \lambda) = 16 - 4\lambda$$
$$\lambda^2 + 4\lambda - 16 = 0$$
$$\lambda = 2.47$$

Alternatively (assuming that the arrival rate is not decreased), VVH could increase the service rate to:

$$L_q = \frac{3^2}{\mu(\mu - 3)} = \frac{3^2}{\mu(\mu - 3)} = 1$$
$$\mu(\mu - 3) = \mu^2 - 3\mu = 3^2 = 9$$
$$\mu^2 - 3\mu - 9 = 0$$
$$\mu = 4.85$$

VVH could also implement some combination of decreasing arrival rate and increasing service rate. In all cases, utilization of the MRI would be reduced to $\rho = \lambda/\mu = 2.47/4.00$, or $3.00/4.85 = 0.62$.

Real systems are seldom as simple as an M/M/1 queuing system and rarely reach equilibrium; often, simulation is needed to study these more complicated systems.

Discrete Event Simulation Details

DES is typically performed using commercially available software packages. Like Monte Carlo simulation, it is possible to perform DES simulation by hand; however, this would be tedious. Two of the more popular software packages are Arena (Rockwell Automation 2012) and Simul8 (Simul8 Corporation 2012).

The terminology and logic of DES are based on queuing theory. A basic simulation model consists of entities, queues, and resources, all of which can have various attributes. Entities are the objects that flow through the system; in healthcare, entities would typically be patients, but they could be any object on which some service or task will be performed. For example, blood samples in the hematology lab could also be entities. Queues are the waiting lines that hold the entities while they are waiting for service. Resources (previously referred to as servers) could be people, equipment, or space for which entities compete.

The logic of a simulation model is based on states (variables that describe the system at a point in time) and events (variables that change the state of the system). Events are controlled by the simulation executive, and data are collected on the state of the system as events occur. The simulation jumps through time from event to event.

A simple example based on the VVH M/M/1 MRI queuing discussion will help to show the logic behind DES software. Exhibit 10.11 contains a list of the events as they happen in the simulation. The arrival rate is three patients per hour, and the service rate is four patients per hour. Random interarrival times are generated using an exponential distribution with a mean of 0.33 hour. Random service times are generated using an exponential distribution with a mean of 0.25 hour (shown at the bottom of Exhibit 10.11).

The simulation starts at time 0.00. The first event is the arrival of the first patient (entity); there is no line (queue), so this patient enters service. Upcoming events are the arrival of the next patient at 0.17 hours (the interarrival between Patients 1 and 2 is 0.17 hour) and the completion of the first patient's service at 0.21 hours.

The next event is the arrival of Patient 2 at 0.17 hours. Because the MRI on Patient 1 is not complete, Patient 2 enters the queue. The MRI has been busy since the start of the simulation, so the utilization of the MRI is

EXHIBIT 10.11 Simulation Event List

Just Finished			Variables		Attributes		Statistics				Upcoming Events		
Entity #	Time	Event Type	Length of Queue	Server Busy	Arrival Time in Queue	Arrival Time in Service	Number Complete Waits in Queue	Total Wait Time in Queue	Average Queue Length	Utilization	Entity #	Time	Event
1	0.00	Arr	0	1	0.00	0.00	0	0	0	0	2	0.17	Arr
											1	0.21	Dep
2	0.17	Arr	1	1	0.17		0	0	0	1.00	1	0.21	Dep
											3	0.54	Arr
1	0.21	Dep	0	1	0.00	0.00	1	0.04	0.19	1.00	3	0.54	Arr
											2	0.77	Dep
3	0.54	Arr	1	1	0.54		1	0.04	0.07	1.00	2	0.77	Dep
											4	0.90	Arr
2	0.77	Dep	0	1	0.17	0.21	2	0.27	0.35	1.00	3	0.79	Dep
											4	0.90	Arr
3	0.79	Dep	0	0		0.77	3	0.27	0.34	1.00	4	0.90	Arr
											4	1.27	Dep
4	0.90	Arr	0	1		0.90	3	0.27	0.30	0.88	4	1.27	Dep
											5	1.49	Arr

			1	2	3	4	5	6	7	8
Interarrival time	Expon (0.33)		0.17	0.37	0.36	0.59	0.14	0.17	0.24	0.06
Time of arrival		0.00	0.17	0.54	0.90	1.49	1.63	1.80	2.04	2.10
Service time	Expon (0.25)	0.21	0.56	0.02	0.37	0.34	0.11	1.02	0.01	0.20

Arr = Arrival; Dep = Departure; Expon = Exponent.

100 percent. Upcoming events are the completion of the first patient's service at 0.21 hours and the arrival of Patient 3 at 0.54 hours (the interarrival between Patients 2 and 3 is 0.37 hour, and Patient 2 arrived at 0.17 hours).

The first patient's MRI is completed at 0.21 hours. There is no one in the queue at this point because once Patient 1 has completed service, Patient 2 can enter service. The total waiting time in the queue for all patients is 0.04 hour (the difference between when Patient 2 entered the queue and entered service). The average queue length is 0.19 patient. There were no people in line for 0.17 hour and one person in line for 0.04 hour.

$$\frac{0 \text{ People} \times 0.17 \text{ Hour} + 1 \text{ Person} \times 0.04 \text{ Hour}}{0.21 \text{ Hour}} = 0.19 \text{ People}$$

Upcoming events are the arrival of Patient 3 at 0.54 hours and the departure of Patient 2 at 0.77 hours (Patient 2 entered service at 0.21 hours, and service takes 0.56 hour).

Patient 3 arrives at 0.54 hours and joins the queue because the MRI is still busy with Patient 2. The average queue length has decreased from the previous event because more time has passed with no one in the queue—there has still only been one person in the queue for 0.04 hour, but total time in the simulation is 0.54 hour. Upcoming events are the departure of Patient 2 at 0.77 hours and the arrival of Patient 4 at 0.90 hours.

Patient 2 departs at 0.77 hours. There is no one in the queue at this point because Patient 3 has entered service. A total of two people have departed the system. The total wait time in the queue for all patients is 0.04 hour for Patient 2 plus 0.17 hour for Patient 3 (0.77 hour − 0.54 hour), a total of 0.21 hour. The average queue length is:

$$\frac{0 \text{ People} \times 0.50 \text{ Hour} + 1 \text{ Person} \times 0.21 \text{ Hour}}{0.77 \text{ Hour}} = 0.35 \text{ People}$$

The MRI utilization is still 100 percent because the MRI has been busy constantly since the start of the simulation. Upcoming events are the departure of Patient 3 at 0.79 hours (Patient 3 arrived at 0.77 hours, and service takes 0.02 hour) and the arrival of Patient 4 at 0.90 hours.

Patient 3 departs at 0.79 hours. Because no patients are waiting for the MRI, it becomes idle. Upcoming events are the arrival of Patient 4 at 0.90 hours and the departure of Patient 4 at 1.27 hours.

Patient 4 arrives at 0.90 hours and enters service. The utilization of the MRI has decreased to 88 percent because it was idle for 0.11 hour of the 0.90 hour the simulation has run. Upcoming events are the departure of

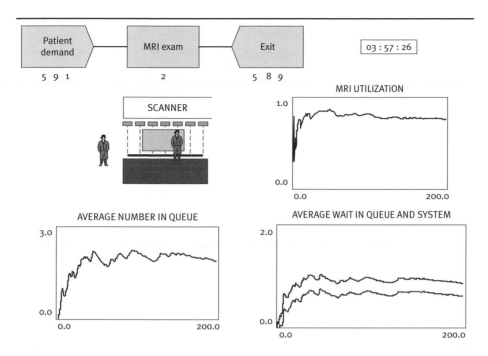

EXHIBIT 10.12
Arena
Simulation
of VVH MRI
M/M/1 Queuing
Example

NOTE: Figure created in Arena®, Rockwell Automation.

Patient 4 at 1.27 hours and the arrival of Patient 5 at 1.49 hours. The simulation continues in this manner until the desired stop time is reached.

Even for this simple model, performing these calculations by hand would obviously take a long time. Additionally, one of the advantages of simulation is that it uses process mapping; many simulation software packages such as Arena are able to import and use Microsoft Visio process and value stream maps. Using DES software makes it possible to build, run, and analyze simple models in limited time. Therefore, Arena was used to build and simulate the present model (Exhibit 10.12).

As before, the arrival rate is three patients per hour, the service rate is four patients per hour, and both are exponentially distributed. Averages over time for queue length, wait time, and utilization for a single replication are shown in the plots in Exhibit 10.12. Each replication of the simulation is run for 200 hours, and there are 30 replications. Replications are needed to determine confidence intervals for the reported values. Some of the output from this simulation is shown in Exhibit 10.13. The sample mean ± the half-width gives the 95 percent confidence interval for the mean. Increasing the number of replications will reduce the half-width.

The results of this simulation agree fairly closely with the calculated steady-state results because the process was assumed to run continuously for a significant period, 200 hours. A more realistic assumption might be that

EXHIBIT 10.13
Arena Output
for VVH MRI
M/M/1 Queuing
Example: 200
Hours

Category Overview

8:22:36 AM   July 26, 2011

Values across all replications

MRI Example

Replications: 30   Time unit: Hours

Key Performance Indicators

System	Average
Number out	601

Entity

Time

Wait Time	Average	Half-Width	Minimum Average	Maximum Average	Minimum Value	Maximum Value
Patient	0.7241	0.08	0.5009	1.3496	0.00	7.3900

Total Time	Average	Half-Width	Minimum Average	Maximum Average	Minimum Value	Maximum Value
Patient	0.9734	0.08	0.7427	1.6174	0.00001961	7.4140

Queue

Other

Number Waiting	Average	Half-Width	Minimum Average	Maximum Average	Minimum Value	Maximum Value
MRI exam queue	2.1944	0.25	1.4326	4.2851	0.00	29.0000

Resource

Usage

Instantaneous Utilization	Average	Half-Width	Minimum Average	Maximum Average	Minimum Value	Maximum Value
MRI	0.7488	0.01	0.6767	0.8513	0.00	1.0000

Arrival rate = 3 patients/hour; service rate = 4 patients/hour.

NOTE: Figure created in Arena®, Rockwell Automation.

MRI procedures are only done for ten hours every day. The Arena simulation was rerun with this assumption, and the results are shown in Exhibit 10.14. The average wait times, queue length, and utilization are lower than the steady-state values.

VVH M/M/1 Queue

VVH determined that a steady-state analysis was not appropriate for its situation because MRIs are only offered ten hours a day. The team decided to analyze this situation using simulation. Once the model was built and run, the model and simulation results were compared with actual data and evaluated by relevant staff to ensure that the model accurately reflected reality. All staff agreed that the model was valid and could be used to determine what needed to be done to achieve the stated goal. If the model had not been thought to be valid, the team would have needed to build and validate a new model.

EXHIBIT 10.14
Arena Output
for VVH MRI
M/M/1 Queuing
Example: 10
Hours

Category Overview

12:19:03 PM   July 26, 2011

Values across all replications

MRI Example

Replications: 30   Time unit: Hours

Key Performance Indicators

System   Average
Number out   28

Entity

Time

Wait Time	Average	Half-Width	Minimum Average	Maximum Average	Minimum Value	Maximum Value
Patient	0.4778	0.15	0.02803444	1.4312	0.00	2.9818

Total Time	Average	Half-Width	Minimum Average	Maximum Average	Minimum Value	Maximum Value
Patient	0.7304	0.16	0.2407	1.7611	0.00082680	3.3129

Queue

Other

Number Waiting	Average	Half-Width	Minimum Average	Maximum Average	Minimum Value	Maximum Value
MRI exam queue	1.5265	0.46	0.2219	4.5799	0.00	10.0000

Resource

Usage

Instantaneous Utilization	Average	Half-Width	Minimum Average	Maximum Average	Minimum Value	Maximum Value
MRI	0.7167	0.05	0.4088	0.9780	0.00	1.0000

Arrival rate = 3 patients/hour; service rate = 4 patients/hour.

NOTE: Figure created in Arena®, Rockwell Automation.

The results of the simulation (Exhibit 10.14) indicate that VVH has an average of 1.5 patients in the queue. To reach the desired goal of an average of only one patient waiting, VVH needs to decrease the arrival rate or increase the service rate. Using trial and error in the simulation, the organization found that decreasing the arrival rate to 2.7 or increasing the service rate to 4.4 would allow the goal to be achieved.

Even using the improvement tools in this text, the team believed that it would only be possible to increase the service rate of the MRI to 4.2 patients per hour. Therefore, to reach the goal the arrival rate must also be decreased. Again using the simulation, VVH found that it would need to decrease the arrival rate to 2.8 patients per hour. Exhibit 10.15 shows the results of this simulation.

The team recommended that a kaizen event be held for the MRI process to increase service rate and that appointments for the MRI be reduced to decrease the arrival rate. However, the team also noted that implementing

EXHIBIT 10.15
Arena Output
for VVH MRI
M/M/1 Queuing
Example:
Decreased
Arrival Rate,
Increased
Service Rate

Category Overview		
8:24:44 AM		July 26, 2011

Values across all replications

MRI Example

Replications: 30   Time unit: Hours

Key Performance Indicators

System   Average
Number out   26

Entity

Wait Time	Average	Half-Width	Minimum Average	Maximum Average	Minimum Value	Maximum Value
Patient	0.3507	0.12	0.02449931	1.4202	0.00	3.4973

Total Time	Average	Half-Width	Minimum Average	Maximum Average	Minimum Value	Maximum Value
Patient	0.6008	0.14	0.1899	1.7825	0.00097591	4.2210

Queue

Other

Number Waiting	Average	Half-Width	Minimum Average	Maximum Average	Minimum Value	Maximum Value
MRI exam queue	1.0342	0.36	0.0928	4.2272	0.00	9.0000

Resource

Usage

Instantaneous Utilization	Average	Half-Width	Minimum Average	Maximum Average	Minimum Value	Maximum Value
MRI	0.6682	0.06	0.3314	0.9456	0.00	1.0000

Arrival rate = 2.8 patients/hour; service rate = 4.2 patients/hour; 10 hours simulated.

NOTE: Figure created in Arena®, Rockwell Automation.

these changes would reduce the average number of patients served from 28 to 26 and reduce the utilization of the MRI from 0.72 to 0.69. More positively, however, average patient wait time would be reduced from 0.48 hour to 0.35 hour.

VVH was able to increase the service rate to 4.2 patients per hour and decrease the arrival rate to 2.8 patients per hour, and the results were as predicted by the simulation. The team also began to look at other solutions that would enable VVH to increase MRI utilization while maintaining wait times and queue length.

Conclusion

Simulation is a powerful tool for modeling processes and systems to evaluate choices and opportunities. As is true of all of the tools and techniques presented in this text, simulation can be used in conjunction with other initiatives, such as Lean or Six Sigma, to enable continuous improvement of systems and processes.

Discussion Questions

1. Think of at least three simulations that you personally have used or been a part of. Why was simulation used? What questions did the simulation help you to answer?
2. Why is simulation not used more extensively in healthcare organizations?
3. What are the advantages of simulation? What are its limitations?
4. Explain the "flaw of averages" and provide a specific example where this flaw adversely affected your organization.
5. Discuss at least three opportunities in your organization in which simulation might be useful in analyzing and improving the situation.
6. Describe several places or times in your organization where people or objects (paperwork, tests, etc.) wait in line. How do the characteristics of each example differ?

Chapter Exercises

1. VVH is considering a pharmacy-managed medication assistance program. This program would help patients who are unable to afford pharmaceuticals obtain free drugs from pharmaceutical manufacturers. VVH would save the cost of the drugs but incur costs to manage the program, and the organization would like to know if the program would be cost beneficial. VVH believes that between 60 and 120 patients will use this program, with equal probability over this range (a uniform distribution); the average value of a patient's drugs obtained per year will most likely be $200, but could be as low as $0 or as high as $1,000 (a triangular distribution). The time to administer the program is expected to follow a normal distribution, with a mean of four hours per week and a standard deviation of 0.5 hour per week (but never less than zero hours). VVH also believes that there is an 80 percent probability the program could be administered by pharmacy research fellows who receive wages and benefits of $30 per hour, but hospital pharmacists may need to administer the program ($60 per hour wages and benefits). Analyze this situation using @Risk. What should VVH do? Why?

2. The hematology lab manager has been receiving complaints that the turnaround time for blood tests is too long. Data from the past month show that the arrival rate of blood samples to one technician in the lab is five per hour and the service rate is six per hour. Use queuing theory and assume that both rates are exponentially distributed and that the lab is at steady state to answer the following questions. What is the capacity utilization of the lab? Average number of blood samples in the lab? Average time that a sample waits in the queue? Average number of blood samples waiting for testing? Average time that a blood sample spends in the lab?

3. Applying one of the previous examples to your organization, develop a model of the process. What data would you need to collect to build a simulation?

APPLICATIONS TO CONTEMPORARY HEALTHCARE OPERATIONS ISSUES

PROCESS IMPROVEMENT AND PATIENT FLOW

Operations Management in Action

The staff of Carondelet St. Mary's Hospital in Tucson, Arizona, undertook an improvement effort aimed at emergency center operations. A number of operational changes were implemented to achieve improvements in patient flow. The hospital

- created a culture for in-house nursing units using "pull system" versus "push system" as a concept to promote patient flow out of the emergency center;
- developed a centralized admitting process with an electronic tracking board;
- implemented a bed-control nurse position;
- developed a mobile admission team to perform bedside admissions;
- developed and implemented a process for direct admit admission labs to improve turnaround time;
- developed and implemented a protocol to bypass the emergency center triage when a bed is available;
- adjusted triage staffing to volume peaks;
- adjusted emergency center staffing to meet volume demand;
- developed physician-driven triage protocols;
- implemented bedside registration in the emergency center when patients bypass triage or arrive by ambulance;
- refocused the inpatient unit charge nurse position to frontline operations with responsibility for unit flow and throughput;
- used the express admission unit as a discharge lounge to open beds and improve patient flow when census is high;

- standardized the channels of communication for follow-up with primary care providers whose patients are cared for by the hospitalist through information systems interfacing;
- provided portal access for physicians to readily obtain patient information;
- opened a fast-track patient care area in the new emergency center to improve flow of low-acuity patients;
- developed a focus team to decrease external and internal transportation delays;
- standardized surgical admission and preadmission testing processes;
- implemented processes to reduce operating room turnover time;
- standardized the recovery process between inpatients and outpatients; and
- developed balancing measures to ensure that changes made to improve patient flow did not adversely affect quality indicators.

These process improvements resulted in the following changes:

- Reduced the emergency center length of stay by 7 percent
- Increased the emergency center's monthly volume by 5 percent
- Increased the inpatient daily census by 20 percent
- Improved the hospital's net operating margin by 1.3 percent above budget

SOURCE: Schmidt and Messer (2005). Reprinted with permission.

Overview

At the core of all organizations are their operating systems. Excellent organizations continuously measure, study, and make improvements to these systems. This chapter provides a methodology for measuring and improving systems using a selected set of the tools presented in the preceding chapters.

The terminology associated with process improvement can be confusing. Typically, tasks combine to form subprocesses, subprocesses combine to form processes, and processes combine to form a system. The boundaries of a particular system are defined by what is of interest. For example, the boundaries of a supply chain system would be more encompassing than a hospital system that is part of that supply chain. The term "process improvement" refers to improvement at any of these levels, from the task level to the systems level. This chapter focuses on process and systems improvement.

Process improvement follows the classic plan-do-check-act (PDCA) cycle (Chapters 8 and 9), with the following, more specific key steps:

- *Plan:* Define the entire process to be improved using process mapping. Collect and analyze appropriate data for each element of the process.
- *Do:* Use process improvement tool(s) to improve the process.
- *Check:* Measure the results of the process improvement.
- *Act to hold the gains:* If the process improvement results are satisfactory, hold the gains (Chapter 15). If the results are not satisfactory, repeat the PDCA cycle.

This chapter discusses the types of problems or issues faced by healthcare organizations, reviews many of the operations tools discussed in earlier chapters, and illustrates how these tools can be applied to process improvement. The relevant tools include

- basic process improvement tools
- Six Sigma and Lean tools and
- simulation with Arena.

Problem Types

Continuous process improvement is essential for organizations to meet the challenges of today's healthcare environment. The theory of swift, even flow (Schmenner 2001, 2004; Schmenner and Swink 1998) asserts that a process is more productive as the stream of materials (customers or information) flows more swiftly and evenly. Productivity rises as the speed of flow through the process increases and the variability associated with that process decreases.

It should be noted that these phenomena are not independent. Often, decreasing system variability will increase flow, and increasing flow will decrease variability. For example, advanced access scheduling increases flow by decreasing the elapsed time between when a patient schedules an appointment and when she has completed her visit to the provider. This can also decrease variability by decreasing the number of patient no-shows.

Solutions to many of the problems facing healthcare organizations can be found in increasing flow or decreasing variability. For example, a key operating challenge in most healthcare environments is the efficient movement of patients within a hospital or clinic, commonly called *patient flow*. Various approaches to process improvement will be illustrated with the patient flow problem. Optimizing patient flow through emergency departments has become a top priority of many hospitals; therefore, the Vincent Valley Hospital and Health System (VVH) example at the end of this chapter will focus on improving patient flow through that organization's emergency department.

Another key issue facing healthcare organizations is the need to increase the level of quality and eliminate errors in systems and processes. In other words, variation must be decreased. Finally, increasing cost pressures result in the need for healthcare organizations not only to improve processes but to do so while reducing costs.

The tools and techniques presented in this book are aimed at enabling cost-effective process improvement. Although this chapter focuses on patient flow and elimination of errors related to patient outcomes, the discussion would be equally applicable to other types of flow problems (e.g., information, paperwork) and other types of errors (e.g., billing). Some tools are more applicable to increasing flow and others to decreasing variation, eliminating errors, or improving quality, but all of the tools can be used for process improvement.

Patient Flow

Efficient patient movement in healthcare facilities can significantly improve the quality of care that patients receive and substantially improve financial performance. A patient receiving timely diagnosis and treatment has a higher likelihood of obtaining a desired clinical outcome. Because most current payment systems are based on fixed payments per episode of treatment, a patient moving more quickly through a system will generate lower costs and, therefore, higher margins.

Patient flow optimization opportunities occur in many healthcare settings. Examples include operating suites, imaging departments, urgent care centers, and immunization clinics. Advanced access (same-day scheduling) is a special case of patient flow and is examined in depth in Chapter 12.

Poor patient flow has several causes, but one culprit discovered by many investigators is variability of scheduled demand. For example, if an operating room is scheduled for a surgery but the procedure does not take place at the scheduled time, or takes longer than it was scheduled to take, the rest of the surgery schedule becomes delayed. These delays ripple through the entire hospital, including the emergency department.

As explained by Dr. Eugene Litvak (IHI 2006):

> You have two patient flows competing for hospital beds—ICU or patient floor beds. The first flow is scheduled admissions. Most of them are surgical. The second flow is medical, usually patients through the emergency department. So when you have a peak in elective surgical demand, all of a sudden your resources are being consumed by those patients. You don't have enough beds to accommodate medical demand.

If scheduled surgical demand varies unpredictably, the likelihood of inpatient overcrowding, emergency department backlogs, and ambulance diversions increases dramatically. Even when patients are admitted into a bed, they may not be receiving a value-added service. A British study (Walley, Silvester, and Steyn 2006) found that, although National Health Service hospitals were running at an occupancy rate of 90 percent, only "60 to 70 percent of the patients occupying those beds were receiving active treatment, and the rest are either waiting for initial visits by doctors, stuck in the system because of delays, or not ill but have not left the hospital for some reason." Clearly, significant opportunities to improve capacity and reduce cost by improving patient flow exist.

A number of management solutions have been introduced to improve patient flow. Separating low-acuity patients into a unique treatment stream can reduce time in the emergency department and improve patient satisfaction (Rodi, Grau, and Orsini 2006). Once a patient is admitted to the hospital, other tools have been employed to improve flow, especially around the discharge process. These include creating a uniform discharge time (e.g., 11:00 a.m.), writing discharge orders the night before, communicating discharge plans early in the patient's care, centralizing oversight of census and patient movement, changing physician rounding times, alerting ancillary departments when their testing procedures are critical to a patient's discharge, and improving discharge coordination with social services (Clark 2005).

However, for patient flow to be carefully managed and improved, the formal methods of process improvement outlined below need to be widely employed.

Quality

Ensuring quality of care became an increasingly important problem for the healthcare industry after it was estimated that in 1999 more than 98,000 individuals died in hospitals because of errors made by healthcare professionals (Institute of Medicine 1999). Both consumers and healthcare providers began to recognize that errors in patient care needed to be reduced or eliminated.

Because the administration and delivery of healthcare involves the interaction of providers and patients, this is a more difficult problem than is encountered in most environments. Human involvement in the "production process" and the intangibility of the resulting product make it difficult to standardize and control healthcare. As noted in *To Err Is Human* (Institute of Medicine 1999), healthcare differs from a systematic production process "mostly because of huge variability in patients and circumstances, the need to adapt processes quickly, the rapidly changing knowledge base, and the importance of highly trained professionals who must use expert judgment in dynamic settings." However, because the consequences of failure—patient injury or death—are so great, the need to reduce or eliminate failures is even more important in healthcare than in manufacturing or other service industries.

Again, to ensure quality and reduce or eliminate errors, the formal methods of process improvement outlined in the next section must be widely employed.

Process Improvement Approaches

Process improvement projects can use a variety of approaches and tools. Typically, they begin with process mapping and measurement. Some simple tools can be initially applied to identify opportunities for improvements. Identifying and eliminating or alleviating bottlenecks in a system (theory of constraints) can quickly improve overall system performance. In addition, the Six Sigma tools described in Chapter 8 can be used to reduce variability in process output, and the Lean tools discussed in Chapter 9 can be used to identify and eliminate waste. Finally, simulation (Chapter 10) provides a powerful tool to understand and optimize flow in a system.

All major process improvement projects should use the formal project management methodology outlined in Chapter 5. An important first step is to identify a system's owner: For a system to be managed effectively over time it must have an owner, someone who monitors the system as it operates, collects performance data, and leads teams to improve the system.

Many systems in healthcare do not have an owner and, therefore, operate inefficiently. For example, a patient may enter an emergency department, see the triage nurse, move to the admitting department, take a chair in the waiting area, be moved to an exam room, be seen by a nurse, have his blood drawn, and finally be examined by a physician. From the patient's point of view this is one system, but many hospital departments may be operating autonomously. System ownership problems can be remedied by multidepartment teams with one individual designated as the overall system or process owner.

Problem Definition and Process Mapping

The first step in improving a system is process description and mapping. However, the team should first ensure that the correct problem is being addressed. Mind mapping or root-cause analysis should be employed to ensure that the problem is identified and framed correctly; much time and money can be wasted finding an optimal solution to something that is not a problem.

For example, suppose that a project team was given the task of improving customer satisfaction with the emergency department. If the team assumes that customer satisfaction is low because of high throughput time, they might proceed to optimize patient flow in the emergency department. However, if an analysis of customer satisfaction showed that customers were dissatisfied because of a lack of parking, the solution to the problem would follow a different path. The problem must be clearly understood and defined to determine what process to map.

Processes can be described in a number of ways. The most common is the written procedure or protocol, typically constructed in the "directions" style, which is sufficient for simple procedures—for example, "Turn right at Elm Street, go two blocks, and turn left at Vine Avenue." Clearly written procedures are an important part of defining standard work, as described in Chapter 9.

However, when processes are linked to form systems they become more complex. These linked processes benefit from process mapping because process maps

- provide a visual representation that offers an opportunity for process improvement through inspection
- allow for branching in a process
- provide the ability to assign and measure the resources in each task in a process and
- are the basis for modeling the process via computer simulation software.

Chapter 6 provides an introduction to process mapping. To review, the steps in process mapping are as follows:

1. Assemble and train the team.
2. Determine the boundaries of the process (where it starts and ends) and the level of detail desired.
3. Brainstorm the major process tasks and list them in order. (Sticky notes are often helpful here.)
4. Once an initial process map (also called a flowchart) has been generated, the chart can be formally drawn using standard symbols for process mapping.
5. The formal flowchart should be checked for accuracy by all relevant personnel.
6. Depending on the purpose of the flowchart, data may need to be collected or more information added.

Process Mapping: VVH Emergency Department

A basic process map illustrating patient flow in the VVH emergency department is displayed in Exhibit 11.1.

EXHIBIT 11.1
VVH Emergency
Department
(ED) Patient
Flow Process
Map

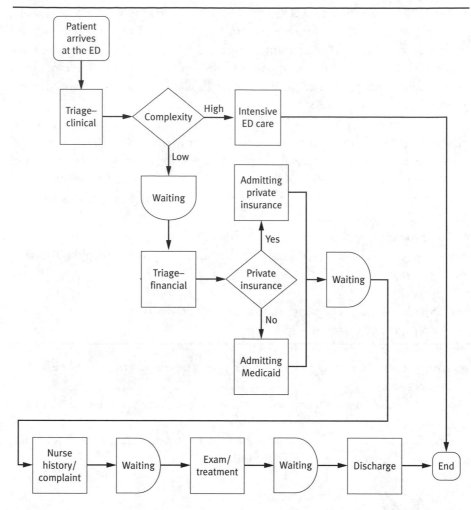

EXHIBIT 11.1
VVH Emergency
Department
(ED) Patient
Flow Process
Map

NOTE: Created with Microsoft Visio®.

In this basic process map, the patient arrives at the emergency department and is examined by the triage nurse. If the patient is very ill (high
complexity level), she is immediately sent to the intensive care section of
the emergency department. If not, she is sent to admitting and then to the
routine care section of the emergency department. The simple process map
shown here ends with this step. In actuality, other processes would now
begin, such as admission into an inpatient bed or a discharge from the emergency department to home with a scheduled clinical follow-up. The VVH
emergency department process improvement project is detailed at the end
of this chapter.

Process Measurements

Once a process map is developed, relevant data should be collected and analyzed. The situation will dictate which specific data and measures should be employed. Important measures and data for possible collection and analysis include the following:

- *Capacity of a process* is the maximum possible amount of output (goods or services) that a process or resource can produce or transform. Capacity measures can be based on outputs or on the availability of inputs. The capacity of a series of tasks is determined by the lowest-capacity task in the series.
- *Capacity utilization* is the proportion of capacity actually being used. It is measured as actual output/maximum possible output.
- *Throughput time* is the average time a unit spends in the process. Throughput time includes both processing time and waiting time and is determined by the critical (longest) path through the process.
- *Throughput rate*, sometimes referred to as drip rate, is the average number of units that can be processed per unit of time.
- *Service time* or *cycle time* is the time to process one unit. The cycle time of a process is equal to the longest task cycle time in that process. The probability distribution of service times may also be of interest.
- *Idle or wait time* is the time a unit spends waiting to be processed.
- *Arrival rate* is the rate at which units arrive to the process. The probability distribution of arrival rates may also be of interest.
- *Work-in-process, things-in-process, patients-in-process,* or *inventory* describe the total number of units in the process.
- *Setup time* is the amount of time spent getting ready to process the next unit.
- *Value-added time* is the time a unit spends in the process where value is actually being added to the unit.
- *Non-value-added time* is the time a unit spends in the process where no value is being added. Wait time is non-value-added time.
- *Number of defects or errors.*

The art in process mapping is to provide enough detail to be able to measure overall system performance, determine areas for improvement, and measure the effect of these changes.

Tools for Process Improvement

Once a system has been mapped, a number of techniques can be used to improve the process. These improvements will result in a reduction in the duration, cost, or waste in a system.

Eliminate Non-Value-Added Activities

The first step after a system has been mapped is to evaluate every element to ascertain whether each one is truly necessary and provides value (to the customer or patient). If a system has been in place for a long period and has not been evaluated through a formal process improvement project, a number of elements of the system can likely be easily eliminated. This step is sometimes termed "harvesting the low-hanging fruit."

Eliminate Duplicate Activities

Many processes in systems have been added on top of existing systems without formally evaluating the total system, frequently resulting in duplicate activities. The most infamous redundant process step in healthcare is asking patients repeatedly for their contact information. Duplicate activities increase both time and cost in a system and should be eliminated whenever possible.

Combine Related Activities

Process improvement teams should examine both the process map and the activity and swim lane map. If a patient moves back and forth between departments, the movement should be reduced by combining these activities so he only needs to be in each department once.

Process in Parallel

Although a patient can only be in one place at one time, other aspects of her care can be completed simultaneously. For example, medication preparation, physician review of tests, and chart documentation could all be done at the same time. As more tasks are executed simultaneously, the total time a patient spends in the process will be reduced. Similar to a chef who has a number of dishes on the stove synchronized to be completed at the same time, much of the patient care process can be completed at the same time.

Another element of parallel processing is the relationship of subprocesses to the main flow. For example, a lab result may need to be obtained before a patient enters the operating suite. Many of these subprocesses can be synchronized through the analysis and use of takt time (Chapter 9). This synchronization will enable efficient process flow and help optimize the process.

Load Balancing

If similar workers perform the same task, a well-tuned system can be designed to balance the work among them. For example, a mass-immunization clinic would want to develop its system so that all immunization stations are active at all times. This could be accomplished by using a single queue with multiple immunization stations.

Load balancing (or load leveling, heijunka) is difficult when employees can only perform a limited set of specific tasks (an unfortunate consequence of the super-specialization of the healthcare professions). When cross-training of employees can be accomplished, load balancing is easier.

Alternative Process Flow Paths and Contingency Plans

The number and placement of decision points in the process should be evaluated and optimized. A system with few decision points has few alternative paths and, therefore, does not respond well to unexpected events. Alternative paths (or contingency plans) should be developed for these types of events. For example, a standard clinic patient rooming system should have alternative paths if an emergency occurs, a patient is late, a provider is delayed, or medical records are absent.

Critical Path

For complex pathways in a system, it is sometimes helpful to identify the critical pathway using tools described in Chapter 5. If a critical path can be identified, execution of processes on the pathway can be improved (e.g., reduce average service time). In some cases, the process can be moved off the critical path and be processed in parallel to it. Either technique will decrease the total time on the critical pathway. In the case of patient flow, this will decrease the patient's total time in the system.

Information Feedback and Real-Time Control

Some systems have a high level of variability in their operations because of variability in the arrival of jobs or customers (patients) into the process and variability of the cycle time of each process in the system. High variability in the system can lead to poor performance. One tool to reduce variability is the control loop (Chapter 1). Information can be obtained from one process and used to drive change in another. For example, the number of patients in the emergency department waiting area can be continuously monitored and if the number reaches a certain level, contingency plans—such as floating in additional staff from other portions of the hospital—can be initiated.

Quality at the Source

Many systems contain multiple reviews, approvals, and inspections. A system in which the task is done right the first time should not require these redundancies. Deming first identified this problem in the process design of manufacturing lines that had inspectors throughout the assembly process (Deming 1998). This expensive and ineffective system was one of the factors that gave rise to the quality movement in Japan and, later, in the United States.

To eliminate inspections, designing systems that embed quality at the source or beginning of a system is important. For example, a billing system that requires a clerk to inspect a bill before it is released does not have quality built into the process. A system that has many inspection steps and does not have quality at the source should be redesigned.

Match Capacity to Demand

A common problem in 24-hour operations is having too few or too many staff for patient care demand. This problem is exacerbated if an organization only allows certain set shifts (e.g., eight hours).

To resolve this problem, first graph and analyze your demand on an hourly and daily basis. Then develop staffing patterns that match this demand. For example a five-hour or seven-hour shift might be needed to correctly meet the demand.

Using the tools in Chapter 7, you should be able to identify patterns of demand (e.g., high emergency department demand on Friday and Saturday evenings). Chapter 12 also provides more details on capacity planning.

Let the Patient Do the Work

The Internet and other advanced information technologies have allowed for more self-service in service industries. Individuals are now comfortable booking their own airline reservations, buying goods online, and checking themselves out at retailers. This trend can be exploited in healthcare with tools that enable patients to be part of the process. For example, online tools are now available that allow patients to make their own clinic appointments. Letting the patient do the work reduces the work of staff and provides an opportunity for quality at the source—if the patients input the data, they are more likely to be correct.

Use Technology

The advent of the electronic health record and other IT tools now provide a platform to automate many tasks that were performed manually. A good rubric to identify these tasks is to examine every daily task and ask where it ranks in complexity based on your professional training. For those tasks that are low on this list, consider ways to automate them.

Today, work is an activity—not a place. The widespread use of smartphones and tablets now enables much work to be done outside the traditional workplace. Consider moving some tasks to these devices to improve your personal productivity.

Theory of Constraints

Chapter 6 discussed the underlying principles and applications of the theory of constraints, which can be used as a powerful process improvement tool. First, the bottleneck in a system is identified, often through the observation of queues forming in front of it. Once a bottleneck is identified, it should be exploited and everything else in the system subordinated to it. This means that other nonbottleneck resources (or steps in the process) should be synchronized to match the output of the constraint. Idleness at a nonbottleneck resource costs nothing, and nonbottlenecks should never produce more than can be consumed by the bottleneck resource. Often, this will cause the bottleneck to shift—a new bottleneck will be identified. However, if the original bottleneck remains, the possibility of elevating the bottleneck needs to be evaluated. Elevating bottlenecks requires additional resources (e.g., staff, equipment), so a comprehensive outcomes and financial analysis needs to be undertaken to determine the trade-offs among process improvement, quality, and costs.

Identify Best Practices and Replicate

Although this is not a formal operations management tool, it must be mentioned as a highly recommended management approach. As health systems expand and grow they are likely to have many similar activities that are replicated in separate geographic sites. Good management practice is to identify high performing sites (e.g., the best primary care clinic in a system) and replicate their core processes throughout the organization.

A similar approach can be taken with individual employees. For example, you can study the best billing clerk in a hospital to understand her processes and then replicate these with all the billers in a department.

The Science of Operations Management

Chapter 10 discussed the use of queuing theory in improving healthcare flow. Queuing theory is interesting because it is based on mathematical equations or scientific fact. Little's law, demonstrated in Chapter 10, is the exact relationship between arrival rate to a system, the time a patient spends in the system, and the number of items in a system. The use of Little's law and queuing theory can greatly benefit in understanding how long patients wait in our healthcare systems, which in turn can yield enormous financial gains.

In a series of studies, queuing theory has been used to analyze flow of emergency departments and operating rooms (Butterfield 2007; McManus et al. 2004). In many instances, surgical suites more than doubled the number of surgeries they have been able to complete in a short time frame. Because surgeries are a prime source of revenue and margin for most hospitals, this improvement makes the hospital more profitable.

Process Improvement in Practice

Six Sigma

If the primary goal of a process improvement project is to improve quality (reduce the variability in outcomes), the Six Sigma approach and tools described in Chapter 8 will yield the best results. As discussed previously, Six Sigma uses seven basic tools: fishbone diagrams, check sheets, histograms, Pareto charts, flowcharts, scatter plots, and run charts. It also includes statistical process control to provide an ongoing measurement of process output characteristics to ensure quality and enable the identification of a problem situation before an error occurs.

The Six Sigma approach also includes measuring process capability—a measure of whether a process is actually capable of producing the desired output—and benchmarking it against other similar processes in other organizations. Quality function deployment is used to match customer requirements (voice of the customer) with process capabilities given that trade-offs must be made. Poka-yoke is employed selectively to mistake-proof parts of a process.

A primary function of Six Sigma programs is to eliminate sources of artificial variance in our processes and systems. Natural variance includes those items that occur naturally in any system, such as heat, temperature, and patients getting sick or breaking a leg. Artificial variance is created by the people within the system and is completely within the control of those in the system. Six Sigma programs identify, eliminate, and remove those sources of artificial variance. For example, scheduling systems, overtime allocations, and business office processing systems can all be changed by people within the system. The secret to a successful Six Sigma program is removing all the artificial variance and focusing on creating value for our customers. Effective Six Sigma systems strategically employ Lean concepts to achieve this goal.

Lean

Process improvement projects focused on eliminating waste and improving flow in the system or process can use many of the tools that are part of the Lean approach (Chapter 9). The kaizen philosophy, which is the basis for Lean, includes the following steps:

1. *Specify value*: Identify activities that provide value from the customer's perspective.
2. *Map and improve the value stream*: Determine the sequence of activities or the current state of the process and the desired future state. Eliminate non-value-added steps and other waste.
3. *Flow*: Enable the process to flow as smoothly and quickly as possible.
4. *Pull*: Enable the customer to pull products or services.
5. *Perfection*: Repeat the cycle to ensure a focus on continuous improvement.

An important part of Lean is value stream mapping, which is used to define the process and determine where waste is occurring. Takt time measures the time needed for the process based on customer demand and can be used to synchronize flow in a process. Standardized work, an important part of the Lean approach, is written documentation of the precise way in which every step in a process should be performed and is a way to ensure that things are done the same way every time in an efficient manner.

Other Lean tools include the five Ss (a technique to organize the workplace) and spaghetti diagrams (a mapping technique to show the movement of customers, patients, workers, equipment, jobs, etc.). Leveling workload (heijunka) so that the system or process can flow without interruption can be used to improve the value stream. Kaizen blitzes or events are Lean tools used to improve the process quickly, when project management is not needed (Chapter 9).

Simulation

Simulation is used to evaluate what-if situations. Usually it is less expensive or speedier than changing the real system and evaluating the effects of those changes. The process of simulation is as follows:

1. *Model development*: Develop a model of the process or situation of interest.
2. *Model validation*: Ensure that the model accurately represents reality.
3. *Simulation and analysis of output*: Run the simulation and analyze the output to determine the answers to the questions asked, optimize the process, or manage risk.

Discrete event simulation (based on queuing theory) is used to model system flows to improve the system. Chapter 10 provides an extensive description of the underlying mathematics and the use of simulation to model operating systems. This chapter applies these concepts more broadly to process improvement, with a specific emphasis on patient flow.

Process Improvement Project: VVH Emergency Department

To demonstrate the power of many of the process improvement tools described previously, an extensive patient-flow process improvement project at VVH will be examined.

VVH identified patient flow in the emergency department as an important area on which to focus process improvement efforts. The goal of the project was to reduce total patient time in the emergency department (both waiting and care delivery) while maintaining or improving financial performance.

The first step for VVH leadership was to charter a multidepartmental team using the project management methods described in Chapter 5. The head nurse for emergency services was appointed project leader. The team felt VVH should take a number of steps to improve patient flow in the emergency department and decided to split the systems improvement project into three major phases. First, team members would perform simple data collection and basic process improvement to identify low-hanging fruit and make obvious, straightforward changes.

Once the team felt comfortable with its understanding of the basics of patient flow in the department, they would work to understand the elements of the system more fully by collecting more detailed data. Then, value stream mapping and the theory of constraints would be used to identify opportunities for improvement. Root-cause analysis would be employed on poorly performing processes and tasks. These changes would be made and their effects measured.

The third phase of the project was the use of simulation. Because the team would have complete knowledge of patient flow in the system, they could develop and test a simulation model with confidence. Once the simulation was validated, the team would continuously test process improvements in the simulation model and implement them in the emergency department.

The team also considered a fourth phase that would implement real-time use of a simulation model and match patient arrivals with emergency department resource needs, then effectively deploy those resources.

The specific high-level tasks in this project were as follows:

Phase I

1. Observe patient flow and develop a detailed process map.
2. Measure high-level patient flow metrics for one week:
   - Patients arriving per hour
   - Patients departing per hour to inpatient

- Patients departing per hour to home
- Number of patients in the emergency department, including the waiting area and exam rooms

3. With the process map and data in hand, use simple process improvement techniques to make changes in the process, then measure the results.

Phase II

4. Set up a measurement system for each individual process and take measurements over one week.
5. Use value stream mapping and the theory of constraints to analyze patient flow and make improvements, then measure the effects of the changes.

Phase III

6. Collect data needed to build a realistic simulation model.
7. Develop the simulation model and validate it against real data.
8. Use the simulation model to conduct virtual experiments on process improvements. Implement promising improvements, and measure the results of the changes.

Phase I

VVH process improvement project team members observed patient flow and recorded the needed data. With the information collected, the team was able to create a detailed process map. They measured the following high-level operating statistics related to patient flow:

- Patients arriving per hour = 10
- Patients departing per hour to inpatient = 2
- Patients triaged to routine emergency care per hour = 8
- Patients departing per hour to home = 8
- Average number of patients in various parts of the system (sampled every 10 minutes) = 20
- Average number of patients in emergency department exam rooms = 4

Using Little's law, the average time in the emergency department (throughput time) is calculated as:

$$\text{Throughput time} = T$$
$$= I/\lambda$$
$$= \frac{24 \text{ Patients}}{8 \text{ Patients/Hour}}$$
$$= 3 \text{ Hours}$$

Hence, each patient spent an average of 3 hours, or 180 minutes, in the emergency department. However, Little's law only gives the average time in the department at steady state. Therefore, the team measured total time in the system for a sample of routine patients and found an average of 165 minutes. They also observed that the number of patients in the waiting room varied from 0 to 20, and that the actual time it took to move through the process varied from 1 to more than 5 hours.

Initially, the team focused on the emergency department admitting subsystem as an opportunity for immediate improvement. Exhibit 11.2 shows the complete emergency department system with the admitting subsystem highlighted.

The team developed the following description of the admitting process from its documentation of patient flow:

> Patients who did not have an acute clinical problem were asked if they had health insurance. If they did not have health insurance, they were sent to the admitting clerk who specialized in Medicaid (to enroll them in a Medicaid program). If they had health insurance, they were sent to the other clerk, who specialized in private insurance. If a patient had been sent to the wrong clerk by triage, he was sent to the other clerk.

The team determined that one process improvement change would be to cross-train the admitting clerks on both private insurance and Medicaid eligibility. This would provide for load balancing, as patients would automatically go to the free clerk and keep the workload balanced. In addition, the system improvement would eliminate triage staff errors in sending patients to the wrong clerk, hence providing quality at the source.

Phase II

Phase I produced some gains in reducing patient time in the emergency department. However, the team felt more detailed data were needed to improve even further. As a first step in collecting these data, the team decided to measure various parameters of the department's processes. Initially, they decided to focus on the time period from 2:00 p.m. to 2:00 a.m., Monday through Thursday, as this is the busy period in the emergency department and demand seemed relatively stable during these times.

EXHIBIT 11.2
VVH Emergency
Department
(ED) Admitting
Subsystem

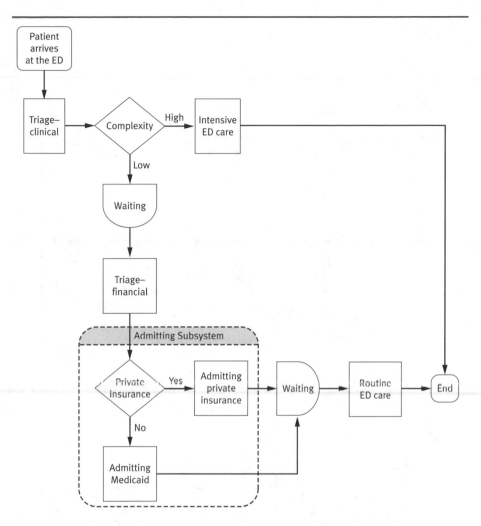

NOTE: Created with Microsoft Visio®.

The team drew a more detailed process map (Exhibit 11.3) and performed value stream mapping of this process (Exhibit 11.4). First, they evaluated each step in the process to determine if it was value-added, non-value-added, or non-value-added but necessary. Then, they measured the time a patient spent at each step in the process. The team found that after a patient had given his insurance information, he spent an average of 30 minutes of non-value-added time in the waiting room before a nurse was available to take his history and record the presenting complaint, a process that took an average of 20 minutes. The percentage of value-added time for these two steps is:

$$(\text{Value-added time}/\text{Total time})100 =$$
$$(20 \text{ Minutes}/[30 \text{ Minutes} + 20 \text{ Minutes}])100 = 40\%$$

EXHIBIT 11.3
VVH Emergency
Department
(ED) Process
Map: Focus on
Waiting and
History

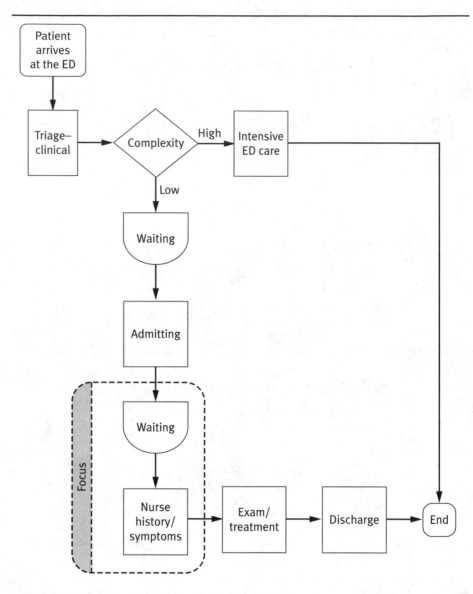

NOTE: Created with Microsoft Visio®.

The team believed the waiting room process could be improved through automation. Patients were given a tablet personal computer in the waiting area and asked to enter their symptoms and history via a series of branched questions. The results were sent via a wireless network to VVH's electronic medical record (EMR). This step usually took patients about 20 minutes. Staff knew which patients had completed the electronic interview by checking the EMR and could then prioritize which patient would be seen next. This new procedure also reduced the time needed by the nurse to 10 minutes because it enabled the nurse to verify, rather than actually record,

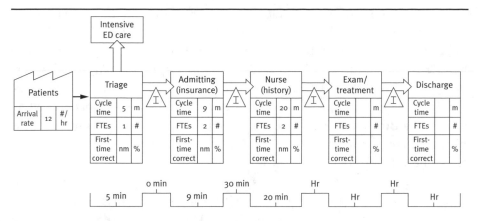

EXHIBIT 11.4
VVH Emergency Department (ED) Value Stream Map: Focus on Waiting and History

NOTE: Created with eVSM software from GumshoeKI, Inc., a Microsoft Visio® add-on.
nm = Number; FTE = full-time equivalent.

presenting symptoms and patient history. The percentage of value-added time for the new procedure is:

$$(\text{Value-added time}/\text{Total time})100 =$$

$$([\text{Patient history time} + \text{Nurse history time}]/[\text{Patient history time} + \text{Wait time} + \text{Nurse history time}])100 =$$

$$([20\ \text{Minutes} + 10\ \text{Minutes}]/[20\ \text{Minutes} + 10\ \text{Minutes} + 10\ \text{Minutes}])]100 = 75\%$$

The average throughput time for a patient in the emergency department was reduced by 10 minutes. The average time for patients to flow through the department (throughput time) prior to this improvement was 155 minutes. Because this step was on the critical path of the complete routine care emergency department process, throughput time for noncomplex patients was reduced to 145 minutes, a 7 percent productivity gain. An analyst from the VVH finance department (a member of the project team) was able to clearly demonstrate that the capital and software costs for the tablet computers would be recovered within 12 months by the improvement in patient flow. This phase of the project used three of the basic process improvement tools discussed in this chapter:

- Have the customer (patient) do it.
- Provide quality at the source.
- Gain information feedback and real-time control.

Although the process improvements already undertaken had a visible effect on flow in the emergency department, the team believed more improvements were possible. There were bottlenecks in the process, as evidenced by two waiting lines, or queues: (1) the waiting room queue, where patients waited before being moved to an exam room; and (2) the most visible queue for routine patients, the discharge area, where patients occasionally had to stand because all of the area's chairs were occupied. In the discharge area, patients waited a significant amount of time for final instructions and prescriptions.

The theory of constraints suggests that the bottleneck should be identified and optimized. However, alleviating or eliminating the patient examination and treatment or discharge bottlenecks would require significant changes in a long-standing process. Because this process improvement step seemed to have the probability of a high payoff but was a significant departure from existing practice, it was decided to move to phase III of the project and use simulation to model different options to improve patient flow in the examination/treatment and discharge processes.

Phase III: Simulation

First, the team reviewed the basic terminology of simulation.

- An *entity* is what flows through a system. Here, the entity is the patient. However, in other systems the entity could be materials (e.g., blood sample, drug) or information (e.g., diagnosis, billing code). Entities usually have attributes that will affect their flow through the system (e.g., male/female, acute/chronic condition).
- Each individual *process* in the system transforms (adds value) to the entity being processed. Each process takes time and consumes resources such as staff, equipment, supplies, and information.
- *Time* and *resource* use can be defined as an exact value (e.g., ten minutes) or a probability distribution (e.g., normal—mean, standard deviation). Chapter 7 discusses probability distributions in detail. Most healthcare tasks and processes will not require the same amount of time each time they are performed—they will require a variable amount of time. These variable usage rates are best described as probability distributions.
- The geographic location of a process is called a *station*. Entities flow from one process to the next via *routes*. The routes can branched based on *decision points* in the process map.
- Finally, because a process may not be able to handle all incoming entities in a timely fashion, *queues* will occur at each process and can be measured and modeled.

EXHIBIT 11.5
VVH Emergency
Department
(ED) Initial State
Simulation
Model

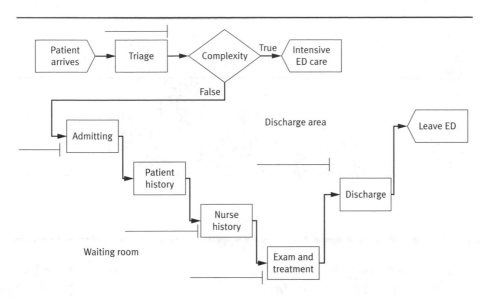

NOTE: Model created in Arena®, Rockwell Automation.

The team next developed a process map and simulation model for routine patient flow (Exhibit 11.5) in the emergency department using Arena simulation software from Rockwell Automation (2012) (see the companion website for links to videos detailing this model and its operation). The team focused on routine patients rather than those requiring

www.ache.org/books/OpsManagement2

intensive emergency care because of the high proportion of routine patients seen in the department. Routine patients are checked in and their self-recorded history and presenting complaint(s) are verified by a nurse. Then, patients move to an exam/treatment room and, finally, to the discharge area. Of the ten patients who come to the emergency department per hour, eight follow this process.

Next, to build a simulation model that accurately reflects this process, the team needed to determine the probability distributions of treatment time, admitting time, nurse history time, discharge time, and arrival rate for routine patients. To determine these probability distributions, they collected data on time of arrival in the department and time to perform each step in the routine patient care process.

Probability distributions were determined using the Input Analyzer function in Arena. Input Analyzer takes raw input data and finds the best-fitting probability distribution for them. Exhibit 11.6 shows the output of Arena Input Analyzer for 500 observations of treatment time for emergency department patients requiring routine care. Input Analyzer suggested that the best-fitting probability distribution for these data was triangular, with a minimum of 9 minutes, mode of 33 minutes, and maximum of 51 minutes.

EXHIBIT 11.6
Examination
and Treatment
Time Probability
Distribution:
Routine
Emergency
Department
Patients

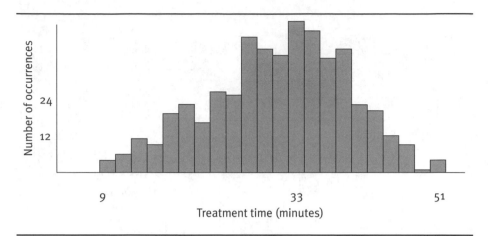

The remaining data were analyzed in the same manner, and the following best-fitting probability distributions were determined:

- Emergency routine patient arrival rate: exponential (7.5 minutes between arrivals)
- Triage time: triangular (2, 5, 7 minutes)
- Admitting time: triangular (3, 8, 15 minutes)
- Patient history time: triangular (15, 20, 25 minutes)
- Nurse history time: triangular (5, 11, 15 minutes)
- Exam/treatment time: triangular (14, 36, 56 minutes)
- Discharge time: triangular (9, 19, 32 minutes)

The Arena model simulation was based on 12-hour intervals (2:00 p.m. to 2:00 a.m.) and replicated 100 times. Note that increasing the number of replications decreases the half-width and, therefore, gives tighter confidence intervals. The number of replications needed depends on the desired confidence interval for the outcome variables. However, as the model becomes more complicated, more replications will take more simulation time; this model is fairly simple, so 100 replications take little time and are more than sufficient.

Most simulation software, including Arena, has the capability of using different arrival rate probability distributions for different times of the day and days of the week, allowing for varying demand patterns. However, the team believed that this simple model using only one arrival-rate probability distribution represented the busiest time for the emergency department, having observed that by 2:00 p.m. on weekdays there were usually no queues in either the waiting room or discharge area. The results of the simulation were reviewed by the team and compared with actual data and observations to ensure that the model was, in fact, simulating the reality of the emergency department. The team was satisfied that the model accurately reflected reality.

Replications: 100   Time Unit: Hours

Total Time	Average	Half-Width	Minimum Average	Maximum Average	Minimum Value	Maximum Value
Routine patient	2.4207	0.08	1.7953	3.4082	1.2004	5.2448

Queue

Time

Waiting Time	Average	Half-Width	Minimum Average	Maximum Average	Minimum Value	Maximum Value
Admitting queue	0.00526930	0.00	0.00048553	0.01668610	0.00	0.2235
Discharge queue	0.3972	0.26	0.06416692	0.8865	0.00	2.0531
Exam and treatment queue	0.3382	0.38	0.04167122	1.1956	0.00	2.5777
Nurse history queue	0.01764541	0.01	0.00272715	0.05309733	0.00	0.3694
Triage queue	0.06437939	0.05	0.01703829	0.1402	0.00	0.6506

Other

Waiting Time	Average	Half-Width	Minimum Average	Maximum Average	Minimum Value	Maximum Value
Admitting queue	0.03458032	0.00	0.00267040	0.1001	0.00	2.0000
Discharge queue	2.2481	0.26	0.2888	5.1713	0.00	13.0000
Exam and treatment queue	2.1930	0.38	0.2062	9.4408	0.00	22.0000
Nurse history queue	0.1136	0.01	0.01298461	0.4069	0.00	5.0000
Triage queue	0.5394	0.05	0.1145	1.7216	0.00	10.0000

Resource

Usage

Instantaneous Utilization	Average	Half-Width	Minimum Average	Maximum Average	Minimum Value	Maximum Value
Discharge nurse 1	0.8285	0.01	0.6715	0.8972	0.00	1.0000
Discharge nurse 2	0.8360	0.01	0.6673	0.9105	0.00	1.0000
Exam room 1	0.8441	0.01	0.6253	0.9497	0.00	1.0000
Exam room 2	0.8329	0.01	0.6548	0.9297	0.00	1.0000
Exam room 3	0.8182	0.02	0.5358	0.9200	0.00	1.0000
Exam room 4	0.8075	0.02	0.6135	0.9156	0.00	1.0000
Financial clerk 1	0.4615	0.01	0.3320	0.5636	0.00	1.0000
Financial clerk 2	0.4580	0.01	0.3286	0.5823	0.00	1.0000
History nurse 1	0.5294	0.01	0.3886	0.6796	0.00	1.0000
History nurse 2	0.5240	0.01	0.3937	0.7107	0.00	1.0000
Triage nurse	0.6267	0.01	0.4861	0.8373	0.00	1.0000

NOTE: Model created in Arena®, Rockwell Automation.

EXHIBIT 11.7
VVH Emergency Department Initial State Simulation Model Output

The focus of this simulation is the queuing occurring at both the waiting room and in the discharge area and the total time in the system. Exhibit 11.7 shows the results of this base (current status) model. On average, a patient spent 2.4 hours in the emergency department.

The team decided to examine the discharge process in depth because patient waiting time was greatest there. The emergency department had two rooms devoted to discharge and used two nurses to handle all discharge tasks, such as making sure prescriptions are given and home care instructions are understood. However, because there were only two nurses and four exam rooms, queuing was inevitable. In addition, the patient treatment information needed to be handed off from the treatment team to the discharge nurse. The process improvement team therefore decided to simulate having the discharge process carried out by the examination and treatment team. Because the examination and treatment team knew the patient information, the handoff task would be eliminated. The team estimated that this change would save about five minutes and, therefore, decided to simulate the new system by eliminating discharge as a separate process.

They estimated the probability distribution of the combined exam/treatment/discharge task by first estimating the probability distribution for handoff as triangular (4, 5, 7 minutes). The team used Input Analyzer to simulate 1,000 observations of exam/treatment time, discharge time, and handoff time using the previously determined probability distributions for each. For each observation, they added exam/treatment time to discharge time and subtracted handoff time to find total time. Input Analyzer found the best-fitting probability distribution for the total time for the new process as triangular (18, 50, 82 minutes).

The team simulated the new process and found that patients would spend an average of 2.95 hours in the emergency department—this change would actually increase time spent there. However, it would also eliminate the need for discharge rooms. The team decided to investigate the effect of converting the former discharge rooms to exam rooms and ran a new simulation incorporating this change (Exhibit 11.8). The result of this simulation is shown in Exhibit 11.9. Both the number of patients in the waiting room (examination and treatment queue) and the amount of time they waited were reduced substantially. The staffing levels were not changed, as the discharge nurses were now treatment nurses. Physician staffing was also not increased, as some delay inside the treatment process itself had always existed due to the need to wait for lab results; this delayed a final physician diagnosis. Having more patients available for treatment filled this lab delay time for physicians with patient care.

The most significant improvement resulting from the process improvement initiative was that total patient throughput time now averaged 1.84 hours (110 minutes). This 33 percent reduction in throughput time exceeded the team's goal and was celebrated by VVH's senior leadership. The summary of process improvement steps is displayed in Exhibit 11.10.

Conclusion

The theory of swift, even flow provides a framework for process improvement and increased productivity. The efficiency and effectiveness of a process

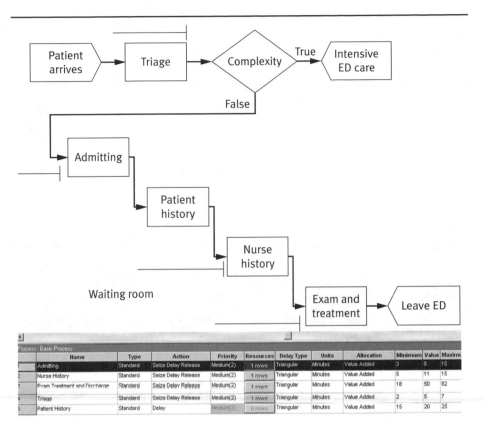

NOTE: Model created in Arena®, Rockwell Automation.

EXHIBIT 11.8
VVH Emergency Department (ED) Proposed Change Simulation Model

The table in the figure reads:

Name	Type	Action	Priority	Resources	Delay Type	Units	Allocation	Minimum	Value	Maximi
1 Admitting	Standard	Seize Delay Release	Medium(2)	1 rows	Triangular	Minutes	Value Added	3	8	15
2 Nurse History	Standard	Seize Delay Release	Medium(2)	1 rows	Triangular	Minutes	Value Added	5	11	15
3 Exam Treatment and Discharge	Standard	Seize Delay Release	Medium(2)	1 rows	Triangular	Minutes	Value Added	18	50	82
4 Triage	Standard	Seize Delay Release	Medium(2)	1 rows	Triangular	Minutes	Value Added	2	5	7
5 Patient History	Standard	Delay	Medium(2)	0 rows	Triangular	Minutes	Value Added	15	20	25

increase as the speed of flow through the process increases and the variability associated with that process decreases.

The movement of patients in a healthcare facility is one of the most critical and visible processes in healthcare delivery. Reducing flow time and variation in processes has a number of benefits:

- Patient satisfaction increases.
- Quality of clinical care improves as patients have reduced waits for diagnosis and treatment.
- Financial performance improves.

This chapter demonstrates many approaches to the challenges of reducing flow time and process variation. Starting with the straightforward process map, many improvements can be found immediately by inspection. In other cases, the powerful tool of computer-based discrete event simulation can provide a road map to sophisticated process improvements.

EXHIBIT 11.9
VVH Emergency
Department
(ED) Proposed
Change
Simulation
Model Output

Category Overview

4:11:35 PM   February 8, 2012

Values Across All Replications

VVH Emergency

Replications: 100   Time Unit: Hours

Entity

Time

Total Time	Average	Half Width	Minimum Average	Maximum Average	Minimum Value	Maximum Value
Routine patient	1.8376	0.05	1.5459	2.8729	1.0063	4.5989

Queue

Time

Waiting Time	Average	Half Width	Minimum Average	Maximum Average	Minimum Value	Maximum Value
Admitting queue	0.00519434	0.00	0.00041085	0.01364095	0.00	0.2235
Exam and treatment and discharge queue	0.2039	0.04	0.00197293	1.1105	0.00	2.2943
Nurse history queue	0.01791752	0.00	0.00244500	0.07537764	0.00	0.3417
Triage queue	0.06635691	0.01	0.01863876	0.2547	0.00	0.8065

Other

Waiting Time	Average	Half Width	Minimum Average	Maximum Average	Minimum Value	Maximum Value
Admitting queue	0.03400433	0.00	0.00218978	0.0946	0.00	3.0000
Exam and treatment and discharge queue	1.3571	0.31	0.00838496	7.8288	0.00	19.0000
Nurse history queue	0.1098	0.01	0.01120623	0.5716	0.00	4.0000
Triage queue	0.5629	0.08	0.1227	2.5046	0.00	11.0000

Resource

Usage

Instantaneous Utilization	Average	Half Width	Minimum Average	Maximum Average	Minimum Value	Maximum Value
Exam room 1	0.7827	0.02	0.5405	0.9303	0.00	1.0000
Exam room 2	0.7644	0.02	0.5468	0.9103	0.00	1.0000
Exam room 3	0.7626	0.02	0.5577	0.9052	0.00	1.0000
Exam room 4	0.7478	0.02	0.4984	0.8993	0.00	1.0000
Exam room 5	0.7859	0.02	0.5420	0.9313	0.00	1.0000
Exam room 6	0.8030	0.02	0.4990	0.9472	0.00	1.0000
Financial clerk 1	0.4606	0.01	0.3250	0.5985	0.00	1.0000
Financial clerk 2	0.4529	0.01	0.2968	0.6119	0.00	1.0000
History nurse 1	0.5236	0.01	0.3642	0.6766	0.00	1.0000
History nurse 2	0.5154	0.01	0.3403	0.6982	0.00	1.0000
Triage nurse	0.6226	0.02	0.4742	0.8185	0.00	1.0000

NOTE: Model created in Arena®, Rockwell Automation.

Process Improvement Change	Throughput Time, Routine Patients
Baseline, before any improvement	165 minutes
Combine admitting functions	155 minutes
Patients enter their own history into computer	145 minutes
Combine discharge tasks into examination and treatment process and convert discharge rooms to treatment rooms	110 minutes

EXHIBIT 11.10
Summary of VVH Emergency Department Throughput Improvement Project

Ensuring quality of care is another critical focus of healthcare organizations. The process improvement tools and approaches in this chapter could also be used to reduce process variation and eliminate errors. Healthcare organizations need to employ the disciplined approach described in this chapter to achieve the needed improvements in flow and quality.

Discussion Questions

1. How do you determine which process improvement tools should be used in a given situation? What is the cost and return of each approach?
2. Which process improvement tool can have the most powerful effect and why?
3. How can barriers to process improvement, such as staff reluctance to change, lack of capital, technological barriers, or clinical practice guidelines, be overcome?
4. How can the EMR be used to make significant process improvements for both efficiency and quality increases?

Chapter Exercises

1. Access the National Guideline Clearinghouse (www.guideline.gov/) and translate one of the guidelines described into a process map. In addition, add decision points and alternative paths to deal with unusual issues that might occur in the process. (Use of Microsoft Visio is encouraged here.)

www.ache.org/books/OpsManagement2

2. Access the following process maps on the companion website:
   - Operating Suite
   - Cancer Treatment Clinic

   Use basic improvement tools, theory of constraints, Six Sigma, and/or Lean tools to determine possible process improvements (Sepúlveda et al. 1999).

3. Access the following Arena models on the companion website:
   - Pharmacy Distribution
   - Clinic Billing

   Develop an improvement plan and use Arena to evaluate it. Compare the results from the base model with your results.

Further Reading

Goldratt, E. M., and J. Cox. 1986. *The Goal: A Process of Ongoing Improvement.* New York: North River Press.

Kelton, W., R. Sadowski, and N. Swets. 2009. *Simulation with Arena.* New York: McGraw-Hill.

SCHEDULING AND CAPACITY MANAGEMENT **12**

Operations Management in Action

"Once upon a time, a patient at Second Street Family Practice in Auburn, Maine, had to wait from 60 to 90 days to be seen for a routine check-up. Then, when the day of the appointment finally arrived, the patient might wait nearly 20 minutes in the waiting room and another 20 for the exam to begin. But thanks to strong leadership, impressive teamwork, and effective tools, patients wanting care from Second Street, even routine check-ups, are now seen the same day they call. The average time patients spend flipping through magazines in the waiting room has dropped to around seven minutes; the exam room wait is down to eight. What's more, staff say they like the new system much better, and patient surveys show that about 90 percent of patients notice and are pleased with the changes as well."

Clinic leadership, "who had been reading and learning about advanced access scheduling, recognized it as the antidote for their frustrations. Developed by Mark Murray, MD, and Catherine Tantau, RN, consultants in Sacramento, California, and promoted by IHI in its office practice programs and on its website, advanced access uses queuing theory to reengineer the standard appointment scheduling system, leaving the majority of slots on any given day open for patients who call that day.

"The benefits of advanced access go beyond improved scheduling, says IHI director Marie Schall. 'It improves quality and continuity,' she says. 'People can get problems checked sooner rather than later, and they see the same provider virtually every time. We know that continuity contributes to better overall quality.' Schall says that, through its Breakthrough Series Collaboratives on Reducing Delays and Waiting Times and its IMPACT network, as well as its work with the Veterans Health Administration on improving access to care, IHI has worked with about 3,000 practices to introduce advanced access."

SOURCE: "Advanced Access: Reducing Waits, Delays, and Frustrations in Maine." Cambridge, MA: Institute for Healthcare Improvement, 2012. (Available on www.ihi.org.)

Overview

Matching the supply of goods or services to the demand for those goods or services is a basic operational problem. In a manufacturing environment, inventory can be used to respond to fluctuations in demand. In the healthcare environment, safety stock can be used to respond to fluctuations in demand for supplies (see Chapter 13), but it is not possible to inventory healthcare services. Capacity must, therefore, be matched to demand. If capacity is greater than demand, resources are underutilized and costs are high. Idle staff, equipment, or facilities increase organizational costs without increasing revenues. If capacity is lower than demand, patients incur long waits or find another provider.

Advanced access scheduling
A method of scheduling outpatient appointments that provides open time slots every day to see a patient on the same day he requests an appointment. Sometimes known as "same day scheduling."

To match capacity to demand, organizations can use demand-influencing strategies or capacity-management strategies. Pricing and promotions are often used to influence demand and demand timing; however, this strategy is often not viable for healthcare organizations. In the past, many healthcare organizations used the demand-leveling strategy of appointment scheduling; more recently, many have begun moving to **advanced access scheduling**. Capacity management strategies allow the organization to adjust capacity to meet fluctuating demand and include using part-time employees, on-call employees, cross-training, and overtime. Effective and efficient scheduling of patients, staff, equipment, facilities, or jobs can help to match capacity to demand and ensure that scarce healthcare resources are utilized to their fullest extent.

This chapter outlines issues and problems faced in scheduling and discusses tools and techniques that can be employed in scheduling patients, staff, equipment, facilities, or jobs. Topics covered include

- hospital census and resource loading,
- staff scheduling,
- job/operation scheduling and sequencing rules,
- patient appointment scheduling models, and
- advanced access patient scheduling.

The scheduling of patients is a unique, but important, subproblem of patient flow. Since the mid-twentieth century, much patient care delivery has moved from the inpatient setting to the ambulatory clinic. Because this trend is likely to continue, matching clinic capacity to patient demand becomes a critical operating skill. In addition, if this capacity can be deployed to meet a patient's desired schedule, marketplace advantage can be gained. Therefore, this chapter focuses on advanced access (same-day scheduling) for ambulatory patients. Topics covered include

- advantages of advanced access,
- implementation steps, and
- metrics to measure the operations of advanced access scheduling systems.

Many of the operations tools and approaches detailed in earlier chapters are employed to optimize the operations of an advanced access clinic.

Hospital Census and Rough Cut Capacity Planning

For many healthcare organizations, the admittance rate and number of occupied beds provide a good indication of the demands being placed on the system. For hospitals, these numbers can often be measured by using the overall patient census. Most hospitals report their census on a daily and hourly basis to manage the available beds in the system. However, what many healthcare organizations fail to understand is that the census gives a good visual of the resource needs to appropriately staff a system. Exhibit 12.1 shows a three-month view of a census for Vincent Valley Hospital and Health System (VVH). The pattern is remarkably similar to most hospitals in that a large amount of variance exists in the patient population on a daily basis. This variance can get magnified when observing the census on an hourly basis.

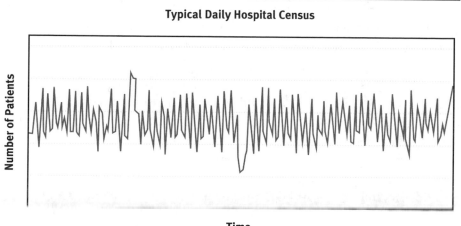

Typical Daily Hospital Census

Number of Patients

Time

EXHIBIT 12.1
Daily Census
at VVH

EXHIBIT 12.2
Hourly Census
at VVH in One
Patient-Care
Unit

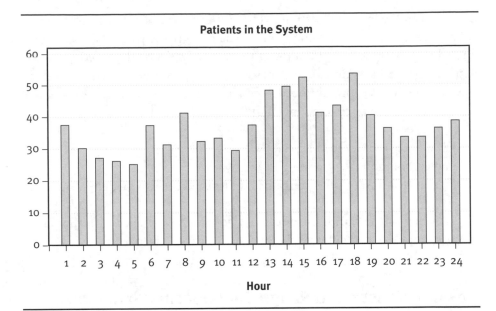

EXHIBIT 12.2
Hourly Census
at VVH in One
Patient-Care
Unit

Rough cut capacity planning
The process of converting the overall production plan into capacity needs for key resources.

Rough cut capacity planning is the process of converting the overall production plan into capacity needs for key resources. For a hospital, it means planning key resources for the demand schedule. While the day-to-day demand in healthcare systems is highly variable, the aggregate demand on a month-to-month basis can be predicted much more precisely. When planning resources, hospitals generally have two types of labor resources: full-time staff and contractors. By examining the census, an administrator should be able to prepare on an aggregate basis the number of contactors needed to protect against high-volume months. Too many healthcare systems leave this planning until the last minute and have not paid enough attention to predictable demand patterns.

A hospital administrator can also use the daily census to assist in preparing workforce schedules on a weekly or daily basis. Exhibit 12.2 shows a spike in the system occurring from hour 13 to hour 19, which in most situations is the middle of the day. Many hospitals are still scheduled using standard morning, evening, and night shifts. If this occurred in this system, doctors and nurses would be ending their shifts at the time of the maximum demand on the system, which could result in increased potential for errors in handing off patients to new doctors, long patient wait times, and medical records not getting finished in a timely manner.

A major cost savings exists for hospitals and clinics by simply matching the resources to the demand patterns in the system. In this case, having many staff doctors and nurses working over the peak times in the middle of the day would be ideal. From an operations perspective, this issue is easy to change; however, in practice there are several obstacles, including unions and doctor block scheduling systems, to deal with.

Staff Scheduling

For small schedule-optimization problems, where demand is reasonably known and staffing requirements can therefore be estimated with certainty, mathematical programming (Chapter 6) can be used to optimize staffing levels and schedules. A simple example of this type of problem is illustrated below. A more detailed problem is illustrated in "Using Linear Programming to Minimize the Cost of Nursing Personnel" (Matthews 2005), and linear programming has been used to help resolve scheduling issues in home health care (Trabelsi, Larbi, and Alouane 2012).

As the problems become larger and more complex, developing and using a mathematical programming model becomes time and cost prohibitive. In those cases, simulation can be used to answer what-if scheduling questions: "What if we added another nurse?" or "What if we cross-trained employees?" See Chapter 11 and the advanced access section of this chapter for examples of these types of applications.

Riverview Clinic Urgent Care Staffing Using Linear Programming

Nurses who staff the Riverview Clinic after-hours urgent care clinic have been complaining about their schedules. They would like to work five consecutive days and have two consecutive days off every seven days. Additionally, different nurses prefer different days off and believe that their preferences should be assigned based on seniority; the most senior nurses should get their most desired days off.

Riverview Urgent Care Clinic (UCC) has collected patient demand data by day of the week and knows how many nurses should be on staff each day to service demand. Riverview UCC management wants to minimize nurse payroll while reducing the nurses' complaints about their schedules. They decide to use **linear programming** to help determine a solution for this problem. Target staffing levels and salary expenses are shown in Exhibit 12.3.

First, Riverview needs to determine how many nurses should be assigned to each possible schedule. There are seven possible schedules (Monday and Tuesday off, Tuesday and Wednesday off, etc.).

Linear programming
A mathematical technique used to find the optimal solution to a linear problem given a set of constrained resources.

	Sunday	Monday	Tuesday	Wednesday	Thursday	Friday	Saturday
Nurses needed/day	5	4	3	3	3	4	6
Salary and benefits/ nurse-day	220	240	240	240	240	240	220

EXHIBIT 12.3
Riverview UCC Target Staffing Level and Salary Expense

The goal is to minimize weekly salary expense, and the objective function is:

$$\text{Minimize: } (\$320 \times \text{Sun. \# of nurses}) + (\$240 \times \text{Mon. \# of nurses}) +$$
$$(\$240 \times \text{Tues. \# of nurses}) + (\$240 \times \text{Wed. \# of nurses}) +$$
$$(\$240 \times \text{Thurs. \# of nurses}) + (\$240 \times \text{Fri. \# of nurses}) +$$
$$(\$320 \times \text{Sat. \# of nurses})$$

The constraints are:

- The number of nurses scheduled each day must be greater than the number of nurses needed each day.

Sunday # of nurses $\geq$ 5	(1)
Monday # of nurses $\geq$ 4	(2)
Tuesday # of nurses $\geq$ 3	(3)
Wednesday # of nurses $\geq$ 3	(4)
Thursday # of nurses $\geq$ 3	(5)
Friday # of nurses $\geq$ 4	(6)
Saturday # of nurses $\geq$ 6	(7)

- The number of nurses assigned to each schedule must be greater than zero and an integer.

# A (B, C, D, E, F, or G) nurses $\geq$ 0	(8–14)
# A (B, C, D, E, F, or G) nurses = integer	(15–21)

Exhibit 12.4 shows the Excel Solver setup of this problem.

EXHIBIT 12.4
Initial Excel
Solver Setup of
Riverview UCC
Optimization

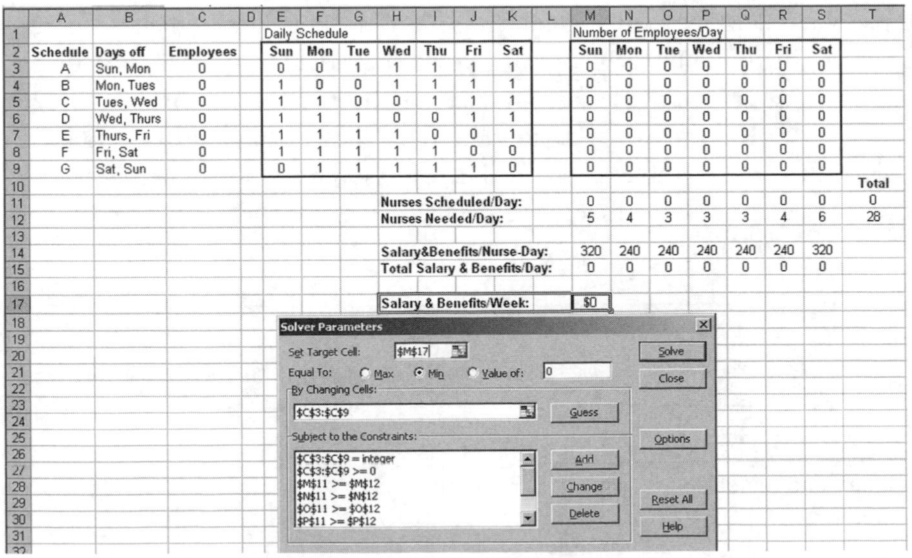

Solver (Exhibit 12.5) finds that the Riverview UCC needs six nurses and should assign one nurse to schedules A, B, C, and D; two nurses to schedule E; and no nurses to schedules F and G. The total salary expense with this optimal schedule is:

$$\text{Minimize: } (\$320 \times 5) + (\$240 \times 4) + (\$240 \times 4) + (\$240 \times 4) + (\$240 \times 3) + (\$240 \times 4) + (\$320 \times 6) = \$8,080/\text{Week}$$

Next, Riverview needs to determine which nurses to assign to which schedule based on their preferences and seniority. Each nurse is asked to rank schedules A through E in order of preference for that particular schedule. The nurses' preferences on a scale of one to five, with five being the most preferred schedule, are then weighted by a seniority factor. Riverview decides to use a seniority weighting factor based on the number of years a particular nurse has worked at the UCC compared with the number of years the most senior nurse has worked at the UCC.

The goal is to maximize the nurses' total weighted preference scores (WPS), and the objective function is:

$$\text{Maximize: Mary's WPS + Anne's WPS + Susan's WPS + Tom's WPS + Cathy's WPS + Jane's WPS}$$

The constraints are:

- Each nurse must either be assigned to a particular schedule or not assigned to that schedule.
  Mary assigned to schedule A (B, C, D, or E) = 0 or 1 (binary)   (1–5)
  Anne assigned to schedule A (B, C, D, or E) = 0 or 1 (binary)   (6–10)
  Susan assigned to schedule A (B, C, D, or E) = 0 or 1 (binary) (11–15)
  Tom assigned to schedule A (B, C, D, or E) = 0 or 1 (binary) (16–20)
  Cathy assigned to schedule A (B, C, D, or E) = 0 or 1 (binary)(21–25)
  Jane assigned to schedule A (B, C, D, or E) = 0 or 1 (binary) (26–30)
- The number of nurses assigned to each schedule must be as required.
  # of nurses assigned to schedule A (B, C, or D) = 1   (31–34)
  # of nurses assigned to schedule E = 2   (35)
- Each nurse can only be assigned to one schedule.
  Mary (Anne, Susan, Tom, Cathy, or Jane) A + B + D + C + E = 1 (36–41)

Exhibit 12.5 Shows the Excel setup of this problem.
Solver (Exhibit 12.6) finds that Mary should be assigned to schedule D (her second choice), Anne to schedule E (her first choice), Susan to schedule C (her first choice), Tom to schedule E (his first choice), Cathy to schedule B (her second choice), and Jane to schedule A (her first choice).

EXHIBIT 12.5
Riverview UCC
Initial Solver
Solution and
Schedule
Preference
Setup

Schedule	Days off	Employees	Daily Schedule							Number of Employees/Day							Total	Preference score
			Sun	Mon	Tue	Wed	Thu	Fri	Sat	Sun	Mon	Tue	Wed	Thu	Fri	Sat		
A	Sun, Mon	1	0	0	1	1	1	1	1	0	0	1	1	1	1	1		
B	Mon, Tues	1	1	0	0	1	1	1	1	1	0	0	1	1	1	1		
C	Tues, Wed	1	1	1	0	0	1	1	1	1	1	0	0	1	1	1		
D	Wed, Thurs	1	1	1	1	0	0	1	1	1	1	1	0	0	1	1		
E	Thurs, Fri	2	1	1	1	1	0	0	1	2	2	2	2	0	0	2		
F	Fri, Sat	0	1	1	1	1	1	0	0	0	0	0	0	0	0	0		
G	Sat, Sun	0	0	1	1	1	1	1	0	0	0	0	0	0	0	0		

| | | | | | | | | | | Nurses Scheduled/Day: | 5 | 4 | 4 | 4 | 3 | 4 | 6 | 30 |
| | | | | | | | | | | Nurses Needed/Day: | 5 | 4 | 3 | 3 | 3 | 4 | 6 | 28 |

| | Salary&Benefits/Nurse-Day: | 320 | 240 | 240 | 240 | 240 | 240 | 320 |
| | Total Salary & Benefits/Day: | 1600 | 960 | 960 | 960 | 720 | 960 | 1920 |

| Salary & Benefits/Week: | $8,080 |

Employee	Seniority (years)	Seniority factor	Preference of employees					Weighted preference of employees					Schedule assigned to						Preference score
			A	B	C	D	E	A	B	C	D	E	A	B	C	D	E	Total	
Mary	5	0.71	3	1	2	4	5	2.14	0.71	1.43	2.86	3.57	0	0	0	0	0	0	0.00
Anne	6	0.86	3	2	1	4	5	2.57	1.71	0.86	3.43	4.29	0	0	0	0	0	0	0.00
Susan	4	0.57	2	3	5	1	4	1.14	1.71	2.86	0.57	2.29	0	0	0	0	0	0	0.00
Tom	7	1.00	3	2	4	1	5	3.00	2.00	4.00	1.00	5.00	0	0	0	0	0	0	0.00
Cathy	3	0.43	3	4	5	2	1	1.29	1.71	2.14	0.86	0.43	0	0	0	0	0	0	0.00
Jane	2	0.29	5	4	3	2	1	1.43	1.14	0.86	0.57	0.29	0	0	0	0	0	0	0.00
Maximum	7												Actual:	0	0	0	0	0	0
													Needed:	1	1	1	1	2	

All of the nurses now have two consecutive days off every seven days and are assigned to either their first or second choice of schedule. Note that even this simple problem has 20 decision variables and 41 constraints.

Job/Operation Scheduling and Sequencing Rules

Job/operation scheduling looks at the problem of how to sequence a pool of jobs (or patients) through a particular operation. For example, a clinic laboratory has many patient blood samples that need to be tested—in what order should the lab work on the samples? Or, a hospital has many surgeries waiting to be performed—in what order should those surgeries occur?

The simplest sequencing problems consist of a pool of jobs waiting for only one resource. Sequencing of those jobs is usually based on a desire to meet due dates (time at which the job is supposed to be complete) by minimizing the number of jobs that are late, minimizing the average amount of

EXHIBIT 12.6
Riverview UCC
Final Solver
Solution for
Individual
Schedules

Employee	Seniority (years)	Seniority factor	Preference of employees					Weighted preference of employees					Schedule assigned to						Preference score
			A	B	C	D	E	A	B	C	D	E	A	B	C	D	E	Total	
Mary	5	0.71	3	1	2	4	5	2.14	0.71	1.43	2.86	3.57	0	0	0	1	0	1	2.86
Anne	6	0.86	3	2	1	4	5	2.57	1.71	0.86	3.43	4.29	0	0	0	0	1	1	4.29
Susan	4	0.57	2	3	5	1	4	1.14	1.71	2.86	0.57	2.29	0	0	1	0	0	1	2.86
Tom	7	1.00	3	2	4	1	5	3.00	2.00	4.00	1.00	5.00	0	0	0	0	1	1	5.00
Cathy	3	0.43	3	4	5	2	1	1.29	1.71	2.14	0.86	0.43	0	1	0	0	0	1	1.71
Jane	2	0.29	5	4	3	2	1	1.43	1.14	0.86	0.57	0.29	1	0	0	0	0	1	1.43
Maximum	7												Actual:	1	1	1	1	2	18.1428559
													Needed:	1	1	1	1	2	

Solver Parameters

Set Target Cell: $W$28

Equal To: ● Max ○ Min ○ Value of: 0

By Changing Cells: $Q$21:$U$26

Subject to the Constraints:
$Q$28 = $Q$29
$R$28 = $R$29
$S$28 = $S$29
$T$28 = $T$29
$U$28 = $U$29
$V$21:$V$26 = 1

[Solve] [Close] [Guess] [Options] [Add] [Change] [Delete] [Reset All] [Help]

time by which jobs will be late, or minimizing the maximum late time of any job. It may also be desirable to minimize the time jobs spend in the system or average completion time.

Various **sequencing rules,** also known as the queuing priority, can be used to schedule jobs through the system. Commonly used rules include:

- *First come, first served (FCFS)*: Jobs are sequenced in the same order in which they arrive.
- *Shortest processing time (SPT)*: The job that takes the least amount of time to complete is first, followed by the job that will take the next least amount time, and so on.
- *Earliest due date (EDD)*: The job with the earliest due date is first, followed by the job with the next earliest due date, and so on.
- *Slack time remaining (STR)*: The job with the least amount of slack (time until due date/processing time) is first, followed by the job with the next least amount of slack time, and so on.
- *Critical ratio (CR)*: The job with the smallest critical ratio (time until due date/processing time) is first, followed by the job with the next smallest critical ratio, and so on.

Sequencing rules
Heuristic rules that indicate the order in which jobs are processed from a queue. Also known as the "queuing priority."

When only one resource or operation for the jobs is to be processed through, the SPT rule will minimize average completion time, and the EDD rule will minimize average lateness and maximum lateness; however, no single rule will accomplish both objectives. When jobs (or patients) must be processed through a series of resources or operations with different possible sequencing at each, the situation becomes more complex, and a particular rule will not result in the same outcome for the entire system as for the single resource. Often, simulation is used to evaluate these more complex systems and help determine optimum sequencing.

For a busy resource, the SPT rule is often used. This rule will complete a greater number of jobs in a shorter amount of time, but some jobs with long completion times may never be finished. To alleviate this problem, the SPT rule is often used in combination with other rules. For example, in some emergency departments, less severe cases (those with a shorter processing time) are separated and fast tracked to free up examination rooms quickly.

For time-sensitive operations, where lateness is not tolerated, the EDD rule is appropriate. Because it is the easiest to apply, the FCFS rule is typically used when the resource has excess capacity and no jobs will be late. In a Lean environment, sequencing rules become irrelevant because the ideal size of the pool of jobs is reduced to one and a kanban system (a form of FCFS) can be used to pull jobs through the system (Chapter 9).

EXHIBIT 12.7
VVH Laboratory
Blood Test
Information

Sample	Processing Time (Minutes)	Due Time (Minutes from Now)	Slack	CR
A	50	100	$100 - 50 = 50$	$100/50 = 2.00$
B	100	160	$160 - 100 = 60$	$160/100 = 1.60$
C	20	50	$50 - 20 = 30$	$50/20 = 2.50$
D	80	120	$120 - 80 = 40$	$120/80 = 1.50$
E	60	80	$80 - 60 = 20$	$80/60 = 1.33$

Vincent Valley Hospital and Health System Laboratory Sequencing Rules

The laboratory at Vincent Valley Hospital and Health System (VVH) recently lost one of its lab technicians, and the lab manager, Jessica Simmons, does not believe she will be able to find a qualified replacement for at least one month. This has greatly increased the workload in the lab, and physicians have been complaining that their requested blood work is not being completed in a timely manner.

In the past, Jessica has divided the blood testing among the technicians and had them complete the tests on an FCFS basis. She is considering using a different sequencing rule to try to satisfy more of the physicians. In anticipation of this change, she requested that each physician put a desired completion time on each request for blood testing. To investigate the effects of changing the sequencing rules, she decides to take the first five requests for blood work from one of the technicians and analyze job completion under various scheduling rules. Note that, for five jobs, there are 120 possible sequences in which the jobs could be completed. Exhibit 12.7 shows the time to complete blood work on each sample and the time when the physician has requested that it be complete.

Exhibit 12.8 shows the order in which jobs will be processed and results under different sequencing rules. Exhibit 12.9 compares the various sequencing rules. The FCFS rule performs poorly on all measures. The SPT rule minimizes average completion time, and the EDD rule minimizes average tardiness. Under both rules, three jobs are tardy and the maximum tardiness is 150 minutes. After looking at these results, Jessica decides to implement the EDD rule for laboratory blood tests to minimize the number of tardy jobs and the average tardiness of jobs. She hopes this will reduce physician complaints until a new technician can be hired.

Sequence	Start Time	Processing Time	Completion Time	Due Time	Tardiness
FCFS					
A	0	50	50	100	
B	50	100	150	160	
C	150	20	170	50	170 − 50 = 120
D	170	80	250	120	250 − 120 = 130
E	250	60	310	80	310 − 80 = 230
		Average	186		(120 + 130 + 230)/5 = 96
SPT					
C	0	20	20	50	
A	20	50	70	100	
E	70	60	130	80	130 − 80 = 50
D	130	80	210	120	210 − 120 = 90
B	210	100	310	160	310 − 160 = 150
		Average	148		(50 + 90 + 150)/5 = 58
EDD					
C	0	20	20	50	
E	20	60	80	80	
A	80	50	130	100	130 − 100 = 30
D	130	80	210	120	210 − 120 = 90
B	210	100	310	160	310 − 160 = 150
		Average	150		(30 + 90 + 150)/5 = 54
STR					
E	0	60	60	80	
C	60	20	80	50	80 − 50 = 30
D	80	80	160	120	160 − 120 = 40
A	160	50	210	100	210 − 100 = 110
B	210	100	310	160	310 − 160 = 150
		Average	164		(30 + 40 + 110 + 150)/5 = 66
CR					
E	0	60	60	80	
D	60	80	140	120	140 − 120 = 20
B	140	100	240	160	240 − 160 = 80
A	240	50	290	100	290 − 100 − 190
C	300	20	310	50	310 − 50 = 260
		Average	208		(20 + 80 + 190 + 260)/5 = 110

EXHIBIT 12.8

VVH Laboratory Blood Test Sequencing Rules

NOTE: All times in table are in minutes.

EXHIBIT 12.9
Comparison of
VVH Blood Test
Sequencing
Rules

Sequencing Rule	Average Completion Time	Average Tardiness	Number of Tardy Jobs	Maximum Tardiness
FCFS	186	96	3*	230
SPT	148*	58	3*	150*
EDD	150	54*	3*	150*
STR	164	66	4	150*
CR	208	110	4	260

*Best values. Times are in minutes.

Patient Appointment Scheduling Models

Appointment scheduling models attempt to minimize patient waiting time while maximizing utilization of the resource (clinician, machine, etc.) the patients are waiting to access. Soriano (1966) classifies appointment scheduling systems into four basic types: block appointment, individual appointment, mixed block-individual appointment, and other.

A block appointment scheme schedules the arrival of all patients at the start of a clinic session. Patients are usually seen FCFS, but other sequencing rules can be used. This type of scheduling system maximizes utilization of the clinician, but patients can experience long wait times. An individual appointment scheme assigns different, equally spaced appointment times to each individual patient. In a common modification of this type of system, different appointment lengths are available and assigned based on the type of patient. This system reduces patient waiting time but decreases utilization of the clinician. Increasing the interval between arrivals results in a reduction of both waiting time and utilization. A mixed block-individual appointment scheme schedules a group of patients to arrive at the start of the clinic session, followed by equally spaced appointment times for the remainder of the session. This type of system can be used to balance the competing goals of increased utilization and decreased waiting time. Other appointment schemes are modifications of the first three types.

Simulation has been used to study the performance of various appointment scheduling models and rules. Although no scheduling rule or scheme was found to be universally superior, the Bailey-Welch rule (Bailey and Welch 1952) performed well under most conditions. This rule schedules two patients at the beginning of a clinic session, followed by equally spaced appointment times for the remainder of the session.

Chow and colleagues (2011) reduced the number of surgery cancellations by using an advanced computer simulation model to better allocate open surgical slots in the appointment system. Using Monte Carlo simulation techniques (Chapter 10), they were able to increase surgical volume by more than 5 percent and reduce bed days over capacity by more than 9 percent.

Kaandorp and Koole (2007b) developed a mathematic model to determine an optimal schedule using a weighted average of expected waiting times of patients, idle time of the clinician, and tardiness (the probability that the clinician has to work later than scheduled multiplied by the average amount of added time) as the objective. This tool uses simulation to compare a user-defined schedule to the optimal schedule found using the model and is available at http://obp.math.vu.nl/healthcare/software/ges/.

Riverview Clinic Appointment Schedule

Physicians at VVH's Riverview Clinic typically see patients for six consecutive hours each day. Each appointment takes an average of 20 minutes; therefore, each clinician is scheduled to see 18 patients per day. Two percent of patients are no-shows. Currently, Riverview is using an individual appointment scheme with appointments scheduled every 20 minutes. However, clinicians have been complaining that they often have to work late but are idle at various points during the course of the day. Riverview decides to use the Optimal Outpatient Appointment Scheduling Tool (Kaandorp and Koole 2007b) to see if a better scheduling model could be used to alleviate these complaints without increasing patient waiting time to an unacceptable level.

Exhibit 12.10 shows the results of this analysis when waiting time weight is 1.5, idle time weight is 0.2, and tardiness weight is 1.0. The optimal schedule follows the Bailey-Welch rule. Under this rule, patient waiting is increased by five minutes, but both idleness and tardiness are decreased. Riverview does not believe that the additional waiting time is unacceptable and decides to implement this new appointment scheduling scheme.

Advanced Access Patient Scheduling

Advanced Access for an Operating and Market Advantage

In the early 1990s, Mark Murray, MD, MPA, and Catherine Tantau, RN, developed the concept of **advanced access scheduling** at Kaiser Permanente in Northern California. Their goal was to eliminate long patient waits for appointments and bottlenecks in clinic operations (Singer 2001). The principles they developed and refined have now been implemented by many leading healthcare organizations globally.

Advanced access scheduling.
A method of scheduling outpatient appointments that provides open time slots every day to see a patient on the same day he requests an appointment. Sometimes known as *same day scheduling*.

EXHIBIT 12.10
Riverview Clinic
Appointment
Scheduling

	Optimal outpatient appointment scheduling tool
Average service time [20] minutes	
Number of intervals [18]	
Length of interval [20] minutes	Press the button to
Total number of arrivals [18]	[compute the solutions]
Percentage no-shows [2] %	Finished searching.
alpha waiting [1.5]	
alpha idle time [0.2]	
alpha tardiness [1]	

Interval	Time	☑ Number of patients of your choice (calc time: several seconds)	☑ ⦿ Small Neighborhood (Suboptimal, calc time: several minutes) ○ Full Neighborhood (Optimal, calc time: several hours)
1	0:00	1	2
2	0:20	1	1
3	0:40	1	1
4	1:00	1	1
5	1:20	1	1
6	1:40	1	1
7	2:00	1	1
8	2:20	1	1
9	2:40	1	1
10	3:00	1	1
11	3:20	1	1
12	3:40	1	1
13	4:00	1	1
14	4:20	1	1
15	4:40	1	1
16	5:00	1	1
17	5:20	1	1
18	5:40	1	0

Waiting time	31 minutes	35.85 minutes	
Idle time	57.53 minutes	40.53 minutes	
Tardiness	52.47	40.96	
Fraction of excess	79.82 %	63.75 %	
Makespan	410.33 minutes	393.33 minutes	
Lateness	50.33 minutes	33.33 minutes	
Object Value	110.47	102.84	

NOTE: Copyright © 2007 Guido Kaandorp and Ger Koole.

Because most clinics today use traditional scheduling systems, long wait times are prevalent, and appointments are only available weeks, or even months, in advance. The further in advance visits are scheduled, the greater the fail (no-show) rate becomes. To compensate, providers double-book or even triple-book appointment slots. Long delays and queues occur when all patients scheduled actually appear for the same appointment slot. This problem is compounded by patients who have urgent needs requiring that they be seen immediately. These patients are either worked into the schedule or sent to an emergency department, decreasing both continuity of care and revenue to the clinic. At the emergency department, patients are frequently told to see their primary care physicians (PCPs) in one to three days, further complicating the problem.

Advanced access is implemented by beginning each day with a large portion of each provider's schedule open for urgent, routine, and follow-up appointments. Patients are seen when they want to be seen. This dramatically reduces the fail rate, as patients do not have to remember clinic visits they booked long ago. Because there is no double- or triple-booking, patients are seen on time and schedules run smoothly inside the clinic. Clinics using advanced access can provide patients with the convenience of walk-in or urgent care, with the added advantage of maintaining continuity of care with their own doctors and clinics.

Parente, Pinto, and Barber (2005) studied the implementation of advanced access in a large Midwestern clinic with a patient panel of 10,000. After implementation of this system, the average number of days between calling for an appointment and being seen by a doctor decreased from 18.7 to 11.8. However, the most significant finding was that 91.4 percent of patients now saw their own PCP, as opposed to 69.8 percent before the implementation of advanced access.

Implementing Advanced Access

Implementing advanced access is difficult. Changing from a long-standing system, albeit a flawed one, is challenging. However, following a few well-prescribed steps increases the probability of success. In a study of large urban public hospitals, Singer (2001) developed the following methodology to implement advanced access.

Obtain Buy-In

Leadership is key to making this major change, and the advanced access system must be supported by senior leaders and providers themselves. Touring other clinics that have implemented advanced access may be helpful to get a sense of how this system can work successfully.

For large systems, starting small in one or two clinical settings is best. Once initial operating problems are resolved and clinic staff is positive about the change, advanced access can be carefully implemented in a number of additional clinics in the system.

Predict Demand

The first quantitative step in implementation is to measure and predict demand from patients. For each day during a study period, demand is calculated as the volume of patients requesting appointments (today or in the future), walk-in patients, patients referred from urgent care clinics or emergency departments, and number of calls deflected to other providers. After initial demand calculations are performed, they can be made more sophisticated by considering day of the week, seasonality, demand for same-day versus scheduled appointments, and even clinical characteristics of patients.

Predict Capacity

The capacity of the clinic needs to be determined once demand is calculated. In general, this is the sum of appointment slots available each day. Capacity can vary dramatically from day to day, as providers usually have obligations for their time other than seeing patients in the clinic.

Determining whether a clinic's capacity can meet expected demand is relatively easy using Little's law (described in detail in Chapter 11). Singer (2001) reported that many public hospital clinics initially felt that demand exceeded capacity in their operations. However, many of these clinics found hidden capacity in their systems by more effectively using providers (e.g., minimizing paperwork) and using for exams space that had been used for storage.

Another opportunity to improve the capacity of a clinic is to standardize and minimize the length of visit times. A clinic with high variability in appointment times may find that it has many small blocks of unused time.

Assess Operations

The implementation of advanced access provides the opportunity to review and improve the core patient flow and operations in a clinic. The tools and techniques of process mapping and process improvement, particularly value stream mapping and the theory of constraints, should be applied before advanced access is implemented.

Work Down the Backlog

Working down the backlog is one of the most challenging tasks in implementing advanced access, as providers must see more patients per day until they have caught up to same-day access. For example, each provider could work one extra hour per day and see three additional patients until the backlog is eliminated. The number of days to work off a backlog can be calculated by:

Days to work down backlog = Current backlog/Increase in capacity

where

Current backlog = Appointments on the books/
Average number of patients seen per day

and

Increase in capacity = (New service rate [Patients/Day]/
Old service rate [Patients/Day]) − 1

Going Live

Once a clinic is ready to go live, it must first determine how many appointment slots to reserve for same-day access. Singer and Regenstein (2003) report that public hospital clinics are leaving 40 percent to 60 percent of their slots available for same-day access, but other clinics have reported leaving up to 75 percent of slots available.

It is important to educate patients, as they will be surprised by the ability to see a provider the day they request an appointment. Many elderly patients may not choose this option, as they may need more time for preparation or to arrange transportation.

No clinic operates in a completely stable environment, so prospectively developing contingency plans in case a provider is ill or called away on an emergency is useful. Contingencies can also be predictable increases in demand such as routine physicals in the weeks preceding the start of school. Good contingency planning will ensure the smooth and efficient operation of an advanced access system.

Metrics

Gupta and colleagues (2006) developed a set of key indicators that can be used to evaluate the performance of advanced access scheduling systems:

- *PCP match*: percentage of same-day patients who see their own PCP
- *PCP coverage*: percentage of same-day patients seen by any physician
- *Wait time for next appointment* (or third next available appointment)
- *Good backlog*: appointments scheduled in advance because of patient preference
- *Bad backlog*: appointments waiting because of lack of slots

Most well-functioning advanced access systems have high PCP match and PCP coverage. Depending on patient mix and preferences the good backlog can be relatively large, but a large or growing bad backlog can be a signal that capacity or operating systems in the clinic need to be improved.

Fears About Advanced Access and Their Practical Resolution

Gregg Broffman, MD, medical director of the 110-physician Lifetime Health Medical Group in Rochester and Buffalo, New York, reported on the effects to his group of same-day scheduling in the late 1990s. Pointing out the realities of same-day scheduling can help reduce physician fears about change and help make an effective change (Olsen 2012):

Three fears are common but actually are unjustified:

1. **Insatiable demand.** Physicians worry that opening their schedule will leave them swamped with work, but this is a false expectation. By carefully measuring and predicting supply and demand, advanced access ensures adequate coverage and can help determine the need to hire new clinicians to handle the workload.

2. **Fewer encounters.** Use of same-day scheduling has been shown to decrease the number of annual encounters with individual patients. At the same time, it boosts the likelihood that patients will see their personal physician, rather than be worked in with the first available clinician. As a result, patients are more satisfied with their visits. Clinical outcomes rise while costs decrease, because a person's regular practitioner is less likely to order unnecessary tests or prescribe medication than a clinician who is unfamiliar with the patient's history.

3. **Lower revenue.** Decreased volume would suggest a dip in practice revenue, but the opposite has proven true. Clinicians that initially saw a 10 percent to 15 percent drop in encounters had about an 8 percent increase in "relative value unit," which is used to measure the robustness (or "dollar value") of an office visit. For example, when a diabetic patient makes an unplanned visit, physicians can look ahead to his next scheduled appointment and "max pack" the initial visit by performing the future check-up that day. The visit can be coded at a higher level, and this leaves an appointment open in two weeks to see a new patient.

Conclusion

Advanced access is a more efficient and patient-friendly method to deliver ambulatory care. However, implementation and maintenance are difficult unless leadership and staff are committed to its success.

Discussion Questions

1. What job sequencing rule do you see most often in healthcare? Why? Can you think of any additional job sequencing rules not described in this text?
2. How could advanced access techniques be used for:
    a. An ambulatory surgery center?
    b. A freestanding imaging center?
3. What are the consequences of using advanced access in a multispecialty clinic? How could these tools be applied to provide same-day scheduling?
4. Can advanced access techniques be used with appointment scheduling schemes? Why or why not?

Chapter Exercises

1. Two of the nurses (Mary and Joe) at Riverview UCC have decided to work part-time rather than full-time. They would like to work only two (consecutive) days per week. Because they would be part-time employees, salary and benefits per nurse-day for these nurses would be reduced to $160 on weekdays and $220 on weekend days. Riverview could hire an additional full-time nurse if needed. Should Riverview UCC agree to this request? If the clinic does agree, will additional nurses need to be hired? Assuming that part-time nurses and any new hires will accept any schedule and preferences for the remainder of the nurses are the same, what new schedule would you recommend for each nurse?
2. The VVH radiology department currently uses FCFS to determine how to sequence patient X-rays. On a typical day, the department collects data related to patient X-rays. Use these data to compare various sequencing rules. Assuming these data are representative, what rule should the radiology department be using and why? (An Excel spreadsheet containing these data can be found on the companion website.)

www.ache.org/books/OpsManagement2

Patient	Processing Time (Minutes)	Due Time (Minutes from Now)
A	35	140
B	15	180
C	35	360
D	25	290
E	30	420
F	25	20
G	35	180
H	30	290
I	20	110
K	25	150
L	15	270
M	30	390
N	20	220
O	20	400
P	10	330
Q	10	80
R	15	230
S	20	370

3. Go to the companion website to use the Optimal Outpatient Appointment Scheduling Tool (Kaandorp and Koole 2007b) to compare various appointment scheduling schemes. First, assume an 8-hour day that can be divided into 10-minute time blocks (48 time intervals), 15-minute service time for patients, 24 patients seen according to the individual appointment scheme (a patient is scheduled to be seen every 20 minutes), and 5 percent no-shows. Compare this to the small neighborhood optimal schedule with waiting time weight of one, idle time weight of one, and tardiness weight of one. What are the differences in the two schedules? Which would you choose? Why? Increase the waiting time weight to three and compute the small neighborhood optimal schedule. How is this optimal schedule different from the previous one? Finally, change the service time to 20 minutes and compare the individual appointment schedule scheme to the small neighborhood optimal schedule with a waiting time weight of one and three. Which schedule would you choose and why?

www.ache.org/books/OpsManagement2

4. A clinic wants to work down its backlog to implement advanced access. The clinic currently has 1,200 booked appointments and sees 100 patients a day. The staff has agreed to extend their schedules and can now see 110 patients per day. What is their current backlog, and how many days will it take to reduce this to zero?

SUPPLY CHAIN MANAGEMENT

13

Operations Management in Action

Chief financial officers searching for ways to cut costs while jump-starting service might want to spend an afternoon with Allen Caudle, vice president of supply chain at Swedish Medical Center in Seattle, Washington. Caudle's supply-chain strategies saved Swedish more than $30 million in 2005. As his peers increasingly rely on group purchasing organizations (GPOs) to get better prices from vendors, Caudle and his team manage Swedish's spending the old-fashioned way, through strict internal buying policies, central purchasing, self-contracting, and tight vendor control.

It wasn't always that way. Swedish switched from the GPO model to self-contracting seven years ago, bucking the strong industry trend that fueled the growth of purchasing powerhouses like Novation, Premier, and Neoforma (now Global Health Exchange). The homegrown system works—94 percent of Swedish's spending is done on contract—partly because internal department heads and vendors alike must abide by the golden rule: Nobody gets paid without an approved purchase order. New-manager orientation includes an hour long supply-chain primer from Caudle to drive the lesson home. After that, "It only takes one time for them to learn. If a manager has a plausible excuse, I give them one 'mulligan.' But I also say, 'Don't ask for another chance.'"

New vendors are adept at finding ways around the rule, but soon realize their reward is nonpayment, he adds. So that there are no surprises, all vendors first have to pass a 10-question quiz on Swedish's contracting arrangements. The first sentence of the document reads, "I understand that I will not be paid if I don't have a purchase order for this project," Caudle says.

A devotee of Toyota's "lean management" approach, he also eyes everything from anesthesiology technicians' work habits to the location of infusion pumps in patient rooms with waste elimination in mind. His slogan is: "Use our minds before we spend our bucks." And though he works for a healthcare provider that encompasses four hospitals, more than a dozen clinics, a home-care service, and affiliated physician offices, his approach could be adapted to most industries, Caudle says.

For instance, an in-house time-and-efficiency study found that Swedish's anesthesiology technicians "spent 34 percent of their time looking for and stocking supplies rather than giving care to patients under sedation...also, 30 percent of the anesthetic drugs were out of date," Caudle reports. Outpatient surgery was another problem child. Clinicians had to leave the operating room area an average of eight times per case to find and retrieve equipment, tools, or supplies. To remedy both the anesthesiology and outpatient surgery dilemmas, Swedish overhauled the physical environment.

"We cleaned up the area and got rid of wasted space. Moved rooms of equipment that were rarely or never used. Put inventories of items that were used right outside the operating rooms, at the point of use. Created case-carts as needed, instead of ahead of time," he explains. "It was like cleaning out your garage. Most of it was pretty basic." Through the reorganization, Caudle says they focused on a general guideline of less variability and greater standardization. No work process escaped scrutiny. Even the clinical "procedure lists"—sort of like recipes naming tools, positioning devices, and the like required to perform a gallbladder removal or hernia repair—were examined for unnecessary items. Now, "go-gets" in outpatient surgery are down from eight to one per case. "My goal is to get mundane supply-chain duties out of their way so they can spend more time with patients," he adds.

Swedish is just one example of how supply chain management can operationally transform healthcare, according to Louis Fierens, senior vice president of supply chain and capital project management for Trinity Health. Based in Novi, Michigan, Trinity is the fourth-largest Catholic health system in the United States, with just under 45,000 employees, 44 hospitals (29 owned, 15 managed), and 379 outpatient clinics. Revenues were $5.7 billion in 2005.

Fierens cites a much-quoted statistic that 31 percent of hospital expenses, on average, are attributed to supplying the facility, which he aptly describes as "an argument for a higher level of management."

But instead of going the Swedish route, many hospitals are turning to companies like Westminster, Colorado–based Global Health Exchange, provider of an electronic trading exchange. Members—buyers and sellers—are healthcare players and include manufacturers, distributors, facilities such as hospitals, nursing homes, clinics and hospices, GPOs, and supply-chain firms.

Global "lets hospitals connect to us once, and connect to providers, kind of like Amazon.com," explains spokeswoman Karen Conway. Hospital members save time and money by handling supply chain functions with multiple trading partners through the exchange's automated environment, she adds. Bottom line, healthcare utilization of companies like Global "can impact the national economy."

That's a big claim, but Conway has numbers to back it up. For instance, according to a study by the Healthcare Distribution Management Association, many hospitals overpay medical/surgical suppliers by 2 to 7 percent. Another industry study found that 40 percent of a hospital buyer's time and 68 percent of an accounts-payable worker's time is spent on "manual processing and rework," she continues. Another common problem is data synchronization, in which the hospital's data and the supplier's data don't match. Conway says there is an average 35 percent inconsistency between hospital and supplier data that, obviously, causes errors and leads to more rework. "The average cost shared by a hospital and supplier to research and correct a single order discrepancy is $15 to $50," she adds.

Then there's the human factor to consider. Many hospitals buy expensive materials management software, but don't get the expected return on investment due to inadequate user training—too little instruction or too short a learning curve—or high turnover among trained personnel. "We forget that it takes time to change," Conway comments, adding that failed IT implementations are often followed by a trip through "the trough of disillusionment."

Going Global offers stunning efficiencies through its process automation, she says: Requisitions are filled three times faster; purchase orders completed seven to 15 times faster; invoices processed twice as fast. Errors go down, too. For instance, Conway cites a 50 percent reduction in purchase-order discrepancy between order initiation, acknowledgment, and invoice. Other customers report spending half as much time researching invoice discrepancies thanks to automation. The goal, she says, is to "boost automation between financials, materials and clinical, and to increase data accuracy."

"This is not a revolution," Conway concludes. "It's definitely an evolution."

SOURCE: Knowledge@W.P. Carey. "Transforming U.S. Health Care: Supply-Chain Makeover Rejuvenates Medical Center." W. P. Carey School of Business, Arizona State University. http://knowledge.wpcarey.asu.edu/index.cfm?fa=viewArticle&id=1223&specialId=42. Reprinted with permission.

Overview

In the world of healthcare and healthcare reform, the supply chain is rarely discussed as a source of improvement and cost savings. However, health spending related to the supply chain represents a substantial opportunity to save capital. A seminal study indicated a potential savings of 2 percent to 8 percent of overall operating costs with an effective supply chain for tangible goods in hospitals and healthcare systems (McKone-Sweet, Hamilton, and Willis 2005). Johnson and Teplitz (2009) demonstrated that procurement costs can be reduced by more than 10 percent and quantity of items purchased by more than 20 percent. With many hospital budgets exceeding $500 million, this savings represents an enormous impact to an organization's bottom line.

As a result, efficient and effective **supply chain management (SCM)** is becoming increasingly important in healthcare. This chapter introduces the concept of SCM and the various tools, techniques, and theories that can enable supply chain optimization. The major topics covered include:

- SCM basics
- Tools for tracking and managing inventory
- Forecasting
- Inventory models
- Inventory systems
- Procurement and vendor relationship management
- Strategic SCM

After completing this chapter, readers should have a basic understanding of SCM, which will help them understand how SCM could be used in their organizations and enable them to begin to employ SCM-related tools, techniques, and theories to optimize supply chains.

Supply Chain Management

The supply chain includes all of the processes involved in getting supplies and equipment from the manufacturer to use in patient care areas. SCM is the management of all activities and processes related to both upstream vendors and downstream customers in the value chain. Because SCM requires managing relationships outside as well as inside an organization, SCM is a broad field of thought.

SCM is aimed at reducing costs and increasing efficiencies associated with the supply chain. Duffy (2009) indicates it is reasonable to assume that the average hospital's expenditure on supplies and on labor to manage supplies is approximately 25 percent of its total operating budget.

Effective SCM is enabled by new technologies and "old" methodologies used to reduce supply-associated costs and effort and to improve the efficiency of supply processes. Many of the techniques used to improve supply chain performance in other industries are applicable to healthcare. Technology-enabled solutions include e-procurement, radio frequency identification (RFID), bar coding, point-of-use data entry and retrieval, and data warehousing and management. These technologies have been used in other industries, and healthcare organizations are increasingly finding that they can reduce cost and increase safety.

A systems view of the supply chain can lead to a better understanding of processes and how best to improve and optimize them. SCM is really about managing relationships with vendors and customers to optimize the entire chain (rather than just pieces of it), and it results in benefits for all members of the chain.

For SCM to be effective, information is needed. Reliable and accurate data are needed to determine where the greatest improvements and gains can be made by improving the supply chain.

Tracking and Managing Inventory

Inventory is the stock of items held by the organization either for sale or to support the delivery of a service. In healthcare organizations, inventory typically includes supplies and pharmaceuticals. This stock allows organizations to cope with variations in supply and demand while making cost-effective ordering decisions.

Inventory management helps determine how much inventory to hold, when to order, and how much to order. Effective and efficient inventory management requires a classification system, an inventory tracking system, a reliable forecast of demand, knowledge of lead times, and reasonable estimates of holding, ordering, and shortage costs.

Inventory Classification System

Not all inventory is equal: Some items may be critical for the organization's operations, some may be costly or relatively inexpensive, and some may be used in large volumes while others are seldom needed. A classification system can enable organizations to manage inventory more effectively by allowing them to focus on the most important inventory items and place less emphasis on less important items.

The ABC classification system divides inventory items into three categories based on the Pareto principle. Vilfredo Pareto studied the distribution of wealth in nineteenth-century Milan and found that 80 percent of the wealth was controlled by 20 percent of the people (Reh 2007). This same idea of the vital few and the trivial many is found in quality management

(Chapter 8) and sales (80 percent of sales come from 20 percent of customers) as well as inventory management. The A items have a high dollar volume (70 percent to 80 percent) but account for only 5 percent to 20 percent of items, B items are moderate dollar (30 percent) and item (15 percent) volume, and C items are low dollar (5 percent to 15 percent) and high item (50 percent to 65 percent) volume. The classification of items is not related to their unit cost; an A item may have high dollar volume because of high usage and low cost or high cost and low usage. Items vital to the organization should be assigned to the A category even if their dollar volume is low to moderate.

The A items are the most important and, therefore, the most closely managed. The B and C items are less important and less closely managed. In a hospital setting, pacemakers are an example of A items and facial tissue might be a C item. The A items are likely ordered more often, and inventory accuracy is checked more often. These items are good candidates for bar coding and point-of-use systems. The C items do not need to be as closely managed and, often, a two-bin system is used for management and control.

Inventory Tracking Systems

An effective inventory management system requires a means of determining how much of a particular item is available. In the past, inventory records were updated manually and were typically not very accurate. Bar coding and point-of-use systems have eliminated much of the data input inaccuracy, but inventory records are still imperfect. A physical count must usually be performed to ensure that the actual and recorded amounts are the same.

Although many organizations perform inventory counts on a periodic basis (e.g., once a month), cycle counting has been found to be more helpful in ensuring accuracy and eliminating errors. More accurate inventory records not only enable efficient inventory management, but they can also help to eliminate the hoarding that occurs when providers are concerned the item will be unavailable when needed. In a typical cycle-counting system, a physical inventory is performed on a rotating schedule based on item classification. The A items might be counted every day and C items only once a month.

Electronic medication orders and matching can not only allow an organization to track demand, it can also result in greater patient safety—the patient and order are matched at the time of administration. Rules can be input into the system to alert providers to adverse drug interactions and, thus, help to eliminate errors. Systems are being developed that allow for complete, current patient records available bedside. The availability of patient and drug history can make care better and safer.

Radio Frequency Identification

RFID is a tool for identifying objects, collecting data about them, and storing that data in a computer system with little human involvement. RFID tags are similar to bar codes, but they emit a data signal that can be read without actually scanning the tag. RFID tags can also be used to determine the location of the object to which they are attached. However, RFID tags are more expensive than bar coding.

The study "RFID in Healthcare" (BearingPoint and National Alliance for Healthcare Information Technology 2006) found that RFID technology is being used in a variety of applications within the healthcare industry, including patient flow management, access control and security, supply chain systems, and smart shelving. Real-time medical equipment tracking systems and patient safety systems, such as those for identification and medication administration, were found to be the major areas where RFID is expected to be used in the future.

PinnacleHealth Hospital in Harrisburg, Pennsylvania, has successfully implemented RFID technology to track and locate expensive medical equipment (Wright 2007). The system can be queried to determine where a particular piece of equipment is located, enabling employees to quickly find the needed equipment rather than search the hospital for it. The hospital's real-time asset tracking program saved the organization $900,000 in its first 12 months (Radianse 2012).

Warehouse Management

Warehouse management systems can enable healthcare organizations to manage and decrease their storage and facility costs. Bar coding and point-of-use systems can reduce the labor needed by automating data entry in receiving. Automated data entry will also reduce errors and allow for more accurate determination of actual inventory held. Information about demand to the warehouse or storage facility can be used to organize that facility so that more heavily demanded items are more accessible and less frequently demanded items are not as accessible. This process can significantly reduce labor costs associated with the storage facility.

Demand Forecasting

Knowledge of demand and demand variation within the system can enable improved demand forecasting, which, in turn, can allow inventory reductions and greater assurance that something will be available when needed. Bar coding and point-of-use systems allow organizations to track when and how many supplies are being consumed, use that information to forecast demand organization-wide, and plan how to meet that demand in the most effective manner.

Forecasting, or time series analysis, is used to predict what will happen in the future, based on data obtained at set intervals in the past. For example, forecasting could be used to predict the number of patients who will be seen in the emergency department in the next year (month, day) based on the number of patients who have been seen there in the past. Time series analysis accounts for the fact that data taken over time may be related to one another and, therefore, violate the assumptions of linear regression. Forecasting methods range from simple to complex. Here, the simpler methods are described; only a brief discussion of the more complicated methods is provided.

Averaging Methods

All averaging methods assume that the variable of interest is stable or stationary—not growing or declining over time and not subject to seasonal or cyclical variation.

Simple Moving Average

A simple moving average (SMA) takes the last p-values and averages them to forecast the value in the next period:

$$F_t = \frac{D_{t-1} + D_{t-2} + \ldots + D_{t-p}}{p}$$

where F_t = forecast for period t (or the coming period), D_{t-1} = value in the previous time period, and p = # of time periods.

Weighted Moving Average

In contrast to the SMA, where all values from the past are given equal weight, a weighted moving average (WMA) weights each of the previous time periods. Typically, the more recent periods are assumed to be more relevant and are given higher weight:

$$F_t = w_1 D_{t-1} + w_2 D_{t-2} + \ldots + w_p D_{t-p}$$

where F_t = forecast for period t (or the coming period), D_{t-1} = value in the previous time period, w_p = weight for time period p, and $w_1 + w_2 + \ldots + w_p = 1$.

Exponential Smoothing

The problem with the previous two methods, SMA and WMA, is that a large amount of historical data are required. With **single exponential smoothing** (SES), the oldest data are eliminated once new data have been added. The forecast is calculated by using the previous forecast as well as the previous actual value with a weighting or smoothing factor, alpha. Alpha can never be greater than one, and higher values of alpha put more weight on the most recent periods:

Single exponential smoothing (SES) A simple forecasting model that smoothes data in a time series to predict the future.

$$F_t = \alpha D_{t-1} + (1-\alpha)F_{t-1}$$

where F_t = forecast for period t (or the coming period), D_{t-1} = value in the previous time period, and α = smoothing constant ≤ 1.

Trend, Seasonal, and Cyclical Models

Holt's Trend-Adjusted Exponential Smoothing Technique

SES assumes that the data fluctuate around a reasonably stable mean (no trend or consistent pattern of growth or decline). If the data contain a trend, Holt's **trend-adjusted exponential smoothing** model can be used.

Trend-adjusted exponential smoothing works much like simple smoothing except that two components—level and trend—must be updated each period. The level is a smoothed estimate of the value of the data at the end of each period, and the trend is a smoothed estimate of average growth at the end of each period. Again, the weighting or smoothing factors, alpha and delta, can never exceed one, and higher values put more weight on more recent time periods:

Trend-adjusted exponential smoothing An extension of a single exponential smoothing model that accounts for a trend when smoothing the data.

$$FIT_t = F_t + T_t$$
and
$$F_t = \alpha D_{t-1} + (1-\alpha)FIT_{t-1}$$
$$T_t = T_{t-1} + \delta(F_{t-1} - FIT_{t-1})$$

where FIT_t =forecast for period t including the trend, F_t =smoothed forecast for period t, T_t = smoothed trend for period t, D_{t-1} =value in the previous time period, $0 \leq \alpha$ = smoothing constant ≤ 1, and $0 \leq \delta$ = smoothing constant ≤ 1.

Linear Regression

Alternatively, when a trend exists in the data, regression analysis (Chapter 7) is often used for forecasting. Demand is the dependent, or Y, variable, and the time period is the predictor, or X, variable. The regression equation

$$\hat{Y} = b(X) + a$$

can be restated using forecasting notation:

$$F_t = b(t) + a$$

where F_t = forecast for period t, b = slope of the regression line, and a = Y intercept. To find b and a, $\overline{D}$ = actual demand, D = average of all actual demands, t = time period, and $\bar{t}$ = average of time periods: $b = \Sigma(t - \bar{t})(D - \overline{D})/\Sigma (t - \bar{t})^2$ and $a = \overline{D} - b\bar{t}$.

In time series forecasting, the predictor variable is time. Regression analysis is also used in forecasting when a causal relationship exists between a predictor variable (not time) and the demand variable of interest. For example, if the number of surgeries to be performed at some future date is known, that information can be used to forecast the number of surgical supplies needed.

Winter's Triple Exponential Smoothed Model

In addition to adjusting for a trend, Winter's triple exponential smoothed model adjusts for a cycle or seasonality.

Autoregressive Integrated Moving Average Models

Autoregressive integrated moving average (ARIMA) models, developed by Box and Jenkins (1976), are able to model a wide variety of time series behavior. However, ARIMA is a complex technique; although it often produces appropriate models, it requires a great deal of expertise to use.

Model Development and Evaluation

Forecasting models are developed based on historical time series data using the previously described techniques. Typically, the "best" model is the simplest model that minimizes the forecast error associated with that model. Mean absolute deviation (MAD) and/or mean squared error (MSE) can be used to determine error levels.

$$MAD = \frac{\sum_{t=1}^{n}|D_t - F_t|}{n}$$

$$MSE = \frac{\sum_{t=1}^{n}(D_t - F_t)^2}{n}$$

t = Period number

D = Actual demand for the period

F = Forecast demand for the period

n = Total number of periods

Many of these forecasting models are available as downloads on the companion website.

www.ache.org/books/OpsManagement2

VVH Diaper Demand Forecasting

Jessie Jones, purchasing agent for Vincent Valley Hospital and Health System (VVH), wants to forecast demand for diapers. She gathers information related to past demand for diapers (Exhibit 13.1) and plots it (Exhibit 13.2). The plot of weekly demand shows no cycles or trends, so Jessie believes that an averaging method would be most appropriate. She compares the forecasts obtained with a five-period SMA; WMA with weights of 0.5, 0.3, and 0.2; and exponentially smoothed forecast with alpha of 0.25.

SMA forecast:

$$F_t = \frac{A_{t-1} + A_{t-2} + \ldots + A_{t-p}}{p}$$

$$F_{14} = \frac{A_{13} + A_{12} + A_{11} + A_{10} + A_9}{5} = \frac{60 + 43 + 53 + 54 + 45}{5} = 51$$

WMA forecast:

$$F_t = w_1 A_{t-1} + w_2 A_{t-2} + \ldots + w_p A_{t-p}$$

$$F_{14} = w_1 A_{13} + w_2 A_{12} + w_3 A_{11} = 0.5 \times 60 + 0.3 \times 43 + 0.2 \times 53 - 53.5$$

Exponentially smoothed forecast:

$$F_t = \alpha A_{t-1} + (1 - \alpha)F_{t-1}$$

$$F_{14} = 0.25 \times A_{13} + 0.75 \times F_{13} = 0.25 \times 60 + 0.75 \times 52 = 54$$

Because each method gives a different forecast, Jessie compares the methods to try to determine which is best. She uses the Excel Forecasting Template (found on the companion website) to perform the calculations

www.ache.org/books/OpsManagement2

EXHIBIT 13.1
VVH Weekly
Diaper Demand

Period	Week of	Cases of Diapers
1	1-Jan	70
2	8-Jan	42
3	15-Jan	63
4	22-Jan	52
5	29-Jan	56
6	5-Feb	53
7	12-Feb	66
8	19-Feb	61
9	26-Feb	45
10	5-Mar	54
11	12-Mar	53
12	19-Mar	43
13	26-Mar	60

EXHIBIT 13.2
Plot of VVH
Weekly Diaper
Demand

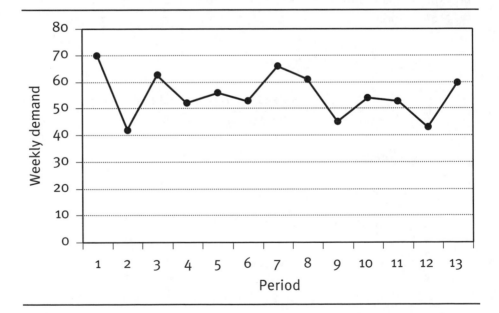

(Exhibit 13.3). She finds that both MAD and MSE are lowest with the WMA method and decides to use that method for forecasting. Therefore, she forecasts that 53.5 cases of diapers will be demanded the week of April 2, period 14.

Simple Moving Average

Periods	5

MAD	7
MSE	86

Period	Actual	Forecast	Error
1	70		
2	42		
3	63		
4	52		
5	56		
6	53	57	4
7	66	53	13
8	61	58	3
9	45	58	13
10	54	56	2
11	53	56	3
12	43	56	13
13	60	51	9
14		51	

Weighted Moving Average (3 periods)

	Weight 3	Weight 2	Weight 1	
Least Recent	0.2	0.3	0.5	Most Recent

MAD	6
MSE	75

Period	Actual	Forecast	Error
1	70		
2	42		
3	63		
4	52	58	6
5	56	53	3
6	53	56	3
7	66	54	12
8	61	60	1
9	45	61	16
10	54	54	0
11	53	53	0
12	43	52	9
13	60	48	12
14		53.5	

Single Exponential Smoothing

á	0.25

MAD	8
MSE	135

Period	Actual	Forecast	Error
1	70		
2	42	70	28
3	63	63	0
4	52	63	11
5	56	60	4
6	53	59	6
7	66	58	8
8	61	60	1
9	45	60	15
10	54	56	2
11	53	56	3
12	43	55	12
13	60	52	8
14		54	

EXHIBIT 13.3

Excel Forecasting Template Output: VVH Diaper Demand

Order Amount and Timing

Inventory management is concerned with the following questions:

- How much inventory should the organization hold?
- When should an order be placed?
- How much should be ordered?

To answer these questions, organizations need to have reasonable estimates of holding, ordering, and shortage costs. Knowledge of lead times and demand forecasts is also essential to determining the best answers to inventory questions.

Economic Order Quantity Model

In 1915, F. W. Harris developed the **economic order quantity (EOQ)** model to answer inventory questions. Although the assumptions of this model limit its usefulness in real situations, it provides important insights into effective and efficient inventory management.

To aid in understanding the model, definitions for some key inventory terms are provided.

- *Lead time* is the interval between placing an order and receiving it.
- *Holding (or carrying) costs* are associated with keeping goods in storage for a period of time, usually one year. The most obvious of these costs are the cost of the space and the cost of the labor and equipment

Economic order quantity (EOQ) An inventory model that indicates an optimal purchase quantity that will minimize total annual inventory costs.

needed to operate the space. Less obvious costs include the opportunity cost of capital and those costs associated with obsolescence, damage, and theft of the goods. These costs are often difficult to measure and are commonly estimated as one-third to one-half the value of the stored goods per year.

- *Ordering (or setup) costs* are the costs of ordering and receiving goods. They may also be the costs associated with changing or setting up to produce another product.
- *Shortage costs* are the costs of not having something in inventory when it is needed.
- *Independent demand* is generated by the customer and is not a result of demand for another good or service.
- *Dependent demand* results from another demand. For example, the demand for hernia surgical kits (dependent) is related to the demand for hernia surgeries (independent).
- *Back orders* cannot be filled when received, but the customer is willing to continue waiting for the order to be filled.
- *Stockouts* occur when the desired good is not available.

The basic EOQ model is based on the following assumptions:

- Demand for the item in question is independent.
- Demand is known and constant.
- Lead time is known and constant.
- Ordering costs are known and constant.
- Back orders, stockouts, and quantity discounts are not allowed.

The EOQ inventory order cycle (Exhibit 13.4) consists of stock or inventory being received at a point in time. An order is placed when the amount of stock on hand is just enough to cover the demand that will be experienced during lead time. The new order arrives at the exact point when the stock is completely depleted. The point at which new stock should be ordered, the reorder point (R), is the quantity of stock demanded during lead time:

$$\text{Reorder point} = R = \bar{d}L$$

where R = reorder point, $\bar{d}$ = average demand per time period, and L = lead time (in the same units as above).

The EOQ inventory order cycle shows that the average amount of inventory held will be:

$$\frac{\text{Order quantity}}{2} = \frac{Q}{2}$$

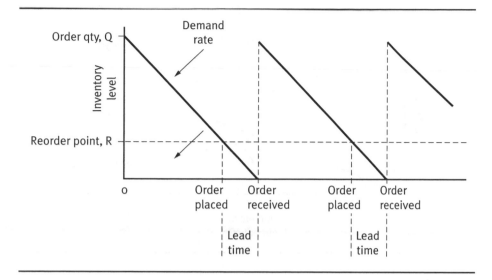

EXHIBIT 13.4
EOQ Inventory
Order Cycle

The number of orders placed in one year will be:

$$\frac{\text{Yearly demand}}{\text{Order quantity}} = \frac{D}{Q}$$

Total costs are the sum of holding and ordering costs. Yearly holding costs are:

Cost to hold one item one year × Average inventory = $h \times Q/2$

Yearly ordering costs are:

Cost to place one order × Yearly number of orders = $o \times D/Q$

Total yearly costs are then:

$$h \times Q/2 + o \times D/Q$$

Exhibit 13.5 illustrates these relationships. An inspection of this graph shows that total cost will be minimized when holding costs equal ordering costs. (This can also be proven using calculus.) The order quantity that will minimize total costs is found when:

$$h \times Q^*/2 = o \times D/Q^*$$

EXHIBIT 13.5
EOQ Model Cost
Curves

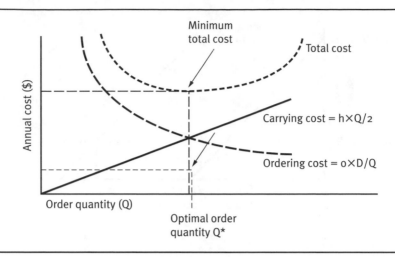

Rearranging this equation, the optimal order quantity is:

$$Q_2 = (2 \times o \times D)/h$$

$$Q^* = \sqrt{\frac{2 \times o \times D}{h}}$$

Several important insights into inventory management can be gained from an examination of this simple model. There are trade-offs between holding costs and ordering costs: As holding costs increase, optimal order quantity decreases, and as ordering costs increase, optimal order quantity increases. Many organizations, including those in the healthcare industry, believe that the costs of holding inventory are much higher than was previously thought. As a consequence, these organizations are decreasing order quantities and working to decrease order costs by streamlining procurement processes.

VVH Diaper Order Quantity

Jessie Jones, VVH's purchasing agent, wants to determine the optimal order quantity for diapers. From her forecasting work, she knows that annual demand for diapers, D, is:

$$\bar{d} \times \text{Time period} = \frac{53.5 \text{ Cases}}{\text{Week}} \times \frac{52 \text{ Weeks}}{\text{Year}} = \frac{2{,}782 \text{ Cases}}{\text{Year}}$$

Each case of diapers costs $5, and Jessie estimates holding costs at 33 percent. It costs $100 to place an order. Lead time for diapers is one week. She calculates the EOQ, Q^*, as:

$$\sqrt{\frac{2 \times o \times D}{h}} = \sqrt{\frac{2 \times \$100 \times 2{,}782 \text{ Cases}}{\$1.67/\text{ Case}}}$$

$$= \sqrt{333{,}174 \text{ Cases}^2} = 577 \text{ Cases}$$

She calculates the reorder point, R, as:

$$\bar{d}L = \frac{53.5 \text{ Cases}}{\text{Week}} \times 1 \text{ Week} = 53.5 \text{ Cases}$$

Jessie will need to place an order for 577 cases of diapers when 53.5 cases remain in stock.

Fixed Order Quantity with Safety Stock Model

The basic EOQ model assumes that demand is constant and known. This means that the amount of stock carried in inventory only needs to match demand. In reality, demand is seldom constant, and excess inventory must be held to meet variations in demand and avoid stockouts. This excess inventory, called safety stock (SS), is the amount of inventory carried over and above expected demand. Exhibit 13.6 illustrates this model.

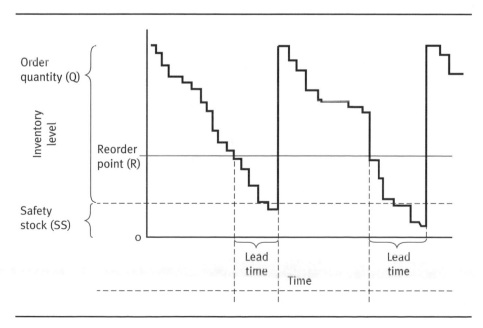

EXHIBIT 13.6
Variable Demand Inventory Order Cycle with Safety Stock

This SS model assumes that demand varies and is normally distributed (Chapter 7). The model also assumes that a fixed quantity equal to EOQ will always be ordered. The EOQ will remain the same as in the basic model, but the reorder point will be different because of the need for SS.

$$R = \bar{d}L + SS$$

Service level
The probability of having an item on hand when needed.

The amount of SS to carry is determined by variation in demand and desired service level. **Service level** is defined as the probability of having an item on hand when needed. For example, suppose that orders are placed at the beginning of a time period and received at the end of that period. If demand is expected to be 100 units in the next time period with a standard deviation of 20 units and 100 units on hand at the start of the period, the probability of stocking out is 50 percent and the service level is 50 percent. If demand is normally distributed, there is a 50 percent probability of its being higher than the mean and a 50 percent probability of its being lower than the mean. Demand would be greater than the stock on hand in half of the time periods.

To increase the service level, SS is needed. For example, if the stock on hand at the start of the time period is 120 units (20 units of SS), the service level would increase to 84 percent and the probability of a stockout would be reduced to 16 percent. Because demand is assumed to follow a normal distribution and 120 units is exactly one standard deviation higher than the mean of 100 units, the probability of being less than one standard deviation above the mean is 84 percent. There is a 16 percent probability of being more than one standard deviation above the mean (Exhibit 13.7). A service level of 95

EXHIBIT 13.7
Service Level and Safety Stock

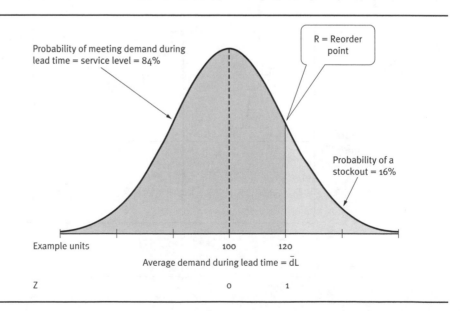

percent is typically used in industry. However, if one stockout every 20 time periods is unacceptable, a higher service level target is needed.

SS is the z-value associated with the desired service level (number of standard deviations above the mean) times the standard deviation of demand during lead time:

$$SS = z \times \sigma_L$$

Note that with this model, the only time demand variability can be a problem is during lead time. Because an order is triggered when a certain level of stock is reached, any variation in demand prior to that time does not affect the reorder point.

This model also provides some important insights into inventory management. Trade-offs exist between the amount of SS held and service level. As the desired service level increases, the amount of SS needed—and therefore the amount of inventory held—increases. As the variation in demand during lead time increases, the amount of SS increases. If demand variation or lead time can be decreased, the amount of SS needed to reach a desired service level will also decrease. Many healthcare organizations are working with their suppliers to reduce lead time and, therefore, SS levels.

VVH Diaper Order Quantity

After learning more about inventory models, Jessie Jones realized that the reorder point that she had decided on using the basic EOQ model would cause the hospital to be out of diapers during 50 percent of the order cycles. Because diapers would be ordered five times per year, this meant that the hospital would be out of diapers at least twice a year. Jessie believed that this was an unacceptable amount of stockouts and decided that SS was needed to avoid them. She decided that a service level of 95 percent, or one stockout every four years, would be acceptable.

Jessie gathered more information related to demand for diapers over the past year and determined that the standard deviation of demand during lead time was 11.5 cases of diapers. She calculated the amount of SS needed as:

$$z \times \sigma_L = 1.64 \times 11.5 = 18.9 \text{ Cases}$$

Her new reorder point is:

$$\overline{dL} + SS = \left(\frac{53.5 \text{ Cases}}{\text{Week}} \times 1 \text{ Week} \right) + 18.9 \text{ Cases} = 72.4 \text{ Cases}$$

EXHIBIT 13.8
VVH 95 Percent
Service Level
Reorder Point

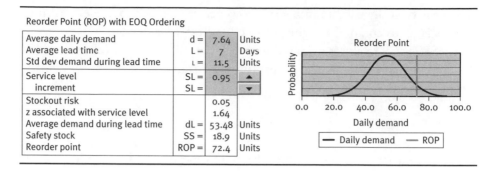

Reorder Point (ROP) with EOQ Ordering			
Average daily demand	d =	7.64	Units
Average lead time	L =	7	Days
Std dev demand during lead time	L =	11.5	Units
Service level	SL =	0.95	▲
increment	SL =		▼
Stockout risk		0.05	
z associated with service level		1.64	
Average demand during lead time	dL =	53.48	Units
Safety stock	SS =	18.9	Units
Reorder point	ROP =	72.4	Units

www.ache.org/books/OpsManagement2

She will need to place an order for 577 cases of diapers when 72.4 cases remain in stock. The forecasting template found on the companion website can be used to perform these calculations, and the output related to Jessie's problem is shown in Exhibit 13.8.

Additional Inventory Models

Many inventory models that address some of the limiting assumptions of the EOQ model have been developed. One that may be of interest is the fixed time period with SS model. In the fixed order quantity with SS model, the order quantity is fixed and the time when the order is placed varies. In the fixed time period with SS model, the order quantity varies and the time when the order is placed is fixed. This type of model is applicable when vendors deliver on a set schedule or if one supplier is used for many different products and orders are bundled and delivered together on a set schedule. Generally, this situation requires more SS because stockouts are possible during the entire time between orders, not just the lead time for the order.

Models that account for quantity discounts and price breaks have also been developed. More information on these higher-level models can be found in most inventory management textbooks.

Inventory Systems

In practice, various types of systems are employed for management and control of inventory. They range from simple to complex, and organizations typically employ a mixture of these systems.

Two-Bin System

The two-bin system is a simple, easily managed system often used for B- and/ or C-type items. In this system, inventory is separated into two bins. These do not necessarily have to be actual bins or containers; a means of identifying the items as being in the first or second bin is simply needed. Inventory is taken from the first bin. When that bin is emptied, an order is placed. Inventory from the second bin is used during the lead time for the order to be received. The amount of inventory held in each bin can be determined from the fixed order quantity with SS model. The amount of inventory held in the first bin would ideally be the EOQ minus the reorder point. The amount of inventory in the second bin would equal the reorder point.

Just-in-Time

Just-in-time (JIT) inventory systems are based on Lean concepts and employ a type of two-bin system called the kanban system. (See Chapter 9 for a description of this type of system.) Because inventory levels are controlled by the number of kanbans in the system and inventory is "waste" in a Lean system, organizations try to decrease the number of kanbans as much as possible.

Material Requirements Planning and Enterprise Resources Planning

Material requirements planning (MRP) systems were first employed by manufacturing organizations in the 1960s when computers became commercially available. These systems were used to manage and control the purchase and production of dependent-demand items.

A simple example illustrates the logic of MRP (Exhibit 13.9). A table manufacturer knows (or forecasts) that 50 tables, consisting of a top and four legs, will be demanded five weeks in the future. The manufacturer knows that it takes one week to produce a table if both the legs and tops are available. The company also knows that there is a two-week lead time for table legs and a three-week lead time for table tops. From this information, MRP determines that for the organization to have 50 tables in week 5, it needs to have 50 table tops and 200 table legs in week 4. The company also needs to order 200 table legs in week 2 and 50 table tops in week 1.

Material requirements planning (MRP) A computer system designed to manage the purchase and control of dependent-demand items.

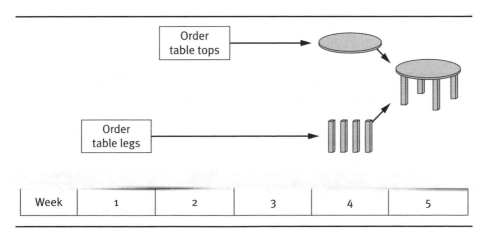

EXHIBIT 13.9
MRP Logic

| Week | 1 | 2 | 3 | 4 | 5 |

The same type of logic can be employed in healthcare for dependent-demand items. For example, if the demand for a particular type of surgery is known or can be forecast, supplies related to this type of surgery can be ordered based on MRP-type logic.

Enterprise resources planning (ERP) systems evolved from these relatively simple systems as computing power grew and software applications became more sophisticated. ERP-type systems found in healthcare today encompass the entire organization and include finance, accounting, human resources, patient records, and so on, in addition to inventory management and control functions. Technology can enable improvement in many aspects of healthcare organizations.

Enterprise resources planning (ERP)
Global information systems that help manage the entire organization, including accounting, operations, and human resources.

Procurement and Vendor Relationship Management

Analyzing the processes used for procurement and improving them can result in significant savings to an organization. Technology can be used to not only streamline processes but also to improve data reliability, accuracy, and visibility. Streamlining procurement processes can reduce associated labor costs. E-procurement is one example of how technology can be employed to make procurement more efficient. The ease of obtaining product information, reduced time associated with the actual procurement process, and increased use of a limited number of suppliers can significantly reduce costs.

Information about supplier reliability can be maintained in these systems to allow organizations to make informed choices about vendors. For example, one vendor may be much less expensive but extremely unreliable, whereas another may be slightly more expensive but more reliable and faster. An analysis may show that it is less costly to use the slightly more expensive vendor because the amount of SS held or the need to expedite shipments may be reduced. Tracking and reviewing supplier performance can aid in ensuring that quality suppliers are being used.

Value-based standardization can be employed to reduce both the number and quantity of items held. Focusing on high-use or high-cost items can leverage the benefits of standardization and reduce the number of suppliers to the organization. Fewer supplies and suppliers can result in both labor and material cost savings.

Outsourcing can be an effective means of ensuring supply availability and reducing internal labor. Distributors can break orders down by point of use and deliver directly to that point as needed rather than having the organization's personnel perform that function. Prepackaged supply packs or surgical carts can reduce the amount of in-house labor needed to organize these supplies and ensure that the correct supplies are available when needed. Vendor-managed inventory is another way to outsource some of the work involved with procurement. Automated supply carts or cabinets and point-of-use systems can enable vendor-managed inventory. GPOs can be employed to increase order quantities and reduce costs.

Disintermediation is another possible means of supply chain improvement. Reducing the number of organizations in the chain can result in lower costs and faster, more reliable delivery.

Strategic View

Most important, effective SCM requires a strategic systems analysis and design. This strategic view enables systems solutions rather than individual solutions. A strategic design will enable systems integration, allowing for improved decision making across the organization.

Successful SCM initiatives require the same things as Six Sigma, Lean, and the Baldrige criteria:

- Top management support and collaboration, including time and money
- Employee buy-in, including clinician support and frontline empowerment
- Evaluation of the structure and staffing of the supply chain to ensure that it will support the desired improvements and that all relevant functions are represented in a meaningful way. Cross-functional teams may be the best way to ensure this.
- Process analysis and improvement, including a thorough and complete understanding of existing systems, processes, and protocols (through process mapping) and their improvement
- Collection and analysis of relevant, accurate data and metrics to determine areas of improvement, means of improvement, and whether improvement was achieved
- Evaluation of technology-enabled solutions in terms of both costs and benefits
- Training in the use of new technologies and techniques. This is essential for broad application and use in the organization and for success
- Internal awareness programs to highlight the need for and benefits of strategic SCM
- Improved inventory management through better understanding of the systems consequences of unofficial inventory, JIT systems, and improved inventory tracking systems

- Enhancement of vendor partnerships through information sharing and the investigation and determination of mutually beneficial solutions. Performance tracking should be employed to determine the best vendors to involve in this process.
- Finally, continuous education by the organization and support for a systemwide view of the supply chain and seek improvement for the system rather than individual departments or organizations in that system

Conclusion

In the past, healthcare organizations did not focus on SCM issues; today, increasing cost pressures are driving them to examine and optimize their supply chains. The ideas and tools presented in this chapter will help the healthcare supply chain professional to achieve these goals.

Discussion Questions

1. Why is SCM important to healthcare organizations?
2. List some inventory items found in your organization. Which of these might be classified as A, B, or C items? Why? How would you manage these items differently depending on their classification?
3. Think of an item for which your organization carries SS. Why is SS needed for this item? Can the amount of SS needed be reduced? How?
4. Describe the ERP system(s) found in your organization. How could they be improved?

Chapter Exercises

www.ache.org/books/OpsManagement2

1. Use the web to investigate and summarize commercially available software solutions for healthcare organizations.
2. This problem uses information from a data set available on the companion website. The data set contains the raw data as well as reduced and reorganized data for ease of analysis.

   Use the forecasting template found on the companion website to forecast total US healthcare expenditures for 2010 using SMA, WMA, SES, trend-adjusted (or double) exponential smoothing, and linear trend.
   a. Which model do you believe gives the best forecast?

b. Do you see any problems with your model?

c. Repeat the above for hospital care, physician services, other professional services, dental services, home health care, prescription drugs, and other. Is any one of these driving the increase in healthcare expense?

3. The Excel inventory template found on the companion website may be helpful for this problem. An Excel spreadsheet with data for the problem can also be downloaded from the companion website.

www.ache.org/books/OpsManagement2

Hospital purchasing agent Abby Smith needs to order examination gloves. Currently, she orders 1,000 boxes of gloves whenever she thinks there is a need. Abby has heard that there is a better way to do this and wants to use EOQ to determine how much to order and when. She collects the following information.

Cost of gloves:	$4.00/box
Carrying costs:	33%, or $_____/box
Cost of ordering:	$150/order
Lead time:	10 days
Annual demand:	10,000 boxes/year

a. What quantity should Abby be ordering? Prove that your order quantity is "better" than Abby's by graphing ordering costs, holding costs, and total costs for 1,000, 1,500, and 2,000 boxes.

b. How often will Abby need to order? About how many days will there be between orders?

c. Assuming that Abby is not worried about SS, when should she place her order? Draw another graph to illustrate why she needs to place her order at that particular point.

d. Abby is concerned that the reorder point she determined is wrong because demand for gloves varies. She gathers the following usage information:

Period (10 Days Each)	Demand
1	274
2	274
3	284
4	274

(continued)

5	254
6	264
7	264
8	284
9	274
10	294
11	274
12	284
13	264
14	274
Average	274

e. Abby decides she will be happy if the probability of a stockout is 5 percent. How much SS should Abby carry?

f. If Abby were to set up a two-bin system for gloves, how many boxes of gloves would be in each bin?

IMPROVING FINANCIAL PERFORMANCE WITH OPERATIONS MANAGEMENT

Operations Management in Action

The ability to create lasting improvement in patient care while reducing waste and managing costs has required nothing short of a cultural upheaval, according to John S. Toussaint, MD, president/CEO emeritus of Theda-Care, Appleton, Wisconsin, a community-owned health system consisting of four hospitals, a large group practice, and other health services, and, with 5,400 employees, the largest employer in Northeast Wisconsin. "If you don't have the fundamental cultural under-pinnings at the heart of what you are doing, then you won't transform the organization and achieve enduring change," he says. "Anybody who is not focused on building the cultural aspects of a continuous improvement transformation will not succeed in bringing about quality improvement."

The transition to a Lean culture has required, among other things, a fundamental shift from the traditional command and control healthcare leadership process to one of continuous improvement management in which senior management's primary role is defining the purpose for which the organization exists and clearly communicating that purpose to every staff member, says Toussaint.

Real change in patient care quality and cost efficiency could not have taken place without this rudimentary alteration in mind-set, he says. "We've had to fundamentally change the way we think and behave. The change has come more naturally to nurses because they are trained in problem solving, but everyone has been expected to make the leap."

As a result of quality initiatives based on Lean, ThedaCare has achieved a 30 percent reduction in the cost of care, 50 percent reductions in Occupational Safety and Health Administration recordable staff injuries, and fall and medication reconciliation rates of zero on its redesigned inpatient units.

SOURCE: Birk (2010, 15).

The Need for Better Tools for Improving Financial Performance

Because Medicare is one of the largest sources of funding in the US healthcare system, its payment policies are used by many other payers. Each year the Medicare Payment Advisory Commission (MedPAC) recommends payment policy changes to the Centers for Medicare & Medicaid Services (CMS) and Congress. In these reports, MedPAC goes to great lengths to examine Medicare beneficiaries' access to care, the number of hospitals going into and out of business, and whether hospitals can make a profit on Medicare revenues.

Because many hospital executives have complained that Medicare payment is insufficient, which results in cost shifting to private payers, the 2011 MedPAC report analyzed Medicare costs and margins for all hospitals from 2006 to 2008 (excluding rural Community Access hospitals) (MedPAC 2011).

In its analysis, MedPAC also excluded hospitals in high-use areas because their volumes are not sustainable over the long term. MedPAC classified 219 hospitals out of 2,171 studied as "relatively efficient." This diverse array of hospitals, including large teaching hospitals and smaller rural hospitals, also reported excellent quality results. The median hospital in the "efficient group" had an overall Medicare margin of +3 percent, while the median hospital in the other group had an overall Medicare margin of –6 percent. MedPAC's implicit conclusion is that because some hospitals do well with Medicare payment levels (see the Floyd Hospital case at the end of this chapter), all others should be able to thrive at these payments levels as well.

This policy direction is woven throughout the Patient Protection and Affordable Care Act (ACA), and the goal of policymakers in the United States is to stabilize or reduce the growth of healthcare costs until it equals the general rate of inflation.

A number of forces have historically worked together to increase the total costs of care beyond inflation:

- Increasing incidence of chronic disease and an aging population
- New diagnostic and treatment technologies

- Increasing complexity of billing and payment systems
- A provider payment system (fee-for-service) that encourages the use of healthcare services

Today's healthcare executive is therefore caught between these two intense environmental pressures—the need to reduce costs in the face of continuing inflationary pressures and little new revenue. This chapter provides a road map to stable or improved financial performance through the use of operations management tools presented in the preceding chapters of this book.

Specifically this chapter

- defines improved financial performance,
- describes a systems view of reducing costs and increasing revenues based on the methodology being used for payment for services,
- details how the operations tools described in this book can be used to optimize costs and revenue for each of these payment methodologies, and
- provides a case example of one hospital that has managed to improve its operations enough to generate a positive margin on Medicare revenues.

Definition of Financial Improvement

Although this textbook is not primarily about financial management, a number of measures are generally accepted as indicators of the successful financial performance of a healthcare enterprise. (For a more comprehensive view, see Gapenski 2011.)

From a balance sheet perspective, three indicators are frequently used to assess an organization's performance (Cleverley and Cleverley 2010):

- Cash on hand
- Percent of debt financed
- Age of plant

Three other key indicators of financial health on the income statement are

- revenue (growth or decline),
- margin, and
- costs (per unit of service).

Because revenue growth per service is likely to grow only slowly (in Medicare's case it may actually decline), the healthcare executive must focus on collecting all available revenue while reducing costs. The approaches described below can achieve these goals. Fortunately, in addition to achiev-

EXHIBIT 14.1 A Systems Approach to Financial Management

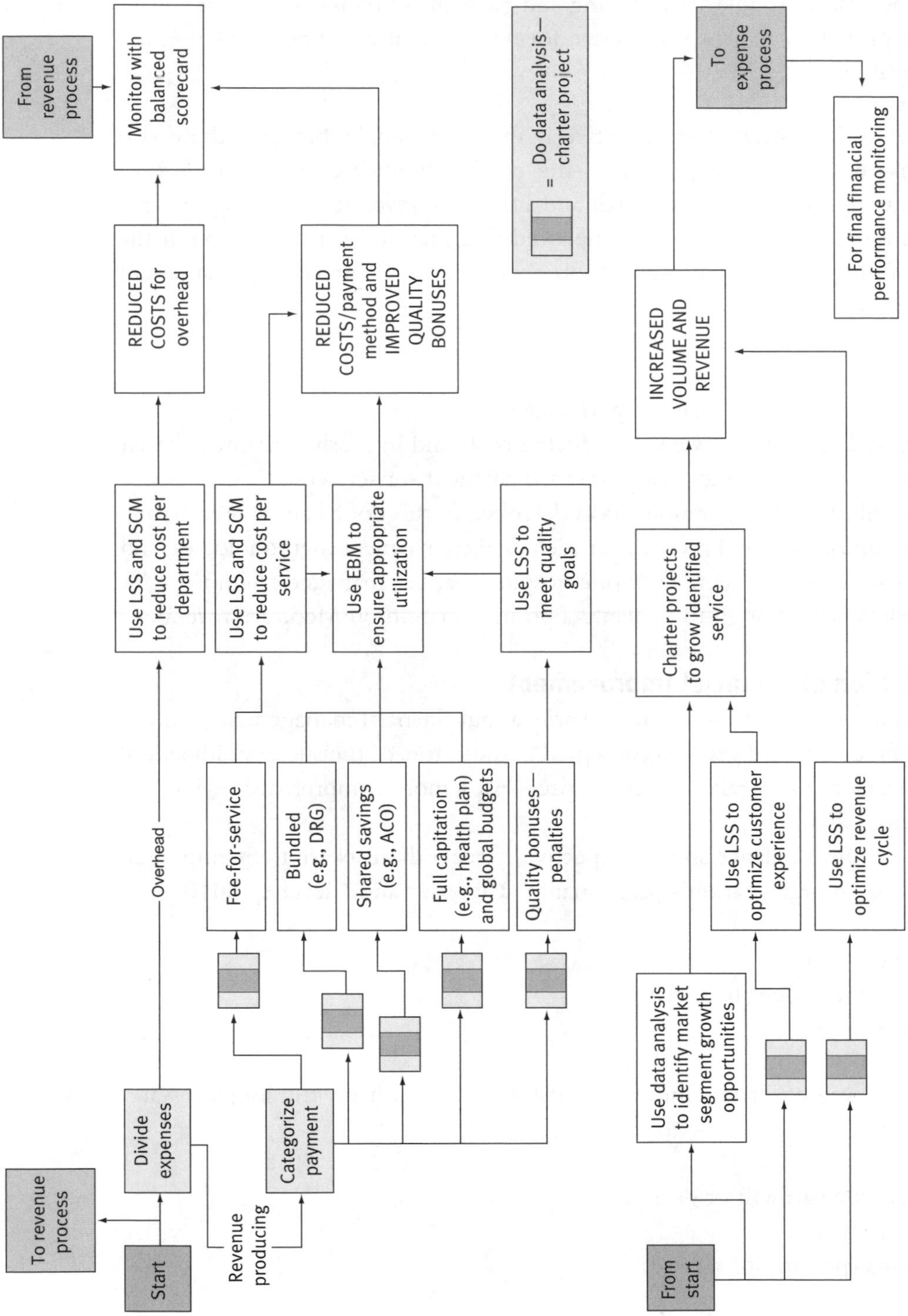

ing these financial goals, the use of operations management tools also almost always results in stable or improved clinical quality and patient satisfaction.

A Systems Approach to Financial Management

Financial goals are part of most healthcare managers' job descriptions, yet most organizations lack a comprehensive approach to support the manager in achieving these goals. Without this type of framework, managers are often required to take measures that may provide immediate results but will foster long-term problems. Some examples include

- across-the-board expense reductions,
- elimination of overtime without changing any processes,
- using less expensive supplies without changes in the supply chain,
- tolerating queuing and long waits for service, and
- outsourcing key activities without quality monitoring systems in place.

A more effective and longer-lasting methodology is a systems approach to financial management (see Exhibit 14.1). First, expenses are divided into those directly related to revenue generation and those considered overhead. Because multiple payment methodologies are in place today and for the foreseeable future, revenue is further divided into these various payment methodologies. Each of these categories can be addressed with the techniques described in this chapter.

Reduction in overhead expenses is more straightforward, and more general techniques can be used. Revenue can be improved and optimized by growing service lines and optimizing the revenue cycle.

Expenses Directly Related to Revenue

All expenses directly related to revenue should be classified into six payment methodologies:

1. Fee-for-service
2. Bundled
3. Shared savings
4. Full capitation
5. Quality bonuses or penalties
6. Global budgets

Next, projects are chartered with a focus on each specific payment methodology and operating unit(s). The first step in the project is to collect data on the current state of service delivery and understand where there is variance in resources used and outcomes achieved. The tools of process improvement, supply chain management, and schedule optimization are then applied to reduce variance and improve outcomes. This approach will reduce costs and, in many instances, will increase throughput.

Fee-for-Service

The most atomic-level area of cost control is individual fee-for-service. In this case the provider renders a bill for a unique service such as an office visit or lab test. Although this billing service unit is the smallest in the current healthcare finance system, each of these services is made up of many smaller components.

Activity-based costing (ABC)
A cost allocation model that assigns a cost to each activity in an organizational unit and then totals the cost for the unit on the basis of the actual consumption of each activity.

Activity-based costing (ABC) is a relatively new tool that can be used to deconstruct the billing service unit and identify opportunities for cost reductions. Gapenski (2011, 208–12) provides a useful example of using ABC to analyze the clinic visit. ABC has five steps:

1. Identify the relevant activities.
2. Determine the cost of each activity, including both direct and indirect.
3. Determine the cost drivers for the activity.
4. Collect activity data for each service.
5. Calculate the total cost of the service by aggregating activity costs.

In Gapenski's example, he assumes that the total annual cost of patient check-in, consisting of clerical labor (direct costs) plus space and other overhead costs (indirect costs) are $50,000 to support 10,000 visits per year. This yields an allocation rate of $5 per visit. Similar calculations are made for each of the components of the office visit, and the allocation rate is then determined for each activity (Exhibit 14.2). Once the allocation rates are determined, the total activity costs for each service can be calculated (Exhibit 14.3).

Each of the cost elements can be optimized with the tools described in this book. Exhibit 14.4 provides examples.

After each activity in a service is analyzed and improved, the total service cost can also be optimized by using Lean and Six Sigma techniques (Chapters 8 and 9). Chapter 11 outlines a number of specific techniques to optimize throughput in a clinic (hence reducing people cost per visit), and Chapter 13 provides a number of supply chain management techniques to reduce supply costs. As costs are reduced at the fee-for-service level, costs at all other levels will decrease as well.

EXHIBIT 14.2   ABC Illustration: Initial Data and Allocation Rate Calculation

			Activity Data			
Activity	Annual Costs	Cost Driver	Service A	Service B	Total	Allocation Rate
Check-in	$ 50,000	Number of visits	5,000	5,000	10,000	$ 5.00
Assessment	75,000	Number of minutes per visit	5	10	75,000	1.00
Diagnosis	250,000	Number of minutes per visit	10	15	125,000	2.00
Treatment	450,000	Number of minutes per visit	10	20	150,000	3.00
Prescription	2,500	Drugs prescribed per visit	0.5	2	12,500	0.20
Check-out	50,000	Number of visits	5,000	5,000	10,000	5.00
Billing	150,000	Number of bills per visit	1	2	15,000	10.00
Total costs	$1,027,500					

SOURCE: Gapenski (2011).

EXHIBIT 14.3 ABC Illustration: Final Aggregation of Activity Costs per Visit

Activity	Cost Driver	Rate	Service A		Service B	
			Consumption	Cost	Consumption	Cost
Check-in	Number of visits	$ 5.00	1	$ 5.00	1	$ 5.00
Assessment	Number of minutes	1.00	5	5.00	10	10.00
Diagnosis	Number of minutes	2.00	10	20.00	15	30.00
Treatment	Number of minutes	3.00	10	30.00	20	60.00
Prescription	Number of drugs	0.20	0.5	0.10	2	0.40
Check-out	Number of visits	5.00	1	5.00	1	5.00
Billing	Number of bills	10.00	1	10.00	2	20.00
Total cost per service				$75.10		$130.40

SOURCE: Gapenski (2011).

Activity	Improvement Tools	Opportunity
Check-in	Process improvement (Lean and Six Sigma, Simulation, etc.) automation	Strong
Assessment	Process improvement	Low
Diagnosis	Evidence-based medicine	Medium
Treatment	Evidence-based medicine	Medium
Prescription	Supply chain management	Strong
Check-out	Process improvement, automation	
Billing	Data mining and analysis, process improvement	Strong

EXHIBIT 14.4
Use of Operations Improvement Tools to Reduce Costs

Bundled Payments

Various fees are frequently bundled together and paid as one amount. The intent of bundling is to give the provider an incentive to minimize costs inside the bundle. Examples of bundled payments in hospitals include the following:

- *Per diem.* All payments for a day in a hospital are paid at one rate.
- *Medicare prospective payment.* All payments for a stay in the hospital are paid at one rate that is adjusted for the complexity of the admission by the diagnosis-related group system.
- *Medicare bundled payments.* All payments for an "episode of care" are paid at one rate adjusted for complexity. This new payment system was first tested in the Medicare acute care episode demonstration (CMS 2012) and is now part of the ACA. The payments for the bundle include hospital services, physicians, outpatient care and testing, and other related services.

To optimize the cost structure of bundled payments, the underlying fee-for-service costs need to be targeted and improved. Because hospitals may have thousands of individual fees, an analysis project should be undertaken to identify which fees need to be targeted. Criteria for targeting can include the following:

- High volume
- High cost compared with benchmarks from other organizations
- High use in bundled payments where costs are highly variable

After reducing the costs for individual services, the tools of evidence-based medicine (EBM) can now be applied. They are particularly useful for optimizing costs in bundled payment models as these protocols reflect the shared wisdom of many clinical studies on the most efficient and effective approach to a particular condition. Chapter 3 outlined contemporary approaches to the use of EBM and the power of clinical decision support systems to support the implementation of EBM.

Shared Savings

The next higher level of payment is the **shared savings model,** which is most prominently featured as the accountable care organization (ACO) in the ACA. Payment in the shared savings model is still made via fee-for-service or bundled payments. However, patients are attributed to the ACO based on their use of primary care providers (e.g., 50 percent of their primary care is provided by an ACO's primary care team). Costs for all patients are then summed for a period, and if these total costs are less than a target set by the payer, the savings are shared with both providers and payer. In the "one-sided" version of ACOs, with low risk to the provider, the lack of savings is not assessed to the ACO. However the bonuses are also lower than the "two-sided model," in which full risk is taken by the ACO (see full capitation in the next section). The one-sided model was developed to provide incentives for improved chronic disease management without the downside of full capitation risk.

Success in the shared savings model requires new data systems to track patients from a longitudinal perspective beyond each episode of service; when higher than expected costs occur, case managers can intervene. The goal of management in this model is to achieve expected expenses per patient per month while achieving quality benchmarks. This type of challenge is well suited for the tools of Six Sigma, such as the following:

- Run and control charts
- Pareto diagrams
- Cause-and-effect diagrams
- Scatter plots
- Regression analysis
- Benchmarking

Six Sigma is detailed in depth in Chapter 8.

The tools of EBM—including chronic disease management, medical home, comparative effectiveness research, and electronic health records with clinical decision support—are also important for the shared savings model.

Full Capitation

The highest level of payment is **full capitation,** which should only be accepted if an organization has already had experience and success with the shared savings model. However, if an organization has successfully implemented a one-sided ACO-type organization and has a stable provider base and market, it could either become a two-sided ACO, a fully state-certified health plan, or a partner with an existing health plan to receive full capitation. In this model the savings or loss per member per month is fully borne by the provider organization.

Full capitation
A methodology in which providers are paid a monthly fee for each patient who receives care in their system.

The key to success in this model is to reduce the use of expensive resources that can be avoided by disciplined attention to improved systems. One of the most successful examples is Group Health Cooperative in Seattle, Washington. Its CEO outlined these initiatives and their outcomes (Vaida 2011):

- *Implement healthcare home*: 10 percent drop in inpatient admissions, 20 percent decline in ER use
- *Implement shared decision making for surgery based on EBM findings*: 12 percent drop in elective surgery
- *Develop new systems to prevent readmissions of Medicare patients through EBM and process improvement*: Reduced readmission rate by 7 percent

Quality Bonuses or Penalties

Chapter 3 reviewed a number of current and anticipated pay-for-performance measures. The policy emphasis has shifted from paying for volume to paying for value. Because these new payment systems are complex and frequently changing, establishing process improvement teams (Chapter 5) and using balanced scorecard techniques (Chapter 4) are important for healthcare leaders in monitoring results. These project teams can use all the tools of process improvement (Lean, Six Sigma, process simulation) to change procedures to improve results. Examples of teams include the following (Healthcare.gov 2012):

- Readmissions reductions
- Length-of-stay management
- Hospital-acquired infections and conditions reduction
- Joint Commission core measures
- Publicly reported quality measures

Monitoring the results of comparative effectiveness research is important to ensure that the provider is using the most current EBM. Fortunately, the Agency for Health Care Research and Quality has provided the Effective

Health Care Program website (http://effectivehealthcare.ahrq.gov/) as an easily accessible guide to the newest discoveries.

Global Payments

The ACA contains a demonstration to evaluate the use of global budgets for hospital payments. In this model, the hospital negotiates one annual budget for its services and then must keep its costs under this budget—regardless of patient volume or acuity. The global payment model is common in many countries other than the United States. The model has the advantage of predictability for both the payers and providers, and it substantially reduces overhead costs for billing systems. However, its shortcoming is that increases in patient demand or new technology cannot be easily, or quickly, accommodated, and in some cases this results in queuing for "elective" services (e.g., hip replacement).

All of the cost management tools contained in this book are useful to succeed in this environment. However the following will have the largest impact:

- Balanced scorecard strategy maps and reporting
- Data mining, benchmarking, and statistical tools to identify opportunities for cost reductions
- Process improvement with Lean and Six Sigma with a special emphasis on services that are developing queues
- Scheduling and capacity management
- Supply chain management

Overhead Expenses

All costs not directly related to revenue are overhead. A number of both general and specific tools can be used to reduce overhead expenses.

Process Improvement

All of the process improvement tools discussed in this book (Chapters 8 through 11) can also be applied to administrative processes in overhead departments. Examples include hiring new employees, marketing campaigns, and processing patient complaints.

Consolidated Activities

Many "miscellaneous" expenses are spread through all departments with no individual in charge of managing their costs. These items can include travel, consulting, and dues. By centralizing management costs, savings can be achieved through bidding and the selection of a prime vendor. The various tools of project management, including earned value analysis, can be useful in holding vendors accountable for results and costs—especially for consulting contracts.

Staffing Layers

As organizations grow, close attention should be given to the layers of management. Symptoms of overlayering include many departmental assistant managers and a proliferation of administrative assistants. These layers can be avoided through the crisp use of strategy maps and scorecards, which are closely linked to the organization's data warehouse.

Meetings, Reports, and Automation Tools

"Why do I need to go to these meetings? I have real work to do." This is a familiar complaint from many healthcare workers—especially clinicians. Meetings should be minimized and the discipline of good meeting management maintained at all times (see Chapter 5). One step in good meeting management is the evaluation of the meeting itself (usually at the end), and one question that should always be asked is, Do we need this meeting in the future?

Historically many organizations have relied on paper reports that are sent to "management." These should be either automated and sent via e-mail or moved to electronic scorecards. The five whys of Lean are useful in evaluating reports:

1. Why am I getting this report?
2. Why do you think I need these numbers?
3. Why can't I use an exception report?
4. Why can't these exceptions be part of a scorecard with an andon indicator (red, yellow, blue)?
5. Why can't the scorecard include a follow-up task with assigned accountability?

As desktop computing, networks, and database design have matured, many automation tools have been developed to improve office and clerical productivity. Web conferences now are a reasonable substitute for face-to-face meetings and can save significant travel time and expense. Calendaring tools make it practical for individuals to efficiently schedule meetings without the aid of assistants. Blogs, social media, and texting are other tools that can be carefully used to improve the productivity and connectivity of managers.

Facility and Capital Costs

The acquisition and deployment of capital is beyond the scope of this book. However, the use of facilities is a significant opportunity for cost reduction. Clinical space use optimization is best done with the patient flow improvement tools in Chapters 11. In addition, storage space can be minimized by the effective application of the Lean tool of the five Ss (page 245).

Administrative space should be evaluated to discern whether employees need to be on-site. Many organizations have developed effective work-at-home policies for employees with high-speed Internet access. A half-step toward completely working at home is *hoteling*. In this model the employee works most of her time at home but comes to the office one or two days per week. When she is at the office, she is given a workspace that is assigned the same way hotel rooms are managed. Hoteling can save up to 80 percent of the space otherwise required for these employees.

Prioritize Departmental Activities

The most aggressive cost reduction technique in a department is to eliminate an existing function. A useful technique is to create a cost/importance chart and locate each function on it (see Exhibit 14.5).

The vertical axis is the importance of a function to accomplishing a department's mission.

The horizontal axis is the cost of the function. It is helpful to use ABC here, as most overhead budgets lump costs into basic expense types (e.g., personnel, supplies, services, miscellaneous). Once the chart is complete, managers can target high-cost, low-importance functions for reduction or elimination (Function D in Exhibit 14.5).

EXHIBIT 14.5
Cost/
Importance
Chart

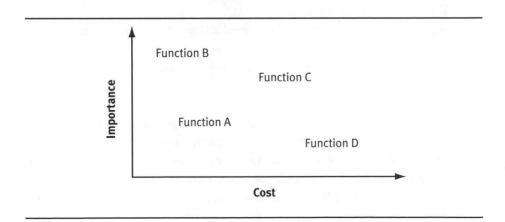

Revenue

The primary focus of this chapter is on cost reduction, but there are also opportunities for improving revenue through the use of operations management tools. The general challenge of increased revenue is addressed in other books from Health Administration Press.

Optimize the Revenue Cycle

Because of the complexity of the US payment system, many of the analytical tools in this book can be applied to optimizing the cycle of billing and collection of charges. Six Sigma in particular is a useful approach, as its goal is to reduce the variability of outcomes in processes. This can be translated in a **revenue cycle** to minimizing the variance in the eventual payment amount and receipt time for the same service.

Revenue cycle
Generating charges, issuing bills, and managing payments and receivables for a defined period.

Current challenges of the revenue cycle include the following:

- Consumer-directed healthcare and the need to collect high deductibles from patients
- Pay-for-performance systems (see Chapter 3)
- Conversion to ICD-10 coding for claims

To succeed in this environment Buysman (2010) suggests five strategies:

1. Providing real-time information to claims processors through data warehouses
2. Using exception-based workflow, in which processes are mapped and automated and only exceptions are handled by staff
3. Providing real-time feedback to clinicians about the effect on reimbursement based on care choices (e.g., medication choice)
4. Automating most tasks in the revenue cycle
5. Enhancing online functionality for customers (i.e., let the consumer do the work—see Chapter 11)

Linking All Cost and Revenue Models Together

Because many opportunities exist for financial improvement, prioritizing improvement efforts is useful. To assist in this task, build a financial model to understand the impact of various improvement projects. Exhibit 14.6 is a simplified financial model for a medium-sized hospital.

As discussed, the revenue is split into its various components and then associated costs determined based on a ratio of costs to charges. The baseline

EXHIBIT 14.6
Hospital
Financial Model

Baseline	Amount $	Cost/charge	IMPROVEMENTS Solver	Baseline	Notes:
Revenue					
Pure fee-for-service	50	0.4	20%	20%	Improvement reduces cost per service
DRG	100	0.8	10%	10%	Improvement reduces number of services
Bundled	10	0.9	5%	5%	Improvement reduces number of services
Shared savings	20	0.9	5%	5%	Improvement reduces number of services
Capitation	40	0.95	3%	3%	Improvement reduces number of services
Overhead	50		1%	1%	Improvement reduces direct costs

Model				
Revenue				
Pure fee-for-service	50.0		50.0	
DRG	100.0		90.0	
Bundled	10.0		9.5	
Shared savings	20.0		20.0	
Capitation	40.0		40.0	
Total	220.0		209.5	207.3
Costs				
Pure fee-for-service	20.0		16.0	
DRG	80.0		57.6	
Bundled	9.0		6.8	
Shared savings	18.0		13.0	
Capitation	38.0		27.4	
Overhead	50.0		49.5	
Total	215.0		170.3	170.3
Net	5.0		39.2	39.2

improvement column shows possible percentage improvements in each segment. Cells D5 to D10 are the variables that affect the bottom line—Cell 37. The user can manually test various improvement strategies to assess their impact on the bottom line. Solver is a more powerful tool to determine the

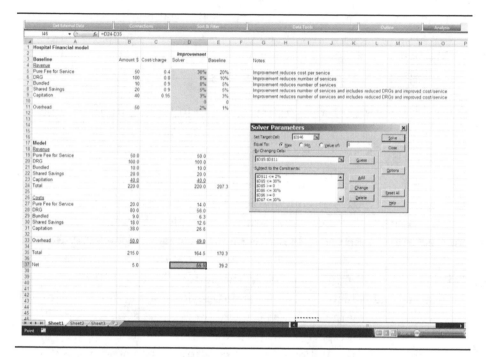

EXHIBIT 14.7
Hospital
Financial Model
Using Solver
to Prioritize
Financial
Improvement
Projects

optimal mix of strategies. However, Solver must be set to make sure its recommended improvement percentages are achievable.

Exhibit 14.7 shows the results of a Solver run with pure fee-for-service savings allowed to go a maximum of 30 percent. The Solver results suggest that this 10 percent increase in improvement from baseline is more important than either the DRG or bundled savings. This is logical because these payment bundles are built out of the fee-for-service costs.

Case Example: Floyd Hospital

Floyd Hospital is a 304-bed stand-alone safety net hospital in northwest Georgia that had 15,328 inpatient admissions, 366,342 emergency visits, and revenue of approximately $300 million in 2009.

They had struggled in prior years and in 1996 they embarked on a journey to improve their financial position and be the provider and employer of choice in their regions.

Initially the hospital began benchmarking other similar institutions to find areas for improvement and then make needed changes. However, the leadership did not feel this approach alone would achieve their long-term goals and instead undertook an extensive Lean Six Sigma program. The five key processes they initially felt needed to be improved were:

- Ensure staffing matches demand ("in quality staffing").
- Discharge inpatients by 2:00 p.m. or earlier 80 percent of the time.
- Maintain emergency care center length of stay for "seen and dismissed" patients at less than three hours and less than four hours for patients who were admitted.
- Match staffing level in the operating room to the length of the surgical procedures.
- Use revenue cycle metrics to meet management's goals.

To achieve these and additional improvement goals, the executive team used a "120-day workout" project management approach. The process proceeded in 30-day increments with each leadership team staff member assigned to come up with at least two improvement projects every 30 days. At the end of each 30-day period, the project improvements were evaluated and their financial impact scored. At the end of the first 120-day workout the hospital had achieved validated annual savings of $2,458,208 with 270 improvements using the tools of Lean and Six Sigma.

An important aspect of each workout was to make the process enjoyable, with a theme throughout and a celebration at the end of the 120 days. Some themes included the Rapids of Change, Hawaiian Blowout, and the Biggest Loser.

From the start of the project through the fall of 2009, Floyd Hospital had 10 cycles of 120-day workouts and 15 major Six Sigma (DMAIC-style) projects. The total validated savings/revenue growth was $16,846,451.

This savings translates into a 5.6 percent improvement in profitability. Floyd is one of the few hospitals in the United States that has maintained a positive Medicare margin (Bakhtiari 2010).

SOURCE: Caldwell, Faulkner, and Stuenkel (2011).

Discussion Questions

1. Why do other payers use Medicare as the benchmark for payment? What are other options?
2. How important is it to involve physicians in financial improvement efforts? What is the best strategy for physician engagement?
3. Compare and contrast three organizational approaches to financial management using operations management tools:
   a. A centralized department that has experts (black belts) who charter and lead projects throughout an organization

b. A centralized department that only does training in process improvement and maintains the project management office. All projects are led by line staff who have been trained in process improvement tools.

c. The use of consultants to lead process improvement projects

Chapter Exercises

1. Use the financial model discussed on page 379 (available on the companion website) to find alternative priorities for financial improvement.

    www.ache.org/books/OpsManagement2

2. Develop a project charter for a bundled payment financial improvement project (see Chapter 5).

3. Develop a strategy map to implement a healthcare home (see Chapters 3 and 4).

PUTTING IT ALL TOGETHER FOR OPERATIONAL EXCELLENCE

HOLDING THE GAINS

Overview

This chapter concludes and integrates this book. It includes

- three strategies to maintain the gains in operational improvement projects: human resources (HR) planning, managerial accounting, and control systems;
- an algorithm that assists practitioners in choosing and applying the tools, techniques, and methods described in this book;
- an examination of how Vincent Valley Hospital and Health System (VVH) used the tools for operational excellence; and
- an optimized healthcare delivery system for the future.

The preceding chapters present an integrated approach to achieving operational excellence. First, strategy execution and change management systems need to be well developed. The balanced scorecard and formal project management techniques are effective methods to employ in these key organizational challenges.

Quantitative tools can now be applied, such as state-of-the-art data collection and analysis tools and problem-solving and decision-making techniques. Processes and scheduling systems can be improved with Six Sigma, Lean, and simulation. Supply chain techniques will maximize value and minimize costs in operations.

The final challenge in achieving healthcare operations excellence is to hold the gains. High energy is usually present when a new initiative is introduced, at the start of a large project, or at the beginning of an effort to solve a problem. However, as time passes, new priorities emerge, team members change, and operations can drift back to unsatisfactory levels.

A strategy for holding the gains must be developed at the beginning of any operations improvement effort. HR planning, managerial accounting, and control systems are the keys to maintaining the gains. Although this book is not focused primarily on HR or finance, these functions are essential to sustaining the improvements achieved. Staff from these support departments should be engaged at the beginning of operations improvement activities and invited to be part of project teams if possible. More extensive information related to these functional areas can be found in *Human Resources in Healthcare—Managing for Success* (Fried and Fottler 2008) and *Healthcare Finance: An Introduction to Accounting and Financial Management* (Gapenski 2011).

Human Resources Planning

The effect of many of the project management and process improvement tools described in this book can be a major change in the work lives of a healthcare organization's employees. Many of these changes will be in the processes of an employee's work, hopefully making it more productive and fulfilling. Some of the more powerful tools, such as Lean, Six Sigma, and simulation, can provide major productivity gains—in some cases, 30 percent to 60 percent increases can be achieved. A clinical process improvement project may significantly change the tasks that fill an employee's workday. In this environment, a disciplined plan for employee redeployment or retraining is essential. Many health care organizations fail at this critical step, as they lack processes to capture and maintain gains in productivity and quality improvement.

As part of the executive function of a healthcare organization, the human resources (HR) department serves as a strategic partner in making effective and long-lasting change. During each annual planning cycle, strategic projects to further the goals of the organization are identified. Many of these initiatives become part of the balanced scorecard. At this point, the HR department should be included to undertake planning, placing the right person in the right job at the right time. This process is shown in Exhibit 15.1.

The HR staff needs to estimate the effect of each project or initiative that will be undertaken during the year. If the project has a goal of providing more service with the same staff, the HR task in the future will be to maintain this staffing level. Broader HR planning can now occur, such as tracking the availability of workers for these positions in external labor pools or identifying and training existing employees to fill these roles if turnover occurs.

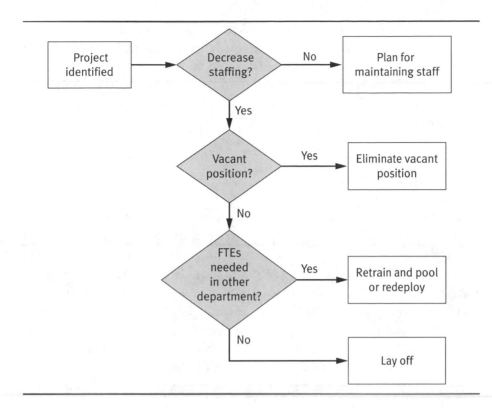

EXHIBIT 15.1
Process for HR
Planning

If, on the other hand, the likely outcome of a project will be to reduce staff in a department, being clear to the organization about the next steps is important. If unfilled positions are no longer needed, the most prudent step is to eliminate them. However, if the position is currently filled, existing employees need to be transferred to different departments in need of full-time equivalents (FTEs). If no openings exist in other departments, these employees may become part of a pool of employees used to fill temporary shortages inside the organization. Retraining for other open positions is also an option if the displaced employee has related skills. Because they have just participated in process improvement projects, these staff members might also receive more training in process improvement tools and be assigned to other departments to aid in their projects.

If none of these options is possible, the last action available to the manager is to lay off the employee. Executing projects that will clearly result in job loss is difficult—getting employees to redesign themselves out of a job is almost impossible. However, layoffs can generally be avoided in health-care, as labor shortages are widespread. In addition, most projects identified should be of the first type, those that will increase throughput with existing staff, as these tend to be the most critical for improved patient access and increases in the quality of clinical care.

The HR planning function should be ongoing and comprehensive. A well-communicated plan for employee reassignment and replacement should be in place. By identifying all potential projects during the annual planning cycle, the HR department can develop an organization-wide staffing plan. Without this critical function, many of the gains in operating improvements will be lost.

Managerial Accounting

Managerial accounting
The field of accounting that focuses primarily on subunit (i.e., departmental) data used internally for managerial decision making.

The second key tool for holding the gains is the use of **managerial accounting** (Gapenski 2011, Chapter 5). In contrast to financial accounting, which is used to prepare financial statements (the past), managerial accounting focuses on the future. Managerial accounting can be used to project the profitability of a particular project that improves patient flow or model the revenue gains from a clinical pay-for-performance (P4P) contract. Even projects that appear to have no financial effect can benefit from managerial accounting. For example, a project to reduce hospital-acquired infections may not only provide higher-quality care, it may also reduce the length of stay for these patients and therefore improve the hospital's profitability. Managerial accounting is a primary analytical tool that must be part of the strategy used to reduce costs and increase revenue as discussed in Chapter 14.

Having a member of the finance staff engaged with operations improvement efforts is useful. This team member should perform an initial analysis of the expected financial results for a project and monitor the financial model throughout the project. She should also ensure that the financial effect of an individual project flows through to the financial results for the entire organization. Monte Carlo simulation (Chapter 10) can be extremely helpful in evaluating the risks and rewards associated with various projects or decisions.

The first step in managerial accounting is to understand an operating unit's revenue source and how it changes with a change in operations. For example, capitation revenue may flow to a primary care clinic; in this case, a reduction in the volume of services will result in a profitability gain. However, if the revenue source for the clinic is fee-for-service payments, the reduction in volume will result in a revenue loss.

Evaluating many revenue sources in healthcare can be complex. For example, understanding inpatient hospital reimbursement via diagnosis-related group can be complicated, as some diagnoses pay substantially more than others. In addition, many other rules affect net reimbursement to the hospital, so a comprehensive analysis needs to be undertaken.

The trend toward consumer-directed healthcare and healthcare savings accounts means that the retail price of some services will also affect net revenue. If a market-sensitive outpatient service is priced too high, net revenue may decline as consumer demand will be lower.

Next, the costs for the operation must be identified and segmented into three categories: variable, fixed, and overhead. Variable costs are those that vary with the volume of the service; a good example is supplies used with a procedure. Fixed costs are those that do not vary with volume and include such items as space costs and equipment depreciation. Employees are usually designated as fixed costs, although they may be variable if the volume of services changes substantially and staffing levels are adjusted based on volume.

The final cost category is overhead, which is allocated to each department or unit in an organization that generates revenue. This allocation pays for costs of departments that do not generate revenue. Overhead formulas are critical to understanding the effect of making operational changes. For example, an overhead rate based on a percentage of revenue will have a substantially different effect than one based on the square footage a department occupies.

Cost-volume-profit (CVP) analysis
A managerial accounting method to evaluate the impact of cost and volume on profit within an organizational unit.

The next step in the managerial accounting process is to conduct a **cost-volume-profit (CVP) analysis**. Exhibit 15.2 illustrates a CVP analysis of two outpatient services at VVH.

EXHIBIT 15.2
Managerial Accounting: CVP Analysis

	Backlogged		Financial Loss	
	Base	Process Improvement Project	Base	Process Improvement Project
Test volume	1,000	1,500	1,000	1,050
Revenue/test	$150	$150	$150	$150
Total revenue	$150,000	$225,000	$150,000	$157,500
Costs				
Variable cost/unit	$38	$38	$38	$38
Fixed costs	$85,000	$85,000	$120,00	$80,000
Overhead	$20,000	$20,000	$20,000	$20,000
Total cost	$143,000	$162,000	$178,000	$139,900
Profit	$7,000	$63,000	($28,000)	$17,600

In the first case, the service is backlogged and current profit (base case) is $7,000 per year. However, if a process improvement project is undertaken, the volume can be increased from 1,000 to 1,500 tests per year. If staffing and other fixed costs remain constant, the net profit is increased to $63,000 per year.

The second example shows a situation where the service is operating at an annual loss of $28,000. In this case, the process improvement goal is to reduce fixed costs (staffing) with a slight increase in volume. The result is a $40,000 reduction in fixed cost, which yields a profit margin of $17,600. HR planning is critical in a project such as this to ensure a comfortable transition for displaced employees.

Control

The final key to holding the gains is a control system. Control systems have two major components: measurement/reporting and monitoring/response.

Chapter 6 discusses many tools for data capture and analysis, with an objective of finding and fixing problems. However, many of the same tools should be deployed for continuous reporting of the results of operations improvement projects. It is important that data collection systems for monitoring outcomes be built into any operations improvement project from the beginning.

Once data collection is under way, results should be displayed both numerically and graphically. The run chart (Chapter 8) is still one of the most effective tools to monitor the performance of a process. Exhibit 15.3 illustrates a simple run chart for birthing center patient satisfaction, where a goal of greater than 90 percent satisfied patients has been agreed upon. This type of chart can show progress over time to ensure that the organization is moving toward its goals.

In addition to a robust data capture and reporting system, a plan for monitoring and response is critical. This plan should include identification of the individual or team responsible for the operation and a method for communicating the reports to them. In some cases, these operations improvement activities are of such strategic importance that they may become part of a departmental or organization-wide balanced scorecard.

A response plan should also be part of the ongoing control system. A procedure or plan should be developed to address situations in which a process fails to perform as it should. Jidoka and andon systems (Chapter 9) can help organizations to discover and correct problems with system performance. Control charts (Chapter 8) can be used to identify out-of-control situations. Once an out-of-control situation is identified, action should be taken to determine the special or assignable cause and eliminate it.

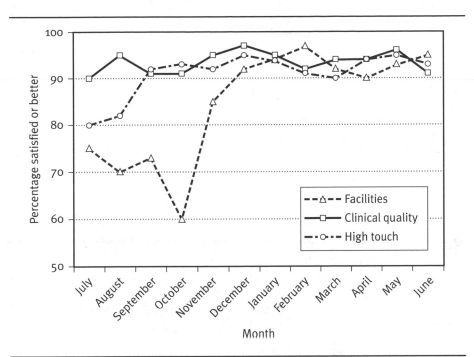

EXHIBIT 15.3
Run Chart
for Birthing
Center Patient
Satisfaction

Which Tools to Use: A General Algorithm

This book presents an array of techniques, tools, and methods to achieve operational excellence. How does the practitioner choose from this broad array? As in clinical care, there is a mix of art and science in choosing the best approach.

A general algorithm for selecting tools is presented below. (The companion website contains an automated and more detailed version of this algorithm.) The general logic discussion at the beginning of this chapter has been expanded to provide a more finely detailed path through the logic (Exhibit 15.4).

www.ache.org/books/OpsManagement2

A. Issue Formulation

First, formulate the issue you wish to address. Determine the current state and a desired state (e.g., competitors have taken 5 percent of our market share in obstetrics and we want to recapture the market, the pediatric clinic lost $100,000 last year and we want to break even next year, public rankings for our diabetes care put our clinic below the median and we want to be in the top quartile). Framing the problem correctly is important to ensure that the outcome is the right answer to the right question rather than the right answer to the wrong question. In particular, all relevant stakeholders should be consulted.

EXHIBIT 15.4   Algorithm for Use of the Tools, Techniques, and Methodologies in This Book

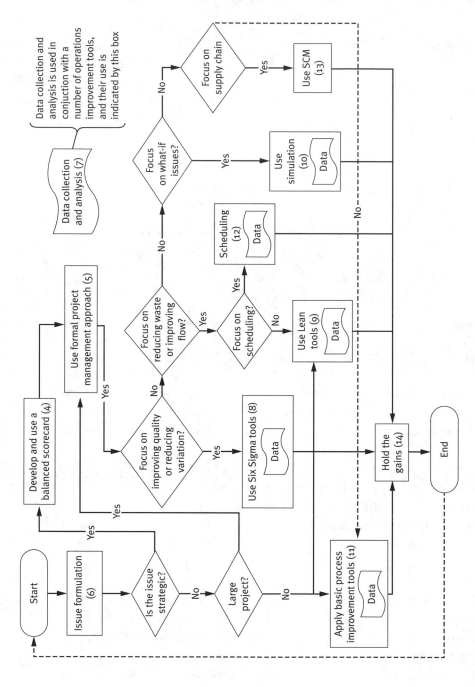

NOTE: Model created in Microsoft Visio
Chapter numbers are in parentheses.

A number of effective decision-making and problem-solving tools can be used to

- frame the question or problem,
- analyze the problem and various solutions to the problem, and
- implement those solutions.

The tools and techniques identified next provide a basis for tackling difficult, complicated problems.

- *The decision-making process*: a generic decision process used for any type of process improvement or problem solving. (Plan-do-check-act [PDCA], define-measure-analyze-improve-control [DMAIC], and project management all follow this same basic outline.)
  - Framing: use to ensure that the "correct" problem or issue is actually being addressed.
  - Gathering intelligence: find and organize the information needed to address the issue (data collection).
  - Coming to conclusions: determine the "solution" to the problem (data analyses).
  - Learning from feedback: ensure that learning is not lost and that the solution actually works (holding the gains).
- *Mapping tools*
  - Mind mapping: use to help formulate and understand the problem or issue.
  - Process mapping, activity mapping, and service blueprinting: use to "picture" the system and process steps.
- *Root-cause analysis (RCA) tools*
  - Five whys technique and fishbone diagrams: use to identify causes and root causes of problems to determine how to eliminate those problems.
  - Failure mode and effects analysis (FMEA): use a more detailed root cause–type analysis to identify and plan for both possible and actual failures.

B. Strategic or Operational Issue

Next, decide whether the issue is strategic (e.g., major resources and high-level staff will be involved) or part of ongoing operations. If the issue is strategic, go to step C; if it is operational, go to step D or E, depending on the size and scope of possible solutions.

C. The Balanced Scorecard for Strategic Issues

To effectively implement a major strategy, develop a balanced scorecard to link initiatives and measure progress. Elements of the balanced scorecard will include:

- *Strategy map*: use to link initiatives or projects to achieve the desired state.
- *Four perspectives*: ensure initiatives and projects span the four main perspectives of the balanced scorecard—financial, customer/patient, operations, and employee learning and growth.
- *Metrics*: use to measure progress; includes both leading (predictive) and lagging (results) measures.

If the balanced scorecard contains a major initiative, go to step D, project management; otherwise, go to step E, basic performance improvement tools.

D. Project Management

The formal project management methodology should be used for initiatives that typically last longer than six months and involve a project team. Project management includes these tools:

- *Project charter*: a document that outlines stakeholders, project sponsor, project mission and scope, a change process, expected results, and estimated resources required
- *Work breakdown structure*: a listing of tasks that will be undertaken to accomplish the project goals, with assigned responsibilities and estimated durations and costs
- *Schedule*: linking of tasks in precedence and relationship and identification of the critical path that determines the overall duration of the project
- *Change control*: a method to formally monitor progress and make changes during the execution of a project
- *Risk management*: an identification of project risks and plans to mitigate each risk

If the project is primarily concerned with improving quality or reducing variation, use the project management technique and tools described in step G, quality and Six Sigma. If the operating issue is large enough for project management and primarily concerned with eliminating waste or improving flow, go to step H, Lean. If the issue is related to evaluating and managing risk or analyzing and improving flow, go to step I, simulation.

If the project is focused on supply chain issues, go to step J, supply chain management (SCM). If the project focus is not encompassed by Six Sigma, Lean, simulation, or SCM, return to step E and use the basic performance improvement tools within the larger project management system.

E. Basic Performance Improvement Tools

Basic performance improvement tools are used to improve and optimize a process. In addition to RCA, the following tools can be helpful in moving toward more effective and efficient processes and systems:

- *Optimization using linear programming*: use to determine the optimal allocation of scarce resources.
- *Theory of constraints (TOC)*: use to identify and manage constraints in the system. The TOC technique consists of five steps:
  1. Identify the constraint (or bottleneck).
  2. Exploit the constraint: Determine how to get the maximum performance out of the constraint without major system changes or capital improvements.
  3. Subordinate everything else to the constraint: Other nonbottleneck resources (or steps in the process) should be synchronized to match the output of the constraint.
  4. Elevate the constraint: Do something (e.g., capital expenditure, staffing increase) to increase the capacity of the constraining resource until it is no longer the constraint. Something else will be the new constraint.
  5. Repeat the process for the new constraint.
- *Force field analysis*: use to identify and manage the forces working for and against change (applicable to any change initiative, including TOC, Six Sigma, and Lean).

If these tools provide an optimal solution, go to step J, holding the gains. However, sometimes the operating issues are so large that they will benefit from the formal project management discipline. In this case, go to step D. If the project is relatively small and focused on eliminating waste, go to step G, Lean, where the kaizen event tool can be used for quick improvements.

F. Quality and Six Sigma

The focus of quality initiatives and the Six Sigma methodology is on improving quality, eliminating errors, and reducing variation.

- *DMAIC*: the process improvement or problem solving technique used in Six Sigma. The DMAIC technique consists of five steps:

1. Define the problem or process (see step A, issue formulation).
2. Measure the current state of the process (see the section Data and Statistics).
3. Analyze the collected data to determine how to fix the problem or improve the process.
4. Improve the process or solve the problem.
5. Control to ensure that changes are embedded in the system (see step J, holding the gains).

Note that at any point in the process it may be necessary to loop back to a previous step. Once the process is complete, start around the loop again.

- *Seven basic quality tools*: in the DMAIC process used to improve the process or solve the problem. The basic quality tools are:
  1. Fishbone diagram: for analyzing and illustrating the root causes of an effect
  2. Check sheet: a simple form used to collect data
  3. Histogram: a graph used to show frequency distributions
  4. Pareto diagram: a sorted histogram
  5. Flowchart: a process map
  6. Scatter plot: a graphic technique to analyze the relationship between two variables
  7. Run chart: a plot of a process characteristic in chronological sequence
- *Statistical process control*: an ongoing measurement of process output characteristics to ensure quality that enables the identification of a problem situation before an error occurs
- *Process capability*: a measure of whether a process is actually capable of producing the desired output
- *Benchmarking*: the determination of what is possible based on what others are doing; used for comparison purposes and goal setting
- *Quality function deployment*: used to match customer requirements (voice of the customer) with process capabilities, given that trade-offs must be made
- *Poka-yoke*: mistake-proofing

Once these tools have produced satisfactory results, proceed to step J, holding the gains.

G. Lean

Lean initiatives are typically focused on eliminating waste and improving flow in the system or process.

- *Kaizen philosophy*: the process improvement technique used in Lean. The kaizen technique consists of the following steps:
  1. Specify value: Identify activities that provide value from the customer's perspective.
  2. Map and improve the value stream: Determine the sequence of activities or the current state of the process and the desired future state and eliminate non-value-added steps and other waste.
  3. Flow: Enable the process to flow as smoothly and quickly as possible.
  4. Pull: Enable the customer to pull products or services.
  5. Perfection: Repeat the cycle to ensure a focus on continuous improvement.
- *Value stream mapping*: used to define the process and determine where waste is occurring
- *Takt time*: a measure of time needed for the process based on customer demand
- *Throughput time*: a measure of the actual time needed in the process
- *Five Ss*: a technique to organize the workplace
- *Spaghetti diagram*: a mapping technique to show the movement of customers (patients), workers, equipment, and so on
- *Kaizen blitz or event*: used to improve the process quickly, when project management is not needed
- *Standardized work*: written documentation of the precise way in which every step in a process should be performed; a way to ensure that things are done the same way every time in an efficient manner
- *Jidoka and andon*: techniques or tools used to ensure that things are "done right the first time" to catch and correct errors
- *Kanban*: scheduling tool used to pull rather than push work
- *Single-minute exchange of die*: a technique to increase the speed of changeover
- *Heijunka*: leveling production (or workload) so that the system or process can flow without interruption

Once these tools have produced satisfactory results, proceed to step J, holding the gains.

H. Simulation

Simulation is used to evaluate what-if situations. Usually simulation is less expensive or speedier than changing the real system and evaluating the effects of those changes.

- *The simulation process* consists of the following steps:
  1. Model development: Develop a model of the process or situation of interest.
  2. Model validation: Ensure that the model accurately represents reality.
  3. Simulate and analyze output: Run the simulation and analyze the output to determine the answers to the questions asked, optimize the process, or manage risk.
- *Monte Carlo simulation*: typically used to evaluate and manage the risks associated with various decisions based on random variables
- *Discrete event simulation*: based on queueing theory; used to model system flows to improve the system

Once these tools have produced satisfactory results, proceed to step J, holding the gains.

I. Supply Chain Management

SCM focuses on all of the processes involved in getting supplies and equipment from the manufacturer to use in patient care areas. SCM is the management of all activities and processes related to both upstream vendors and downstream customers in the value chain. Effective and efficient management of the supply chain requires an understanding of all of the following:

- Tools for tracking and managing inventory
- Forecasting
- Inventory models
- Inventory systems
- Procurement and vendor relationship management
- Strategic SCM

Once these tools have produced satisfactory results, proceed to step J, holding the gains.

J. Holding the Gains

Once successful operational improvements have been completed, three tools can be used to ensure that these changes will endure:

1. *HR planning*: a plan to use employees in new ways after an improvement project is completed
2. *Managerial accounting*: a study of the expected financial consequences and gains after an operations improvement project has been implemented

3. *Control systems*: a set of tools to monitor the performance of a new process and methods to take corrective action if desired results are not achieved

Data and Statistics

All of the aforementioned tools, techniques, and methodologies require data and data analysis. Tools and techniques associated with data collection and analysis include the following:

- *Data collection techniques*: used to ensure that valid data are collected for further analysis
- *Graphic display of data*: used to "see" the data
- *Mathematic descriptions of data*: used to compare sets of data and for simulation
- *Statistical tests*: used to determine whether differences in data exist
- *Regression analyses*: used to investigate and define relationships among variables
- *Forecasting*: used to predict future values of random variables

Operational Excellence

Many leading hospitals, medical groups, and health plans are using the tools and techniques contained in this book. Unfortunately, these tools have not seen widespread use in healthcare, nor have they been as comprehensively applied as in other sectors of the economy. The authors have developed a scale for the application of these tools to gauge progress toward comprehensive operational excellence in healthcare.

Level 1

There are no organized operations monitoring or improvement efforts at level 1. Quality efforts are aimed at compliance and the submission of data to regulating agencies.

Level 2

At level 2, the organization has begun to use operations data for decision making. Pockets of process improvement activities occur where process mapping and PDCA or rapid prototyping are employed. Evidence-based medicine (EBM) guidelines are used in some clinical activities.

Level 3

Senior management has identified operations improvement efforts as a priority by level 3. The organization conducts operations improvement experiments, uses a disciplined project management methodology, and maintains a comprehensive balanced scorecard. Some P4P bonuses are received, and the organization obtains above-average scores on publicly reported quality measures.

Level 4

A level 4 organization engages in multiple process improvement efforts using a combination of project management, Six Sigma, Lean, and simulation tools. It has trained a significant number of employees in the advanced use of these tools, and these individuals lead process improvement projects. EBM guidelines are comprehensively used, and all P4P bonuses are achieved.

Level 5

Operational excellence is the primary strategic objective of an organization at level 5. The executive leadership team has embraced operational excellence as a key component of the organization's strategic plan and demonstrates knowledge in all of its tools. Operations improvement efforts are underway in all departments, led by departmental staff who have been trained in advanced tools. The organization uses real-time simulation to control patient flow and operations. New EBM guidelines and best practices for administrative operations are developed and published by this organization, which scores in the top 5 percent of any national ranking on quality and operational excellence.

A few leading organizations currently are at level 4, but most reside between levels 2 and 3. Our friends at VVH are at the top of level 3 and moving toward 4.

VVH Strives for Operational Excellence

As can be recalled from Chapter 3, VVH leadership felt it had a number of opportunities to succeed with the Medicare Value-Based Purchasing Program and added the program as an initiative to its corporate balanced scorecard: "Conduct projects to optimize Medicare Value-Based Purchasing Program to generate at least a 2 percent increase in inpatient revenue." VVH reorganized its structure to combine a number of operations and quality activities into a new organization-wide department known as operations management and quality.

One team targeted the following specific measures for improvement:

- Pneumonia patients assessed and given pneumococcal vaccination
- Pneumonia patients whose initial emergency room blood culture was performed prior to the administration of the first hospital dose of antibiotics
- Pneumonia patients given smoking cessation advice and counseling
- Pneumonia patients given initial antibiotic(s) within six hours after arrival
- Pneumonia patients given the most appropriate initial antibiotic(s)
- Pneumonia patients assessed and given influenza vaccination

The first step in the project was to identify this team and develop a project charter and schedule (Chapter 5). Both the HR and finance departments were included in the project team to model financial consequences (new revenues, possible new costs, capital requirements) and the potential effect on staffing levels.

The project team began by collecting data on current performance and summarizing them using visual and mathematic techniques to determine where performance was not meeting goals (Chapter 7). A process map was constructed and analyzed to determine where processes could be improved to achieve the desired results. Various Six Sigma tools (fishbone diagrams, check sheets, Pareto diagrams, and scatter plots) were employed to further analyze and improve the process (Chapter 8).

The clinicians on the project team performed a careful analysis to determine which areas of the treatment of patients the risk of pneumonia could be standard and which needed customization. The standard modules were then examined for both effectiveness and efficiency using value stream mapping (Chapter 9). Patient flow for the standard care modules was also modeled and entered into a simulation model to test various patient movement options (Chapter 10).

Changes were identified, many of them requiring either a staffing change or a change in VVH's electronic medical record. Because many options were available and it was not clear which would achieve the desired results, a decision tree (Chapter 6) was constructed to identify the optimal process improvements. Finally, once the project team began to implement these process improvements, the results were monitored with control charts (Chapter 7).

EXHIBIT 15.5
An Optimized
Healthcare
Delivery System
of the Future

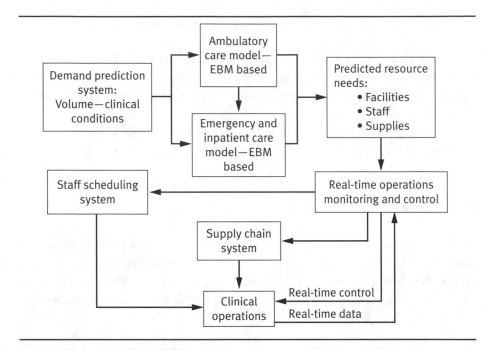

The Healthcare Organization of the Future

A future healthcare organization operating at level 5 is illustrated in Exhibit 15.5. This care delivery system would use many of the tools and techniques contained in this text. A demand prediction model (Chapter 13) would generate predictions of demand for inpatient and ambulatory care services. Because much of the care delivered in these sites would be through the use of EBM guidelines (Chapter 3) that have optimized processes (Chapters 7 to 9), the resource requirements could be predicted as well; these predictions would drive scheduling and supply chain systems.

A key component of this future system is a real-time operations monitoring and control system. This system would use the simulation and modeling techniques described in Chapter 10 to monitor, control, and optimize patient flow and diagnostic and treatment resources. Macro-level control systems such as the balanced scorecard (Chapter 4) would ensure that this system meets the organization's strategic objectives. The result would be a finely tuned healthcare delivery system providing high-quality clinical care in the most efficient manner possible.

Conclusion

We hope that this text is helpful to you and your organization on your journey toward level 5. We are interested in your progress whether you are a new member of the health administration team, a seasoned department head, or a physician leader—please use the e-mail addresses on the companion website to inform us of your successes and let us know what we could do to make this a better text.

Because many of the tools discussed in this text are evolving, we will continuously update the companion website with revisions and additions; check there frequently. We too are striving to reach level 5.

www.ache.org/books/OpsManagement2

Discussion Questions

1. Identify methods to reduce employees' resistance to change during an operations improvement project.
2. What should be the key financial performance indicator used to analyze performance changes for hospitals? Clinics? Health plans? Public health agencies?
3. Describe tools (other than control charts) that can be used to ensure that processes achieve their desired results.
4. Describe the tools, methods, and techniques in this book that would be used to address the following operating issues:
    a. A hospital laboratory department provides results that are late and frequently erroneous.
    b. A clinic's web-based patient information system is not being used by the expected number of patients.
    c. An ambulatory clinic is financially challenged but has a low staffing ratio compared with similar clinics.

Case Study: VVH

VVH has a serious problem: A major strategic objective of the health system was to grow its ambulatory care network, but the organization is facing a number of challenges. Although a new billing system was installed and various reimbursement-maximization strategies were executed, total costs in the system exceed revenue. This was occurring even though the clinic staff felt busy and backlog appointments were growing. Analysis of clinic data also indicated an increasing number of patients were canceling appointments or were no-shows.

In addition, a new group of multispecialty and primary care physicians had been created from the merger of three separate groups; this clinic is aggressively competing with VVH for privately insured patients. The new large clinic is making same-day clinic appointments available and heavily advertising them.

The board of VVH asked the chief executive officer (CEO) to develop a plan to address this growing concern. The CEO first formed a small strategy team to lead improvement efforts; its first step was to assign the chief operating officer, chief financial officer, and medical director to direct the planning and finance staff on the improvement team.

www.ache.org/books/OpsManagement2

VVH ultimately decided that it needed to increase the number of patients seen by clinicians and begin to implement advanced access in its clinics. Because VVH believes in knowledge-based management and sharing in improved methods of delivering health services, the organization has made its data and information available on the companion website. VVH invited students and practitioners to help them improve this system.

1. Frame the original issue for VVH. Mind maps and RCA may be useful here.
2. How would you address the no-shows and cancellations issue?
3. Develop a project charter for one project associated with VVH's problems.
4. Develop a balanced scorecard for VVH's clinics.
5. If VVH decided that it should focus on increasing throughput in the system, how would you go about doing this? Be specific.
6. Would simulation be a useful tool in VVH's quest to implement advanced access? Why or why not? How would you go about implementing advanced access? Be specific.

GLOSSARY

Activity-based costing (ABC). A cost allocation model that assigns a cost to each activity in an organizational unit and then totals the cost for the unit on the basis of the actual consumption of each activity.

Advanced access scheduling. A method of scheduling outpatient appointments that provides open time slots every day to see a patient on the same day he requests an appointment. Sometimes known as "same day scheduling."

Agency for Healthcare Research and Quality (AHRQ). A federal agency that is part of the Department of Health and Human Services. It provides leadership and funding to identify and communicate the most effective methods to deliver high-quality healthcare in the United States.

Andon. A visual or audible signaling device used to indicate a problem in the process, typically used in conjunction with jidoka.

Archimedes model. A full-scale mathematical simulation of human physiology that can be used to test the effect of diseases and their treatments.

Balanced scorecard. A system of strategy links and reporting that supports effective strategy execution.

Bayes' theorem. A formula used to revise the calculation of conditional probability as new information is obtained in the situation.

Business intelligence. The combination of data and analytical tools to find meaningful and actionable information. It includes the creation of data warehouses in order to support data mining.

Capacity utilization. The percentage of time that a resource (worker, equipment, space, etc.) or process is actually busy producing or transforming output.

Care path. A sequence of best practices for healthcare staff to follow for a diagnosis or procedure, designed to minimize waste and maximize quality of care.

Central limit theorem. A theory demonstrating that as the sample size from a population becomes sufficiently large, the sampling distribution of the means will approach normality, no matter the distribution of the original variable.

Coefficient of determination. The measure of how well a model fits the data.

Coefficient of variation. A measure of variation in the data relative to the measure of central tendency in the data.

Confidence interval (CI). The probability that a population parameter falls between two values.

Consumer-directed healthcare. In general it means the consumer (patient) is well informed about healthcare prices and quality and makes her personal buying decisions based on this information. The health savings account is frequently included as a key component of consumer-directed healthcare.

Contingency tables. A tool used to examine the relationships between qualitative or categorical variables.

Continuous quality improvement (CQI). A comprehensive quality improvement and management system with three key components: quality planning, control, and improvement.

Control limits. Common variation limits that are ±3 standard deviations from the mean.

Correlation coefficient. A measure of the linear relationship between two variables.

Cost of quality. The costs associated with producing poor-quality goods and services, including tangible costs, such as scrap and rejects, and intangible costs, such as lost customer goodwill.

Cost performance index. The ratio of budgeted costs of work performed to actual costs of work performed.

Cost-volume-profit (CVP) analysis. A managerial accounting method to evaluate the impact of cost and volume on profit within an organizational unit.

Critical index. The product of the cost performance index and the schedule performance index.

Critical path method (CPM). The critical path is the longest path through a graph of linked tasks within a project. The critical path method is used to reduce the total time of a project by reducing the duration of tasks on the critical path.

Cross-functional process map. A map that follows the flow of a process through the various departments of the organization using dashed lines to show the work being completed by a particular department or individual in the process. Also called a *swim lane process map*.

Cycle time. The time it takes to accomplish a task in a system.

Data mining. An analytical approach to retrieving data from data warehouses to discover new patterns and relationships to support management decision making.

Data warehouse. A separate but connected computer system designed for accurate data storage, performance reporting, and data mining.

Decision analysis. A structured process for examining and evaluating decisions.

Decision tree. A graphic representation of the order of future and current events of how decisions are made.

Discrete event simulation (DES). A simulation technique that uses probability distributions to represent random variables.

Dot plot. A chart in which frequency is represented by a dot. Useful for displaying small data sets with positive values.

Earned value analysis. Provides one number that can be used to track the duration and cost of a project as compared to plan.

Economic order quantity (EOQ). An inventory model that indicates an optimal purchase quantity that will minimize total annual inventory costs.

Enterprise resources planning (ERP). Global information systems that help manage the entire organization, including accounting, operations, and human resources.

Evidence-based medicine (EBM). The conscientious and judicious use of the best current evidence in making decisions about the care of individual patients.

Failure mode and effects analysis (FMEA). A technique developed by the US military to identify the ways in which a process (or piece of equipment) might potentially fail and identify ways to mitigate those risks.

Fishbone diagram. A graphical technique used to display the relationship between the potential causes of problems and the effect created by the problem. Sometimes called an *Ishikawa diagram.*

Five whys. A technique that uses a series of logical questions to find the root cause of a problem.

Force field analysis. A graphical technique that demonstrates all the forces for and against making a key decision.

Full capitation. A methodology in which providers are paid a monthly fee for each patient who receives care in their system.

Gantt chart. A scheduling tool that lists project tasks with bars indicating start and end dates for each task.

Healthcare home. Care that is accessible, continuous, comprehensive, family-centered, coordinated, compassionate, and culturally effective.

Health savings accounts (HSAs). Personal accounts that can only be used for healthcare expenses. The funds are not taxed, and the balance can be rolled over from year to year. HSAs are normally used with high-deductible health insurance plans.

Heijunka. The process of eliminating variations in volume and variety of production to reduce waste.

Histogram. A graph summarizing discrete or continuous data. Histograms visually display how much variation exists in the data.

Hypothesis testing. The process of testing a statistical distribution parameter against that of another distribution parameter to assess if statistical differences exist in the data.

Institute of Medicine (IOM). The healthcare arm of the National Academy of Sciences; an independent, nonprofit organization providing unbiased and authoritative advice to decision makers and the public.

Ishikawa diagram. See *fishbone diagram.*

ISO 9001. Standards developed by the International Organization for Standardization to give organizations guidelines to develop and maintain effective quality systems.

Jidoka. The ability to prevent defects by stopping a process when an error occurs.

Just-in-time (JIT). An inventory management system designed to improve efficiency and reduce waste. Part of Lean manufacturing.

Kaizen. Continuous improvement based on the belief that everything can be improved and that incremental changes result in a better system.

Kaizen event. A focused, short-term project aimed at improving a particular process.

Kanban. A visual signal that triggers the movement of inventory or product in a system.

Knowledge-based management (KBM). The use of data and information, rather than feelings or intuition, to support management decisions.

Knowledge hierarchy. The foundation of knowledge-based management, comprising five categories of learning: data, information, knowledge, understanding, and wisdom.

Lagging indicator. A performance measurement that assesses the outcome of existing actions.

Leading indicator. A performance measurement that predicts the future and is specific to an initiative or to organizational strategy. Also called a performance driver.

Linear programming. A mathematical technique used to find the optimal solution to a linear problem given a set of constrained resources.

Little's law. The relationship between arrival rate to a system, the time a patient spends in the system, and the number of items in a system.

Malcolm Baldrige National Quality Award. An annual award established by Congress in 1987 to recognize US organizations for their achievements in quality.

Managerial accounting. The field of accounting that focuses primarily on subunit (i.e., departmental) data used internally for managerial decision making.

Material requirements planning (MRP). A computer system designed to manage the purchase and control of dependent-demand items.

Mind mapping. A nonlinear technique used to develop thoughts and ideas by placing pictures or phrases on a map to show logical connections.

Mitigation plan. A set of tasks intended to reduce or eliminate the effect of risk in a project.

Monte Carlo simulation. A mathematical technique that allows a modeler to enter input variables as probability distributions that will create output variables with probabilistic outcomes.

Network diagram. A scheduling tool that connects tasks in order of precedence.

Observed probability. The number of times an event occurred divided by the total number of trials.

Optimization. A technique used to determine the optimal allocation of limited resources (such as people, money, or equipment) given a desired goal. Also called mathematical programming.

Pareto diagram. A rank-ordered frequency chart that indicates the number of times a particular item occurs in a situation.

Pareto principle. Developed by Italian economist Vilfredo Pareto in 1906 based on his observation that 80 percent of the wealth in Italy was owned by 20 percent of the population.

Patient care microsystem. The level of healthcare delivery that includes providers, technology, and treatment processes.

Patient Protection and Affordable Care Act (ACA). The Patient Protection and Affordable Care Act was passed by Congress in 2010 and signed into law by President Obama. It contains policies to increase access to health insurance and to improve the operations and outcomes of the American healthcare system. Its common name has been shortened to the Affordable Care Act or ACA.

Plan-do-check-act (PDCA). A core process-improvement tool with four elements: Plan your change to a process; do the change; check to make sure it is working as expected; act to make sure this change is sustainable.

Poka-yoke. A mechanism that prevents mistakes or makes them immediately obvious to prevent adverse outcomes.

Practical significance. The differences in the parameters of two data sets are large enough to be meaningful for the person or organization studying the situation whether or not it is statistically significant.

Prevention quality indicator (PQI). A set of measures that can be used with hospital discharge data to identify patients who may have hospitalizations or complications that could be avoided with the use of evidence-based ambulatory care.

Process capability. A measure of how well a process can produce output that meets desired standards or specifications.

Process map. A graphic depiction of a process showing the sequence of events, including tasks, decisions, and other activities from inputs to outputs (i.e., a flowchart).

Program evaluation and review technique (PERT). PERT is a graphic technique used to link and analyze all tasks within a project. This graph can then be used to optimize the project's schedule.

Project Management Body of Knowledge (PMBOK). A book of science-based, field-tested guidelines for successful project management, developed by the Project Management Institute.

Project management professional (PMP). Professional certification of a project manager by the Project Management Institute.

Public reporting. A statement of healthcare quality made by hospitals, long-term care facilities, and clinics. May also include patient satisfaction and provider charges.

Quality function deployment (QFD). A technique that translates customer requirements into specific product or process requirements.

Quality trilogy. A comprehensive quality improvement and management system with three key components: quality planning, control, and improvement.

Queue discipline. In queuing theory, the method by which customers are selected from the queue to be served.

Queuing theory. The mathematical study of wait lines.

Range (R) chart. Measures process performance of sample ranges for continuous data.

RASIC. A chart delineating all project team members' roles for each task in a project. The acronym comes from the members' roles: Responsible, Approval, Support, Informed, Consult.

Revenue cycle. Generating charges, issuing bills, and managing payments and receivables for a defined period.

Risk adjustment. Raising or lowering fees paid to providers on the basis of factors that may increase medical costs, such as age, sex, or illness.

Risk management. Within a project, the identification of possible risks that will affect the execution of the project and a plan to mitigate these risks.

Rolled throughput yield. The probability that a unit (of product or service) will pass through all process steps free of defects.

Root-cause analysis (RCA). A generic term describing structured, step-by-step techniques for problem solving.

Rough cut capacity planning. The process of converting the overall production plan into capacity needs for key resources.

Scatter plot. A graph displaying two variables and whether they are related, how strongly they are related, and the direction of the relationship.

Schedule performance index. The ratio of the budgeted cost of work performed to the budgeted cost of work scheduled.

Scientific management. A disciplined approach to studying a system or process and then using data to optimize it to be more efficient or effective.

Sensitivity analysis. A tool that examines the effect of independently changing input variables to see the impact on the output of a model.

Sequencing rules. Heuristic rules that indicate the order in which jobs are processed from a queue. Also known as the "queuing priority."

Service blueprinting. A process map that separates actions into onstage (visible to the customer) and backstage (not visible to the customer).

Service level. The probability of having an item on hand when needed.

Shared savings model. A model of healthcare delivery that includes an organized system of delivery, accountability for the quality and costs of services, and a sharing of savings with the payer for these services.

Shewhart's rule. An outlier exists in bell-shaped data if a data point is greater than three standard deviations from the mean.

Simple linear regression. An equation that relates two variables using a slope and intercept in a linear fashion.

Single exponential smoothing (SES). A simple forecasting model that smoothes data in a time series to predict the future.

Spaghetti diagram. A visual representation of the movement or travel of materials, employees, or customers.

Standard deviation. A measurement of variation around the mean.

Standardized work. Documentation of the precise way in which every step in a process should be completed.

Stakeholder. Anyone who has a vested interest in the outcome of a project, including (but not limited to) employees, customers, users, partner organizations, project sponsors, and the project manager.

Statement of work (SOW). A detailed set of tasks, expected outcomes, dates, and costs of a project undertaken by an external contractor.

Statistical process control (SPC). A scientific approach to controlling the performance of a process by measuring the process outputs and then using statistical tools to determine whether this process is meeting expected performance.

Statistical significance. The differences in two parameters of two data sets are large enough to reject the null hypothesis using hypothesis testing.

Strategy map. A set of initiatives that are graphically linked by if-then statements to describe an organization's strategy.

Supply chain management (SCM). The management of all supplier, vendor, and distribution activities related to the production of value to end consumers.

Systems thinking. A view of reality that emphasizes the relationships and interactions of each part of the system to all of the other parts.

Taguchi methods. The idea that product development should focus on "perfect" rather than on conformance to specifications.

Takt time. The speed with which customers must be served to satisfy demand for the service.

Theoretical probability. The number of times an event will occur divided by the total number of possible outcomes.

Theory of constraints (TOC). The idea that every organization and process is subject to at least one constraint that limits it from moving toward or achieving its goal.

Throughput time. The time for an item to complete the entire process, including waiting time and transport time.

Tornado graph. A sensitivity graph used to display relative strength of variables in a simulation model.

Total quality management (TQM). A management philosophy or program aimed at ensuring quality (defined as customer satisfaction) by focusing on quality throughout the organization and product/service life cycle.

Toyota Production System (TPS). A quality improvement system developed by Toyota for its auto manufacturing lines. TPS has broad applicability beyond auto manufacturing and is now commonly known as Lean manufacturing.

Transformation. The process of converting a variable by linear regression into a format that is more readily usable.

Trend-adjusted exponential smoothing. An extension of a single exponential smoothing model that accounts for a trend when smoothing the data.

Tukey's rule. An outlier exists in a skewed data set if a data point is greater than q1 − one step or q3 + one step.

Type I, or α, error. The probability of rejecting the null hypothesis when it is true.

Type II, or β, error. The probability of accepting the null hypothesis when it is false.

Variance. A statistical term that indicates how much a measurement varies around the mean.

Value proposition. A marketing term summarizing the relative cost, features, and quality of a service or a good.

Value purchasing. A system using payment as a means to reward providers who publicly report results and achieve high levels of clinical care.

Value stream map. An overview of how a system transforms supplies into finished goods for the customer.

Work breakdown structure (WBS). A list of the tasks that need to be accomplished, their relationship to each other, and the resources required for a project to meet its goals.

X-bar chart. Measures process performance of sample means for continuous data.

REFERENCES

Ackoff, R. L. 1989. "From Data to Wisdom." *Journal of Applied Systems Analysis* 16: 3–9.

Agency for Healthcare Research and Quality (AHRQ), US Department of Health and Human Services. 2012a. "Effective Healthcare Program: Helping You Make Better Treatment Choices." *AHRQ.* Accessed January 25. www.effective healthcare.ahrq.gov.

———. 2012b. "National Guideline Clearinghouse FAQ." *AHRQ.* Accessed January 25. www.guideline.gov/faq.aspx.

———. 2012c. "Prevention Quality Indicators Overview." *AHRQ.* Accessed February 27. www.qualityindicators.ahrq.gov/modules/pqi_overview.aspx.

———. 2007. *Managing and Evaluating Rapid-Cycle Process Improvements as Vehicles for Hospital System Redesign.* AHRQ Publication No. 07-0074-EF, September 2007. Rockville, MD: Agency for Healthcare Research and Quality.

———. 2006. "Guide to Prevention Quality Indicators: Hospital Admission for Ambulatory Care Sensitive Conditions." *AHRQ.* Accessed May 30. www .qualityindicators.ahrq.gov/downloads/pqi/pqi_guide_v30a.pdf.

Aiello, A. E., G. F. Murray, V. Perez, R. M. Coulburn, B. M. Davis, M. Uddin, D. K. Shay, S. H. Waterman, and A. S. Monto. 2010. "Mask Use, Hand Hygiene, and Seasonal Influenza-Like Illness Among Young Adults: A Randomized Intervention Trial." *Journal of Infectious Diseases* 201 (4): 491–98.

American Academy of Family Physicians (AAFP), American Academy of Pediatrics (AAP), American College of Physicians (ACP), and American Osteopathic Association (AOA). 2007. "Joint Principles of the Patient-Centered Medical Home." *American Academy of Family Physicians.* Published February 21. www.aafp.org/online/etc/medialib/aafp_org/documents/policy/fed/ jointprinciplespcmh0207.Par.0001.File.dat/022107medicalhome.pdf.

American Productivity and Quality Center (APQC). 2005. "Glossary of Benchmarking Terms." *APQC.* Accessed January 30, 2006. www.apqc.org/portal/apqc/ ksn/Glossary%20of%20Benchmarking%20Terms.pdf?paf_gear_id=content gearhome&paf_dm=full&pageselect=contentitem&docid=119519.

Archimedes Incorporated. 2012. "What Is the Archimedes Model?" *Archimedes.* Accessed May 17. http://archimedesmodel.com/archimedesmodel.html.

Auerbach, A. D. 2001. "Making Health Care Safer: A Critical Analysis of Patient Safety Practices." In *Localizing Care to High-Volume Centers. Evidence Report/Technology Assessment: No. 43*, AHRQ Publication No. 01-E058. Rockville, MD: AHRQ.

Axelrod, R. 2006. "Advancing the Art of Simulation in the Social Sciences." In *Handbook of Research on Nature-Inspired Computing for Economics and Management*, edited by J. Rennard. 3-4. Hershey, PA: Idea Group Reference.

Baiardini, I., F. Braido, M. Bonini, E. Compalati, and G. W. Canonica. 2009. "Why Do Doctors and Patients Not Follow Guidelines?" *Current Opinion in Allergy and Clinical Immunology* 9 (3): 228–33.

Bailey, N. T. J., and J. D. Welch. 1952. "Appointment Systems in Hospital Outpatient Departments." *Lancet* 259: 1105–08.

Bakhtiari, E. 2010. "Can Hospitals Break Even with Medicare?" *Health Leaders Media*. December 13. www.healthleadersmedia.com/page-2/MAG-259987/Can-Hospitals-Break-Even-with-Medicare.

Baldrige National Quality Program. 2006a. "1988–2004 Award Recipients' Contacts and Profiles." *National Institute of Standards and Technology*. Accessed January 15. www.quality.nist.gov/Contacts_Profiles.htm.

———. 2006b. *2006 Criteria for Performance Excellence*. Gaithersburg, MD: National Institute of Standards and Technology.

———. 2005. "Frequently Asked Questions About the Malcolm Baldrige National Quality Award." *National Institute of Standards and Technology*. Accessed January 15, 2006. www.nist.gov/public_affairs/factsheet/baldfaqs.htm.

Baldrige Performance Excellence Program. 2011. "Four U.S. Organizations Honored with the 2011 Baldrige National Quality Award." *National Institute of Standards and Technology*. Accessed May 19, 2012. www.nist.gov/baldrige/baldrige_recipients2011.cfm.

Barry, R., A. Murcko, and C. E. Brubaker. 2002. *Six Sigma Book for Healthcare: Improving Outcomes by Reducing Errors*. Milwaukee, WI: ASQ Quality Press.

BearingPoint and National Alliance for Healthcare Information Technology. 2006. *RFID in Healthcare: Poised for Growth. Bearing Point*. Accessed February 15, 2007. www.bearingpoint.com.

Beaver, R. 2004. "Six Sigma Success in Health Care." *Quality Digest* (March): 31–34.

Bednarz, T. F. 2012. "Strategies and Solutions for Solving Team Problems: Teams That Run Smoothly Can Concentrate on Their Primary Goals." *Quality Digest*. Published February 2. www.qualitydigest.com/inside/quality-insider-article/strategies-and-solutions-solving-team-problems.html.

Belardi, F. G., S. Weir, and F. W. Craig. 2004. "A Controlled Trial of an Advanced Access Appointment System in a Residency Family Medicine Center." *Family Medicine* 36 (5): 341–45.

Bellis, M. 2006. "Henry Ford (1863–1947)." *About.com*. Accessed June 8. http://inventors.about.com/library/inventors/blford.htm.

Belohlav, J. A., L. S. Cook, J. R. Olson, and D. E. Drehmer. 2010. "Core Values in Hospitals: A Comparative Study." *Quality Management Journal* 17 (4): 36–50.

Berlekamp, E. R., J. H. Conway, and R. K. Guy. 2003. *Winning Ways (for Your Mathematical Plays)*, 2nd edition, Vol. 2. Wellesley, MA: AK Peters.

Birk, S. 2010. "Quality Cost Efficiency: The New Quality-Cost Imperative." *Healthcare Executive* 25 (2): 14–19.

Bisognano, M. A., and C. Caldwell. 1995. "Best Practices in Quality Leadership." *Quality Letter for Healthcare Leaders* 7 (6): 16–21.

Bloomquist, P., and J. Yeager. 2008. "Using Balanced Scorecards to Align Organizational Strategies." *Healthcare Executive* 23 (1): 24–28.

Bohmer, R. M. J. 2005. "Medicine's Service Challenge: Blending Custom and Standard Care." *Health Care Management Review* 30 (4): 322–30.

Box, G. E. P., and G. M. Jenkins. 1976. *Time Series Analysis: Forecasting and Control*, 2nd ed. San Francisco: Holden-Day.

Bureau of Economic Analysis, US Department of Commerce (BEA). 2006. "Benchmark Input-Output Accounts." *BEA*. Accessed December 20. http://bea.gov/bea/dn2/home/benchmark.htm.

Butterfield, S. 2007. "A New Rx for Crowded Hospitals: Math." *ACP Hospitalist* (December). www.acphospitalist.org/archives/2007/12/math.htm#sb1.

Buysman, L. 2010. "Five Things to Look for in a Next-Generation Revenue Cycle Management System." *Healthcare Financial Management* 64 (8): 40–43.

Buzan, T. 1991. *Use Both Sides of Your Brain*. New York: Plume.

Buzan, T., and B. Buzan. 1994. *The Mind Map Book: How to Use Radiant Thinking to Maximize Your Brain's Untapped Potential*. New York: Dutton.

Caldwell, C., T. Faulkner, and K. M. Stuenkel. 2010. "Aggressive Cost Reduction: Taking Lean to the Next Level." Lecture at the ACHE Congress on Healthcare Leadership, March.

Caldwell, C., J. Brexler, and T. Gillem. 2005. *Lean-Six Sigma for Healthcare: A Senior Leader Guide to Improving Cost and Throughput*. Milwaukee, WI: ASQ Quality Press.

Carden, L., and T. Egan. 2008. "Does Our Literature Support Sectors Newer to Project Management? The Search for Quality Publications Relevant to Non-traditional Industries." *Project Management Journal* 39 (3): 6–27.

Cayirli, T., and E. Veral. 2003. "Outpatient Scheduling in Health Care: A Review of the Literature." *Production and Operations Management* 12 (4): 519–49.

Center for the Study of Healthcare Management. 2002. "Deploying Six Sigma in a Healthcare System." *University of Minnesota School of Public Health*. Accessed August 13, 2006. www.hpm.umn.edu/research/centerline/8260.pdf.

Centers for Disease Control and Prevention (CDC). 2010. "2009 H1N1 Flu: Situation Update." *CDC.* Published June 18. www.cdc.gov/h1n1flu/update.htm.

Centers for Medicare & Medicaid Services (CMS). 2012. "Medicare Acute Care Episode Demonstration for Orthopedic and Cardiovascular Surgery." CMS. Accessed May 15. www.cms.gov/Medicare/Demonstration-Projects/DemoProjectsEvalRpts/downloads//ACE_web_page.pdf.

———. 2011. "Medicare Program; Hospital Inpatient Value-Based Purchasing Program." *Federal Register.* Published January 13. www.federalregister.gov/articles/2011/01/13/2011-454/medicare-program-hospital-inpatient-value-based-purchasing-program#p-8.

———. 2010. "National Health Expenditure Projections 2009–2019 (September 2010)." *Centers for Medicare & Medicaid Services.* Accessed May 17, 2012. www.cms.gov/NationalHealthExpendData/downloads/NHEProjections2009to2019.pdf.

Chalice, R. 2005. *Stop Rising Healthcare Costs Using Toyota Lean Production Methods: 38 Steps for Improvement.* Milwaukee, WI: ASQ Quality Press.

Chaplin, E. M. D., and J. Terninko. 2000. *Customer Driven Healthcare: QFD for Process Improvement and Cost Reduction.* Milwaukee, WI: American Society for Quality Press.

Chase, R. B. 1978. "Where Does the Customer Fit in a Service Operation?" *Harvard Business Review* 56 (6): 137–42.

Chassin, M. R., and J. M. Loeb. 2011. "The Ongoing Quality Improvement Journey: Next Stop, High Reliability." *Health Affairs* 30 (4): 559–68.

Cheang, B., H. Li, A. Lim, and B. Rodrigues. 2003. "Nurse Rostering Problems— A Bibliographic Survey." *European Journal of Operational Research* 151 (1): 447–60.

Chow, V. S., M. L. Puterman, N. Salehirad, W. Huang, and D. Atkins. 2011. "Reducing Surgical Ward Congestion Through Improved Surgical Scheduling and Uncapacitated Simulation." *Production and Operations Management* 20 (3): 418–30.

Clark, J. J. 2005. "Unlocking Hospital Gridlock." *Healthcare Financial Management* 59 (11): 94–104.

Cleveland, H. 1982. "Information as a Resource." *Futurist* 16 (Dec.): 34–39.

Cleverley, W. O., and J. O. Cleverley. 2010. "Critical Financial Questions for Healthcare Executives." Presented at ACHE Congress on Healthcare Leadership, March.

Cleverley, W. O., and R. K. Harvey. 1992. "Is There a Link Between Hospital Profit and Quality?" *Healthcare Financial Management* 46 (9): 40–44.

Cohen, I. B. 1984. "Florence Nightingale." *Scientific American* 250 (3): 128–37.

Connolly, C. 2005. "Cedars-Sinai Doctors Cling to Pen and Paper." *Washington Post*, March 21, A01.

Cook, D. P., C. Goh, and C. H. Chung. 1999. "Service Typologies: A State of the Art Survey." Production and Operations Management 8 (3): 318–38.

Cooper, R. B. 1981. *Introduction to Queueing Theory*, 2nd ed. New York: North-Holland.

Council of Supply Chain Management Professionals (CSCMP). 2006. "Supply Chain Management/Logistics Management Definitions." *CSCMP*. Accessed December 20. www.cscmp.org/Website/AboutCSCMP/Definitions/Definitions.asp.

Crosby, P. B. 1979. *Quality Is Free: The Art of Making Quality Certain*. Boston: McGraw-Hill.

Curtright, J. W., and S. C. Stolp-Smith. 2000. "Strategic Performance Management: Development of a Performance Measurement System at the Mayo Clinic." *Journal of Healthcare Management* 45 (1): 58–68.

Defeo, J. 2010. *Juran's Quality Handbook: The Complete Guide to Performance Excellence*, 6th ed. New York: McGraw-Hill.

DeLia, D. 2007. "Hospital Capacity, Patient Flow, and Emergency Department Use in New Jersey." *Rutgers Center for State Health Policy*. Accessed May 18, 2012. www.cshp.rutgers.edu/Downloads/7510.pdf.

De Mast, J., B. Kemper, R. J., M. M. Does, M. Mandjes, and Y. van der Bijl. 2011. "Process Improvement in Healthcare: Overall Resource Efficiency." *Quality and Reliability Engineering International*. Accessed May 18, 2012. www1.fee.uva.nl/pp/bin/forthcomingpublication633fulltext.pdf.

Deming, W. E. 2000. *Out of the Crisis*. Cambridge, MA: MIT Press.

———. 1998. "The Deming Philosophy." *Deming-Network*. Accessed June 9, 2006. http://deming.ces.clemson.edu/pub/den/deming_philosophy.htm.

———. 1994. *The New Economics for Industry, Government, Education*, 2nd ed. Cambridge, MA: MIT Press.

———. 1986. *Out of the Crisis*. Cambridge, MA: Cambridge University Press.

De Nies, Y., J. Pirone, and K. Santichen. 2009. "Hand Sanitizer: Good Hygiene or Just Hype?" *ABC News*. Published December 6. http://abcnews.go.com/GMA/Weekend/america-obsessed-hand-sanitizer/story?id=9260788#.T51Hvdmlt8E.

Detsky, A. S., G. M. Naglie, M. D. Krahn, D. M. Naimark, and D. A. Redelmeier. 1997. "Primer on Medical Decision Analysis: Parts 1 to 5." *Medical Decision Making* 17 (2): 123–59.

Donabedian, A. 1985. *Exploration in Quality Assessment and Monitoring, Volume 3. The Methods and Findings of Quality Assessment and Monitoring: An Illustrated Analysis*. Chicago: Health Administration Press.

———. 1982. *Exploration in Quality Assessment and Monitoring, Volume 2. The Criteria and Standards of Quality*. Chicago: Health Administration Press.

———. 1980. *Exploration in Quality Assessment and Monitoring, Volume 1. Definition of Quality and Approaches to Its Assessment*. Chicago: Health Administration Press.

————. 1966. "Evaluating the Quality of Medical Care." *Milbank Memorial Fund Quarterly* 44 (3): 166–206.

Duffy, M. 2009. "Is Supply Chain the Cure for Rising Healthcare Costs?" *Supply Chain Management Review* 13 (6): 28–35.

Environmental Protection Agency (EPA). 2011. "Lean and Environment Toolkit." *Environmental Protection Agency.* Accessed May 21, 2012. www.epa.gov/lean/environment/toolkits/environment/ch5.htm.

Ettinger, W. H. 2001. "Six Sigma: Adapting GE's Lessons to Health Care." *Trustee* 54 (8): 10–15.

Farrell, B., and T. Simas. 2005. "Tracking Quality Improvement in Health Care." *Quality Digest.* Accessed May 22, 2012. www.qualitydigest.com/sept05/articles/02_article.shtml.

Fineberg, H. 2012. "A Successful and Sustainable Health System: How to Get There from Here." *New England Journal of Medicine* 366: 1020–27.

Finnie, W. 1997. "Strategies, Systems, and Organizations: An Interview with Russell L. Ackoff." *Strategy and Leadership* 25 (2): 22–28.

Fox, M. 2009. "Swine Flu Death Rate Similar to Seasonal Flu: Expert." *Reuters.* Accessed May 17, 2012. www.reuters.com/article/2009/09/17/us-flu-deaths-idUSTRE58E6NZ20090917.

Freitas, A. 2011. "Building Cost-Sensitive Decision Trees for Medical Applications." *AI Communications.* Accessed May 18, 2012. http://iospress.metapress.com/content/f274348171742t66.

Fried, B. J., and M. D. Fottler, eds. 2008. *Human Resources in Healthcare: Managing for Success*, 3rd ed. Chicago: Health Administration Press.

Gapenski, L. C. 2011. *Healthcare Finance: An Introduction to Accounting and Financial Management*, 5th ed. Chicago: Health Administration Press.

Garvin, D. A. 1987. "Competing on the Eight Dimensions of Quality." *Harvard Business Review* 65 (6): 101–10.

Gawande, A. 2009. *The Checklist Manifesto.* New York: Metropolitan Books.

George, M. 2002. *Lean Six Sigma: Combining Six Sigma Quality with Lean Production Speed.* New York: McGraw-Hill.

Gilbreth, F. B., and E. G. Carey. 1948. *Cheaper by the Dozen.* New York: T.Y. Crowell Co.

Goldratt, E. M., and J. Cox. 1986. *The Goal: A Process of Ongoing Improvement.* New York: North River Press.

Goldstein, S. M., and A. R. Iossifova. 2011. "Ten Years After: Interference of Hospital Slack in Process Performance Benefits of Quality Practices." *Journal of Operations Management* 20 (1–2): 44–54.

Grenvik, A., and J. Schaefer. 2004. "From Resusci-Anne to Sim-Man: The Evolution of Simulators in Medicine." *Critical Care Medicine* 32 (2 Suppl.): S56–S57.

Gupta, D., S. Potthoff, D. Blowers, and J. Corlett. 2006. "Performance Metrics for Advanced Access." *Journal of Healthcare Management* 51 (4): 246–59.

Haavik, S. 2000. "Building a Demand-Driven, Vendor-Managed Supply System." *Healthcare Financial Management* 54 (2): 56–61.

Hackman, J. R., and R. Wageman. 1995. "Total Quality Management: Empirical, Conceptual, and Practical Issues." *Administrative Science Quarterly* 40 (2): 309–42.

Haley, L. 2005. "Simulation Aims to Speed Patients Through Surgeries." *Medical Post* 41 (1): 2–3.

Halm, E. A., C. Lee, and M. R. Chassin. 2002. "Is Volume Related to Outcome in Health Care? A Systematic Review and Methodologic Critique of the Literature." *Annals of Internal Medicine* 137 (6): 511–20.

Harris Poll Online. 2006. "Two Gigantic Blunders in the History of Election Polling." *Harris Poll Online*. Accessed August 8. www.harrispollonline.com/uk/history.asp#blunders.

Hayes, R. H., and S. C. Wheelwright. 1979. "Link Manufacturing Process and Product Life Cycles." *Harvard Business Review* 57 (1): 133–40.

Healthcare Financial Management Association. 2005. *HFMA's 2005 Supply Chain Benchmarking Survey*. HFMA. Accessed August 9, 2006. www.hfma.org/library/accounting/costcontrol/2005_Supply_Chain_Benchmk.htm.

———. 2002. *Resource Management: The Healthcare Supply Chain 2002 Survey Results*. HFMA. Accessed February 19, 2007. www.hfma.org/library/accounting/costcontrol/Supply_Chain_2002_Survey.htm.

———. 2001. *Resource Management Update: Healthcare Supply Chain*. HFMA. Accessed February 19, 2007. www.hfma.org/library/accounting/costcontrol/Update_Healthcare_Supply_Chain.htm.

Healthcare.gov. 2012. "Comparing Care Providers. Tools to Help You Assess the Quality of Care You're Getting." *Healthcare.gov*. Accessed May 15. www.healthcare.gov/compare/index.html.

Hefkin, D. C. 1993. "The Navy's Quality Journey: Operational Implementation of TQL." Executive Research Project CS5. Washington, DC: Industrial College of the Armed Forces.

Henry J. Kaiser Family Foundation. 2012. "US Healthcare Costs: Background." *KaiserEDU.org*. Accessed May 17.www.kaiseredu.org/Issue-Modules/US-Health-Care-Costs/Background-Brief.aspx.

Heskett, J. L. 2003. *Shouldice Hospital Ltd. Harvard Business School Case 9-683-068*. Boston: Harvard Business School Publishing.

Hillestad, R., J. Bigelow, A. Bower, F. Girosi, R. Meili, R. Scoville, and R. Taylor. 2005. "Can Electronic Medical Record Systems Transform Health Care? Potential Health Benefits, Savings, and Costs." *Health Affairs* 24 (5): 1103–17.

Homa-Lowry, J., D. Bertin-Epp, and P. L. Spath. 2002. "Enhance Pursuit of Excellence by Integrating ISO 9000, Baldrige: National Baldrige Winners Often

Use ISO as Platform." *HealthCare Benchmarks and Quality Improvement* 9 (9): 25–29.

Hutzschenreuter, A. 2004. "Waiting Patiently: An Analysis of the Performance Aspects of Outpatient Scheduling in Healthcare Institutes." Master's thesis, Virje Universiteit, Amsterdam.

Inamdar, N., and R. S. Kaplan. 2002. "Applying the Balanced Scorecard in Healthcare Provider Organizations." *Journal of Healthcare Management* 47 (3): 179–95.

Institute for Clinical Systems Improvement (ICSI). 2012. "Diagnostic Imaging." *Institute for Clinical Systems Improvement.* Accessed January 26. www.icsi.org/health_care_redesign_/diagnostic_imaging_35952.

———. 2010a. "Health Care Home Operational Definition." *Institute for Clinical Systems Improvement.* Accessed May 22, 2012. www.icsi.org/health_care_home_operational_definition/health_care_home_operational_definition__.html.

———. 2010b. "ICSI High Tech Diagnostic Imaging Enrollment and Next Steps." *ICSI.* Accessed May 18, 2012. www.icsi.org/htdi_slide_presentation__35982/htdi_slide_presentation_.html.

———. 2009. "Transforming High-Tech Diagnostic Imaging: Appropriate, Easy, and Efficient Ordering of Scans at the Point of Care." *ICSI.* Accessed May 18, 2012. www.icsi.org/overview_of_icsi_s_htdi_solution/htdi_brochure.html.

Institute for Healthcare Improvement (IHI). 2012. "Advanced Access: Reducing Waits, Delays, and Frustration in Maine." *IHI.* Accessed May 18. www.ihi.org/knowledge/Pages/ImprovementStories/AdvancedAccessReducingWaitsDelaysandFrustrationinMaine.aspx.

———. 2006a. "Flow." *IHI.* Accessed July 17. www.ihi.org/IHI/Topics/Flow.

———. 2006b. "Managing Patient Flow: Smoothing OR Schedule Can Ease Capacity Crunch, Researchers Say." *IHI.* Accessed July 12. www.ihi.org/IHI/Topics/Flow/PatientFlow/ImprovementStories/ManagingpatientflowSmoothingORschedulecaneasecapacitycrunchesresearcherssay.htm.

———. 2006c. "Primary Care Access." *IHI.* Accessed July 17. www.ihi.org/IHI/Topics/OfficePractices/Access.

———. 2006d. "Protecting 5 Million Lives from Harm." *IHI.* Accessed June 20, 2007. www.ihi.org/IHI/Programs/Campaign/Campaign.htm.

———. 2005. "Failure Mode and Effects Analysis Tool." *IHI.* Accessed January 1, 2006. www.ihi.org/ihi/workspace/tools/fmea.

———. 2003. *Optimizing Patient Flow: Moving Patients Smoothly Through Acute Care Settings.* Boston: Institute for Healthcare Improvement.

Institute of Medicine. 2001. *Crossing the Quality Chasm—A New Health System for the 21st Century.* Washington, DC: National Academies Press.

———. 1999. *To Err Is Human: Building a Safer Health System.* Washington, DC: National Academies Press.

International Organization for Standardization (ISO). 2006. "ISO Homepage." *ISO*. Accessed January 15. www.iso.org/iso/en/ISOOnline.frontpage.

———. 2005. "IWA 1, Quality Management Systems—Guidelines for Process Improvements in Health Service Organizations." *ISO*. Accessed October 29, 2007. www.iso.org.

International Work Simplification Institute. 1968. "Pioneers in Improvement and Our Modern Standard of Living." *IW/SI News*, Sept. 18. Accessed June 8, 2006. http://gilbrethnetwork.tripod.com/bio.html.

Ishikawa, K. 1985. *What Is Total Quality Control?* Translated by D. J. Lu. Englewood Cliffs, NJ: Prentice-Hall Inc.

iSixSigma. 2005. "Six Sigma Project Selection: How Organizations Choose the Most Important Projects." *iSixSigma*. Accessed January 10, 2006. www.isixsigma.com/library/content/dfss.asp.

Johnson, C., and C. Teplitz. 2009. "Applying Collaborative Contracting to the Supply Chain Department of a Regional Health Care Provider." *The Journal of Applied Business Research* 25 (2): 41–50.

Joint Commission, The. 2012. "Sentinel Event." *The Joint Commission*. Accessed May 21. www.jointcommission.org/sentinel_event.aspx.

———. 2005a. "New Standard LD.3.11." *The Joint Commission*. Accessed July 17, 2006. www.jcrinc.com/subscribers/perspectives.asp?durki=6640&site=10&return=6065.

———. 2005b. "Sentinel Event Forms and Tools." *The Joint Commission*. Accessed January 1, 2006. www.jointcommission.org/SentinelEvents/Forms.

———. 2005c. "Sentinel Event Policy and Procedures." *The Joint Commission*. Accessed January 1, 2006. www.jointcommission.org/SentinelEvents/Policy and Procedures.

———. 2001. "Patient Safety Standards—Hospitals." *The Joint Commission*. Accessed January 1, 2006. www.jcrinc.com/subscribers/perspectives.asp?durki=2973&site=10&return=2897.

———. 1999. *Florence Nightingale: Measuring Hospital Care Outcomes*. Oakbrook Terrace, IL: The Joint Commission.

Juran, J. M. 1986. "The Quality Trilogy." *Quality Progress* 19 (8): 19–24.

Juran, J. M., and A. B. Godfrey. 1998. *Juran's Quality Handbook*, 5th ed. New York: McGraw-Hill.

Kaandorp, G. C., and G. Koole. 2007a. "Optimal Outpatient Appointment Scheduling." *Health Care Management Science* 10 (3): 217–29.

———. 2007b. "Optimal Outpatient Appointment Scheduling Tool." *VU University Amsterdam*. Accessed June 24. http://obp.math.vu.nl/healthcare/software/ges.

Kansal, B. B., and P. C. K. Rao. 2006. *Preface to Management*. New Delhi, India: Paragon Books.

Kaplan, R. S., and D. P. Norton. 2001. *The Strategy-Focused Organization: How Balanced Scorecard Companies Thrive in the New Business Environment*. Boston: Harvard Business School Press.

———. 1996. *The Balanced Scorecard: Translating Strategy into Action*. Boston: Harvard Business School Press.

Kassean, H. K., and Z. B. Jagoo. 2005. "Managing Change in the Nursing Handover from Traditional to Bedside Handover: A Case Study from Mauritius." *BMC Nursing* 4 (1): 1.

Kennedy, J. G., and J. T. Hsu. 2003. "Implementation of an Open Access Scheduling System in a Residency Training Program." *Family Medicine* 35 (9): 666–70.

Kenney, J. M. 1988. "Hypothesis Testing: Guilty or Innocent." *Quality Progress* 21 (1): 55–57.

Knowledge@W.P.Carey. 2006. "Transforming U.S. Health Care: Supply-Chain Makeover Rejuvenates Medical Center." *W. P. Carey School of Business, Arizona State University*. Published April 6. http://knowledge.wpcarey.asu .edu/index.cfm?fa=viewArticle&id=1223& specialId=42.

Landrigan, C. P., G. J. Parry, C. B. Bones, A. D. Hackbarth, D. A. Goldmann, and P. J. Sharek. 2010. "Temporal Trends in Rates of Patient Harm Resulting from Medical Care." *New England Journal of Medicine* 363 (22): 2124–34.

Lang, W. 1950. *Cheaper by the Dozen*. Beverly Hills, CA: Twentieth Century Fox Film Corporation.

Laszlo, C. 2003. *The Sustainable Company: How to Create Lasting Value Through Social and Environmental Performance*. Washington, DC: Island Press.

Lazarus, I. R., and B. Stamps. 2002. "The Promise of Six Sigma (Special Report)." *Managed Healthcare Executive* 12 (1): 27–30.

Levy, S. 2003. *Cheaper by the Dozen*. Beverly Hills, CA: Twentieth Century Fox.

Lewin, K. 1951. *Field Theory in Social Science: Selected Theoretical Papers*, edited by D. Cartwright. New York: Harper.

Lim, T. O. 2003. "Statistical Process Control Tools for Monitoring Clinical Performance." *International Journal for Quality in Health Care* 15 (1): 3–4.

Lohr, S. 2008. "Health Care That Puts a Computer on the Team." *New York Times*. Published December 26. www.nytimes.com/2008/12/27/business/27record .html?pagewanted=1&_r=2&sq=Marshfield clinic&st=cse&scp=1.

Lowe, G., V. Plummer, A. P. O'Brien, and L. Boyd. 2012. "Time to Clarify— The Value of Advanced Practice Nursing Roles in Health Care. *Journal of Advanced Nursing* 68 (3): 677–85.

Mankins, M. C., and R. Steele. 2005. "Turning Great Strategy into Great Performance." *Harvard Business Review* 83 (7): 64–72.

Mason, C. C. 1980. *If Japan Can, Why Can't We?* New York: NBC.

Matthews, C. H. 2005. "Using Linear Programming to Minimize the Cost of Nurse Personnel." *Journal of Healthcare Finance* 32 (1): 37–49.

Mayo, E. 1933. *The Human Problems of an Industrial Civilization*. New York: Mac-Millan.

Mazur, G., J. Gibson, and B. Harries. 1995. "QFD Applications in Health Care and Quality of Work Life." Paper presented at the First International Symposium on QFD, Tokyo, Japan, November 11.

McCormick, M. 2006. "Immanuel Kant (1724–1804) Metaphysics." *Internet Encyclopedia of Philosophy*. Accessed June 8. www.iep.utm.edu/k/kantmeta.htm.

McKone-Sweet, K., P. Hamilton, and S. Willis. 2005. "The Ailing Healthcare Supply Chain: A Prescription for Change." *Journal of Supply Chain Management* 41 (1): 4–17.

McManus, M., M. Long, A. Cooper, and E. Litvak. 2004. "Queuing Theory Accurately Models the Need for Critical Care Resources." *Anesthesiology* 100 (5): 1271–76.

Medicare Payment Advisory Commission (MedPAC). 2011. "Report to the Congress: Medicare Payment Policy March 2011." *MedPAC*. Accessed May 18, 2012. www.medpac.gov/documents/mar11_entirereport.pdf.

Metropolis, N. C. 1987. "The Beginning of the Monte Carlo Method." *Los Alamos Science* 15 (Special Issue): 125 30.

Microsoft Corp. 2003. *Microsoft Office Project Professional, Help Screens*. Redmond, WA: Microsoft Corp.

Midwest Business Group on Health. 2003. *Reducing the Costs of Poor-Quality Health Care Through Responsible Purchasing Leadership*. Chicago: Midwest Business Group on Health, PPNEW04.

Milstein, A., and E. Gilbertson. 2009. "American Medical Home Runs." *Health Affairs* 28 (5): 1317–26.

Mostashari, F., M. Tripathi, and M. Kendall. 2009. "A Tale of Two Large Community Electronic Health Record Extension Projects." *Health Affairs* 28 (2): 345–56.

Mountain States Group. 2003. "Balanced Scorecards for Small Rural Hospitals: Concept Overview and Implementation Guidance." Publication No. ORHP00346. *Health Resources and Services Administration, US Department of Health and Human Services*. Accessed August 15, 2006. http://tasc.rural health.hrsa.gov/documents/Final%20BSC%20Manual%20edits%2010.18F .pdf.

Moy, E., M. Barrett, and K. Ho. 2011. "Potentially Preventable Hospitalizations: United States, 2004–2007." *CDC Morbidity and Mortality Weekly Report* 60 (1): 80–83

Murray, M., and D. M. Berwick. 2003. "Advanced Access: Reducing Waiting and Delays in Primary Care." *JAMA* 290 (3): 332–34.

Murray, M., T. Bodenheimer, D. Rittenhouse, and K. Grumbach. 2003. "Improving Timely Access to Primary Care: Case Studies in the Advanced Access Model." *JAMA* 289 (8): 1042–46.

National Academy of Engineering and Institute of Medicine. 2005. *Building a Better Delivery System: A New Engineering/Health Care Partnership*, edited by P. P. Reid, W. D. Compton, J. H. Grossman, and G. Fanjiang. Washington, DC: National Academies Press. Accessed July 28, 2006. www.nap.edu/catalog/11378.html.

National Guideline Clearinghouse (NGC). 2011. "Home." *US Department of Health and Human Services.* Accessed January 29, 2012. www.guideline.gov.

National Quality Forum. 2002. "Serious Reportable Events in Healthcare: A National Quality Forum Consensus Report." Publication No. NQFCR01-02. Washington, DC: National Quality Forum.

NationMaster.com. 2004. "Venetian Arsenal." *NationMaster.* Accessed June 8, 2006. www.nationmaster.com/encyclopedia/Venetian-Arsenal.

Nelson, D. 1980. *Frederick Taylor and the Rise of Scientific Management.* Madison, WI: University of Wisconsin Press.

NetMBA.com. 2005. "Frederick Taylor and Scientific Management." *NetMBA.* Accessed June 8, 2006. www.netmba.com/mgmt/scientific.

Neuhauser, D. 2003. "Florence Nightingale Gets No Respect: As a Statistician That Is." *Quality and Safety in Health Care* 12 (4): 317.

Nietert, P. J., A. M. Wessell, R. G. Jenkins, C. Feifer, L. S. Nemeth, and S. M. Ornstein. 2007. "Using a Summary Measure for Multiple Quality Indicators in Primary Care: The Summary QUality InDex (SQUID)." *Implementation Science* 2: 11.

Nightingale, F. 1858. *Notes on Matters Affecting the Health, Efficiency and Hospital Administration of the British Army.* Presented by request to the Secretary of State for War. Privately printed for Miss Nightingale by Harrison and Sons.

Niven, P. R. 2002. *Balanced Scorecard Step-by-Step: Maximizing Performance and Maintaining Results.* New York: John Wiley & Sons.

Nuwash, P. 2010. Presentation at Midwest Healthcare Business Intelligence Summit. October 19.

O'Hare, C. D., and J. Corlett. 2004. "The Outcomes of Open-Access Scheduling." *Family Practice Management* 11 (2): 35–38.

Olsen, K. 2012. "Nothing to Fear: The Myths of Same-Day Scheduling." *Health Leaders Media.* Accessed May 18. www.healthleadersmedia.com/content/MAG-87221/Nothing-to-Fear-The-Myths-of-SameDay-Scheduling.

Olson, J. R., J. A. Belohlav, L. S. Cook, and J. M. Hays. 2008. "Examining Quality Improvement Programs: The Case of Minnesota Hospitals." *Health Services Research* 43 (5): 1781–86.

Omachonu, V., and P. Barach. 2005. "QFD in a Managed Care Organization." *Quality Progress* 38 (11): 36–41.

Oracle Corporation. 2012. "Crystal Ball." *Oracle Corporation.* Accessed May 25. www.decisioneering.com.

Palisade Corporation. 2012. "@Risk 5.7." *Pallisade Corporation*. Accessed April 17. www.palisade.com/risk.

Panchak, P. 2003. "Lean Health Care? It Works." *Industry Week* 252 (11): 34–38.

Parasuraman, A., V. A. Zeithaml, and L. L. Berry. 1988. "SERVQUAL: A Multiple-Item Scale for Measuring Consumer Perceptions of Service Quality." *Journal of Retailing* 64 (4): 12–40.

Parente, D. H., M. B. Pinto, and J. C. Barber. 2005. "A Pre-Post Comparison of Service Operational Efficiency and Patient Satisfaction Under Open Access Scheduling." *Health Care Management Review* 30 (3): 220–28.

Pascal, D. 2007. *Lean Production Simplified*, 2nd ed. New York: Productivity Press.

Patient Protection and Affordable Care Act (ACA). 2010. *Federal Register Online* via the Government Printing Office (www.gpo.gov). [FR Doc No: 2011-10568] [[Page 26489]] Vol. 76 Friday, No. 88 May 6, 2011 Part V.

Perkins, J. S. 1997. "Frank B. Gilbreth's Research: The Quest of the One Best Way." *THE QUEST, Newsletter of the Gilbreth Network*. Accessed October 29, 2007. http://gilbrethnetwork.tripod.com/qv1n2.html.

Poundstone, W. 1985. *The Recursive Universe*. Chicago: Contemporary Books.

Powell, T. C. 1995. "Total Quality Management as Competitive Advantage: A Review and Empirical Study." *Strategic Management Journal* 16 (1): 15–37.

Praxel, T. A. 2009. "Quality Improvement in the Marshfield Clinic." Presentation at the Institute for Clinical Systems Improvement Annual Meeting, Oct. 26.

Proctor, P., W. Reid, D. Compton, J. H. Grossman, and G. Fanjiang. 2005. *Building a Better Delivery System: A New Engineering/Health Care Partnership*. Washington, DC: Institute of Medicine.

Project Management Institute (PMI). 2008. *A Guide to the Project Management Body of Knowledge*. Newtown Square, PA: Project Management Institute.

Quality Assurance Project. 2003. "Dimensions of Quality." *Quality Assurance Project*. Accessed January 15, 2006. www.qaproject.org/methods/resdimension.html.

Radel, S. J., A. M. Norman, J. C. Notaro, and D. R. Horrigan. 2001. "Redesigning Clinical Office Practices to Improve Performance Levels in an Individual Practice Association Model HMO." *Journal of Healthcare Quality* 23 (2): 11–15.

Radianse. 2012. "Success Stories: Pinnacle Health System." *Radianse*. Accessed May 21. www.radianse.com/success_stories_pinnacle.html.

Ransom, S. B., J. S. Maulik, and D. B. Nash (eds.). 2005. *The Healthcare Quality Book: Vision, Strategy, and Tools*. Chicago: Health Administration Press.

Reh, F. J. 2007. "Pareto's Principle—The 80-20 Rule." *About.com*. Accessed February 15. http://management.about.com/cs/generalmanagement/a/Pareto081202.htm.

Reid, S. 2000. "Using the 'Theory of Constraints' Methodology to Increase, Improve Services to Patients." *ImpAct* 6 (March/April).

Ressler, T., and M. Ahrens. 2006. *The Decision Making Book*. Minneapolis, MN: University of St. Thomas.

Revere, L., and A. K. Black. 2003. "Integrating Six Sigma with Total Quality Management: A Case Example for Measuring Medication Errors." *Journal of Healthcare Management* 48 (6): 377–91.

Ribas, V. J., J. C. Lopez, J. C. Ruiz-Rodriguez, A. Ruiz-Sanmartin, J. Rello, and A. Vellido. 2011. "On the Use of Decision Trees for ICU Outcome Prediction in Sepsos Patients Treated with Statins." *IEEE.* Accessed May 18, 2012. http://ieeexplore.ieee.org/xpl/freeabs_all.jsp?arnumber=5949439&abstract Access=no&userType=inst.

Rockwell Automation. 2012. "Arena." *Rockwell Automation.* Accessed April 17. www.arenasimulation.com/Products_Basic_Edition.aspx.

Rodi, S. W., M. V. Grau, and C. M. Orsini. 2006. "Evaluation of a Fast Track Unit: Alignment of Resources and Demand Results in Improved Satisfaction and Decreased Length of Stay for Emergency Department Patients." *Quality Management in Healthcare* 15 (3): 163–70.

Roos, R. 2011. "Study Puts Global 2009 H1N1 Infection Rate at 11% to 21%." *Center for Infectious Disease Research and Policy.* Published August 8. www.cidrap .umn.edu/cidrap/content/influenza/swineflu/news/aug0811serologic.html.

Ross, J. E., and S. Perry. 1999. *Total Quality Management: Text, Cases and Readings.* Oxford, UK: CRC Press.

Rotter, T., L. Kinsman, E. L. James, A. Machotta, H. Gothe, J. Willis, P. Snow, and J. Kugler. 2010. "Clinical Pathways: Effects on Professional Practice, Patient Outcomes, Length of Stay and Hospital Costs." *Cochrane Database of Systematic Reviews* 3: CD006632.

Ruland, C. 2002. "Patient Preferences in Health Care Decision Making." *Columbia University Biomedical Informatics.* Accessed January 7, 2006. www.dbmi .columbia.edu/homepages/cmr7001/sdm/html/methods.htm.

Russo, J. E., and P. J. H. Schoemaker. 1989. *Decision Traps: The Ten Barriers to Brilliant Decision-Making and How to Overcome Them.* New York: Doubleday.

Samson, D., and M. Terziovski. 1999. "The Relationship Between Total Quality Management Practices and Operational Performance." *Journal of Operations Management* 17 (4): 393–409.

Sarker, S., A. Al Masud, M. A. Habib, and A. K. M. Masud. 2010. "Application of QFD for Improving Customer Perceived Quality of Synthetic Fiber: A Case of Beximco Synthetics Ltd." *Journal of Business.* Accessed May 18, 2012. www.journalofbusiness.org/index.php/GJMBR/article/view/133.

Savage, S. 2002. "The Flaw of Averages." *Harvard Business Review* 80 (11): 20–21.

Schmenner, R. W. 2004. "Service Businesses and Productivity." *Decision Sciences* 35 (3): 333–47.

———. 2001. "Looking Ahead by Looking Back: Swift, Even Flow in the History of Manufacturing." *Production and Operations Management* 10 (1): 87–96.

———. 1986. "How Can Service Businesses Survive and Prosper?" *Sloan Management Review* 27 (3): 21–32.

Schmenner, R. W., and M. L. Swink. 1998. "On Theory in Operations Management." *Journal of Operations Management* 17 (1): 97–113.

Schmidt, C., and M. Messer. 2005. "A Pragmatic Approach to Improving Patient Efficiency Throughput." *Institute for Healthcare Improvement.* Accessed June 15, 2006. www.ihi.org/IHI/Topics/Flow/PatientFlow/Improvement Stories/APragmaticApproachtoImprovingPatientEfficiencyThroughput.htm.

Schneider, E. C., P. S. Hussey, and C. Schnyer. 2011. *Payment Reform: Analysis of Models and Performance Measurement Implications.* Santa Monica, CA: RAND Corporation–RAND Health.

Schyve, P. M. 2000. "A Trio for Quality: Accreditation, Baldrige and ISO 9000 Can Play a Role in Reducing Medical Errors." *Quality Progress* 33 (6): 53–55.

Senge, P. M. 1990. *The Fifth Discipline: The Art and Practice of the Learning Organization.* New York: Doubleday.

Sepúlveda, J. A., W. J. Thompson, F. F. Baesler, M. I. Alvarez, and L. E. Cahoon III. 1999. "The Use of Simulation for Process Improvement in a Cancer Treatment Center." In *Proceedings of the 31st Conference on Winter Simulation: Simulation—A Bridge to the Future,* Vol. 2. New York: ACM Press.

Sharma, J. R., and A. M. Rawani. 2010. "From Customers Requirements to Customers Satisfaction: Quality Function Deployment in Service Sector." *International Journal of Productivity and Quality Management* 5 (4): 428–39.

Shewhart, W. A. 1931. *Economic Control of Quality of Manufactured Product.* New York: D. Van Nostrand Company, Inc.

Shewhart, W. A., and W. E. Deming. 1939. *Statistical Method from the Viewpoint of Quality Control.* Washington, DC: The Graduate School, US Department of Agriculture.

Shingo, S. 1985. *A Revolution in Manufacturing: The SMED System.* Translated by A. Dillon. New York: Productivity Press.

Shortell, S. M., J. L. O'Brien, J. M. Carman, R. W. Foster, E. F. Hughes, H. Boerstler, and E. J. O'Connor. 1995. "Assessing the Impact of Continuous Quality Improvement/Total Quality Management: Concept Versus Implementation." *Health Services Research* 30 (2): 377–401.

Shostack, G. L. 1984. "Designing Services That Deliver." *Harvard Business Review* 62 (1): 133–39.

Simkin, J. 2005. "Henry Ford." *Spartacus.* Accessed June 8, 2006. www.spartacus.schoolnet.co.uk/USAford.htm.

Simul8 Corporation. 2012. "Simul8 Software Products." *Simul8.* Accessed April 17. www.simul8.com/products/index.htm.

Singer, I. A. 2001. *Advanced Access: A New Paradigm in the Delivery of Ambulatory Care Services.* Washington, DC: National Association of Public Hospitals and Health Systems.

Singer, I. A., and M. Regenstein. 2003. *Advanced Access: Ambulatory Care Redesign and the Nation's Safety Net.* Washington, DC: National Association of Public Hospitals and Health Systems.

Slack, M. P. 2005. Personal communication, August 15.

Sochalski, J., T. Jaarsma, H. M. Krumholz, A. Laramee, J. J. V. McMurray, M. D. Naylor, M. W. Rich, B. Riegel, and S. Stewart. 2009. "What Works in Chronic Care Management: The Case of Heart Failure." *Health Affairs* 28 (1): 179–89.

Society for Healthcare Strategy and Market Development and American College of Healthcare Executives. 2012. *Futurescan: Healthcare Trends and Implications 2011–2016.* Chicago: Health Administration Press.

Soriano, A. 1966. "Comparison of Two Scheduling Systems." *Operations Research* 14 (3): 388–97.

Spear, S. J. 2005. "Fixing Health Care from the Inside, Today." *Harvard Business Review* 83 (9): 78–91.

Stratton, R. and A. Knight. 2010. "Managing Patient Flow Using Time Buffers." *Journal of Manufacturing Technology Management.* Accessed May 18, 2012. http://stamps.ntu.ac.uk/nbs/document_uploads/94590.pdf.

Sunol, R. 2000. "Avedis Donabedian." *International Journal for Quality in Health Care* 12 (6): 451–54.

Suver, J. D., B. R. Neumann, and K. E. Boles. 1992. "Accounting for the Costs of Quality." *Healthcare Financial Management* 46 (9): 28–37.

Sytsma, S. 1997. "Quality and Statistical Process Control." *Systma.* Accessed February 4, 2006. www.sytsma.com/tqmtools/ctlchtprinciples.html.

Taguchi, G., S. Chowdhury, and Y. Wu. 2004. *Taguchi's Quality Engineering Handbook.* Hoboken, NJ: Wiley-Interscience.

Tarí, J. J. 2005. "Components of Successful Total Quality Management." *TQM Magazine* 17 (2): 182–94.

Taylor, F. W. 1911. *The Principles of Scientific Management.* New York: Harper and Row.

Trabelsi, S., R. Larbi, and A. Alouane. 2012. "Linear Integer Programming for Home Health Care." *Lecture Notes in Business Information Processing* 100 (2): 143–51.

Trajano, D., S. Mattson, and M. Sanford. 2011. "Using Lean to Improve Outcomes and Decrease Waste." Presented at the Total Cost of Care Forum, November 15. www.icsi.org/breakout_session__using_lean_to_improve_outcomes_and_decrease_waste/slides_by_daniel_trajano__md_and_steve_mattson.html.

Truelsen, T., and M. Grønbæk. 1999. "Wine Consumption and Cerebrovascular Disease Mortality in Spain." *Stroke* 30 (1): 186–88.

Tufte, E. R. 1997. *Visual Explanations: Images and Quantities, Evidence and Narrative.* Cheshire, CT: Graphics Press.

———. 1990. *Envisioning Information.* Cheshire, CT: Graphics Press.

———. 1983. *The Visual Display of Quantitative Information*. Cheshire, CT: Graphics Press.

Vaida, B. 2011. "How Group Health Is Holding Costs Down: A KHN Interview With CEO Scott Armstrong." *Kaiser Health News*. Published February 14. www.kaiserhealthnews.org/Stories/2011/February/14/group-health-scott-armstrong-coops.aspx.

Vesely, R. 2011. "Pilot Payment Plan Cuts Costs; Non-Traditional Model also Improving Quality." *Modern Healthcare* 41 (5): 14–15.

Veterans Affairs National Center for Patient Safety. 2006. "Healthcare Failure Mode and Effect Analysis (HFMEA)." *US Department of Veterans Affairs*. Accessed January 7. www.patientsafety.gov/SafetyTopics.html#HFMEA.

Wagner, E. H. 2000. "The Role of Patient Care Teams in Chronic Disease Management." *British Medical Journal* 320 (7234): 569–72.

Wagner, E. H., B. T. Austin, C. Davis, M. Hindmarsh, J. Schaefer, and A. Bonomi. 2001. "Improving Chronic Illness Care: Translating Illness into Action." *Health Affairs* 20 (6): 64–78.

Walley, P., K. Silvester, and R. Steyn. 2006. "Managing Variation in Demand: Lessons from the UK National Health Service." *Journal of Healthcare Management* 51 (5): 309–22.

Werner, R. M., and E. T. Bradlow. 2010. "Public Reporting on Hospital Process Improvements Is Linked to Better Patient Outcomes." *Health Affairs* 29 (7): 1319–24.

Werner, R. M., and R. A. Dudley. 2009. "Making the 'Pay' Matter in Pay-for-Performance: Implications for Payment Strategies." *Health Affairs* 28 (5): 1498–508.

Wheelwright, S., and J. Weber. 2004. *Massachusetts General Hospital: CABG Surgery (A)*. Harvard Business Review Case 9-696-015. Boston: Harvard Business School Publishing.

Winston, W. L., and S. C. Albright. 2005. *Practical Management Science: Spreadsheet Modeling and Applications* (with CD-ROM Update), 2nd ed. Belmont, CA: Duxbury.

Wolstenholme, E. 1999. "A Patient Flow Perspective of UK Health Services: Exploring the Care for New 'Intermediate Care' Initiatives." *System Dynamics Review* 15 (3): 253–71.

Womack, J. P., A. P. Byrne, O. J. Fiume, G. S. Kaplan, and J. Toussaint. 2005. *Going Lean in Health Care*. Cambridge, MA: Institute for Healthcare Improvement.

Womack, D., and S. Flowers. 1999. "Improving System Performance: A Case Study in the Application of the Theory of Constraints." *Journal of Healthcare Management* 44 (5): 397–405.

Womack, J., and D. Jones. 1999. *Learning to See*. Brookline, MA: The Lean Enterprise Institute.

Womack, J. P., D. T. Jones, and D. Roos. 1990. *The Machine That Changed the World: Based on the Massachusetts Institute of Technology 5-Million Dollar 5-Year Study on the Future of the Automobile.* New York: Rawson Associates.

World Health Organization (WHO). 2003. "Influenza: Overview." *World Health Organization.* Accessed May 17, 2012. www.who.int/mediacentre/factsheets/2003/fs211/en.

Wright, C. M. 2007. "Where's My Defibrillator? More Effectively Tracking Hospital Assets." *APICS* 17 (1): 28–33.

Wysocki, B., Jr. 2004. "To Fix Health Care, Hospitals Take Tips from Factory Floor." *Wall Street Journal*, April 9, A1–A5.

Yabroff, K. R., C. N. Klabunde, G. Yuan, T. S. McNeel, M. L. Brown, D. Casciotti, D. W. Buckman, and S. Taplan. 2010. "Are Physicians' Recommendations for Colorectal Cancer Screening Guideline-Consistent?" *Journal of General Internal Medicine* 26 (2): 177–84.

Yule, G. U. 1926. "Why Do We Sometimes Get Nonsense-Correlations Between Time-Series?—A Study in Sampling and the Nature of Time-Series." *Journal of the Royal Statistical Society* 89 (1): 1–63.

Zeleny, M. 1987. "Management Support Systems: Towards Integrated Knowledge Management." *Human Systems Management* 7 (1): 59–70.

Zelman, W. N., G. H. Pink, and C. B. Matthias. 2003. "Use of the Balanced Scorecard in Health Care." *Journal of Health Care Finance* 29 (4): 1–15.

INDEX

ABOUT THE AUTHORS

Daniel B. McLaughlin, MHA, is the director of the Center for Health and Medical Affairs in the Opus College of Business at the University of St. Thomas in Minneapolis, Minnesota. He is active in teaching, research, and speaking at the university, with a special emphasis on healthcare operations and policy. He is the author of a number of textbooks and management guides published by Health Administration Press, including *Make It Happen: Effective Execution in Healthcare Leadership* and *Responding to Healthcare Reform: A Strategy Guide for Healthcare Leaders.*

From 1984 to 1992, Mr. McLaughlin was the administrator and CEO of Hennepin County Medical Center, the level 1 trauma center in Minneapolis. He served as the chair of the National Association of Public Hospitals and Health Systems and served on President Clinton's Task Force on Health Care Reform in 1993. In 2000, he helped establish and direct the National Institute of Health Policy at St. Thomas. He holds degrees in electrical engineering and healthcare administration from the University of Minnesota.

John R. Olson is a professor at the University of St. Thomas in the Operations and Supply Chain Management Department. He holds his PhD in operations and supply chain management from the University of Nebraska. He has published many articles and books in leading operations management journals and has consulted with many Fortune 500 companies as well as many firms in the public sector. Over the past 10 years, he has consulted with several healthcare organizations implement their continuous improvement programs, including Six Sigma and Lean initiatives. He is a master black belt in Six Sigma and a Lean Sensei.